NORTH AMERICAN INDIAN LEGENDS

Selected and Edited by
Allan A. Macfarlan

Illustrated by
Everett Gee Jackson

DOVER PUBLICATIONS, INC.
Mineola, New York

The American Indian legends in this book have been taken from the writings of Henry R. Schoolcraft, George Bird Grinnell, Franz Boas, and others.

Copyright

Copyright © 1968 by The George Macy Companies, Inc.
All rights reserved under Pan American and International Copyright Conventions.

Published in Canada by General Publishing Company, Ltd., 895 Don Mills Road, 400-2 Park Centre, Toronto, Ontario M3C 1W3.
Published in the United Kingdom by David & Charles, Brunel House, Forde Close, Newton Abbot, Devon TQ12 4PU.

Bibliographical Note

This Dover edition, first published in 2001, is an unabridged republication of the work published as *American Indian Legends* by the Heritage Press, New York, in 1968. This edition is published by arrangement with the Limited Editions Book Club, New York.

Library of Congress Cataloging-in-Publication Data

American Indian legends.
    North American Indian legends / selected and edited by Allan A. Macfarlan ; illustrated by Everett Gee Jackson.
        p. cm.
    Originally published: American Indian legends. Los Angeles : Printed for the members of the Limited Editions Club at the Ward Ritchie Press, 1968.
    ISBN 0-486-41947-9 (pbk.)
    1. Indians of North America—Folklore. 2. Tales—North America. 3. Legends—North America. I. Macfarlan, Allan A. II. Title.

E98.F6 M13 2001
398.2'089'97—dc21

2001032357

Manufactured in the United States of America
Dover Publications, Inc., 31 East 2nd Street, Mineola, N.Y. 11501

TABLE OF CONTENTS

INTRODUCTION

AMERICAN INDIAN LEGENDS soared to the stars with the smoke of campfire and council fire from the tepees of the Indians of the Plains, the long-houses of the Woodland Indians, the cliff dwellings of the Pueblo People, the hogans of the Navaho, and the magnificent cedar houses of the Indians of the North Pacific Coast. The legends selected for this book were chosen from many hundreds as among the most interesting, varied, and representative.

The way of life of the many Indian nations was well illustrated by their legends and folk tales, which often reveal the habitat, habits, and principal occupations of the tribes which told them. They also reveal some of the inner workings of the Indian mind, their beliefs, hopes, fears, and what they lived, fought, and died for. Because of their beliefs in mystery, magic, signs, and omens, Indians lived in a fascinating world of their own until it was shattered by the invasion of the white man, whose actions and influence, coupled with diseases formerly unknown in this hemisphere, proved the most devastating, disruptive, and debasing happening in the long history of the American Indians.

Prior to the arrival of the white man, the Indians, "spartans of the plains and forests," lived happy, healthy, and adventurous lives. They were brave, stoic, simple and complex, warlike and peaceful, loyal, and self-sacrificing for family and friends. The code of the Great Confederation of the Iroquois, followed by the hundreds of their chiefs, was to be brave, truthful, patient, unselfish, chivalrous, generous to a fault, helpful to their people in every way without accepting anything in return, and to work united for peace and in all things, calling upon the Creator to help them in their undertakings.

American Indian storytellers and their tales date from the time that the Indian was able to communicate intelligibly and intelligently. Many of the "modern" retellings of these legends, myths, and folk tales date from 1600 to 1760, when they were collected by the Jesuits. Since the early seventeenth century, legends have also been gathered by English, French, Dutch, and Spanish explorers and travelers, and set down as told by native storytellers. The tales have not materially changed, in reliable retellings, up to the twentieth century. This is remarkable, since setting down legends accurately was often difficult, chiefly because reliable interpreters were scarce. The early chroniclers had to be wary of would-be interpreters who ignored objectivity and sometimes embellished the tales passed down by the ancient storytellers or tried to build into them some of their own personality or beliefs.

In translations made by white men who had insufficient knowledge of the Indian language, some legends lost authenticity, meaning, and Indian flavor. Fortunately, the majority of such misleading tales have been discredited through study and comparison with legends set down in the Annual Reports of the Bureau of American Ethnology and other anthropological and scientific sources.

An amusing instance of taking liberties with translation occurred when the editor of this volume set down the legend of "The First Blackfish" for his book, *Talking Stick Tales*. The old Tlingit chief relating the tale said that the hunter rode on a sea lion's back. Having previously heard the legend from a well-known Haida storyteller, the author suggested that it was not a sea lion but a gull. The Tlingit reluctantly replied: "What you heard about sea gull may be right; but because you write story for white people, maybe they believe it more if you say hunter went on back of sea lion—he much stronger than sea gull."

American folklorists are greatly indebted to Henry Rowe Schoolcraft, a pioneer in the field, who collected many tales and legends during his thirty years' stay with the Indians. His first book of Indian legends was published in 1839. Several of his best stories appear in this book. But it was probably Longfellow's lengthy narrative poem (of rather un-Indian tempo), *The Song of Hiawatha* (1855), that first aroused public interest in the Indians of North America.

The authentic records of unlettered peoples are usually short-lived, reaching back only in the memories of their oldest men. Among the Indian tribes, traditions and folklore were handed down orally and entrusted to those who showed a special aptitude in remembering them. Regarded as tribal historians, these men in turn instructed the boys.

The Indians evinced little or no interest in recording unvarnished historical facts, hence they were often embellished by fantasy or embroidered with the supernatural, so that it was almost impossible to separate fancy from reality. The differences and distortions apparent in legend variants were often due to reinterpretations.

Many long, detailed, verbal accounts of legendary lore have been almost entirely lost because only certain chiefs, medicine men, and storytellers were privileged to recite and explain some classes of traditions, especially sacred ones. Tribal rites, customs, songs, and dances were often based on such legends and myths. Some folklore was preserved in the form of songs adapted for use on suitable occasions. The primary myths, regarded as having sacred association and significance, were highly respected and were usually told in hushed voices, after dark, by specially appointed storytellers, many of whom embellished their tales with prayer, song, dance, and wonderful mimicry. Some legends are of the classical type and display real literary art in their composition.

Most tribal myths and legends can be divided into specific categories, such as sacred and creation myths, historical legends, traditions, and local legends. In these folk tales of so long ago, legends, myths, traditions, and folk tales have often merged and become almost inseparable. There is little use in trying to differentiate between myth, legend, and tradition, or to delve into the origins, since little or no proof can be offered to substantiate the majority of them, though in some cases legends have been supported by archaeological research. All in all, the records of the myths and legends of the North American Indians are perhaps the most authentic in existence of those of any primitive peoples.

Some tales, many of them told by tribal Merry Makers, were of a simple naiveté, conceived and told with only one purpose in mind, to entertain. In such tales, told in the spirit of fun, nothing is gained by trying to analyze them in search of subtle meanings—they do not exist.

Far-flung Indian legends, similar despite their wide distribution, might lead one to suppose they were carried thousands of miles by tribal nomads. Emissaries of some Indian "prophets" spread their creation myths throughout North America. Tribal alliances also added to the spread of myths. Few legends worth relating were confined to a single tribe. Tales of the Haida, of the Queen Charlotte Islands, were equally popular among the Tlingit of Alaska, and many Raven legends were known by the various groups of Eskimo. It is difficult to guess how the unusual themes of some legends were spread over vast distances. For instance, in "Kwanokasha," a Choctaw legend included here, one reads that this little man-spirit headed the trio who gave little children, lost in the forest, an I. Q. test which had a marked similarity to the one given by high Tibetan lamas when testing and choosing a child as their new Dalai Lama!

Motifs often used in American Indian mythology and legend were many and varied. Some of those most commonly used follow:

Repetition, to create suspense or make clear what was happening.

A boy or girl, living with an old grandparent or uncle. These relatives either cherished and helped the children or were jealous and plotted against them.

Visits to stars, sky, supernatural lands (underground or elsewhere), and the upper and lower world. In primitive mythology the transformation of humans into stars or star groups was a common motif, as was *escape* to or from stars. Sky windows and sky ropes often figure in such themes.

Transformation of humans into stars, mountains, rocks, trees, or other natural features, and into animals and everyday objects, by tricksters and enemies possessing magic power. Besides transformers, those with special powers became almost anything, including a tuft of down or a feather, as an escape device or to travel on the wind. At the end of the flight, they became human again.

Disguises of many kinds, such as trees, animals, or people, used by medicine men, transformers, tricksters, and the protagonists in the legends, who also used the skins of animals and humans in order to effect the change. They used their magic powers to assume the walk and voice of the person or animal, and the deception was nearly always successful.

Invisibility, and the use of shrouding mist and magic cloaks and caps.

Etiquette, which was very strict and demanding, and protocol meticulously observed.

Inexhaustible food supply, springing from hunger and starvation which many Indian tribes often experienced.

Contests and challenge games, with varying prizes—often the chief's beautiful daughter—sometimes won by culture heroes and supernatural beings disguised, who easily defeated all human contestants by skill, abnormal strength, cunning, or magic. This involved shooting with bow and arrow, climbing, swimming, diving, harpooning, trapping, tree-pulling, wrestling, racing, and feats of magic.

Dreams sending someone on a dangerous quest from which he was unlikely to return, and unpopular or unwanted youths, sent to slay dangerous animals, persons, or monsters, in the hope that they would not survive the mission.

Numskull motifs (such as in "The Old Man's Lessons to His Nephew" in this book), telling how someone does everything wrong, to his and everyone else's confusion. These were popular with Indian audiences, who had a good sense of humor and saw themselves as the bumbling protagonist. One can detect a European slant in some of these tales, though usually the influence is not marked.

Strenuous personal programs in endurance and fortitude, since the Indian way of life was always hard. Legends often said, "He trained himself in the mountains, for he wished to become great."

Taboos, such as going northward or in some other direction. To disregard this meant grave difficulties or even death.

Resurrection, rejuvenation, and becoming beautiful.

Enchanted objects pointing the way or giving advice.

Pointing at people or animals to cause their death.

Reading people's minds or knowing their thoughts, a feat which went unquestioned.

Power of thought, of which the Indians were well aware. Some legendary figures had their wishes granted because they "kept their minds" on what they wished to achieve or obtain. In some legends, people were saved by "the power of thought" and the same power made impossible things possible.

Snapping door-traps, on the North Pacific Coast, where doors were many and massive.

Tall tales of superhuman men and superhuman feats (as in our "Kwasind"). They remind one of Paul Bunyan, legendary hero of American tall tales; of Baron Munchausen, German adventurer extraordinary; of Jonathan Swift's Gulliver, and of Shakespeare's Falstaff . . . as well as of the modern Superman and Batman!

Human relationship, including love, marriage, and responsibility. Such legends could be called fairy tales for adults. (Some children's fairy tales —of the Haida, for instance—would make a white man's hair stand on end.)

Magic weapons; invisible, and specific weapons—as in "Kwasind."

European motifs such as "Pandora's Box" and others were hit upon by Indian storytellers long before European tales reached the New World. After the arrival of the white man, more than fifty European legends, folk tales, and fairy tales were added to the Indian repertoire of legends; some were told in their entirety, and portions of others were woven into the Indian tales.

The Greek influence predominates in many Indian legends, the Orpheus and Eurydice theme frequently occurring, as in "The White Stone Canoe," and the Achilles' heel motif, as in "Kwasind." In "The Red Swan," the fate of the would-be lovers is reminiscent of that of Penelope's suitors.

"The Magical Food, Belt, and Flute" appears to be partly of European origin, a combination of "Jack and the Beanstalk" and "Making the Princess Laugh" being easily seen in the fabric of this tale. "Oochigeopch" is obviously a version of "Beauty and the Beast." "The Poor Turkey Girl" has been likened to a realistic version of "Cinderella." Wishes unintentionally or foolishly wasted are a recurrent theme in Indian legends as in European and Oriental tales.

Some tales of the Indians of the Southwest are of Spanish origin; and some legends of Negro origin were told in the Apache and other tribes, who believed they were entirely Indian.

"The Prince and the Peasant Girl," a Micmac legend, is based on a European tale. As to royalty among the American Indians, there were no "princesses" among the tribes of the Plains, Woodland, or Southwest, nor was the term ever used by them. Only the tribes of the North Pacific Coast had genuine princesses, also known as "noble girls," and their families, "noble families." When used in reference to women of other habitats the term "princess" is a misnomer, coined by newspaper men and press agents as a publicity stunt and for box-office appeal. In "The Princess and the Mouse" and "The Princess Who Rejected Her Cousin," however, since these are Tsimshian legends, the term is correct.

On the North Pacific Coast especially, many of the legends have a hint of Siberian folklore interwoven with other motifs. This is not surprising, considering the trek of the American Indian tribes across what is now Bering Strait to North America.

Fortunately, American myth and legend have become part of the living literature of the world and are being studied and compared by modern scientists with those of Europe and the Orient.

The many variants occurring in myths and legends have been well illustrated by an old Blackfoot who pulled up a ragweed, pointed to its stem and said, "All parts of this weed branch from the same stem. The branches go in different ways, but all have the same root. So it is with the different versions of myths and legends." Though there may be several variations of a legend, many will prove to be in substantial agreement. A number of Indian tribes, such as the San Carlos Apache, have many versions of the same legend. Or a legend may be composed of incidents common to several other stories. The Pueblo People regard some of their tales as being Mexican in origin.

"Brother Birch," a Blackfoot legend, is known in at least one other version in which the tree is *scarred*, not beautified, by Manabozho, because it interrupted his "playing with the wind."

As told by the Tsimshian, "The Hunter and His Wooden Wife" has a happy ending; versions told by the Tlingit of Alaska, the Iroquois, and other tribes have sad endings. And "The Dog and the Stick," a Blackfoot legend, is a variant of "The Release of the Buffalo," a Comanche tale.

In the creation myths, though a number of variants occur, many of them tell that the world was formed of mud brought to the surface by diving animals or birds, the duck, loon, otter, muskrat, and turtle, usually being among the wild creatures sent down by various transformers. Bible stories became a part of American Indian legends.

The Rip Van Winkle theme was popular in various Indian legends long before it was introduced by Washington Irving in 1819. Compared to some of the Indian "sleeps," Rip's was only a cat-nap.

Transformers, tricksters, and culture heroes are frequently the protagonists of Indian legends. These strange beings, endowed with even stranger powers, were charlatans, cheats, mischief-makers, mountebanks, and wonder-workers, motivated by greed, lust, and vainglory, to whom altruism was unknown. Most of their services to the Indians were performed unintentionally, merely to gratify their whims or feed their intense egos. Their adventures and misadventures provide tribal folklore with a comic element.

All of the tricksters possessed, to a certain degree, wit that was not wisdom and an exaggerated and distorted sense of humor. Few possessed real wit and insight. Their characters varied so, noble and ignoble traits mingling, that in some trickster tales, culture heroes and tricksters merge. Some had a dual nature, human and animal, the animal predominating and always ready to come to the surface, to the misfortune of anyone or anything they encountered. Manabozho, transformer and trickster of the Central Woodland groups, and Raven, of the Northwest Coast, were outstanding examples.

In considering these Indian makers of magic and mischief, let us remember that Europe, too, had its share of legendary male and female tricksters, of whom Morgan Le Fay, King Arthur's fairy half-sister, and the wizard Merlin are good examples. Women transformers often appear in Indian legends, and their treachery and tricks equal or surpass those of their English prototype. Wolf Woman, of the Pawnee, and Deer Woman, of the Teton, in the guise of beautiful maidens, seduced many young warriors, who died soon after.

Since the trickster and transformer Manabozho was known to the Iroquois, Ojibwa, Menomini, Ottawa, and Fox, among other tribes, by different names, the one given him throughout the legends in this book has been standardized. As a transformer, he was among the busiest. A glance at his "family tree," as told in Indian legends, is interesting: His grandmother was a daughter of the moon; her daughter was ravaged by the West Wind, and while dying gave birth to a flint (which the Menomini blame for her death), a wolf cub, and Manabozho, who was to become a scourge to both man and beast.

Raven too was known by a number of names, some of them unprintable. The Tsimshian, of the North Pacific Coast, called him Txäm'sëm (pronounced *Tchem*sem) * and also Giant. Raven and the term "Mocker," often used to describe him, are synonymous.

Old Man, in many Blackfoot legends and others, was a powerful transformer and trickster who usually practiced his magic at the expense of humans and animals alike. He set a record as a transformer by becoming an animal (a wolf) only once, though like all other transformers he was adept at disguises.

The twin gods of the Zuñi, Withio of the Cheyenne, animal tricksters such as Coyote of the Southwest, Rabbit, and other, lesser tricksters, were, like their confreres, a combination of boastfulness, stupidity, and wisdom of a sort.

In their better moments, transformers often taught the tribes arts and crafts and hunting skills, which brings us to the noblest transformer of them all, Glooscap, hero-god of the Northeast Woodland groups, such as Micmac, Abenaki, Penobscot, and Passamaquoddy. Some Glooscap tales smack of old Norse legends. Glooscap, genial giant, magician, transformer, lover of peace, and consistent doer-of-good, was credited with knowing and teaching every art needful to the North American Indians. He had a superb sense of humor but never used it to injure anyone or anything.

It is well to turn from transformers and tricksters, who lived only in the vivid imaginations of the Indian storytellers and their avid listeners, to real legendary figures.

*The transliteration of American Indian proper nouns is beset by so many special diacritical marks that even the best-equipped printer would find it difficult to set the type. Even then, they would not help to suggest the correct pronunciation except to ethnologists. Because of this, such marks have not been used in the printing of this book, which is why a difficult name like Txäm'sëm appears in translation as "Raven" in our text.

Hiawatha, a great and modest chief of the Onondaga, was forced by them to go on an almost impossible mission to the Mohawk, who later adopted him. Called Hi-ant-wat-ha by the Iroquois, he was also known as "He Who Clears Rivers," among other titles, though that of Teacher best fits the man and his works. His achievements, recorded in history, were factual, epic, and legendary.

Hiawatha was a great statesman and, though he has become a legendary figure, should not be confused with tricksters such as Manabozho. Hiawatha achieved psychologically what legend credits him with doing by magic powers. Modern Iroquoian storytellers explain that his great "white stone canoe" was really made of white birch, and the reason for the "magic" emptying of the wampum-lined lake, told in "Hiawatha and the Iroquois Wampum," was the breaking of a beaver dam. When the beavers repaired the dam, the lake filled again. Given proper understanding, legend and logic can, at times, be synonymous.

After five years of effort, Hiawatha accomplished his mission when, around 1452,* he and Deganawida, a Huron later adopted by the Mohawk, founded the mighty Confederacy of the Iroquois, which began as the Five Nations. These became the Six Nations in 1722 with the admission of the Tuscarora, driven from the South by the whites. It took over a hundred years to build and weld the invincible Confederacy, one of the greatest po-

*It is impossible to substantiate the date when Hiawatha worked with Deganawida in founding the League of the Iroquois, as the leading authorities disagree. A spokesman for the Smithsonian Institution hazards a guess that the date was somewhere around "1600, plus or minus 30 years," while the ethnohistorian of the National Museum of Canada states that estimates vary from ca. 1450 to ca. 1600. The Encyclopedia Britannica cites 1452, the date I favor as probably closest to actuality.

Apart from historical data, I base my opinion on the firm belief of my Indian friends, the late Dr. Arthur C. Parker, a leading Iroquoian authority, and Aren Akweks (some of whose legends appear in this book), both of whom give the date as approximately 1452—a figure that is founded on an ancient record. According to this, one or two of the Iroquoian Nations had hesitated about joining the League, and Deganawida said he would show them a celestial sign: "Look at the sun!" he told them. The corn was knee-high, it is recorded, and the sun went out, whereupon the doubting nations immediately sent messengers to say that they would join. Investigation of astronomical records reveals that the only total eclipse to occur when the corn was knee-high in western New York within hundreds of years of that date was in 1452.

litical organizations ever achieved. The democratic laws on which the Great Peace was founded merit careful study, since the unprecedented handiwork of its two founders proved so outstanding that it was greatly admired by Benjamin Franklin and other erudite American colonists who were so much impressed and influenced by it that they used it as a basis for the Constitution of the United States of America.

The object of the League was to assure peace, prosperity, power, and equality for all its members. The Iroquois Confederacy was so powerful and its social order and system of government so far advanced in theory and practice from any that Europeans had known, that it became a magnet to the officially appointed ambassadors from the courts of the most enlightened European nations.

After an uninterrupted reign of over three centuries, the League of the Six Nations ceremoniously extinguished its council fire on January 19, 1777. It has recently, however, been rekindled, and will be kept burning as in the days of legend.

Another historical figure is the Pima chief, Morning Green, of Casa Grande, in "How Turquoises Were Obtained," and "Women Enticed by Magic Song." Renowned in fact and fiction, he was regarded by the Pima as an historic personage and worker of miracles.

Most American Indian tribes had firm beliefs and strong taboos regarding certain legends. Some could be told only at certain seasons and special times, as when the moon was round, or when the forest was covered with the dark blanket of night, for fear that the telling would anger powerful spirits or call up ghosts. However, the readers who hold *American Indian Legends* in their hands are immune from even the most powerful spells and taboos. As they open this book, the Teller of Tales stands before them and begins, "When I was a boy, the old men told me . . ."

ALLAN A. MACFARLAN

ACKNOWLEDGMENTS

ACKNOWLEDGMENT for permission to include the copyrighted selections in this volume is gratefully given by the publisher and the editor to the following:

To Aren Akweks, secretary of Akwesasne, Six Nations Museum, Onchiota, New York, for six of his legends: "The Discovery of Fire," "The Flying Head," "The Great Gift," "The Hermit Thrush," "How Man Was Created," and "The Thunder Boy."

To Dodd, Mead and Company and Allan Macfarlan for four of the latter's legends in *Indian Adventure Trails* (copyright 1953): "Brother Birch," "The First False Face," "The Four Winds," and "The Loon's Necklace."

To the *Journal of American Folklore* for "The Story of Jack and His Brothers" (originally entitled "Little Poucet"); to the Queen's Printer for "Wemicus Tests His Son-in-Law" from *Memoirs of the Geological Survey of Canada* (1915); to Yale University Press for "The Mouse's Children" in George Bird Grinnell's *By Cheyenne Campfires* (copyright 1926). Other legends retold by Grinnell have been taken from his *Blackfoot Lodge Tales* and *Pawnee Hero Stories and Folk Tales*.

To the *Anthropological Papers of the Field Museum* for "The Origin of the Buffalo and of Corn" and "The Origin of the Medicine-Arrows"; to the *Bulletin of the American Museum of Natural History* for "How the Earth Began"; to the *Memoirs of the American Folk Lore Society* for "The Coyote and His Guests."

"Manabozho" and a dozen other stories are from *The Myth of Hiawatha and Other Oral Legends of the North American Indians* by Henry Rowe Schoolcraft. The *Annual Reports* of the United States Bureau of American Ethnology are the source of a great many of the legends in this volume; these include numerous tales collected by Dr. Franz Boas. Among the others whose work has been drawn upon are Rev. William M. Beauchamp, Frank H. Cushing, Charles G. Leland, Charles F. Lummis, Arthur C. Parker, Rev. Silas T. Rand, and Zitkala-Sa.

We also gratefully acknowledge the unstinting helpfulness of Paulette Macfarlan (Deer Woman), as well as the courtesies of the staffs of the New York Public Library, the Library of the American Museum of Natural History, and the Museum of the American Indian, Heye Foundation.

HABITATS OF NATIONS
AND TRIBES REPRESENTED

Central Eskimo: Arctic coasts

Tsimshian: north Pacific coast

Thompson: southern British Columbia

Maidu: northeast California

Pima, Pueblo, Zuñi: southwest United States

Blackfoot, Cheyenne, Dakota, Pawnee, Sioux: Great Plains

Cherokee, Choctaw, Shawnee: southeast United States

The remaining tribes represented by legends in this volume inhabited the vast woodland area, principally east of the Mississippi. Besides the *Micmac*, who lived in Nova Scotia and the Maritime Provinces of Canada, these include two large groups:

In the Iroquoian territory, chiefly from southwest Quebec and southeast Ontario to upper New York State and the eastern Great Lakes: *Iroquois, Mohawk, Oneida, Onondaga, Seneca.*

In the central section, comprising south-central Canada and the north-central area of the Ohio-Mississippi valley: *Algonquin, Chippewa, Maskego, Menomini, Ojibwa, Ottawa, Timagami-Ojibwa.*

Most of the above locations are to be understood in a general way, as habitats shifted in the course of time.

1

WHEN THE WORLD WAS YOUNG

HOW THE EARTH BEGAN

IN THE BEGINNING there was no sun, no moon, no stars. All was dark, and everywhere there was only water. A raft came floating on the water. It came from the north, and in it were two persons—Turtle (Anosma) and Father-of-the-Secret-Society (Peheipe). The stream flowed very rapidly. Then from the sky a rope of feathers, called *Pokelma*, was let down, and down it came Earth-Initiate. When he reached the end of the rope, he tied it to the bow of the raft, and stepped in. His face was covered and was never seen, but his body shone like the sun. He sat down, and for a long time said nothing.

At last Turtle said, "Where do you come from?" and Earth-Initiate answered, "I come from above." Then Turtle said, "Brother, can you not make for me some good dry land, so that I may sometimes come up out of the water?" Then he asked another time, "Are there going to be any people in the world?" Earth-Initiate thought awhile, then said, "Yes." Turtle asked, "How long before you are going to make people?" Earth-Initiate replied, "I don't know. You want to have some dry land: well, how am I going to get any earth to make it of?" Turtle answered, "If you will tie a rock about my left arm, I'll dive for some."

Earth-Initiate did as Turtle asked, and then, reaching around, took the end of a rope from somewhere, and tied it to Turtle. When Earth-Initiate came to the raft, there was no rope there: he just reached out and found one. Turtle said, "If the rope is not long enough, I'll jerk it once, and you must haul me up; if it is long enough, I'll give two jerks, and then you must pull me up quickly, as I shall have all the earth that I can carry." Just as Turtle went over the side of the boat, Father-of-the-Secret-Society began to shout loudly.

Turtle was gone a long time. He was gone six years; and when he came up, he was covered with green slime, he had been down so long. When he reached the top of the water, the only earth he had was a very little under his nails: the rest had all washed away. Earth-Initiate took with his right

3

hand a stone knife from under his left armpit, and carefully scraped the earth out from under Turtle's nails. He put the earth in the palm of his hand, and rolled it about till it was round; it was as large as a small pebble. He laid it on the stern of the raft. By and by he went to look at it: it had not grown at all. The third time that he went to look at it, it had grown so that it could be spanned by the arms. The fourth time he looked, it was as big as the world, the raft was aground, and all around were mountains as far as he could see. The raft came ashore at Tadoiko, and the place can be seen today.

When the raft had come to land, Turtle said, "I can't stay in the dark all the time. Can't you make a light, so that I can see?" Earth-Initiate replied, "Let us get out of the raft, and then we will see what we can do." So all three got out. Then Earth-Initiate said, "Look that way, to the east! I am going to tell my sister to come up." Then it began to grow light, and day began to break; then Father-of-the-Secret-Society began to shout loudly, and the sun came up. Turtle said, "Which way is the sun going to travel?" Earth-Initiate answered, "I'll tell her to go this way, and go down there." After the sun went down, Father-of-the-Secret-Society began to cry and shout again, and it grew very dark. Earth-Initiate said, "I'll tell my brother to come up." Then the moon rose. Then Earth-Initiate asked Turtle and Father-of-the-Secret-Society, "How do you like it?" And they both answered, "It is very good." Then Turtle asked, "Is that all you are going to do for us?" and Earth-Initiate answered, "No, I am going to do more yet." Then he called the stars each by its name, and they came out.

When this was done, Turtle asked, "Now what shall we do?" Earth-Initiate replied, "Wait, and I'll show you." Then he made a tree grow at Tadoiko, the tree called *Hukimtsa*; and Earth-Initiate and Turtle and Father-of-the-Secret-Society sat in its shade for two days. The tree was very large, and had twelve different kinds of acorns growing on it.

After they had sat for two days under the tree, they all went off to see the world that Earth-Initiate had made. They started at sunrise, and were back by sunset. Earth-Initiate traveled so fast that all they could see was a ball of fire flashing about under the ground and the water. While they were gone, Coyote (Olali) and his dog Rattlesnake (Kaudi or Sola) came up out of the ground. It is said that Coyote could see Earth-Initiate's face. When

4

Earth-Initiate and the others came back, they found Coyote at Tadoiko. All five of them then built huts for themselves, and lived there at Tadoiko, but no one could go inside of Earth-Initiate's house. Soon after the travelers came back, Earth-Initiate called the birds from the air, and made the trees and then the animals. He took some mud, and of this made first a deer; after that, he made all the other animals. Sometimes Turtle would say, "That does not look well: can't you make it some other way?"

Some time after this, Earth-Initiate and Coyote were at Marysville Buttes (Estobusin Yamani). Earth-Initiate said, "I am going to make people." In the middle of the afternoon he began, for he had returned to Tadoiko. He took dark red earth, mixed it with water, and made two figures, one a man, and one a woman. He laid the man on his right side, and the woman on his left, inside his house. Then he lay down himself, flat on his back, with his arms stretched out. He lay thus and sweated all the afternoon and night. Early in the morning the woman began to tickle him in the side. He kept very still, and did not laugh. By and by he got up, thrust a piece of pitch-wood into the ground, and fire burst out. The two people were very white. No one today is as white as they were. Their eyes were pink, their hair was black, their teeth shone brightly, and they were very handsome.

It is said that Earth-Initiate did not finish the hands of the people, as he did not know how it would be best to do it. Coyote saw the people, and suggested that they ought to have hands like his. Earth-Initiate said, "No, their hands shall be like mine." Then he finished them. When Coyote asked why their hands were to be like that, Earth-Initiate answered, "So that, if they are chased by bears, they can climb trees." This first man was called Kuksu, and the woman, Morning-Star Woman (La Idambulum Kule).

When Coyote had seen the two people, he asked Earth-Initiate how he had made them. When he was told, he thought, "That is not difficult. I'll do it myself." He did just as Earth-Initiate had told him, but could not help laughing, when, early in the morning, the woman poked him in the ribs. As a result of his failing to keep still, the people were glass-eyed. Earth-Initiate said, "I told you not to laugh," but Coyote declared he had not. This was the first lie.

By and by there came to be a good many people. Earth-Initiate had wanted to have everything comfortable and easy for people, so that none

5

of them should have to work. All fruits were easy to obtain, no one was ever to get sick and die. As the people grew numerous, Earth-Initiate did not come as often as formerly, he only came to see Kuksu in the night. One night he said to him, "Tomorrow morning you must go to the little lake near here. Take all the people with you. I'll make you a very old man before you get to the lake." So in the morning Kuksu collected all the people, and went to the lake. By the time he had reached it, he was a very old man. He fell into the lake, and sank down out of sight. Pretty soon the ground began to shake, the waves overflowed the shore, and there was a great roaring under the water, like thunder. By and by Kuksu came up out of the water, but young again, just like a young man. Then Earth-Initiate came and spoke to the people, and said, "If you do as I tell you, everything will be well. When any of you grow old, so old that you cannot walk, come to this lake, or get someone to bring you here. You must then go down into the water as you have seen Kuksu do, and you will come out young again." When he had said this, he went away. He left in the night, and went up above.

All this time food had been easy to get, as Earth-Initiate had wished. The women set out baskets at night, and in the morning they found them full of food, all ready to eat, and lukewarm. One day Coyote came along. He asked the people how they lived, and they told him that all they had to do was to eat and sleep. Coyote replied, "That is no way to do: I can show you something better." Then he told them how he and Earth-Initiate had had a discussion before men had been made; how Earth-Initiate wanted everything easy, and that there should be no sickness or death, but how he had thought it would be better to have people work, get sick, and die. He said, "We'll have a burning." The people did not know what he meant; but Coyote said, "I'll show you. It is better to have a burning, for then the widows can be free." So he took all the baskets and things that the people had, hung them up on poles, made everything all ready. When all was prepared, Coyote said, "At this time you must always have games." So he fixed the moon during which these games were to be played.

Coyote told them to start the games with a foot race, and everyone got ready to run. Kuksu did not come, however. He sat in his hut alone, and was sad, for he knew what was going to occur. Just at this moment Rattlesnake came to Kuksu, and said, "What shall we do now? Everything is spoiled!" Kuksu did not answer, so Rattlesnake said, "Well, I'll do what I think is best." Then he went out, along the course that the racers were to go over, and hid himself, leaving his head just sticking out of a hole. By this time all the racers had started, and among them Coyote's son. He was Coyote's only child, and was very quick. He soon began to outstrip all the runners, and was in the lead. As he passed the spot where Rattlesnake had hidden himself, however, Rattlesnake raised his head and bit the boy in the ankle. In a minute the boy was dead.

Coyote was dancing about the home-stake. He was very happy, and was shouting at his son and praising him. When Rattlesnake bit the boy, and he fell dead, everyone laughed at Coyote, and said, "Your son has fallen down, and is so ashamed that he does not dare to get up." Coyote said, "No, that is not it. He is dead." This was the first death. The people, however, did not understand, and picked the boy up, and brought him to Coyote. Then Coyote began to cry, and everyone did the same. These were the first tears. Then Coyote took his son's body and carried it to the lake of which Earth-Initiate had told them, and threw the body in. But there was no noise, and nothing happened, and the body drifted about for four days on the surface, like a log. On the fifth day Coyote took four sacks of beads and brought them to Kuksu, begging him to restore his son to life. Kuksu did not answer. For five days Coyote begged, then Kuksu came out of his house bringing all his beads and bearskins, and calling to all the people to come and watch him. He laid the body on a bearskin, dressed it, and wrapped it up carefully. Then he dug a grave, put the body into it, and covered it up. Then he told the people, "From now on, this is what you must do. This is the way you must do till the world shall be made over."

About a year after this, in the spring, all was changed. Up to this time everybody spoke the same language. The people were having a burning, everything was ready for the next day, when in the night everybody suddenly began to speak a different language. Each man and his wife, however, spoke the same. Earth-Initiate had come in the night to Kuksu, and had told him about it all, and given him instructions for the next day.

So, when morning came, Kuksu called all the people together, for he was able to speak all the languages. He told them each the names of the different animals, in their languages, taught them how to cook and to hunt, gave them all their laws, and set the time for all their dances and festivals. Then he called each tribe by name, and sent them off in different directions, telling them where they were to live. He sent the warriors to the north, the singers to the west, the flute-players to the east, and the dancers to the south. So all the people went away, and left Kuksu and his wife alone at Tadoiko. By and by his wife went away, leaving in the night, and going first to Marysville Buttes. Kuksu stayed a little while longer, and then he also left. He too went to the Buttes, went into the spirit house (*Kukinim Kumi*), and sat down on the south side. He found Coyote's son there, sitting on the north side. The door was on the west.

Coyote had been trying to find out where Kuksu had gone, and where his own son had gone, and at last found the tracks, and followed them to the spirit house. Here he saw Kuksu and his son, the latter eating spirit food (*Kukinim pe*). Coyote wanted to go in, but Kuksu said, "No, wait there. You have just what you wanted, it is your own fault. Every man will now have all kinds of troubles and accidents, will have to work to get his food, and will die and be buried. This must go on till the time is out, and Earth-Initiate come again, and everything will be made over. You must go home, and tell all the people that you have seen your son, that he is not dead." Coyote said he would go, but that he was hungry, and wanted some of the food. Kuksu replied, "You cannot eat that. Only ghosts may eat that food." Then Coyote went away and told all the people, "I saw my son and Kuksu, and he told me to kill myself." So he climbed up to the top of a tall tree, jumped off, and was killed. Then he went to the spirit house, thinking he could now have some of the food; but there was no one there, nothing at all, and so he went out, and walked away to the west, and was never seen again. Kuksu and Coyote's son, however, had gone up above.

HOW MAN WAS CREATED

AFTER SAT-KON-SE-RI-IO, the Good Spirit, had made the animals, birds, and other creatures and had placed them to live and multiply upon the earth, he rested. As he gazed around at his various creations, it seemed to him that there was something lacking. For a long time the Good Spirit pondered over this thought. Finally he decided to make a creature that would resemble himself.

Going to the bank of a river he took a piece of clay, and out of it he fashioned a little clay man. After he had modeled it, he built a fire and, setting the little clay man in the fire, waited for it to bake. The day was beautiful. The songs of the birds filled the air. The river sang a song and, as the Good Spirit listened to this song, he became very sleepy. He soon fell asleep beside the fire. When he finally awoke, he rushed to the fire and removed the clay man. He had slept too long. His little man was burnt black. According to the Mohawks, this little man was the first Negro. His skin was black. He had been overbaked.

The Good Spirit was not satisfied. Taking a fresh piece of clay, he fashioned another man and, placing him in the fire, waited for him to bake, determined this time to stay awake and watch his little man to see that he would not be overbaked. But the river sang its usual sleepy song. The Good Spirit, in spite of all he could do, fell asleep. But this time he slept only a little while. Awakening at last, he ran to the fire and removed his little man. Behold, it was half baked. This, say the Mohawks, was the first white man. He was half baked!

The Good Spirit was still unsatisfied. Searching along the riverbank he hunted until he found a bed of perfect red clay. This time he took great care and modeled a very fine clay man. Taking the clay man to the fire, he allowed it to bake. Determined to stay awake, the Good Spirit stood beside the fire, after a while Sat-kon-se-ri-io removed the clay man. Behold, it was just right—a man the red color of the sunset sky. It was the first Mohawk Indian.

THE GENESIS OF THE WORLDS, OR THE BEGINNING OF NEWNESS

BEFORE THE BEGINNING of the new-making, Awonawilona—the Maker and Container of All, the All-father Father—solely had being. There was nothing else whatsoever throughout the great space of the ages save everywhere black darkness in it, and everywhere void desolation.

In the beginning of the new-made, Awonawilona conceived within himself and thought outward in space, whereby mists of increase, steams potent of growth, were evolved and uplifted. Thus, by means of his innate knowledge, the All-container made himself in person and form of the Sun, whom we hold to be our father and who thus came to exist and appear. With his appearance came the brightening of the spaces with light, and with the brightening of the spaces, the great mist clouds were thickened together and fell, whereby was evolved water in water; yea, and the world-holding sea.

With his substance of flesh outdrawn from the surface of his person, the Sun-father formed the seed-stuff of twain worlds, impregnating therewith the great waters, and lo! in the heat of his light these waters of the sea grew green and scums rose upon them, waxing wide and weighty until, behold! they became *Awitelin Tsita*, the "Fourfold-containing Mother-earth," and *Apoyan Tachu*, the "All-covering Father-sky."

THE GENESIS OF MEN AND THE CREATURES

FROM THE LYING TOGETHER of these twain upon the great world waters, so vitalizing, terrestrial life was conceived; whence began all beings of earth, men and the creatures, in the Fourfold Womb of the World, *Awiten Tehuhena Kwi*.

Thereupon the Earth-mother repulsed the Sky-father, growing big and sinking deep into the embrace of the waters below, thus separating from the Sky-father in the embrace of the waters above. As a woman forebodes evil for her first-born ere born, even so did the Earth-mother forebode, long withholding from birth her myriad progeny and meantime seeking counsel with the Sky-father. "How," said they to one another, "shall our children, when brought forth, know one place from another, even by the white light of the Sun-father?"

Now like all the surpassing beings the Earth-mother and the Sky-father were changeable, even as smoke in the wind; transmutable at thought, manifesting themselves in any form at will, as dancers may by mask-making.

Thus, as a man and woman, spake they, one to the other. "Behold!" said the Earth-mother as a great terraced bowl appeared at hand and within it water, "this is as, upon me, the homes of my tiny children shall be. On the rim of each world country they wander in, terraced mountains shall stand, making in one region many, whereby country shall be known from country, and within each, place from place. Behold, again!" said she as she spat on the water and rapidly smote and stirred it with her fingers. Foam formed, gathering about the terraced rim, mounting higher and higher. "Yea," said she, "and from my bosom they shall draw nourishment, for in such as this shall they find the substance of life whence we were ourselves sustained, for see!" Then with her warm breath she blew across the terraces; white flecks of the foam broke away, and, floating over above the water, were shattered by the cold breath of the Sky-father attending, and forthwith shed downward abundantly fine mist and spray! "Even so, shall white clouds float up from the great waters at the borders of the world, and clustering about the mountain terraces of the horizons be borne aloft and abroad by the breaths of the surpassing of soul-beings, and of the children, and shall hardened and broken be by thy cold, shedding downward, in rain spray, the water of life, even into the hollow places of my lap! For therein chiefly shall nestle our children mankind and creature-kind, for warmth in thy coldness."

Lo! even the trees on high mountains near the clouds and the Sky-father crouch low toward the Earth-mother for warmth and protection! Warm is the Earth-mother, cold the Sky-father, even as woman is the warm, man the cold being!

"Even so!" said the Sky-father. "Yet not alone shalt *thou* helpful be unto

11

our children, for behold!" And he spread his hand abroad with the palm downward and into all the wrinkles and crevices thereof he set the semblance of shining yellow corn grains; in the dark of the early world-dawn they gleamed like sparks of fire, and moved as his hand was moved over the bowl, shining up from and also moving in the depths of the water therein. "See!" said he, pointing to the seven grains clasped by his thumb and four fingers, "by such shall our children be guided; for behold, when the Sun-father is not nigh, and thy terraces are as the dark itself (being all hidden therein), then shall our children be guided by lights—like to these lights of all the six regions turning round the midmost one—as in and around the midmost place, where these our children shall abide, lie all the other regions of space! Yea! and even as these grains gleam up from the water, so shall seed grains like to them, yet numberless, spring up from thy bosom when touched by my waters, to nourish our children." Thus and in many other ways devised they for their offspring.

THE ORIGIN OF DAYLIGHT

GIANT FLEW INLAND toward the east. He went on for a long time, and finally he was very tired, so he dropped down on the sea the little round stone which his father had given to him. It became a large rock way out at sea. Giant rested on it and refreshed himself, and took off the raven skin.

At that time there was always darkness. There was no daylight then. Again Giant put on the raven skin and flew toward the east. Now, Giant reached the mainland and arrived at the mouth of Skeena River. There he stopped and scattered the salmon roe and trout roe. He said while he was scattering them, "Let every river and creek have all kinds of fish!" Then he took the dried sea-lion bladder and scattered the fruits all over the land, saying, "Let every mountain, hill, valley, plain, the whole land, be full of fruits!"

The whole world was still covered with darkness. When the sky was clear, the people would have a little light from the stars; and when clouds were in the sky, it was very dark all over the land. The people were distressed by this. Then Giant thought that it would be hard for him to obtain his food if it were always dark. He remembered that there was light in heaven, whence he had come. Then he made up his mind to bring down the light to our world. On the following day Giant put on his raven skin, which his father the chief had given to him, and flew upward. Finally he found the hole in the sky, and he flew through it. Giant reached the inside of the sky. He took off the raven skin and put it down near the hole of the sky. He went on, and came to a spring near the house of the chief of heaven. There he sat down and waited.

Then the chief's daughter came out, carrying a small bucket in which she was about to fetch water. She went down to the big spring in front of her father's house. When Giant saw her coming along, he transformed himself into the leaf of a cedar and floated on the water. The chief's daughter dipped it up in her bucket and drank it. Then she returned to her father's house and entered.

After a short time she was with child, and not long after she gave birth to a boy. Then the chief and the chieftainess were very glad. They washed the boy regularly. He began to grow up. Now he was beginning to creep about. They washed him often, and the chief smoothed and cleaned the floor of the house. Now the child was strong and crept about every day. He began to cry, "*Hama, hama!*" He was crying all the time, and the great chief was troubled, and called in some of his slaves to carry about the boy. The slaves did so, but he would not sleep for several nights. He kept on crying, "*Hama, hama!*" Therefore the chief invited all his wise men, and said to them that he did not know what the boy wanted and why he was crying. He wanted the box that was hanging in the chief's house.

This box, in which the daylight was kept, was hanging in one corner of the house. Its name was *Ma*. Giant had known it before he descended to our world, so the child cried for it. The chief was annoyed, and the wise men listened to what the chief told them. When the wise men heard the child crying aloud, they did not know what he was saying. He was crying all the time, "*Hama, hama, hama!*"

One of the wise men, who understood him, said to the chief, "He is crying for the *ma*." Therefore the chief ordered it to be taken down. The man put it down. They put it down near the fire, and the boy sat down near it

and ceased crying. He stopped crying, for he was glad. Then he rolled the
ma about inside the house. He did so for four days. Sometimes he would
carry it to the door. Now the great chief did not think of it. He had quite
forgotten it. Then the boy really took up the *ma*, put it on his shoulders,
and ran out with it. While he was running, someone said, "Giant is running away with the *ma!*" He ran away, and the hosts of heaven pursued
him. They shouted that Giant was running away with the *ma*. He came to
the hole of the sky, put on the skin of the raven, and flew down, carrying
the *ma*. Then the hosts of heaven returned to their houses, and he flew down
with it to our world.

At that time the world was still dark. He arrived farther up the river, and
went down river. Giant had come down near the mouth of Nass River. He
went to the mouth of Nass River. It was always dark, and he carried the
ma about with him. He went on, and went up the river in the dark. A little
farther up he heard the noise of the people, who were catching *olachen* in

bag nets in their canoes. There was much noise out on the river, because they were working hard.

Giant, who was sitting on the shore, said, "Throw ashore one of the things that you are catching, my dear people!" After a while, Giant said again, "Throw ashore one of the things you are catching!" Then those on the water scolded him. "Where did you come from, great liar, whom they call Raven?" The animal people knew that it was Giant. Therefore they made fun of him. Then Giant said again, "Throw ashore one of the things that you are catching, or I shall break the *ma!*" And all those who were on the water answered, "Where did you get what you are talking about, you liar?" Giant said once more, "Throw ashore one of the things that you are catching, my dear people, or I shall break the *ma* for you!" One person replied, scolding him.

Giant had repeated his request four times, but those on the water refused what he had asked for. Therefore Giant broke the *ma*. It broke, and it was daylight. The north wind began to blow hard; and all the fishermen, the frogs, were driven away by the north wind. All the frogs who had made fun of Giant were driven away down river until they arrived at one of the large mountainous islands. Here the frogs tried to climb up the rock; but they stuck to the rock, being frozen by the north wind, and became stone. They are still on the rock. The fishing frogs named him Raven, and all the world had the daylight.

OLD MAN MAKES THE LAND AND THE PEOPLE

ALL ANIMALS of the plains at one time heard and knew him, and all birds of the air heard and knew him. All things that he had made understood him, when he spoke to them—the birds, the animals, and the people.

Old Man was traveling about, south of here, making the people. He came from the south, traveling north, making animals and birds as he passed along. He made the mountains, prairies, timber, and brush first. So he went along, traveling northward, making things as he went, putting rivers here and there, and falls on them, putting red paint here and there in the ground, fixing up the world as we see it today. He made the Milk River, the Teton, and crossed it, and being tired, went up on a little hill and lay down to rest.

As he lay on his back, stretched out on the ground, with arms extended, he marked himself out with stones—the shape of his body, head, legs, arms, and everything. There you can see those rocks today. After he had rested, he went on northward, and stumbled over a knoll and fell down on his knees. Then he said, "You are a bad thing to be stumbling against"; so he raised up two large buttes there, and named them the Knees, and they are called so to this day. He went on farther north, and with some of the rocks he carried with him he built the Sweet Grass Hills.

Old Man covered the plains with grass for the animals to feed on. He marked off a piece of ground, and in it he made to grow all kinds of roots and berries—camas, wild carrots, wild turnips, sweetroot, bitterroot, service berries, bullberries, cherries, plums, and rosebuds. He put trees on the ground. He put all kinds of animals on the ground. When he made the bighorn with its big head and horns, he made it out on the prairie. It did not seem to travel easily on the prairie; it was awkward and could not go fast. So he took it by one of its horns, and led it up into the mountains, and turned it loose; and it skipped about among the rocks, and went up fearful places with ease. So he said, "This is the place that suits you; this is what you are fitted for, the rocks and the mountains." While he was in the mountains, he made the antelope out of dirt, and turned it loose, to see how it would go. It ran so fast that it fell over some rocks and hurt itself. He saw that this would not do, and took the antelope down on the prairie, and turned it loose; and it ran away fast and gracefully, and he said, "This is what you are suited to."

One day Old Man determined that he would make a woman and a child; so he formed them both—the woman and the child, her son—of clay. After he had molded the clay in human shape, he said to the clay, "You must be people," and then he covered it up and left it, and went away. The next morning he went to the place and took the covering off, and saw that the clay shapes had changed a little. The second morning there was still more change, and the third still more. The fourth morning he went to the place, took the covering off, looked at the images, and told them to rise and walk; and they did so. They walked down to the river with their Maker, and then he told them that his name was Napi, Old Man.

As they were standing by the river, the woman said to him, "How is it? Will we always live, will there be no end to it?" He said, "I have never thought of that. We will have to decide it. I will take this buffalo chip and throw it in the river. If it floats, when people die, in four days they will become alive again; they will die for only four days. But if it sinks, there will be an end to them." He threw the chip into the river, and it floated. The woman turned and picked up a stone, and said, "No, I will throw this stone in the river; if it floats we will always live, if it sinks people must die, that they may always be sorry for each other." The woman threw the stone into the water, and it sank. "There," said Old Man, "you have chosen. There will be an end to them."

It was not many nights after, that the woman's child died, and she cried a great deal for it. She said to Old Man, "Let us change this. The law that you first made, let that be a law." He said, "Not so. What is made law must be law. We will undo nothing that we have done. The child is dead, but it cannot be changed. People will have to die."

That is how we came to be people. It is he who made us.

The first people were poor and naked, and did not know how to get a living. Old Man showed them the roots and berries, and told them that they could eat them; that in a certain month of the year they could peel the bark off some trees and eat it, that it was good. He told the people that the animals should be their food, and gave them to the people, saying, "These are your herds." He said, "All these little animals that live in the ground—rats, squirrels, skunks, beavers—are good to eat. You need not fear to eat of their flesh." He made all the birds that fly, and told the people that there was no harm in their flesh, that it could be eaten. The first people that he created he used to take about through the timber and swamps and over the prairies, and show them the different plants. Of a certain plant he would say, "The root of this plant, if gathered in a certain month of the year, is good for a certain sickness." So they learned the power of all herbs.

In those days there were buffalo. Now the people had no arms; but those black animals with long beards were armed; and once, as the people were moving about, the buffalo saw them, and ran after them, and hooked them, and killed and ate them. One day, as the Maker of the people was traveling over the country, he saw some of his children, that he had made, lying dead, torn to pieces and partly eaten by the buffalo. When he saw this he was very sad. He said, "This will not do. I will change them. The people shall eat the buffalo."

He went to some of the people who were left, and said to them, "How is it that you people do nothing to these animals that are killing you?" The people said, "What can we do? We have no way to kill these animals, while they are armed and can kill us." Then said the Maker, "That is not hard. I will make you a weapon that will kill these animals." So he went out, and cut some service-berry shoots, and brought them in, and peeled the bark off them. He took a larger piece of wood, and flattened it, and tied a string to it, and made a bow. Now, as he was the master of all birds and could do with them as he wished, he went out and caught one, and took feathers from its wing, and split them, and tied them to the shaft of wood. He tied four feathers along the shaft, and tried the arrow at a mark, and found that it did not fly well. He took these feathers off, and put on three; and when he tried it again, he found that it was good. He went out and began to break sharp pieces off the stones. He tried them, and found that the black flint stones made the best arrow points, and some white flints. Then he taught the people how to use these things.

Then he said, "The next time you go out, take these things with you, and use them as I tell you, and do not run from these animals. When they run at you, as soon as they get pretty close, shoot the arrows at them, as I have taught you; and you will see that they will run from you or will run in a circle around you."

Now, as people became plenty, one day three men went out onto the plain to see the buffalo, but they had no arms. They saw the animals, but when the buffalo saw the men, they ran after them and killed two of them, but one got away. One day after this, the people went on a little hill to look about, and the buffalo saw them, and said, "*Saiyah*, there is some more of our food." And they rushed on the people. This time the people did not run. They began to shoot at the buffalo with the bows and arrows Napi had given them, and the buffalo began to fall; but in the fight a person was killed.

At this time these people had flint knives given them, and they cut up the bodies of the dead buffalo. It is not healthful to eat the meat raw, so Old Man gathered soft dry rotten driftwood and made punk of it, and then got a piece of hardwood, and drilled a hole in it with an arrow point. He gave the people the pointed piece of hardwood, and taught them how to make a fire with fire sticks, and to cook the flesh of these animals and eat it.

They got a kind of stone that was in the land, and then took another harder stone and worked one upon the other, and hollowed out the softer one, and made a kettle of it. This was the fashion of their dishes.

Also Old Man said to the people, "Now, if you are overcome, you may go and sleep, and get power. Something will come to you in your dreams, that will help you. Whatever these animals tell you to do, you must obey them, as they appear to you in your sleep. Be guided by them. If anybody wants help, if you are alone and traveling, and cry aloud for help, your prayer will be answered. It may be by the eagles, perhaps by the buffalo, or by the bears. Whatever animal answers your prayer, you must listen to him."

That was how the first people got through the world, by the power of their dreams.

After this, Old Man kept on, traveling north. Many of the animals that he had made followed him as he went. The animals understood him when he spoke to them, and he used them as his servants. When he got to the north point of the Porcupine Mountains, there he made some more mud images of people, and blew breath upon them, and they became people. He made men and women. They asked him, "What are we to eat?" He made many images of clay in the form of buffalo. Then he blew breath on these, and they stood up; and when he made signs to them, they started to run. Then he said to the people, "Those are your food." They said to him, "Well, now, we have those animals; how are we to kill them?" "I will show you," he said. He took them to a cliff, and made them build two lines of rock piles so that they slanted together toward a small opening at the edge of the cliff. He made the people hide behind these piles of rocks, and said, "When I lead the buffalo this way, as I bring them opposite to you, rise up."

After he had told them how to act, he started on toward a herd of buffalo. He began to call them, and the buffalo started to run toward him, and they followed him until they were inside the lines. Then he dropped back; and as the people rose up, the buffalo ran in a straight line and jumped over the cliff. He told the people to go and take the flesh of those animals. They tried to tear the limbs apart, but they could not. They tried to bite pieces out, and could not.

So Old Man went to the edge of the cliff, and broke some pieces of stone with sharp edges, and told them to cut the flesh with these. When they had taken the skins from these animals, they set up some poles and put the hides on them, and so made a shelter to sleep under. There were some of these buffalo that went over the cliff that were not dead. Their legs were broken, but they were still alive. The people cut strips of green hide, and tied stones in the middle, and made large mauls, and broke in the skulls of the buffalo, and killed them.

After he had taught those people these things, he started off again, traveling north, until he came to where the Bow and Elbow rivers meet. There he made some more people, and taught them the same things. From here he again went on northward. When he had come nearly to the Red Deer's River, he reached the hill where the Old Man sleeps. There he lay down and rested himself. The form of his body is to be seen there yet.

When he awoke from his sleep, he traveled farther northward and came to a fine high hill. He climbed to the top of it, and there sat down to rest. He looked over the country below him, and it pleased him. Before him the hill was steep, and he said to himself, "Well, this is a fine place for sliding; I will have some fun," and he began to slide down the hill. The marks where he slid down are to be seen yet, and the place is known to all people as the Old Man's Sliding Ground.

This is as far as the Blackfeet followed Old Man. The Crees know what he did farther north.

In later times once, Napi said, "Here I will mark you off a piece of ground," and he did so. Then he said: "There is your land, and it is full of all kinds of animals, and many things grow in this land. Let no other people come into it. This is for you five tribes (Blackfeet, Bloods, Piegans, Gros Ventres, Sarcees). When people come to cross the line, take your bows and arrows, your lances and your battle-axes, and give them battle and keep them out. If they gain a footing, trouble will come to you."

Our forefathers gave battle to all people who came to cross these lines, and kept them out. Of late years we have let our friends, the white people, come in, and you know the result. We, his children, have failed to obey his laws.

HOW THE TRIBES BEGAN

MANY GENERATIONS AGO Aba, the Good Spirit above, created many men, all Choctaw, who spoke the language of the Choctaw, and understood one another. These came from the bosom of the earth, being formed of yellow clay, and no men had ever lived before them. One day all came together and, looking upward, wondered what the clouds and the blue expanse above might be. They continued to wonder and talk among themselves and at last determined to endeavor to reach the sky.

So they brought many rocks and began building a mound that was to have touched the heavens. That night, however, the wind blew strong from above, and the rocks fell from the mound. The second morning they again began work on the mound, but as the men slept that night, the rocks were again scattered by the winds. Once more, on the third morning, the builders set to their task. But once more, as the men lay near the mound that night, wrapped in slumber, the winds came with so great force that the rocks were hurled down on them.

The men were not killed, but when daylight came, and they made their way from beneath the rocks and began to speak to one another, all were astounded as well as alarmed; they spoke various languages and could not understand one another. Some continued thenceforward to speak the original tongue, the language of the Choctaw, and from these sprang the Choctaw tribe. The others, who could not understand this language, began to fight among themselves. Finally they separated. The Choctaw remained the original people; the others scattered, some going north, some east, and others west, and formed various tribes. This explains why there are so many tribes throughout the country at the present time.

II

HERO AND CULTURE-HERO TALES

GLOOSCAP AND THE THREE
SEEKERS OF GIFTS

OF OLD TIME. Now when it was noised abroad that whoever besought Glooscap could obtain the desire of his heart, there were three men who said among themselves, "Let us seek the Master." So they left their home in the early spring when the bluebird first sang, and walked till the fall frosts, and then into winter, and ever on till the next midsummer. And having come to a small path in a great forest, they followed it, till they came out by a very beautiful river; so fair a sight they had never seen, and so went onward till it grew to be a great lake. And so they kept to the path which, when untrodden, was marked by blazed trees, the bark having been removed, in Indian fashion, on the side of the trunk which is opposite the place where the wigwam or village lies toward which it turns. So the mark can be seen as the traveler goes toward the goal, but not while leaving it.

Then after a time they came to a long point of land running out into the lake, and having ascended a high hill, they saw in the distance a smoke, which guided them to a large, well-built wigwam. And entering, they found seated on the right side a handsome, healthy man of middle age, and by the other a woman so decrepit that she seemed to be a hundred years old. Opposite the door, and on the left side, was a mat, which seemed to show that a third person had there a seat.

And the man made them welcome, and spoke as if he were well pleased to see them, but did not ask them whence they came or whither they were going, as is wont among Indians when strangers come to their homes or are met in travel. Ere long they heard the sound of a paddle, and then the noise of a canoe being drawn ashore. And there came in a youth of fine form and features and well clad, bearing weapons as if from hunting, who addressed the old woman as *Kejoo*—or mother—and told her that he had brought game. And with sore ado—for she was feeble—the old dame tottered out and brought in four beavers; but she was so much troubled to cut them up that the elder, saying to the younger man, *"Uoh-keen!—My brother,"* bade him do the work. And they supped on beaver.

So they remained for a week, resting themselves, for they were sadly worn with their wearisome journey, and also utterly ragged. And then a wondrous thing came to pass, which first taught them that they were in an enchanted land. For one morning the elder man bade the younger wash their mother's face. And as he did this all her wrinkles vanished, and she became young and very beautiful; in all their lives the travelers had never seen so lovely a woman. Her hair, which had been white and scanty, now hung to her feet, dark and glossy as a blackbird's breast. Then, having been clad in fine array, she showed a tall, lithe, and graceful form at its best.

And the travelers said to themselves, "Truly this man is a great magician!" They all walked forth to see the place. Never was sunshine so pleasantly tempered by a soft breeze; for all in that land was fair, and it grew fairer day by day to all who dwelt there. Tall trees with rich foliage and fragrant flowers, but without lower limbs or underbrush, grew as in a grove, wide as a forest, yet so far apart that the eye could pierce the distance in every direction.

Now when they felt for the first time that they were in a new life and a magic land, he that was host asked them whence they came and what they sought. So they said that they sought Glooscap. And the host replied, "Lo, I am he!" And they were awed by his presence, for a great glory and majesty now sat upon him. As the woman had changed, so had he, for all in that place was wonderful.

Then the first, telling what he wanted, said, "I am a wicked man, and I have a bad temper. I am prone to wrath and reviling, yet I would fain be pious, meek, and holy."

And the next said, "I am very poor, and my life is hard. I toil, but can barely make my living. I would fain be rich."

Now the third replied, "I am of low estate, being despised and hated by all my people, and I wish to be loved and respected." And to all these the Master made answer, "So shall it be!"

And taking his medicine bag he gave unto each a small box, and bade them keep it closed until they should be once more at home. And on returning to the wigwam he also gave to each of them new garments; in all their lives they had never seen or heard of such rich apparel or such ornaments as they now had. Then when it was time to depart, as they knew not the way to their home, he arose and went with them. Now they had been more than a year in coming. But he, having put on his belt, went forth, and they followed, till in the forenoon he led them to the top of a high mountain, from which in the distance they beheld yet another, the blue outline of which could just be seen above the horizon. And having been told that their way was unto it, they thought it would be a week's journey to reach it. But they went on, and in the middle of the afternoon of the same day they were there, on the summit of the second mountain. And looking from this afar, all was familiar to them—hill and river, and wood and lakes—all was in their memory. "And there," said the Master, pointing unto it, "there is your village!" So he left them alone, and they went on their way, and before the sun had set were safe at home.

Yet when they came, no one knew them, because of the great change in their appearance and their fine attire, the like of which had never been seen by man in those days. But having made themselves known to their friends, all that were there of old and young gathered together to gaze upon and hear what they had to say. And they were amazed.

Then each of them, having opened his box, found therein an unguent, rich and fragrant, and with this they rubbed their bodies completely. And they were ever after so fragrant from the divine anointing that all sought to be near them. Happy were they who could but sniff at the blessed smell which came from them.

Now he who had been despised for his deformity and weakness and meanness became beautiful and strong and stately as a pine tree. There was no man in all the land so graceful or of such good behavior.

And he who had desired abundance had it, in all fullness, his wish. For the moose and caribou came to him in the forest, the fish leaped into his nets; all men gave unto him, and he gave unto all freely, to the end.

And he that had been wicked and of evil mind, hasty and cruel, became meek and patient, good and gentle, and he made others like himself. And he had his reward, for there was a blessing upon him as upon all those who had wished wisely even unto the end of their days.

GENETASKA, THE PEACEMAKER QUEEN

KIENUKA, the peace home, was deserted. The ancient fire no longer burned there. All was cold and desolate. No friendly voice welcomed the fugitive; no persuasive words kept peace between hostile warriors who met there and laid aside their anger and their arms. The broad paths from every direction were untrod by human feet. They were left to the woodland animals, and serpents hissed and wolves howled where men sought wise counsels in hours of doubt and danger. The house of the peace queen was in a ruinous state, within and without, for she had abandoned her office and there was no one to take her place. Men had come there with angry thoughts, and no one was found to judge between them. Blood had been shed in Kienuka, and the Great Spirit no longer smiled upon it.

When the wise Hiawatha spoke his last words to his friends, he told them to choose from their maidens one gifted with wisdom, who should be their peacemaker. For her they should build a house and in it she should dwell. Doors were to be made at each side and end. Broad paths were to be made to these, so that all might find a welcome, no matter whence they came. More than a welcome, for she was to judge equitably between them, turn danger into safety, and hatred into love. This was to be her great and honorable office.

Then all the maidens were brought together at the great council place, and to them were submitted the questions in dispute among their brothers. Whoever decided the most of these justly should be the Peacemaker Queen, and dwell in the strong house provided. The house was built, the queen enthroned. When the Great Spirit called her to Eskanane, she was mourned by all, and none entered Kienuka till her successor had been chosen.

In this way there came to the peace home Genetaska, the Seneca maiden, whose wisdom and kindness were known to all, and whose beauty was like that of the summer days. She was the most famous of all the Peacemaker Queens, and the red men said that Hiawatha's daughter came often from the sky, borne by the great white bird, and gave her advice and guidance. Whoever went to Kienuka disputing departed from thence, when they had rested and eaten, with no anger in their hearts, for Genetaska soothed them by her gentle voice. To the sick and wounded she ministered with the best medicinal herbs; to those inflamed with anger she told of the Great Spirit which taught them moderation. Disputes were so adjusted that the hunters and warriors who came there with anger and war in their hearts left her doors as brothers.

One day there came to Kienuka two young chiefs, one from the Onondagas, one an Oneida. Each claimed that his arrow had slain a mighty buck they had been following in the forest. When they had tried their skill with weapons, agreeing that the victor should have the slain animal, neither had any advantage. Then said the Onondaga, "I will fight thee, O, Oneida chief, and he who survives may bear to his village the great buck and the scalp lock of his enemy."

But the Oneida said, "O, Onondaga, thou must remember the words that thou hast heard from the old men who heard the teachings of Hiawatha, that when two hunters of the Five Nations dispute in the forest, they shall not fight, but tell their disputes to the Peacemaker. I will go with thee to Kienuka."

When they had eaten and rested there, the hunters were told that each of them should take half of the buck to his village. "For," said the Peacemaker, "it is large, and with half of it one hath enough for his wife and little ones." "The Oneida is alone in his home," said the Oneida chief. "I carry the meat to the old men and the women who have no sons. The Oneida has seen no maiden he would take to his lodge till he beheld Genetaska, the Peace Queen."

Then said the Onondaga, "The home of the Onondaga is desolate since the plague entered its walls. He is a great and powerful chief, for he was never overcome in the chase or in war. The Peacemaker has made his heart weak. He will never be strong again unless she will come to his lodge."

But Genetaska replied, "Go ye, my brothers, and think no more of the Peace Queen, who is chosen by all and may be the wife of no one. Seek ye other maidens who will gladly be your wives." But when they were gone she had no more peace, for the Oneida's form was ever before her eyes.

When the autumn came, when its glories tinged the forests, the Oneida came at sunset, and stood boldly before the Peace Queen saying, "The Oneida has built a lodge in the summer land, where the Five Nations care not to go. He has filled it with robes and supplied it with food, and it awaits the Seneca maiden who loves the Oneida. The tribes will choose another Peace Queen when thou art gone. Thy life will no longer be heavy with the burdens of all who come to thee. Wilt thou go?"

She looked in his face and said, "Genetaska will go."

They left Kienuka, embarked in his canoe on the river, glided swiftly down the stream and were lost to their people forever.

The peace home was left desolate. To its doors two men came running in the darkness, full of hatred and rage. No one restrained them and they died.

HI-NUN AND NIAGARA

A BEAUTIFUL INDIAN MAIDEN was about to be compelled by her family to marry a hideous old Indian. Despair was in her heart. She knew that there was no escape for her, so in desperation she leaped into her canoe and pushed it from shore on the roaring waters of Niagara. She heeded not that she was going to her death, preferring the angry waters to the arms of her detested lover.

Now, the God of Cloud and Rain, the great deity Hi-Nun, who watches over the harvest, dwelt in a cave behind the rushing waters. From his home he saw the desperate launching of the maiden's canoe, saw her going to almost certain destruction. He spread out his wings and flew to her rescue, and caught her just as her frail bark was dashing on the rocks below.

The grateful Indian girl lived for many weeks in Hi-Nun's cave. He taught her many new things. She learned from him why her people died so often—why sickness was always busy among them. He told her how a snake lay coiled up under the ground beneath the village, and how he crept out and poisoned the springs, because he lived on human beings and craved their flesh more and more, so that he could never get enough if they died from natural causes.

Hi-Nun kept the maiden till he learned that the ugly old suitor was dead. Then he bade her return and tell her tribe what she had learned of the great Hi-Nun.

She taught them all he had told her and begged them to break up their

settlement and travel nearer to the lake; and her words prevailed. For a while sickness ceased, but it broke out again, for the serpent was far too cunning to be so easily outwitted. He dragged himself slowly but surely after the people, and but for Hi-Nun's influence would have undermined the new settlement as he had the former one. Hi-Nun watched him until he neared the creek, then he launched a thunderbolt at him. A terrible noise awoke all the dwellers by the lake, but the snake was only injured, not killed. Hi-Nun was forced to launch another thunderbolt, and another and another, before, finally, the poisoner was slain.

The great dead snake was so enormous that when the Indians laid his body out in death it stretched over more than twenty arrow flights; and as he floated down the waters of Niagara it was as if a mountain appeared above them. His corpse was too large to pass the rocks, so it became wedged in-between them, and the waters rose over it mountains high. As the weight of the monster pressed on the rocks they gave way and thus the horseshoe form, that remains to this day, was fashioned. But the Indians had no more fever in their settlement.

THE MAIDEN OF THE YELLOW ROCKS

IN THE DAYS of the ancients, when our ancestors lived in the Village of the Yellow Rocks, also in the Salt City, also in the Village of the Winds, and also in the Village of the White Flowering Herbs, and also in the Village of Odd Waters, where they come forth, when in fact all these broken-down villages were inhabited by our ancients, there lived in the Village of the Yellow Rocks a very beautiful maiden, the daughter of the high priest.

Although a woman, she was wonderfully endowed by birth with the magic knowledge of the hunt and with the knowledge of all the animals who contribute to the sustenance of man—game animals. And, although a woman, she was also somewhat bad in her disposition, and selfish, in that, possessing this knowledge above all other men and women, she concluded she would have all these animals—the deer, antelope, rabbits—to herself.

So, through her wonderful knowledge of their habits and language, she communicated with them and charmed them, and on the top of the mountain—where you will see to this day the ancient figures of the deer cut in the rock—she built a huge corral, and gathered one after another all the deer and antelope and other wild animals of that great country. And the hunters of these villages hunted in vain. They trailed the deer and the antelope, but they lost their trails and always came home with nothing save the weapons they took with them. But this maiden, whenever she wished for deer, would go to her corral and kill whatever animal she wanted. So she and her family always had plenty of meat, while others were without it; always had plenty of buckskins with which to make moccasins and apparel, while others were every day wearing out their old supply and never able to replenish it.

Now, this girl was surpassingly beautiful, and was looked upon by many a young man as the flower of his heart and the one on whom he would ultimately concentrate his thoughts for life. Among these young men, the first to manifest his feelings was a youth from the Village of the Winds.

One day he said to his old people, "I am going courting." And they observed that he made up a bundle of various precious things for women's dress and ornamentation—necklaces, snow-white buckskin moccasins and leggings, and embroidered skirts and mantles—and, taking his bundle on his shoulders, he started off for the Village of the Yellow Rocks.

When he reached the village he knew the home of the maiden by the beauty of the house. Among other houses it was alone of its kind. Attached to the ladder was the crosspiece carved as it is in these days, but depending from it was a fringe of black hair (not scalp locks) with which they still ornament certain houses when they have sacred ceremonies; and among this fringe were hung hollow stalactites from a sacred cave on the Colorado Chiquito, which sounded, when the wind blew them together, like little bells. This fringe was full of them, so that when a stranger came to this important chief priest's house he no sooner touched the ladder rung at the foot than the bells tinkled, and they knew someone was coming.

As he placed his foot on the lowermost rung of the ladder, *chi-la-li* sang the bells at the top.

Said the people within, "Someone is coming."

Step after step he went up, and still the bells made music at the top, and as he stepped over on the roof, *thud, thud*, his footsteps sounded as he walked

33

along; and when he reached the door, those within said, "Thou comest?" And he replied, "I come. Draw me in"; by which expression he meant that he had brought with him a present to the family. Whenever a man has a bundle to hand down, it is the place of the woman to take it; and that is called "drawing a man in," though she only takes his bundle, and he follows. In this case he said, "Draw me in," and the maiden came to the top of the ladder and took the bundle and dropped it on the floor. They knew by the appearance of the bundle what the object of the visit was.

The old man was sitting by the fireplace—it was nighttime—and as the stranger entered, said, "Thou hast come?"

The young man answered, "Yes."

Said the old man, "It is not customary for a stranger to visit the house of a stranger without saying something of what may be in his thoughts."

"It is quite true," said the youth; "I come thinking of this maiden, your daughter. It has occurred to me that I might happily and without fear rest my thoughts and hopes on her; therefore I come."

The daughter brought forth food for the young man and bade him eat. He reached forth his hand and partook of the food. She sat down and took a mouthful or two, whereby they knew she was favorably disposed. She was favorably disposed to all appearance, but not in reality. When he had finished eating, she said, "As you like, my father. You are my father." She answered to her own thoughts, "Yes, you have often reproached me for not treating with more gentleness those who come courting me."

Finally said the father, "I give ye my blessing and sacred speech, my children. I will adopt thee as my child."

"My children," said the father, after a while, when he had smoked a little, "the stranger, now a son, has come a long distance and must be weary."

So the maiden led him to an upper chamber, and said, "Rest here; you are not yet my husband. I would try you in the morning. Get up early, when the deer are most plentiful, and go forth and slay me a fine one, and then indeed shall we rest our hopes and thoughts on each other for life."

"It is well," said the youth; and he retired to sleep, and in the morning arose early. The maiden gave into his hands the food for the day; he caught up his bows and arrows and went forth into the forests and mountains, seeking for the deer. He found a superb track and followed it until it suddenly disappeared, and though he worked hard and followed it over and over again, he could find nothing.

While the young man was out hunting and following the tracks for nothing, the young girl went out, so as to be quite sure that none of her deer should get out. And what did she do? She went into the river and followed it against the current, through the water beyond the village and where the marked rocks stand, up the canyon to the place where her deer were gathered. They were all there, peaceful and contented. But there were no tracks of the girl; no one could follow where she went.

The young man hunted and hunted, and at nighttime, all tired out and hungry, took his way back to the home of the maiden. She was there.

"Ha!" said she, "what good fortune today?"

And the young man with his face dragged down and his eyes not bright, answered, "I found no game today."

"Well," said the girl, "it is too bad; but under the circumstances we cannot rest our thoughts and hopes on each other for life."

"No, I suppose not," said the young man.

"Here is your bundle," said the girl. She raised it very carefully and handed it to him. He took it over his shoulder, and after all his weary work went on his way home.

The very next day a young man named Halona, when he heard of this, said, "Ha! ha! What a fool he was! He didn't take her enough presents; he didn't please her. I am said to be a very pleasant fellow" (he was a very conceited young man); "I will take her a bundle that will make things all right."

So he put into a bundle everything that a woman could reasonably want —for he was a wealthy young man, and his bundle was very heavy—put on his best dress, and with fine paint on his face started for the home of the maiden. Finally, his foot touched the lowermost rung of the ladder; the stalactites went jingling above as he mounted, and *thud* went his bundle as he dropped it on the roof.

"Somebody has come," said the people below. "Listen to that!"

The maiden shrugged her shoulders and said, "Thou comest?"

"Yes," answered the young man, "draw me in."

35

So she reached up and pulled the huge bundle down into the room, placing it on the floor, and the young man followed it down.

Said the old man, who was sitting by the fire, for it was night, "Thou comest. Not thinking of nothing doth one stranger come to the house of another. What may be thy thoughts?"

The young man looked at the maiden and said to himself, "What a magnificent creature she is! She will be my wife, no fear that she will not." Then said he aloud, "I came, thinking of your daughter. I would rest my hopes and thoughts on her."

"It is well," said the old man. "It is the custom of our people and of all people, that they may possess dignity, that they may be the heads of households; therefore, young men and maidens marry and establish themselves in certain houses. I have no objection. What dost thou think, my daughter?"

"I have no objection," said the daughter.

"Ah, what did I tell you?" said the youth to himself, and ate with a great deal of satisfaction the meal placed before him.

The father laid out the cornhusks and tobacco, and they had a smoke. Then he said to his daughter, "The stranger who is now my son has come a long way, and should not be kept sitting up so long."

As the daughter led him to another room, he thought, "What a gentle creature she is! How softly she steps up the ladder."

When the door was reached, she said, "Here we will say good night."

"What is the matter?" he asked.

Said she: "I would like to know of my husband this much, that he is a good hunter; that I may have plenty of food all my days, and plenty of buckskins for my clothing. Therefore I must ask that in the morning you go forth and hunt the deer, or bring home an antelope for me."

The young man quickly recovered himself, and said, "It is well," and lay himself down to rest.

So the next morning he went out, and there was the maiden at the top of the house watching him. He couldn't wait for daylight; he wanted the Sun, his father, to rise before his time, and when the Sun did rise he jumped out of bed, tied his quiver to his belt, took his bow in his hand, and with a little luncheon the maiden had prepared for him, started off.

As he went down the river he saw the maiden was watching him from the top of the house. So he started forward and ran until he was out of sight, to show how fine a runner he was and how good a hunter, because he was reputed to be a very strong and active young man. He hunted and hunted, but did not find any deer, nor even any tracks.

Meanwhile, the maiden went up the stream as before and kept watch of the corral; and he fared as the other young man had fared. At night he came home, not quite so downcast as the other had been, because he was a young man of more self-reliance.

She asked him, as she met him, "Haven't you got any deer today?"

He answered, "No."

She said, "I am sorry, but under the circumstances, I don't see how we can become husband and wife."

So he carried his bundle home.

The next day there was a young man in the City of Salt who heard of this; not all of it, but he heard that day after day young men were going to the home of this maiden to court her, and she turned them all away. He said, "I dare say they didn't take enough with them." So he made up two bundles and went to the home of the maiden, and he said to himself, "This time it will be all right."

When he arrived, much the same conversation was gone through as before with the other young men, and the girl said, when she lighted him to the door of his room, "My young friend, if you will find a deer for me tomorrow I will become your wife and rest my hope only on you."

"Mercy on me!" thought the young man to himself, "I have always been called a poor hunter. What shall I do?"

The next morning he tried, but with the same results.

Now, this girl was keeping the deer and antelope and other animals so long closed up in the corral that the people in all the villages round about were ready to die of hunger for meat. Still, for her own gratification she would keep these animals shut up.

The young man came back at evening, and she asked him if he had found a deer for her.

"No," said he. "I could not even find the trail of one."

"Well," she said, "I am sorry, for your bundles are heavy."

He took them up and went home with them.

Finally, this matter became so much talked about that the two small gods on the top of Thunder Mountain, who lived with their grandmother where our sacrificial altar now stands, said, "There is something wrong here; we will go and court this maiden." Now, these gods were extremely ugly in appearance when they chose to be—mere pigmies who never grew to man's stature. They were always boys in appearance, and their grandmother was always crusty with them; but they concluded one night that they would go the next day to woo this maiden.

Said one to the other, "Suppose we go and try our luck with her." Said he, "When I look at you, you are extremely handsome."

Said the other to him, "When I look at you, you are extremely handsome."

They were the ugliest beings in human form, but in reality were among the most magnificent of men, having power to take any form they chose.

Said the elder one, "Grandmother, you know how much talk there is about this maiden in the Village of the Yellow Rocks. We have decided to go and court her."

"You miserable, dirty, ugly little wretches! The idea of your going to court this maiden when she has refused the finest young men in the land!"

"Well, we will go," said he.

"I don't want you to go," replied she. "Your names will be in the mouths of everybody; you will be laughed and jeered at."

"We will go," said they. And without paying the slightest attention to their grandmother, they made up their bundle—a very miserable bundle it was. The younger brother put in little rocks and sticks and bits of buckskins and all sorts of worthless things, and they started off.

"What are you carrying this bundle for?" asked Ahaiyuta, the elder brother.

"I am taking it as a present to the maiden," said Matsailema, the younger one.

"She doesn't want any such trash as that," said the other. "They have taken very valuable presents to her before; we have nothing to take equal to what has been carried to her by others."

They decided to throw the bundle away altogether, and started out with absolutely nothing but their bows and arrows.

As they proceeded they began to kill wood rats, and continued until they had slaughtered a large number and had a long string of them held up by their tails.

"There!" exclaimed the younger brother. "There is a fine present for the girl." They knew perfectly well how things were, and were looking out for the interests of their children in the villages round about.

"Oh, my younger brother!" said the elder. "These will not be acceptable to the girl at all; she would not have them in the house!"

"Oh, yes, she would," said the younger. "We will take them along as a present to her."

So they went on, and it was hardly noon when they arrived with their strings of rats at the white cliffs on the southern side of the canyon opposite the village where the maiden lived.

"Here, let us sit down in the shade of this cliff," said the elder brother, "for it is not proper to go courting until evening."

"Oh, no," said the younger, "let us go along now. I am in a hurry! I am in a hurry!"

"You are a fool!" said the elder brother. "You should not think of going courting before evening. Stay here patiently."

So they sat down in the shade of the cliff. But the younger kept jumping up and running out to see how the sun was all the afternoon, and he would go and smooth out his string of rats from time to time, and then go and look at the sun again. Finally, when the sun was almost set, he called out, "Now, come on!"

"Wait until it is wholly dark," said the other. "You never did have any patience, sense, or dignity about you."

"Why not go now?" asked the younger.

So they kept quarreling, but the elder brother's wish prevailed until it was nearly dark, when they went on.

The elder brother began to get very bashful as they approached the village. "I wonder which house it is," said he.

"The one with the tallest ladder in front of it, of course," said the other.

Then the elder brother said in a low voice, "Now, do behave yourself; be dignified."

"All right!" replied the younger.

When they got to the ladder, the elder one said in a whisper, "I don't want to go up here; I don't want to go courting; let's go back."

"Go along up," said the younger.

"Keep still; be quiet!" said the elder one. "Be dignified!"

They went up the ladder very carefully, so that there was not a tinkle from the bells.

The elder brother hesitated, while the younger one went on to the top, and over the edge of the house.

"Now!" cried he.

"Keep still!" whispered the other; and he gave the ladder a little shake as he went, and the bells tinkled at the top.

The people downstairs said, "Who in the world is coming now?"

When they were both on the roof, the elder brother said, "You go down first."

"I will do nothing of the kind," said the other, "you are the elder."

The people downstairs called out, "Who comes there?"

"See what you have done, you simpleton!" said the elder brother. Then with a great deal of dignity he walked down the ladder. The younger one came tumbling down, carrying his string of rats.

"Throw it out, you fool; they don't want rats!" said the elder one.

"Yes, they do," replied the other. "The girl will want these; maybe she will marry us on account of them!"

The elder brother was terribly disturbed, but the other brought his rats in and laid them in the middle of the floor.

The father looked up, and said, "You come?"

"Yes," said the two odd ones.

"Sit down," said the old man. So they sat down, and food was placed before them.

"It seems," said the father, "that ye have met with luck today in hunting," as he cast his eyes on the string of rats.

"Yes," said the two.

So the old priest went and got some prayer meal, and, turning the faces of the rats toward the east, said a short prayer.

"What did I tell you?" said the younger brother. "They like the presents we have brought. Just see!"

Presently the old man said, "It is not customary for strangers to come to a house without something in mind."

"Quite so," said the younger brother.

"Yes, my father," said the elder one, "we have come thinking of your daughter. We understand that she has been wooed by various young men, and it has occurred to us that they did not bring the right kind of presents."

"So we brought these," said the younger brother.

"It is well," said the old man. "It is the custom for maidens and youths to marry. It rests with my daughter."

So he referred the matter to his daughter, and she said, "As you think, my father. Which one?"

"Oh, take us both!" said the younger brother.

This was rather embarrassing to the maiden, but she knew she had a safe retreat. So when the father admonished her that it was time to lead the two young men up into the room where the others had been placed, she told them the same story.

They said, "It is well."

They lay down, but instead of sleeping spent most of the night speculating as to the future.

"What a magnificent wife we will have," said one to the other.

"Don't talk so loud; everyone will hear you; you will be covered with shame!"

After a while they went to sleep, but were awake early the next morning. The younger brother began to talk to the elder one, who said, "Keep quiet; the people are not awake; don't disturb them!"

The younger one said, "The sun is rising."

"Keep quiet," said the other, "and when they are awake they will give us some luncheon to take with us."

But the younger one jumped up and went rushing about the house, calling out, "The sun is rising. Get up!"

The luncheon was provided, and when they started off the maiden went out on the housetop and asked them which direction they would take.

Said they, "We will go over to the south and will get a deer before long, although we are very small and may not meet with very good luck."

So they descended the ladder, and the maiden said to herself, "Ugly, miserable little wretches; I will teach them to come courting me this way!"

The brothers went off to the cliffs, and while pretending to be hunting, they ran back through the thickets near the house and waited to see what the maiden would do.

Pretty soon she came out. They watched her and saw that she went down the valley and presently ran into the river, leaving no trail behind, and took her course up the stream. They ran on ahead, and long before she had ascended the river found the path leading out of it up the mountain. Following this path, they came to the corral, and looking over it, they saw thousands of deer, mountain sheep, antelope, and other animals wandering around in the enclosure.

"Ha, here is the place!" the younger brother exclaimed. "Let us go at them now!"

"Keep quiet! Be patient! Wait till the maiden comes," said the elder one. "If we should happen to kill one of these deer before she comes, perhaps she has some magic power or knowledge by which she would deprive us of the fruits of our efforts."

"No, let us kill one now," said the other. But the elder one kept him curbed until the maiden was climbing the cliff, when he could restrain him no longer, and the youth pulled out his bow and let fly an arrow at the largest deer. One arrow, and the deer fell to the ground. And when the maiden appeared on the spot the deer was lying dead not far away.

The brothers said, "You come, do you? And here we are!"

She looked at them, and her heart went down and became as heavy as a stone, and she did not answer.

"I say, you come!" said the younger brother. "You come, do you?"

She said, "Yes." Then she said to herself, "Well, I suppose I shall have to submit, as I made the arrangement myself." Then she looked up and said, "I see you have killed a deer."

"Yes, we killed one; didn't have any difficulty at all," said the younger brother. "Come and help us skin him; we are so little and hungry and tired we can't do it. Come on."

So the girl went slowly forward, and in a dejected way helped them skin the deer. Then they began to shoot more deer, and attempted to drag them out; but the men were so small they could not do it, and the girl had to help them. Then they cut up the meat and made it into bundles. She made a large one for herself, and they made two little ones for themselves.

"Now," said they, wiping their brows, "we have done a good day's work, haven't we?" and they looked at the maiden with twinkling eyes.

"Yes," said she; "you are great hunters."

"Shall we go toward home?" asked the younger brother of the maiden. "It would be a shame for you to take such a bundle as that. I will take it for you."

"You little conceited wretch!" cried the elder brother. "Haven't I tried to restrain you? And now you are going to bury yourself under a bundle of meat!"

"No," said the younger brother, "I can carry it."

So they propped the great bundle of meat against a tree. The elder brother called on the maiden to help him; the younger one stooped down and received it on his back. They had no sooner let go of it than it fell on the ground and completely flattened the little man out.

"Mercy! Mercy! I am dying; help me out of here!" cried he.

So they managed to roll the thing off, and he got up and rubbed his back, complaining bitterly (he was only making believe), and said, "I shall have to take my little bundle."

So he shouldered his little bundle, and the maiden took the large one; but before she started she turned to the animals and said, "Oh, my children! these many days, throwing the warm light of your favor upon me, you have rested contented to remain away from the sight of men. Now, hereafter you shall go forth whithersoever you will, that the earth may be covered with your offspring, and men may once more have of your flesh to eat and of your pelts to wear." And away went the antelope, the deer, the mountain sheep, the elk, and the buffalo over all the land.

Then the young gods of war turned to the maiden and said, "Now, shall we go home?"

"Yes," said she.

"Well, I will take the lead," said the younger brother.

"Get behind where you belong," said the other; "I will precede the party." So the elder brother went first, the maiden came next, and the younger brother followed behind, with his little bag of meat.

So they went home, and the maiden placed the meat to dry in the upper rooms of the house.

While she was doing this, it was yet early in the day. The two brothers were sitting together, and whispering, "And what will she say for herself now?"

"I don't see what she can say for herself."

"Of course, nothing can she say for herself."

And when the meat was all packed away in the house and the sun had set, they sat by themselves talking this over, "What can she say for herself?"

"Nothing whatever; nothing remains to be done."

"That is quite so," said they, as they went in to the evening meal and sat with the family to eat it.

Finally the maiden said, "With all your hunting and the labors of the day, you must be very weary. Where you slept last night you will find a resting place. Go and rest yourselves. I cannot consent to marry you, because you have not yet shown yourselves capable of taking care of and dressing the buckskins, as well as of killing deer and antelope and such animals. For a long time buckskins have been accumulating in the upper room. I have no brothers to soften and scrape them; therefore, if you two will take the hair off all my buckskins tomorrow before sunset, and scrape the underside so that they will be thin and soft, I will consent to be the wife of one of you, or both."

And they said, "Oh mercy, it is too bad!"

"We can never do it," said the younger brother.

"I don't suppose we can; but we can try," said the elder.

So they lay down.

"Let us take things in time," said the elder one, after he had thought of it. And they jumped up and called to the maiden, "Where are those buckskins?"

"They are in the upper room," said she.

She showed them the way to the upper room. It was packed to the rafters with buckskins. They began to make big bales of these and then took them down to the river. When they got them all down there they said, "How in the world can we scrape so many skins? There are more here than we can clean in a year."

"I will tell you what," said the younger brother; "we will stow away some in the crevices of the rocks, and get rid of them in that way."

"Always hasty, always hasty," said the elder. "Do you suppose that woman put those skins away without counting every one of them? We can't do that."

They spread them out in the water that they might soak all night, and built a little dam so they would not float away. While they were thus engaged they heard someone talking, so they pricked up their ears to listen.

Now, the hill that stands by the side across from the Village of the Yellow Rocks was, and still is, a favorite home of the field mice. They are very prolific, and have to provide great bundles of wool for their families. But in the days of the ancients they were terrible gamblers and were all the time betting away their nests, and the young mice being perfectly bare, with no wool on them at all, died of cold. And still they kept on betting, making little figures of nests and betting these away against the time when they should have more. It was these mice which the two gods overheard.

Said the younger brother, "Listen to that! Who is talking?"

"Someone is betting. Let us go nearer."

They went across the river and listened, and heard the tiny little voices calling out and shouting.

"Let us go in," said the younger brother. And he placed his foot in the hole and descended, followed by the other. They found there an enormous village of field mice in human form, their clothes, in the shape of mice, hanging over the sides of the house. Some had their clothing all off down to their waists, and were betting as hard as they could and talking with one another.

As soon as the two brothers entered, they said, "Who comes?"

The two answered, "We come."

"Come in, come in," cried the mice; they were not very polite. "Sit down and have a game. We have not anything to bet just now, but if you trust us we will bet with you."

"What had you in mind in coming?" said an old field mouse with a broken tail.

They answered that they had come because they heard voices. Then they told their story.

45

"What is this you have to do?" asked the mice.

"To clean all the hair off those pelts tomorrow."

The mice looked around at one another; their eyes fairly sparkled and burned.

"Now then, we will help you if you will promise us something," said they; "but we want your solemn promise."

"What is that?" asked the brothers.

"That you will give us all the hair."

"Oh, yes," said the brothers; "we will be glad to get rid of it."

"All right," said they; "where are the skins?" Then they all began to pour out of the place, and they were so numerous that it was like water, when the rain is falling hard, running over a rock.

When they had all run out, the two War-gods drew the skins on the bank, and the field mice went to nibbling the hair and cleaning off the underside. They made up little bundles of the flesh from the skins for their food, and great parcels of the hair. Finally they said, "May we have them all?"

"No," said the brothers, "we must have eight reserved, four for each, so that we will be hard at work all day tomorrow."

"Well," said the mice, "we can't consent to leaving even so many, unless you promise that you will gather up all the hair and put it somewhere so that we can get it."

The two promised that, and said, "Be sure to leave eight skins, will you? And we will go to bed and rest ourselves."

"All right, all right!" responded the field mice.

So the brothers climbed up the hill to the town, and up the ladder, and slept in their room.

The next morning the girl said, "Now, remember, you will have to clean every skin and make it soft and white."

So they went down to the river and started to work. The girl had said to them that at midday she would go down and see how they were getting along. They were at work nearly all the forenoon on the skins. While the elder brother shaved the hair off, the younger one scraped them thin and softened them.

46

When the maiden came at noon, she said, "How are you getting along?"

"We have finished four and are at work on the fifth."

"Remember," said she, "you must finish all of them today, or I shall have to send you home."

So they worked away until a little before the sun set, when she appeared again. They had just finished the last. The field mice had carefully dressed all the others (they did it better than the men), and there they lay spread out on the sands like a great field of something growing, only white.

When the maiden came down she was perfectly overcome; she looked and looked and counted and recounted. She found them all there. Then she got a long pole and fished in the water, but there were none.

Said she, "Yes, you shall be my husbands; I shall have to submit."

She went home with them, and for a long time they all lived together, the woman with her two husbands. They managed to get along very comfortably, and the two brothers didn't quarrel any more than they had done before.

Finally, there were born little twin boys, exactly like their fathers, who were also twins, although one was called the elder and the other the younger.

After a time the younger brother said, "Now, let us go home to our grandmother. People always go home to their own houses and take their families with them."

"No," said the elder one, "you must remember that we have been only pretending to be human beings. It would not do to take the maiden home with us."

"Yes," said the other, "I want her to go with us. Our grandmother kept making fun of us; called us little, miserable, wretched creatures. I want to show her that we amount to something!"

The elder brother could not get the younger one to leave the wife behind, and like a dutiful wife she said, "I will go with you." They made up their bundles and started out. It was a very hot day, and when they had climbed nearly to the top of Thunder Mountain, the younger brother said, "Ahem! I am tired. Let us sit down and rest."

"It will not do," said the elder brother. "You know very well it will not do to sit down; our father, the Sun, has forbidden that we should be among mortals. It will not do."

"Oh, yes, it will; we must sit down here," said the younger brother. And again his wish prevailed and they sat down.

At midday the Sun stood still in the sky, and looked down and saw this beautiful woman, and by the power of his withdrawing rays quickly snatched her from them while they were sitting there talking, she carrying her little children.

The brothers looked around and said, "Where is our wife?"

"Ah, there she is," cried the younger. "I will shoot her."

"Shoot your wife!" cried the elder brother. "No, let her go! Serves you right!"

"No," said the younger, "I will shoot her!" He looked up and drew his arrow, and as his aim was absolutely unerring, *swish* went the arrow directly to her, and she was killed. The power of life by which the Sun was drawing her up was gone, the thread was cut, and she fell over and over and struck the earth.

The two little children were so very small, and their bones so soft, that the fall did not hurt them much. They fell on the soft bank, and rolled and rolled down the hill, and the younger brother ran forward and caught them up in his arms, crying, "Oh, my little children!" and brought them to the elder brother, who said, "Now, what can be done with these little babies, with no mother, no food?"

"We will take them home to grandmother," said the younger brother.

"Your grandmother cannot take care of these babies," said the elder brother.

"Yes, she can, of course," said the younger brother. "Come on, come on! I didn't want to lose my wife and children, too; I thought I must still have the children; that is the reason why I shot her."

So one of them took one of the children, and the other one took the other, and they carried them up to the top of Thunder Mountain.

"Now then," said the elder brother, "we went off to marry; we come home with no wife and two little children, and with nothing to feed them."

"Oh, grandmother!" called out the younger brother.

The old woman hadn't heard them for many a day, for many a month, even for years. She looked out and said, "My grandchildren are coming," and she called to them, "I am so glad you have come!"

"Here, see what we have," said the younger brother. "Here are your grandchildren. Come and take them!"

"Oh, you miserable boy, you are always doing something foolish. Where is your wife?" asked the grandmother.

"Oh, I shot her!" was the response.

"Why did you do that?"

"I didn't want my father, the Sun, to take them away with my wife. I knew you would not care anything about my wife, but I knew you would be very fond of the grandchildren. Here they are."

But she wouldn't look at all. So the younger brother drew his face down, and taking the poor little children in his arms said, "You unnatural grandmother, you! Here are two nice little grandchildren for you!"

She said, "How shall I feed them? Or what shall I do with them?"

He replied, "Oh, take care of them, take care of them!"

She took a good look at them, and became a true grandmother. She ran and clasped the little ones, crying out, "Let me take you away from these miserable children of mine!" She made some beds of sand for them, as Zuñi mothers do today, got some soft skins for them to lie on, and fed them with a kind of milk made of corn toasted and ground and mixed with water, so that they gradually enlarged and grew up to be nice children.

HIAWATHA AND THE IROQUOIS WAMPUM

IN ONE OF HIS MISSIONS into the country of the Mohawks, Hiawatha once came upon the borders of a lake. While deliberating in what manner he should cross it, the whole sky became filled with wild ducks, all of which finally alighted upon the surface of the water.

After quenching their thirst and soaking their plumage, they ascended again into the air in one great mass, and lo! the lake had become dry, while its bed was filled with shells.

From these the wise chief and counselor proceeded to make the wampum which afterward so firmly cemented the union of the six tribes, thereby forming the great Iroquois Confederacy.

WEMICUS TESTS HIS SON-IN-LAW

WEMICUS, the animal transformer-trickster, had a son-in-law who was a man. This man's wife, the daughter of Wemicus, had had a great many husbands, because Wemicus had put them to so many different tests that they had been all killed off except this one. He, however, had succeeded in outwitting Wemicus in every scheme that was tried on him.

Wemicus and this man hunted beaver in the spring of the year by driving them all day with dogs. The man's wife warned him before they started out to hunt, saying, "Look out for my father; he might burn your moccasins in camp. That's what he did to my other husbands." That night in camp Wemicus said, "I didn't tell you the name of this lake. It is called Burnt Moccasins Lake." When the man heard this, he thought that Wemicus was up to some sort of mischief and was going to burn his moccasins. Their moccasins were hanging up before a fire to dry and, while Wemicus was not looking, the man changed the places of Wemicus' moccasins and his own, and then went to sleep. Soon the man awoke and saw Wemicus get up and throw his own moccasins into the fire. Wemicus then said, "Say! something is burning; it is your moccasins." Then the man answered, "No, not mine, but yours." So Wemicus had no moccasins, and the ground was covered with snow. After this had happened, the man slept with his moccasins on.

The next morning the man started on and left Wemicus there with no shoes. Wemicus started to work. He got a big boulder, made a fire, and placed the boulder in it until it became red hot. He then wrapped his feet with spruce boughs and pushed the boulder ahead of him in order to melt the snow. In this way he managed to walk on the boughs. Then he began to sing, "Spruce is warm, spruce is warm." When the man reached home he told his wife what had happened. "I hope Wemicus will die," she said. A little while after this they heard Wemicus coming along singing, "Spruce is warm, spruce is warm." He came into the wigwam, and as he was the head man, they were obliged to get his meal ready.

The ice was getting bad by this time, so they stayed in camp a while. Soon Wemicus told his son-in-law, "We'd better go sliding." He then went to a hill where there were some very poisonous snakes. The man's wife warned her husband of these snakes and gave him a split stick holding a certain kind of magic tobacco, which she told him to hold in front of him so that the snakes would not hurt him. Then the two men went sliding. At the top of the hill Wemicus said, "Follow me," for he intended to pass close by the snakes' lair. So when they slid, Wemicus passed safely, and the man held his stick with the tobacco in it in front of him, thus preventing the snakes from biting him. The man then told Wemicus that he enjoyed the sliding.

The following day Wemicus said to his son-in-law, "We had better go to another place." When she heard this, the wife told her husband that, as it was getting summer, Wemicus had in his head many poisonous lizards instead of lice. She said, "He will tell you to pick lice from his head and crack them in your teeth. But take low-bush cranberries and crack them instead." So the man took cranberries along with him. Wemicus took his son-in-law to a valley with a great ravine in it. He said, "I wonder if anybody can jump across this?" "Surely," said the young man, "I can." Then the young man said, "Closer," and the ravine narrowed, and he jumped across easily. When Wemicus tried, the young man said, "Widen," and Wemicus fell into the ravine. But it did not kill him, and when he made his way to the top again, he said, "You have beaten me." Then they went on.

They came to a place of hot sand and Wemicus said, "You must look for lice in my head." "All right, father," replied the son-in-law. So Wemicus lay down and the man started to pick the lice. He took the cranberries from inside his shirt, and each time he pretended to catch a louse, he cracked a cranberry and threw it on the ground. So Wemicus was fooled a second time that day. Then they went home, and Wemicus said to his son-in-law, "There are a whole lot of eggs on that rocky island where the gulls are. We will go get the eggs, come back, and have an egg supper." As Wemicus was the head man, his son-in-law had to obey him.

So they started out in their canoe and soon came to the rocky island. Wemicus stayed in the canoe and told the man to go ashore and to bring the eggs back with him and fill the canoe. When the man reached the shore, Wemicus told him to go farther back on the island, saying, "That's where the former husbands got their eggs. There are their bones." Then he started the canoe off in the water by singing, without using his paddle. Then Wemicus told the gulls to eat the man, saying to them, "I give you him to eat."

The gulls started to fly about the man, but the man had his paddle with him, and he killed one of the gulls with it. He then took the gull's wings and fastened them on himself, filled his shirt with eggs, and started flying over the lake by the aid of the wings.

When he reached the middle of the lake, he saw Wemicus going along and singing to himself. Wemicus, looking up, saw his son-in-law but mistook him for a gull. Then the man flew back to camp and told his wife to cook the eggs, and he told his children to play with the wings. When Wemicus reached the camp, he saw the children playing with the wings and said, "Where did you get those wings?" "From father," was the reply. "Your father? Why the gulls ate him!" Then he went to the wigwam, and there he saw the man smoking. Then Wemicus thought it very strange how the man could have got home, but no one told him how it had been done. Thought he, "I must try another scheme to do away with him."

One day Wemicus said to his son-in-law, "We'd better make two canoes of birchbark, one for you and one for me. We'd better get bark." So they started off for birchbark. They cut a tree almost through and Wemicus said to his son-in-law, "You sit on that side and I'll sit on this." He wanted the tree to fall on him and kill him. Wemicus said, "You say, 'Fall on my father-in-law,' and I'll say, 'Fall on my son-in-law,' and whoever says it too slowly or makes a mistake will be the one on whom it will fall." But Wemicus made the first mistake, and the tree fell on him and crushed him. However, Wemicus was a Manito and was not hurt.

They went home with the bark and made the two canoes. After they were made, Wemicus said to his son-in-law, "Well, we'll have a race in our two canoes, a sailing race." Wemicus made a big bark sail, but the man did not make any, as he was afraid of upsetting. They started the race. Wemicus went very fast, and the man called after him, "Oh, you are beating me." He kept on fooling and encouraging Wemicus, until the wind upset Wemicus' canoe and that was the end of Wemicus. When the man sailed over the spot where Wemicus had upset, he saw a big pike there, into which Wemicus had been transformed when the canoe upset. This is the origin of the pike.

THE RABBIT HUNTRESS AND HER ADVENTURES

IT WAS LONG AGO, in the days of the ancients, that a poor maiden lived at Kyawana Tehua-tsana—Little Gateway of Zuñi River. You know there are black stone walls of houses standing there on the tops of the cliffs of lava, above the narrow place through which the river runs, to this day.

In one of these houses there lived this poor maiden alone with her feeble old father and her aged mother. She was unmarried, and her brothers had all been killed in wars, or had died gently. So the family lived there helplessly, so far as many things were concerned, from the lack of men in their house.

It is true that in making the gardens—the little plantings of beans, pumpkins, squashes, melons, and corn—the maiden was able to do very well; and thus mainly on the products of these things the family were supported. But, as in those days of our ancients we had neither sheep nor cattle, the hunt was depended upon to supply the meat; or sometimes it was procured by barter of the products of the fields to those who hunted mostly. Of these things, this little family had barely enough for their own subsistence; hence, they could not procure their supplies of meat in this way.

Long before, it had been a great house, for many were the brave and strong young men who had lived in it; but the rooms were now empty, or at best contained only the leavings of those who had lived there, much used and worn out.

One autumn day, near wintertime, snow fell, and it became very cold. The maiden had gathered brush and firewood in abundance, and it was piled along the roof of the house and down underneath the ladder which descended from the top. She saw the young men issue forth the next morning in great numbers, their feet protected by long stockings of deerskin, the fur turned inward, and they carried on their shoulders and stuck in their belts stone axes and rabbit sticks.

As she gazed at them from the roof, she said to herself, "O that I were a man and could go forth, as do these young men, hunting rabbits! Then my poor old mother and father would not lack for flesh with which to duly season their food and nourish their lean bodies." Thus ran her thoughts, and before night, as she saw these same young men coming in, one after another, some of them bringing long strings of rabbits, others short ones, but none of them empty-handed, she decided that, woman though she was, she would set forth on the morrow to try what luck she might find in the killing of rabbits herself.

It may seem strange that, although this maiden was beautiful and young, the youths did not give her some of their rabbits. But their feelings were not friendly, for no one of them would she accept as a husband, although one after another of them had offered himself for marriage.

Fully resolved, the girl that evening sat down by the fireplace, and turning toward her aged parents, said, "O my mother and father, I see that the snow has fallen, whereby easily rabbits are tracked, and the young men who went out this morning returned long before evening heavily laden with strings of this game. Behold, in the other rooms of our house are many rabbit sticks, and there hang on the walls stone axes, and with these I might perchance strike down a rabbit on his trail, or, if he run into a log, split the log and dig him out. So I have thought during the day, and have decided to go tomorrow and try my fortunes in the hunt, woman though I be."

"Naiya, my daughter," quavered the feeble old mother, "you would surely be very cold, or you would lose your way, or grow so tired that you could not return before night, and you must not go out to hunt rabbits, woman as you are."

"Why, certainly not," insisted the old man, rubbing his lean knees and shaking his head over the days that were gone. "No, no; let us live in poverty rather than that you should run such risks as these, O my daughter."

But say what they would, the girl was determined. And the old man said at last, "Very well! You will not be turned from your course. Therefore, O daughter, I will help you as best I may." He hobbled into another room, and found there some old deerskins covered thickly with fur; and drawing them out, he moistened and carefully softened them, and cut out for the maiden long stockings, which he sewed up with sinew and the fiber of the yucca leaf. Then he selected for her from among the old possessions of his brothers and sons, who had been killed or perished otherwise, a number of rabbit sticks and a fine, heavy stone axe. Meanwhile, the old woman busied herself in preparing a lunch for the girl, which was composed of little cakes of corn meal, spiced with pepper and wild onions, pierced through the middle, and baked in the ashes. When she had made a long string of these by threading them like beads on a rope of yucca fiber, she laid them down not far from the ladder on a little bench, with the rabbit sticks, the stone axe, and the deerskin stockings.

That night the maiden planned and planned, and early on the following morning, even before the young men had gone out from the town, she had put on a warm, short-skirted dress, knotted a mantle over her shoulder and thrown another and larger one over her back, drawn on the deerskin stockings, had thrown the string of corncakes over her shoulder, stuck the rabbit sticks in her belt, and carrying the stone axe in her hand sallied forth eastward through the Gateway of Zuñi and into the plain of the valley beyond, called the Plain of the Burnt River, on account of the black, roasted-looking rocks along some parts of its sides. Dazzlingly white the snow stretched out before her—not deep, but unbroken—and when she came near the cliffs with many little canyons in them, along the northern side of the valley, she saw many a trail of rabbits running out and in among the rocks and between the bushes.

Warm and excited by her unwonted exercise, she did not heed a coming snowstorm, but ran about from one place to another, following the trails of the rabbits, sometimes up into the canyons, where the forests of piñon and cedar stood, and where here and there she had the good fortune sometimes to run two, three, or four rabbits into a single hollow log. It was little work to split these logs, for they were small, as you know, and to dig out the rabbits and slay them by a blow of the hand on the nape of the neck, back of the ears. As she killed each rabbit she raised it reverently to her lips, and breathed from its nostrils its expiring breath, and tying its legs together, placed it on the string, which after a while began to grow heavy on her shoulders.

Still she kept on, little heeding the snow which was falling fast; nor did she notice that it was growing darker and darker, so intent was she on the hunt, and so glad was she to capture so many rabbits. Indeed, she followed the trails until they were no longer visible, as the snow fell all around her, thinking all the while, "How happy will be my poor old father and mother that they shall now have flesh to eat! How strong will they grow! And when this meat is gone, that which is dried and preserved of it also, lo! another snowstorm will no doubt come, and I can go hunting again."

At last the twilight came, and looking around, she found that the snow had fallen deeply, there was no trail, and that she had lost her way. True, she turned about and started in the direction of her home, as she supposed, walking as fast as she could through the soft, deep snow. Yet she reckoned not rightly, for instead of going eastward along the valley, she went southward across it; and entering the mouth of the Descending Plain of the Pines, she went on and on, thinking she was going homeward, until at last it grew dark and she knew not which way to turn.

"What harm," thought she, "if I find a sheltered place among the rocks? What harm if I remain all night, and go home in the morning when the snow has ceased falling, and by the light I shall know my way?"

So she turned about to some rocks which appeared, black and dim, a short distance away. Fortunately, among these rocks is the cave which is known as Taiuma's Cave. This she came to, and peering into that black hole, she saw in it, back some distance, a little glowing light. "Ha, ha!" thought she, "perhaps some rabbit hunters like myself, belated yesterday, passed the night here and left the fire burning. If so, this is greater good fortune than I could have looked for." So, lowering the string of rabbits which she carried on her shoulder, and throwing off her mantle, she crawled in, peering well into the darkness, for fear of wild beasts; then, returning, she drew in the string of rabbits and the mantle.

Behold! there was a bed of hot coals buried in the ashes in the very middle of the cave, and piled up on one side were fragments of broken wood. The girl, happy in her good fortune, issued forth and gathered more sticks from the cliff side, where dead piñons are found in great numbers, and bringing them in little armfuls one after another, she finally succeeded in gathering a store sufficient to keep the fire burning brightly all the night through. Then she drew off her snow-covered stockings of deerskin and the bedraggled mantles, and building a fire, hung them up to dry and sat down to rest herself. The fire burned up and glowed brightly, so that the whole cave was as light as a room at night when a dance is being celebrated. By and by, after her clothing had dried, she spread a mantle on the floor of the cave by the side of the fire, and sitting down, dressed one of her rabbits and roasted it, and, untying the string of corncakes her mother had made for her, feasted on the roasted meat and cakes.

She had just finished her evening meal, and was about to recline and watch the fire for a while, when she heard away off in the distance a long, low cry of distress—*"Ho-o-o-o thlaia-a!"*

"Ah," thought the girl, "someone, more belated than myself, is lost; doubtless one of the rabbit hunters." She got up, and went nearer to the entrance of the cavern.

"Ho-o-o-o thlaia-a!" sounded the cry, nearer this time. She ran out, and as it was repeated again, she placed her hand to her mouth, and cried, woman though she was, as loudly as possible, *"Li-i thlaia-a!* Here!"

The cry was repeated near at hand, and presently the maiden, listening first, and then shouting, and listening again, heard the clatter of an enormous rattle. In dismay and terror she threw her hands into the air, and, crouching down, rushed into the cave and retreated to its farthest limits, where she sat shuddering with fear. For she knew that one of the Cannibal Demons of those days, perhaps the renowned Atahsaia of the east, had seen the light of her fire through the cave entrance, with his terrible staring eyes, and assuming it to be a lost wanderer, had cried out, and so led her to guide him to her place of concealment.

On came the Demon, snapping the twigs under his feet and shouting in a hoarse, loud voice, *"Ho lithlsh ta ime!*—Ho, there! So you are in here, are you?" *Kothl!* clanged his rattle, while almost fainting with terror, closer to the rock crouched the maiden.

The old Demon came to the entrance of the cave and bawled out, "I am cold, I am hungry! Let me in!" Without further ado, he stooped and tried to get in; but behold! the entrance was too small for his giant shoulders to pass. Then he pretended to be wonderfully civil, and said, "Come out, and bring me something to eat."

"I have nothing for you," cried the maiden. "I have eaten my food."

"Have you no rabbits?" "Yes."

"Come out and bring me some of them."

But the maiden was so terrified that she dared not move toward the entrance.

"Throw me a rabbit!" shouted the old Demon.

The maiden threw him one of her precious rabbits at last, when she could rise and go to it. He clutched it with his long, horny hand, gave one gulp and swallowed it. Then he cried out, "Throw me another!" She threw him another, which he also immediately swallowed; and so on until the poor maiden had thrown all the rabbits to the voracious old monster. Everyone she threw him he caught in his huge, yellow-tusked mouth, and swallowed, hair and all, at one gulp.

"Throw me another!" cried he, when the last had already been thrown to him.

So the poor maiden was forced to say, "I have no more."

"Throw me your overshoes!" cried he.

She threw the overshoes of deerskin, and these like the rabbits he speedily devoured. Then he called for her moccasins, and she threw them; for her belt, and she threw it; and finally, wonderful to tell, she threw even her mantle, and blanket, and her overdress, until, behold, she had nothing left!

Now, with all that he had eaten, the old Demon was swollen hugely at the stomach, and though he tried and tried to squeeze himself through the mouth of the cave, he could not by any means succeed. Finally, lifting his great flint axe, he began to shatter the rock about the entrance to the cave, and slowly but surely he enlarged the hole and the maiden now knew that as soon as he could get in he would devour her also, and she almost fainted at the sickening thought. Pound, pound, pound, pound, went the great axe of the Demon as he struck the rocks.

In the distance the two War-gods were sitting in their home at Thla-uthla —the Shrine amid the Bushes—beyond Thunder Mountain, and though far off, they heard thus in the middle of the night the pounding of the Demon's hammer axe against the rocks. And of course they knew at once that a poor maiden, for the sake of her father and mother, had been out hunting; that she had lost her way, and finding a cave where there was a little fire, entered it, rebuilt the fire, and rested herself; that attracted by the light of her fire, the Cannibal Demon had come and besieged her retreat, and only a little time hence would he so enlarge the entrance to the cave that he could squeeze even his great over-filled paunch through it and come at the maiden to destroy her. So, catching up their wonderful weapons, these two War-gods flew away into the darkness and in no time they were approaching the Descending Plain of the Pines.

Just as the Demon was about to enter the cavern, and the maiden had fainted at seeing his huge face and gray shock of hair and staring eyes, his yellow, protruding tusks, and his horny, taloned hand, they came upon the old beast; and each one hitting him a welt with his war club, they "ended his daylight," and then hauled him forth into the open space. They opened his huge paunch and withdrew from it the maiden's garments, and even the rabbits which had been slain. The rabbits they cast away among the soapweed plants that grew on the slope at the foot of the cliff. The garments they spread out on the snow, and by their knowledge cleansed and made them perfect, even more perfect than they had been before.

Then, flinging the huge body of the giant Demon down into the depths of the canyon, they turned them about, and calling out gentle words to the maiden, entered and restored her. And she, seeing in them not their usual ugly persons, but handsome youths (as like to one another as are two deer born of the same mother), was greatly comforted; and bending low, and breathing upon their hands, thanked them over and over for the rescue they had brought her. But she crouched herself low with shame that her garments were but few. When, behold! the youths went out and brought in to her the garments they had cleaned by their knowledge, restoring them to her.

Then, spreading their mantles by the door of the cave, they slept there that night, in order to protect the maiden, and on the morrow wakened her. They told her many things, and showed her many things which she had not known before, and counseled her thus, "It is not fearful that a maiden should marry; therefore, O maiden, return unto thy people in the Village of the Gateway of the River of Zuñi. This morning we will slay rabbits un-numbered for you, and start you on your way, guarding you down the snow-covered valley; and when you are in sight of your home we will leave you, telling you our names."

So, early in the morning the two gods went forth; and flinging their sticks among the soapweed plants, behold! as though the soapweed plants were rabbits, so many lay killed on the snow before these mighty hunters.

And they gathered together great numbers of these rabbits, a string for each one of the party. And when the sun had risen clearer in the sky, and his light sparkled on the snow around them, they took the rabbits to the maiden and presented them, saying, "We will carry each one of us a string of these rabbits." Then taking her hand, they led her out of the cave and down the valley, until, beyond on the high black mesas at the Gateway of the River of Zuñi, she saw the smoke rise from the houses of her village. Then turned the two War-gods to her, and they told her their names. And again she bent low, and breathed on their hands. Then, dropping the strings of rabbits which they had carried close beside the maiden, they swiftly disappeared.

Thinking much of all she had learned, she continued her way to the home of her father and mother. And as she went into the town, staggering under her load of rabbits, the young men and the old men and women and children beheld her with wonder; and no hunter in that town thought of comparing himself with the Maiden Huntress of Kyawana Tehua-tsana. The old man and the old woman, who had mourned the night through and sat up anxiously watching, were overcome with happiness when they saw their daughter returning; and as she laid the rabbits at their feet, she said, "Behold! my father and my mother, foolish have I been, and much danger have I passed through, because I forgot the ways of a woman and assumed the ways of a man. But two wondrous youths have taught me that a woman may be a huntress and yet never leave her own fireside. Behold! I will marry, when some good youth comes to me, and he will hunt rabbits and deer for me, for my parents and my children."

So, one day, when one of those youths who had seen her come in laden with rabbits, and who had admired her time out of mind, presented himself with a bundle at the maiden's fireside, behold! she smilingly and delightedly accepted him. And from that day to this, when women would hunt rabbits or deer, they marry, and behold, the rabbits and deer are hunted.

Thus shortens my story.

III

LEGENDS OF THE LITTLE PEOPLE, GIANTS, AND MONSTERS

TWO FACES, THE EVIL ONE

THE INDIANS used to hear an Anung-ite—Two Faces—pass along kicking the ground. When he kicked the ground with one foot, bells rang and an owl hooted, and when he kicked with the other, it seemed as if a buffalo bull was there, snorting as he does when about to charge. At the next step, a chickadee was heard, and when he moved the other foot, he made all kinds of animals cry out. The Indians had heard this Anung-ite and were afraid of him. Now and then when a man, who thought himself strong, was alone, the Anung-ite surprised him by catching him and throwing him into one of his ears. These ears were so large that each could hold three men.

No person knew where the Anung-ite made his abode, and no one cared to follow him; no one dared to go out of doors at night. Now, there was an old man and his wife who had a lodge to themselves, and their only child was a willful boy. One night he was particularly ill-behaved, and when his mother told him to do something, he disobeyed her. So she said, "I will put you out of the lodge, and the Anung-ite will toss you into his ear." She did not believe this, and merely said it to frighten her son into obedience. Finding him heedless, she seized his arm and, though he began to cry, pushed him out of the lodge and fastened the entrance securely. The poor boy ran crying around the lodge, but soon there was silence. The mother in turn began to cry, and went to seek him, but she did not find him outside the lodge.

The next morning she and her husband, weeping, went to seek him among the people in the neighboring camp, asking everyone about him, but no one had seen him. So they returned to their lodge, and they wept many days for their son. One night when the mother was weeping, she heard someone say, "*Hin! Hin!* You said to me, 'Ghost, take that one.' *Hin! Hin!*" This was said often, and she noticed a rattling of small bells as the being walked along. Just then she said, "Husband, I think now that a ghost has taken my son." The husband said, "Yes; you gave the boy to the ghost, and, of course, the ghost took him. Why should you complain? It serves you right."

Then the mother cried aloud, so that her voice might have been heard

65

at a distance. Then said she, "Husband, tomorrow night I will lie hid by the woodpile, and if the ghost comes I will have a knife in my hand, and after I catch it by the leg I will call to you. Be ready to come at once. You must aid me, and I will recover my son, because I know that the ghost threw him into his ear."

So the next night she lay in wait for the monster. By and by something was coming, crying out *"Hin!"* and making all kinds of birds and animals cry out as it walked. She saw a very large being come and stand by the lodge. He was very tall, his head being above the smoke hole, down which he peeped into the lodge. Suddenly the mother called to her husband, and seized one leg of the monster with both hands. Then she and her husband gashed the legs in many places, and after tying a thong to one leg, they pulled down the monster and bound him securely. They guarded him till it was day. Then they beheld a hideous monster covered with thick hair, except on his two faces.

They split his ears with a knife, and within one they found their long-lost son, who was very lean and unable to speak. He had a thick coat of long hair on him from his legs up to his head, but his head and face were smooth. And he would have become an Anung-ite had he not been rescued. He did not survive very long. After the parents had taken their son from the ear of the monster, they put many sticks of wood on a fire, and on this they laid the monster. He soon was in flames, and they stood looking on. Many things were sent flying out of the fire in all directions, just like sparks. These were porcupine quills, bags, all kinds of feathers, arrows, pipes, birds, axes, war clubs, flints, stones for sharpening knives, stone balls resembling billiard balls, necklaces of *tuki* shells, flints for striking tinder, flint hide scrapers, whips, tobacco pouches, and all kinds of beads.

KWASIND, THE STRONG MAN

PAUWATING was a village where the young men amused themselves very much in ancient times, in sports and ball-playing.

One day, as they were engaged in their sports, one of the strongest and most active, at the moment he was about to succeed in a trial of lifting, slipped and fell upon his back. "Ha! ha! ha!" cried the lookers-on, "you will never rival Kwasind." He was deeply mortified, and when the sport was over, these words came to his mind. He could not recollect any man of this name. He thought he would ask the old man, the storyteller of the village, the next time he came to the lodge. The opportunity soon occurred.

"My grandfather," said he, "who was Kwasind? I am very anxious to know what he could do."

"Kwasind," the old man replied, "was a listless idle boy. He would not play when the other boys played, and his parents could never get him to do any kind of labor. He was always making excuses. His parents took notice, however, that he fasted for days together, but they could not learn what spirit he supplicated, or had chosen as the guardian spirit to attend him through life. He was so inattentive to his parents' requests, that he, at last, became a subject of reproach.

"'Ah,' said his mother to him one day, 'is there any young man of your age, in all the village, who does so little for his parents? You neither hunt nor fish. You take no interest in anything, whether labor or amusement, which engages the attention of your equals in years. I have often set my nets in the coldest days of winter without any assistance from you. And I have taken them up again while you remained inactive at the lodge fire. Are you not ashamed of such idleness? Go, I bid you, and wring out that net, which I have just taken from the water.'

"Kwasind saw that there was a determination to make him obey. He did not, therefore, make any excuses, but went out and took up the net. He carefully folded it, doubled and redoubled it, forming it into a roll, and then with an easy twist of his hands wrung it short off, with as much ease as if every twine had been a thin brittle fiber. Here they at once saw the secret of his reluctance. He possessed supernatural strength.

67

"After this, the young men were playing one day on the plain, where there was lying one of those large, heavy, black pieces of rock, which Manabozho is said to have cast at his father. Kwasind took it up with much ease, and threw it into the river. After this, he accompanied his father on a hunting excursion into a remote forest. They came to a place where the wind had thrown a great many trees into a narrow pass. 'We must go the other way', said the old man, 'it is impossible to get the burdens through this place'. He sat down to rest himself, took out his smoking apparatus, and gave a short time to reflection. When he had finished, Kwasind had lifted away the largest pine trees, and pulled them out of the path.

"Sailing one day in his canoe, Kwasind saw a large furred animal, which he immediately recognized to be the king of beavers. He plunged into the water in pursuit of it. His companions were in the greatest astonishment and alarm, supposing he would perish. He often dove down and remained a long time under water, pursuing the animal from island to island; and at last returned with the kingly prize. After this, his fame spread far and wide, and no hunter would presume to compete with him.

"He helped Manabozho to clear away the obstructions in the streams, and to remove the great windfalls of trees from the valleys, the better to fit them for the residence of man.

"He performed so many feats of strength and skill that he excited the envy of the Puck Wudj Ininees, the fairies, who conspired against his life. 'For', said they, 'if this man is suffered to go on, in his career of strength and exploits, we shall presently have no work to perform. Our agency in the affairs of men must cease. He will undermine our power, and drive us, at last, into the water, where we must all perish, or be devoured by the wicked water spirit, Neebanawbaig'.

"The strength of Kwasind was all concentrated in the crown of his head. This was, at the same time, the only vulnerable part of his body; and there was but one species of weapon which could be successfully employed in making any impression upon it. The fairies carefully hunted through the woods to find this weapon. It was the burr or seed vessel of the white pine. They gathered a quantity of this article, and waylaid Kwasind at a point on the river where the red rocks jut into the water forming rude castles—a point which he was accustomed to pass in his canoe. They waited a long time, making merry upon these rocks, for it was a highly romantic spot. At last the wished-for object appeared; Kwasind came floating calmly down the stream, on the afternoon of a summer's day, languid with the heat of the weather, and almost asleep. When his canoe came directly beneath the cliff, the tallest and stoutest fairy began the attack. Others followed his example. It was a long time before they could hit the vulnerable part, but success at length crowned their efforts, and Kwasind sank, never to rise more.

"Ever since this victory, the Puck Wudj Ininees have made that point of rock a favorite resort. The hunters often hear them laugh, and see their little plumes shake as they pass this scene on light summer evenings."

THE POLESTAR

A LARGE PARTY of Indians, while moving in search of new hunting grounds, wandered on for many moons, finding but little game. At last they arrived at the banks of a great river, entirely unknown to them, where they had to stop, not having the material to build boats. Lost and nearly famished with hunger, the head chief was taken very ill, and it was decided to hold a council to devise means for returning to their old homes. During the dance, and while the tobacco was burning, a little being like a child came up, saying she was sent to be their guide. Accordingly they broke up their camp and started with her that night. Preceding them, with only a *gi-wah*, a small war club, she led them on until daylight, and then commanded them to rest while she prepared their food. This they did, and when awakened by her they found a great feast in readiness for them. Then she bade them farewell, with the assurance of returning to them again in the evening.

True to her word, at evening she reappeared, bringing with her a skin jug, from which she poured out some liquid into a horn cup, and bade them each to taste of it. At first they feared to do so, but at last yielding they began to feel very strong. She then informed them that they had a long journey to make that night. Again they followed her, and in the early morn arrived at a great plain, where she bade them rest again for the day, with

the exception of a few warriors who were to be shown where they could find plenty of game.

Two of the warriors had accompanied her but a short distance when they encountered a herd of deer, of which she bade them kill all they wished in her absence, and then, again promising to return at night, she took leave of them. At nightfall she returned, saying her own chief would soon follow her to explain to them how they could reach their own homes in safety. In a short time he arrived, with a great number of his race, and immediately all held council together and informed the Indians that they were now in the territory of the pigmies, who would teach them a sign, already in the sky, which would be to them a sure guide whenever they were lost. The pigmies pointed out the polestar and told them that in the north, where the sun never goes, while other stars moved about, this particular star should stand still, as the Indian's guide in his wanderings, and that they were then but to follow its light and they would soon return to their tribe, where they would find plenty of game.

The warriors thanked the good pigmies, and traveled every night until they arrived safely in their homes, where, when they had recounted all their adventures, the head chief called a meeting of all the tribes and said they ought to give this star a name. So they called it *ti-yn-sou-da-go-err*— the star which never moves—by which name it is called unto this day.

PUCK WUDJ ININEES,
OR THE VANISHING LITTLE MEN

THERE WAS A TIME when all the inhabitants of the earth had died, excepting two helpless children, a baby boy and a little girl. When their parents died, these children were asleep. The little girl, who was the elder, was the first to wake. She looked around her, but seeing nobody besides her little brother, who lay asleep, she quietly resumed her bed. At the end of ten days, her brother moved without opening his eyes. At the end of ten days more, he changed his position, lying on the other side.

The girl soon grew up to woman's estate, but the boy increased in stature very slowly. It was a long time before he would even creep. When he was able to walk, his sister made him a little bow and arrows, and suspended around his neck a small shell, saying, "You shall be called Wa-Dais-Ais-Imid—He of the Little Shell."

Every day he would go out with his little bow, shooting at the small birds. The first bird he killed was a tomtit. His sister was highly pleased when he took it to her. She carefully skinned and stuffed it, and put it away for him. The next day he killed a red squirrel. His sister preserved this too. The third day he killed a partridge (*Peena*), which she stuffed and set up. After this, he acquired more courage, and would venture some distance from home. His skill and success as a hunter daily increased, and he killed the deer, bear, moose, and other large animals inhabiting the forest. In fine, he became a great hunter.

He had now arrived to maturity in years, but remained an infant in stature. One day, walking about, he came to a small lake. It was in the winter season. He saw a man on the ice killing beavers. The man appeared to be a giant. Comparing himself to this great man he appeared no bigger than an insect. He seated himself on the shore, and watched the man's movements. When the large man had killed many beavers, he put them on a hand sled and went home.

When he saw him retire, Wa-Dais-Ais-Imid followed him, and wielding his magic shell, cut off the tail of one of the beavers, and ran home with his trophy. When the tall stranger reached his lodge, with his sled load of beavers, he was surprised to find the tail of one of them gone, for he had not observed the movements of the little hero of the shell.

The next day Wa-Dais-Ais-Imid went to the same lake. The man had already fixed his load of beavers on his *odawbon*, his sled, and commenced his return. But Wa-Dais-Ais-Imid nimbly ran forward, and overtaking him, succeeded by the same means in securing another of the beavers' tails. When the man saw that he had lost another of this most esteemed part of the animal, he was very angry. "I wonder," said he, "what dog it is that has thus cheated me. Could I meet him, I would make his flesh quiver at the point of my lance."

Next day he pursued his hunting at the beaver dam near the lake, and was followed again by the little man of the shell. On this occasion, the hunter had worked so fast that he had accomplished his object and nearly reached his home before our tiny hero could overtake him, but he nimbly drew his shell and cut off another beaver's tail. In all these pranks our hero availed himself of his power of invisibility, and thus escaped observation. When the man saw that the trick had been so often repeated, his anger was greater than ever. He gave vent to his feelings in words. He looked carefully around to see whether he could discover any tracks. But he could find none. His unknown visitor had stepped so lightly as to leave no track.

Next day the hunter resolved to disappoint him by going to his beaver pond very early. When Wa-Dais-Ais-Imid reached the place, he found the fresh traces of his work, but the hunter had already returned. Our hero followed his tracks, but failed to overtake him. When he came in sight of the lodge, the hunter was in front of it, employed in skinning his beavers. As he stood looking at him, he thought, "I will let him see me." Presently the man, who proved to be no less a personage than Manabozho, looked up and saw him. After regarding him with attention, "Who are you, little man?" said Manabozho. "I have a mind to kill you." The little hero of the shell replied, "If you were to try to kill me, you could not do it."

When he returned home he told his sister that they must separate. "I must go away," said he, "it is my fate. You too," he added, "must go away soon. Tell we where you would wish to dwell." She said, "I would like to go to the place of the breaking of daylight. I have always loved the east. The earliest glimpses of light are from that quarter and it is, to my mind, the most beautiful part of the heavens. After I get there, my brother, whenever you see the clouds in that direction of various colors, you may think that your sister is painting her face."

"And I," said he, "my sister, shall live on the mountains and rocks. There I can see you at the earliest hour, and there the streams of water are clear, and the air pure. And I shall ever be called Puck Wudj Ininee, or the little wild man of the mountains. But before we part forever, I must go and try to find some Manitoes." He left her, and traveled over the surface of the globe, and then went far down into the earth. He had been treated well wherever he went.

At last he found a giant Manito, who had a large kettle which was forever boiling. The giant regarded him with a stern look, and then took him up in his hand, and threw him unceremoniously into the kettle. But by the protection of his personal spirit, our hero was shielded from harm, and with much ado got out of the kettle and escaped.

He returned to his sister, and related his rovings and misadventures. He finished his story by addressing her thus, "My sister, there is a Manito at each of the four corners of the earth. There is also one above them, far in the sky; and last," continued he, "there is another, and wicked one, who lives deep down in the earth. We must now separate. When the winds blow from the four corners of the earth you must then go. They will carry you to the place you wish. I go to the rocks and mountains, where my kindred will ever delight to dwell."

He then took his ball stick, and commenced running up a high mountain, whooping as he went. Presently the winds blew, and as he predicted, his sister was borne by them to the eastern sky, where she has ever since been, and her name is the Morning Star.

> Blow, winds, blow! my sister lingers
>   For her dwelling in the sky,
> Where the morn, with rosy fingers,
>   Shall her cheeks with vermil dye.
>
> There, my earliest views directed,
>   Shall from her their color take,
> And her smiles, through clouds reflected,
>   Guide me on, by wood or lake.
>
> While I range the highest mountains,
>   Sport in valleys green and low,
> Or beside our Indian fountains
>   Raise my tiny *hip holla.*

THE FLYING HEAD

LONG AGO before the white man came to this island there was a settlement of Oneida Indians near Oneida Lake. In this village lived a famous Indian hunter named Wolf Marked. Wolf Marked lived in a bark house at the edge of the village. His only companions were two large wolflike dogs who never left their master's side. They were his constant friends, and it was said that, while hunting, these swift-running dogs would drive the game to Wolf Marked. This famous hunter was never known to have returned from the trail empty-handed. He was well liked by other members of his nation. A portion of all game brought down by his arrows was given to the needy, the widow, and the orphan. No one was fleeter of foot than this young man, and often the chiefs of his nation sent him with wampum messages down the long trail that bound one end of the Long House Country to the other. He was a great ballplayer and many times his strong arm and fleet foot carried the ball through the goal posts of a neighboring tribe. In feats of endurance and strength he excelled all others of his people.

One day Wolf Marked made preparations for a long hunt. With a new quiver of arrows and a pouch of provisions, he left the village traveling toward the west. On each side of him trotted one of his faithful dogs. All day he traveled, his eyes ever alert for signs of game. But on this day all life in the forests seemed to have vanished. Over the entire countryside a deep silence had fallen. Not a bird sang a note. Not a rabbit crossed the trail. No squirrel barked at him from the branches of a tree. Even the brook that he occasionally crossed refused to make a murmur. The very forest seemed to have fallen asleep. No leaf waved or rustled in the wind.

Wolf Marked wondered because never before had he traveled such a distance without seeing some sign of game. He wondered also why his two faithful dogs traveled so close to his feet. He wondered why their hair rose on their backs, why their tails lay curled beneath their bodies as if they feared something. Never before had his brave dogs acted in this manner. Bravely they had often charged the largest of the bear tribe, and even a mountain lion caused no fear in their eyes. Yet today, instead of running into the forest in search of game, as was their usual practice, they stayed close to their master's side. Occasionally they would sniff the air, look toward the north and utter low and fierce growls. Wolf Marked tried to urge them to hunt, but it was no use. They would not leave his side. In this manner they traveled the entire day.

As the sun neared the western horizon, Wolf Marked came to a little stream. Throwing down his pack he prepared to make camp for the night. As he gathered wood for a fire, his dogs growled again. Looking up, Wolf Marked thought that he heard a strange wailing cry coming from the north. His two dogs shivered and pressed against his legs. One of the dogs moved in front of his master, and looking Wolf Marked in the face, the dog spoke. "Master, do not be surprised that we can speak to you in your own language. Never before have we done this, though we have the power to do so. You have been kind to us, never allowing us to go cold or hungry, but always sharing with us. For that reason we are going to break our silence and warn you. We cannot describe to you the terrible monster that is coming toward your camp. Do not delay but hurry back to the village. This creature is master in the woods. No one can harm him here in the forest. Only in clearings is he helpless. It is of no use to stay and fight this thing. Your arrows would be useless against his thick skin. Your war club would bounce from him. Your only hope is to run and try to reach the village clearing before the monster catches up with you. If he catches you, there is no hope. The creature travels like the wind. Even now it may be too late, for he has scented you."

There was no mistaking the terror in the eyes of his dogs. With a bound, Wolf Marked flung his pack aside and ran down the trail toward the village, his dogs following on either side. As Wolf Marked ran he heard again the terrible wail of the monster. It was a high, long-drawn-out, piercing wail. It was a cry that Wolf Marked had never heard before. Sometimes it reminded him of the scream of a mountain lion. Again it resembled the howl of a wolf, or the roar of the north wind screaming through the forest. As Wolf Marked ran, the wail got nearer and nearer. The creature was fast gaining on him. Once, while at the foot of a long hill, he glanced back. What he saw startled him so much that he almost froze in his tracks. For a moment he could not run. A great fiery Head with large, round yellow eyes, a long hooked beak, and large open mouth appeared over the brow of the hill. The creature had fiery hair that flowed in a long wavy streak as the monster traveled. It had no body, but fastened to the bottom of the huge head were two scale-covered paws, on the ends of which were long curved, ugly-looking claws. The monster traveled in a peculiar fashion. It would jump to the foot of a tree, climb the tree, and then bound to the foot of another tree. In this way it traveled very rapidly. There was a wide burned path cutting back through the forest where the creature had traveled.

As the monster looked down the hill and saw Wolf Marked, it opened its mouth and showed its huge teeth. From its mouth came the terrible cry that Wolf Marked had heard. With a chopping snap, the monster closed its huge teeth on the trunk of a tree, and with one bite cut it in two. Then with a bound it headed for the hunter. Wolf Marked turned and ran on.

One of the dogs spoke again, "Throw away your shirt, master. It will delay the creature for a while." The hunter tore off his shirt. Throwing it behind him he ran on. In a little while he heard the creature give a roar, and he knew that it was chewing up his shirt. Soon the wail was again heard. Nearer and nearer it came, until Wolf Marked could feel the hot breath of his pursuer on the back of his neck. One of the dogs again spoke to him, "Master, the creature is almost upon us. I am going to fight it. I can delay it a little while, but I will never see you again. Farewell, kind and good master." Saying this, the dog turned and ran back.

Wolf Marked heard barking and growling and then a yelp of pain. He knew that his faithful dog was dead and was being eaten by the Head. He ran on. The village was just around the bend of a hill. If he could only make it, he knew that he would be safe. Again he heard the wailing cry of the creature. Nearer and nearer it sounded. He could feel the hot breath of the Head singe his hair. Sparks from its fiery mouth fell around him. The remaining dog said, "Master, the creature is almost upon us. Perhaps I can delay it until you reach the village. I am going back to fight it. I will never see you again on this earth. Farewell, kind and faithful master." Saying this, the dog turned and ran back over the trail.

Wolf Marked heard barking and growling and then a yelp of pain. He knew that his second faithful dog was dead and was being eaten by the monster. He was very tired, but ahead of him he could see the sky lit up by the fires of the village. He ran on and after a brief silence he again heard the terrible wail of the monster. He could hear the creature getting nearer and nearer as it cut a burning path through the forest. He could feel the hot breath of the monster burn his back. He could sense its huge eyes upon him. With a staggering run, he entered the large clearing in the center of which was the village. Running across the field, he finally came to a stop and with his startled people looked back over his trail. A great Head came bounding to the edge of the forest. Showers of sparks shot from its mouth. Its great yellow eyes glared in fiery hatred at the people. With a mighty bound and a terrible cry of anger, it turned and disappeared over the dark forest, traveling toward the north.

(In ancient days this story was told to show the fidelity of a dog, man's best friend. It was a belief of the old people that a person who was cruel to dogs could never reach the Land of Happy Spirits.)

IV

MYSTERY, MEDICINE, AND MAGIC

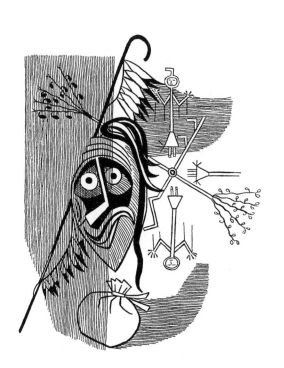

THE ORIGIN OF THE MEDICINE SOCIETY

THERE WAS in old times a young chief who was a hunter of great cunning, but though he killed many animals he never took advantage of their positions. He never shot a swimming deer or a doe with a fawn, he never killed an animal fatigued by a long run nor took one unawares. Before the hunt he always threw tobacco and made a ceremony to ask permission to kill game. Nor was he ever ungrateful to the animals of the woods who had been his friends for so many years. The flesh that was useless he left for the wolves and birds, calling to them as he left it, "Come, my friends, I have made a feast for you." Likewise when he took honey from a tree, he left a portion for the bears, and when he had his corn harvested, he left open ears in the field for the crows, that they might not steal the corn sprouts at the next planting. He fed the fish and water animals with entrails and offal. No ruthless hunter was he but thoughtful. He threw tobacco for the animals in the woods and water, and made incense for them with the *oyenkwaonwe*, the sacred tobacco, and threw it even for the trees.

He was a well-loved chief, for he remembered his friends and gave them meat. All the animals were his friends, and all his people were loyal to him. All this was because he was good, and he was known as the "protector of the birds and beasts." So he was called. It is supposed that his own name was His-hand-is-red.

The southwest country is a land of mysteries. There are many unknown things in the mountains there and also in the waters. The wildest people have always lived there, and some were very wise and made different things. When, many years ago, the Ongwe honwe, the Iroquois, began to make excursions to this distant country they encountered many nations that were friendly and more that were hostile. The Iroquois used to like to go to this country for there they learned new things and found new plants and new kinds of corn and beans, and when they would fight and destroy a tribe they would carry away curiously made things and some captives back to their own country.

While one of these exploring parties was in the far southwest looking for war and new things, a band of very savage people attacked them. The young chief, the friend of the animals, was with the party, and being separated from the rest of his party, was struck down by a tomahawk blow The enemy cut a circle around his scalp lock and tore it off. He could not fight strong because he was tired and very hungry from the long journey, so he was killed. The enemy knew him because he had been a brave fighter and killed a good many of their people in former battles, so they were glad when they killed him and prized his scalp. Now he lay dead in a thicket, and none of his warriors knew where he was, but the enemy showed them his scalp. So they knew he was dead, but they did not kill all the Iroquois.

Black night came and alone upon the red and yellow leaves the chief lay dead, and his blood was clotted upon the leaves where it had spilled. The night birds scented the blood and hovered over the body, the owl and the whippoorwill flew above it, and Oshadagea, the dew eagle, swooped down from the regions over the clouds. "He seems to be a friend," they said. "Who can this man be?" A wolf sniffed the air and thought he smelled food. Skulking through the trees he came upon the body, dead and scalped. His nose was upon the clotted blood, and he liked blood. Then he looked into the face of the dead man and leaped back with a long yelping howl—the dead man was the friend of the wolves and the animals and birds.

His howl was a signal call and brought all the animals of the big woods, and the birds dropped down around him. All the medicine animals came— the bear, the deer, the fox, the beaver, the otter, the turtle, and the big horned deer (moose). Now the birds around him were the owl, the whippoorwill, the crow, the buzzard, the swift hawk, the eagle, the snipe, the white heron, and also the great chief of all birds, Oshadagea, who is the eagle that flies in the world of our Creator above the clouds.

These are all the great medicine people, and they came in council about their killed friend. Then they said, "He must not be lost to us. We must restore him to life again." Then a bird said, "He is our friend, he always fed us. We cannot allow our friend to die. We must restore him." Then the wolf came up to the body and said, "Here is our friend, he always gave us food in time of famine. We called him our father, now we are orphans. It is our duty to give him life again. Let each one of us look in our medicine packets and take out the most potent ingredient. Then let us compound a medicine and give it." Then the owl said, "A living man must have a scalp."

So the animals made a wonderful medicine, and in its preparation some gave their own lives and mixed them with the medicine roots. When the medicine was made, all of it was contained in the bowl of an acorn. So they poured it down the throat of the man, and the bear, feeling over the body, found a warm spot over his heart. Then the bear hugged him close in his hairy arms and kept him warm. The crow had flown away for the scalp but could not find it. Then the white heron went, but while flying over a bean field thought herself hungry and stopped to eat and when filled was too heavy to rise again. Then the pigeon hawk, the swiftest of the birds, said that he would go and surely find it.

By this time the enemy had become aware that the animals were holding a council over their friend whom they had slain, and so they carefully guarded the scalp which they stretched upon a hoop and swung on a thong over the smoke hole of a lodge. The pigeon hawk, impatient at delay shot upward into the air and flying in wide circles discovered the scalp dangling over the fire drying in the hot smoke. Hovering over the lodge for a moment he dropped down, and snatching the scalp shot back upward into the clouds, faster and farther than the arrows that pursued him swift from the strong bows of the angered enemy. Back he flew, his speed undiminished by his long flight, and placed the scalp in the midst of the council. It was smoky and dried and would not fit the head of the man. Then big crow (buzzard) emptied his stomach on it to clean it of smoke and make it stick fast, and Oshadagea plucked a feather from his wing and dipped it in the pool of dew that rests in the hollow of his back and sprinkled the water upon it. The dew came down in round drops and refreshed the dry scalp as it does a withered leaf. The man had begun faintly to breathe when the animals placed the scalp back in his head, and they saw that truly he would revive. Then the man felt a warm liquid trickling down his throat, and with his eyes yet shut he began to talk the language of the birds and animals.

And they sang a wonderful song, and he listened and remembered every word of the song. This song the animals told him was the charm song of the medicine animals, and that when he wished the favor of the great medicine people, and when he felt grateful, to make a ceremony and sing the song. So also they told him that they had a dance and a dance song, and that they would teach him the dance. So they danced and some shook rattles made of the squashes (gourds), and though his eyes were closed he saw the dance and he knew all the tunes.

Then the animals told him to form a company of his friends and on certain occasions to sing and dance this ceremony, for it was a great power and called all the medicine animals together, and when the people were sick, they would devise a medicine for them. Now they said that he must not fail to perform the ceremony and throw tobacco for them. Now the name of the ceremony was *Hadidos*.

Then the chief asked the medicine people what the ingredients of the medicine were, and they promised to tell him. At a time the animals should choose they would notify him by the medicine song. Now, he could not receive the secret because he had been married. Only *hoyahdiwadoh*—virgin men—may receive the first knowledge of mysteries. Now, the chief greatly wished for the medicine, for he thought it would be a great charm and a cure for the wounds received in war. After a time the chief was lifted to his feet by the hand of the bear. Then he recovered his full life, and when he opened his eyes he found himself alone in the midst of a circle of tracks. He made his way back to his people and related his adventure. He gathered his warriors together and in a secret place sang the medicine song of the animals, the *Hadidos*. So they sang the song, and each had a song and they danced.

After some time, the chiefs decided to send another war party against the enemy in the southwest to punish the hostile people who were attacking them. Then the friend of the birds and animals said, "It is well that we destroy them for they are not a reasonable people," and so he went with his party.

Now after a certain number of days, the party stopped in an opening in the forest to replenish their stock of food. Now the place where they stopped was grassy and a good place for camp. Now a short distance away, a half day's journey, was a deer lick and near it a clear spring and a brook that ran from it, and to this place all the animals came to drink. The party wanted fresh meat and so dispatched two young men, *hoyahdiwadoh*, to the lick for game. As they approached it, they heard the sound of a distant song, and drawing near to the lick, they sat down on the bank over the spring and listened to the song. It was a most wonderful song and floated through the air to them. At a distance away, the animals came and drank, but so entranced were the young men by the music that they killed none. Through the entire night, they sat listening to the song, and learned sections of the song.

In the morning, they returned to the camp and reported what they had heard to their chief. Then said the chief, "That song is for the good of the medicine. You must find the source of the song and discover the medicine that will make us powerful in war and cure all our ills. You must purge yourselves and go again on the morrow." So the young men did as directed and went again to the spring and threw tobacco upon its surface. As night came on they listened, and again heard the great song. It was louder and more distinct than before. Then they heard a voice singing from the air and telling them the story of their lives and they marveled greatly. The song grew louder, and as they listened they discovered that it emanated from the summit of a mountain. So they returned in the morning and reported to their chief and sang to him parts of the song. Then he said, "You must cleanse yourselves again, and this time do not return until you have the medicine, the song, and the magic."

So the young men cleansed themselves again and went to the spring. As the thick night came on, they heard the singing voices clear and loud, ringing from the mountaintop. Then said one of the young men, "Let us follow the sound to its source," and they started in the darkness.

After a time they stumbled upon a windfall, a place where the trees had been blown down in a tangled mass. It was a difficult place to pass in the darkness, for they were often entrapped in the branches, but they persevered, and it seemed that someone was leading them. Beings seemed to be all about them, yet they could not see them, for it was dark. After they had extricated themselves from the windfall, they went into a morass, where their footsteps were guided by the unseen medicine animals.

Now the journey was a very tedious one, and they could see nothing. They approached a gulf and one said, "Let us go up and down the gulf and try to cross it," and they did and crossed one gulf. Soon they came to another,

85

where they heard the roaring of a cataract and the rushing of waters. It was a terrifying place, and one of the young men was almost afraid. They descended the slope and came to a swift river. Its waters were very cold, but they plunged in and would have been lost if someone unseen had not guided them. So they crossed over, and on the other side was a steep mountain which they must ascend, but could not because it was too steep. Then one of the young men said, "Let us wait here awhile and rest ourselves for we may need our strength for greater dangers." So he said. But the other said, "I am rested, we must go onward somehow."

When he had so spoken, a light came flying over and sang for them to follow it. So they followed the winged light and ascended the mountain, and they were helped. The winged light kept singing, "Follow me, follow me, follow me!" And they were safe when they followed and were not afraid. Now the singing, flying beacon was the whippoorwill. He led them. After a time the light disappeared, but they struggled up the mountainside unaided by its guidance. The way became very stony, and it seemed that no one was helping them now. Then they wished that their unseen friends would help them, so they made a prayer and threw sacred tobacco on the path. Then the light came again, and it was brighter; it glowed like the morning, and the way was lighted up. The singing continued all this while; they were nearing its source, and they reached the top of the mountain.

They looked about for they heard the song near at hand, but there was no one there. They saw nothing but a great stalk of corn springing from a flat rock. Its four roots stretched in the four directions, north, east, south, and west. They listened and discovered that the music emanated from the cornstalk. It was wonderful. The corn was a mystically magic plant, and life was within it. Then the winged light sang for them to cut the root and take a piece for medicine. So they made a tobacco offering and cut the root. Red blood like human blood flowed out from the cut, and then the wound immediately healed. Then the unseen speaker said, "This root is a great medicine, and now we will reveal the secret of the medicine." So the voices told them the composition of the medicine that had healed the chief and instructed them how to use it. They taught the young men the *Ganota*, the medicine song that would make the medicine strong and preserve it. They said that, unless the song was sung, the medicine would become weak, and the animals would become angry because of the neglect of the ceremonies that honored their medicine. Therefore, the holders of the medicine must sing the all-night song for it. And they told them all the laws of the medicine, and the singing light guided them back to the spring, and it was morning then. The young men returned to their chief and told him the full story of their experiences, and he was glad for he said, "The medicine will heal all wounds."

It was true, the medicine healed the cuts and wounds made by arrows and knives, and not one of the Iroquois was killed in their battle with the enemy. When they returned home, the chief organized the lodges of the medicine and the medicine people, and the name of the society was *Hadidos*. The medicine was called *niganigaa*—little dose—because its dose was so small.

KWANOKASHA, THE SPIRIT OF MEDICINE

KWANOKASHA is the name of a little spirit—a man, but no larger than a child two or three years of age. His home is in a cave under large rocks, in a rough, broken part of the country.

Now, when a child is two or three or even four years old, it is often sick, and then runs away from its home and goes among the trees. When the little one is well out of sight of home, Kwanokasha, who is on the watch, seizes it and leads it away to his dwelling place. In many instances they have to travel a considerable distance through the country. When Kwanokasha and the child enter the spirit's home they are met by three other spirits, all very old, with white hair.

Approaching the child the first offers it a knife; the second a bunch of herbs, all poisonous; the third a bunch of herbs yielding good medicine. Now, if the child accepts the knife he is certain to become a bad man, and may even kill his friends. If he takes the bunch of poisonous herbs, he will never be able to cure or otherwise help others; but if he waits and accepts the good herbs, then he is destined to become a great doctor and an important and influential man of his tribe, and to have the confidence of all his people. In this event, Kwanokasha and the three old spirits tell him how to make use of the herbs—the secrets of making medicines of the roots and leaves and of curing and treating various fevers and pains.

The child remains with the spirits three days, after which he returns to his home, but does not tell where he has been or what he has seen and heard. Not until the child has become a man will he make use of the knowledge gained from the spirits; but never will he reveal to others how it was acquired.

The Choctaw say that few children wait to accept the offering of the good herbs from the third spirit, and hence there are comparatively few great doctors and other men of influence among them.

THE FIRST FALSE FACE

THE POWERFUL Spirit Medicine Man of the Seneca was making magic. All the night before he had led the All Night Medicine Singing, but he was not tired. He stood in a lovely valley which nestled in the mountains. This Medicine Man had suffered much to gain his great skill. He knew all of the magic rites and had even attended the Dark Dance Feast of the Little People. Spirit Medicine Man truly loved people, birds, and animals. For that the Great Good Spirit had granted him vast power.

On this day, Spirit Medicine Man had wonderful power. He made bright flowers flutter from their stems and join the breeze-borne butterflies. When a daring butterfly declared that flowers should not fly, the Medicine Man changed that gleaming jewel of the air into a brilliant flower. The sunflowers begged to see a star, although the sun still rode high in the serene sky. The Medicine Man raised his hand high to the east and west and begged the Great Spirit to grant the wish of the sunflowers. Almost immediately a great star shone brightly in the cloudless sky above the valley and, for the first time, the faces of the sunflowers turned from the sun to a star.

The heart of the Medicine Man was glad that day, and the birds and beasts came close to him to be caressed. Suddenly alarm spread among the wild things. They swiftly left their friend and hid in the trees and bushes. A stranger was coming across the valley toward them. The Spirit Medicine Man was sorry to be disturbed. He wished to be far from mankind just then and had come to this hidden valley to seek solitude. Still, he greeted the stranger courteously, hoping that he would continue on his way. This was not to be.

"O mighty Spirit Medicine Man, I have traveled for many moons to greet you," said the stranger. "From the wise ones of the plains and hills I have learned much magic. At last I knew all that they could teach me. Then they told me that among the woodland people I would find a maker of magic more powerful far than they. He whom they spoke of was you. So come I to try my magic against yours. You will find that I too have great power," the stranger added boastfully.

Spirit Medicine Man disliked boasting. Still, he believed that the stranger must have considerable skill or he would not have asked for the chance to test it. Well, he would soon see how powerful the magic of the stranger really was. Perhaps in such a test of power he would learn things which he did not now know. Despite his great knowledge, Spirit Medicine Man was humble and always willing to learn.

"Friend, I did not come to this peaceful valley to try my skill against yours nor that of any other medicine man. As you have come, let us make tests for the time it takes the sun to travel the width of a lodge pole, that you may leave with a happy heart. What, O stranger, will you have the test be?"

"Let us try to move one of these mountains," suggested the stranger calmly.

Spirit Medicine Man smiled in surprise. "You would start at the top and reach the bottom of magic-making last!" he exclaimed.

"All other tests will be too simple for magicians such as we," asserted the stranger. As he spoke, he crooked his right forefinger, and two fully grown red foxes ran from their den beneath a great boulder. One climbed onto his right shoulder and the other onto his left. "Such a small test is easy for a

89

maker of magic such as I," boasted the stranger. "This medicine I do not make often because their tails tickle my nose," he confided.

"The wild things must love you well to come so close," remarked Spirit Medicine Man.

"They never leave me until they have my permission to go," replied the stranger.

Spirit Medicine Man moved a pace toward the stranger and crooked his left forefinger. Instantly the two foxes sprang from the shoulders of the stranger and landed on his own.

"Go!" commanded Spirit Medicine Man as the foxes sat motionless on his shoulders. "Your tails tickle my nose."

Silent as shadows, the foxes leaped to the ground and raced to their den.

"Is it still your wish to move a mountain?" inquired Spirit Medicine Man.

"I would like to try," replied the stranger, but his voice was no longer boastful.

"Try first," suggested Spirit Medicine Man, pointing to the mountain that was closest to them. "First let us turn our backs to the mountain as we make our magic. It is good medicine to do so."

They turned their faces from the peak, and the stranger stretched his arms out in front of him, hands open, palms up. "Come to me, mountain!" he commanded.

After a moment the medicine men turned to look at it. The mountain had moved slightly, of that both men felt sure. Loosened rocks were still rolling down its sides from the movement.

"Try once more," advised Spirit Medicine Man kindly. "Your medicine is powerful. You lack only complete faith, not skill."

"After you have made the test I will try again," promised the stranger. He was trembling violently and sweat poured down his face.

Again they turned their backs to the mountain.

High above his head went the arms of Spirit Medicine Man. A serene smile hovered on his lips. "Come!" he ordered gently.

Instantly there was a mighty rumbling. The earth trembled and shook close to his feet. Spirit Medicine Man was calm and did not move. The stranger swung sharply around. His face struck the side of the mountain with a sickening thud, because the mountain now stood directly behind him. The boastful stranger had learned a hard lesson. His face and mouth were terribly twisted, and his nose was broken and hung to one side. From then on he was called Old Broken Nose.

Spirit Medicine Man took pity on the injured stranger, and when his wounds were healed, taught him how to care for sick people and to cure illness, but Old Broken Nose's face always remained twisted to one side.

Soon the strange, distorted face became a sign of healing, as Old Broken Nose often cured very sick people by blowing hot ashes over them with his twisted mouth. The women of the tribe made little masks resembling the face of the healer and used them as charms and the Dance of the False Faces was started in his honor.

THE GHOST'S BUFFALO

A LONG TIME AGO there were four Blackfeet, who went to war against the Crees. They traveled a long way, and at last their horses gave out, and they started back toward their homes. As they were going along, they came to the Sand Hills; and while they were passing through them, they saw in the sand a fresh travois trail, where people had been traveling.

One of the men said, "Let us follow this trail until we come up with some of our people. Then we will camp with them." They followed the trail for a long way, and at length one of the Blackfeet, named E-kus-kini—a very powerful person—said to the others, "Why follow this longer? It is just nothing." The others said, "Not so. These are our people. We will go on and camp with them." They went on, and toward evening, one of them found a stone maul and a dog travois. He said, "Look at these things, I know this maul and this travois. They belonged to my mother, who died. They were buried with her. This is strange." He took the things. When night overtook the men, they camped.

Early in the morning, they heard, all about them, sounds as if a camp of people were there. They heard a young man shouting a sort of war cry, as young men do; women chopping wood; a man calling for a feast, asking people to come to his lodge and smoke—all the different sounds of the camp. They looked about, but could see nothing; and then they were frightened and covered their heads with their robes. At last they took courage, and started to look around and see what they could learn about this strange thing. For a little while they saw nothing, but pretty soon one of them said, "Look over there. See that *piskun.** Let us go over and look at it." As they were going toward it, one of them picked up a stone-pointed arrow. He said, "Look at this. It belonged to my father. This is his place." They started to go on toward the *piskun*, but suddenly they would see no *piskun*. It had disappeared all at once.

A little while after this, one of them spoke up, and said, "Look over there. There is my father running buffalo. There! he has killed. Let us go over to him." They all looked where this man pointed, and they could see a person on a white horse, running buffalo. While they were looking, the person killed the buffalo, and got off his horse to butcher it. They started to go over toward him, and saw him at work butchering, and saw him turn the buffalo over on its back; but before they got to the place where he was, the person got on his horse and rode off, and when they got to where he had been skinning the buffalo, they saw lying on the ground only a dead mouse. There was no buffalo there. By the side of the mouse was a buffalo chip, and lying on it was an arrow painted red. The man said, "That is my father's arrow. That is the way he painted them." He took it up in his hands; and when he held it in his hands, he saw that it was not an arrow but a blade of spear grass. Then he laid it down, and it was an arrow again.

Another Blackfoot found a buffalo rock, *I-nis-kim*.

Some time after this, the men got home to their camp. The man who had taken the maul and the dog travois, when he got home and smelled the smoke from the fire, died, and so did his horse. It seems that the shadow of the person who owned the things was angry at him and followed him home. Two others of these Blackfeet have since died, killed in war; but E-kus-kini is alive yet. He took a stone and an iron arrow point that had belonged to

*Buffalo corral at the foot of a cliff.

his father, and always carried them about with him. That is why he has lived so long. The man who took the stone arrow point found near the *pis-kun*, which had belonged to his father, took it home with him. This was his medicine. After that he was badly wounded in two fights, but he was not killed; he got well.

The one who took the buffalo rock, *I-nis-kim*, it afterward made strong to call the buffalo into the *piskun*. He would take the rock and put it in his lodge close to the fire, where he could look at it, and would pray over it and make medicine. Sometimes he would ask for a hundred buffalo to jump into the *piskun*, and the next day a hundred would jump in. He was powerful.

THE RED SWAN

THREE BROTHERS were left destitute, by the death of their parents, at an early age. The eldest was not yet able to provide fully for their support, but did all he could in hunting, and with his aid, and the stock of provisions left by their father, they were preserved and kept alive, rather, it seems, by miraculous interposition than the adequacy of their own exertions. For the father had been a hermit, having removed far away from the body of the tribe, so that when he and his wife died they left their children without neighbors and friends, and the lads had no idea that there was a human being near them. They did not even know who their parents had been, for the eldest was too young, at the time of their death, to remember it.

Forlorn as they were, they did not, however, give up to despondency, but made use of every exertion they could, and in process of time, learned the art of hunting and killing animals. The eldest son soon became an expert hunter, and was very successful in procuring food. He was noted for his skill in killing buffalo, elk, and moose, and he instructed his brothers in the arts of the forest as soon as they became old enough to follow him. After they had become able to hunt and take care of themselves, the elder brother proposed to leave them, and go in search of habitations, promising to return as soon as he could procure them wives. In this project he was overruled by his brothers, who said they could not part with him. Maujeekewis, the second eldest, was loud in his disapproval, saying, "What will you do with *those you propose to get*—we have lived so long without them, and we can still do without them." His words prevailed, and the three brothers continued together for a time.

One day each agreed to kill a male of the kind of animal he was most expert in hunting, for the purpose of making quivers from their skins. They did so, and immediately commenced making arrows to fill their quivers, that they might be prepared for any emergency. Soon after, they hunted on a wager, to see who should come in first with game, and prepare it so as to regale the others. They were to shoot no other animal, but such as each was in the habit of killing. They set out different ways; Odjibwa, the youngest, had not gone far before he saw a bear, an animal he was not to kill, by the agreement. He followed him close, and drove an arrow through him, which brought him to the ground.

Although contrary to the bet, he immediately commenced skinning him, when suddenly something red tinged all the air around him. He rubbed his eyes, thinking he was perhaps deceived, but without effect, for the red hue continued. At length he heard a strange noise at a distance. It first appeared like a human voice, but after following the sound for some distance, he reached the shores of a lake, and soon saw the object he was looking for.

At a distance out in the lake, sat a most beautiful Red Swan, whose plumage glittered in the sun, and who would now and then make the same noise he had heard. He was within long bowshot, and pulling the arrow from the bowstring up to his ear, took deliberate aim and shot. The arrow took no effect; and he shot and shot again till his quiver was empty. Still the swan remained, moving around and around, stretching its long neck and dipping its bill into the water, as if heedless of the arrows shot at it.

Odjibwa ran home, and got all his own and his brothers' arrows, and shot them all away. He then stood and gazed at the beautiful bird. While standing, he remembered his brothers' saying that in their deceased father's medicine sack were three magic arrows. Off he started, his anxiety to kill the swan overcoming all scruples. At any other time, he would have deemed it sacrilege to open his father's medicine sack, but now he hastily seized the

95

three arrows and ran back, leaving the other contents of the sack scattered over the lodge.

The swan was still there. He shot the first arrow with great precision, and came very near to it. The second came still closer. As he took the last arrow, he felt his arm firmer, and drawing it up with vigor, saw it pass through the neck of the swan a little above the breast. Still it did not prevent the bird from flying off, which it did, however, at first slowly, flapping its wings and rising gradually into the air, and then flying off toward the sinking of the sun.

Odjibwa was disappointed; he knew that his brothers would be displeased with him. He rushed into the water and rescued the two magic arrows, the third was carried off by the swan; but he thought that it could not fly very far with it, and let the consequences be what they might, he was bent on following it.

Off he started on the run; he was noted for speed, for he would shoot an arrow, and then run so fast that the arrow always fell behind him. "I can run fast," he thought, "and I can get up with the swan some time or other." He thus ran over hills and prairies, toward the west, till near night, and was only going to take one more run, and then seek a place to sleep for the night, when suddenly he heard noises at a distance, which he knew were from people; for some were cutting trees, and the strokes of their axes echoed through the woods. When he emerged from the forest, the sun was just falling below the horizon, and he felt pleased to find a place to sleep in, and get something to eat, as he had left home without a mouthful. All these circumstances could not damp his ardor for the accomplishment of his object, and he felt that if he only persevered, he would succeed.

At a distance, on a rising piece of ground, he could see an extensive town. He went toward it, but soon heard the watchman, Mudjee-Kokokoho, who was placed on some height to overlook the place, and give notice of the approach of friends or foes, crying out, "We are visited"; and a loud holla indicated that they all heard it. The young man advanced, and was pointed by the watchman to the lodge of the chief, "It is there you must go in," he said, and left him. "Come in, come in," said the chief, "take a seat there," pointing to the side where his daughter sat. "It is there you must sit." Soon they gave him something to eat, and very few questions were asked him, being a stranger. It was only when he spoke that the others answered him.

"Daughter," said the chief, after dark, "take our son-in-law's moccasins, and see if they be torn; if so, mend them for him, and bring in his bundle." The young man thought it strange that he should be so warmly received, and married instantly, without his wishing it, although the young girl was pretty. It was some time before she would take his moccasins, which he had taken off. It displeased him to see her so reluctant to do so, and when she did reach them, he snatched them out of her hand and hung them up himself. He laid down and thought of the swan, and made up his mind to be off by dawn. He awoke early, and spoke to the young woman, but she gave no answer. He slightly touched her. "What do you want?" she said, and turned her back toward him. "Tell me," said he, "what time the swan passed. I am following it, and come out and point the direction." "Do you think you can catch up to it?" she said. "Yes," he answered. "*Naubesah*—foolishness," she said. She, however, went out and pointed in the direction he should go.

The young man went slowly till the sun arose, when he commenced traveling at his accustomed speed. He passed the day in running, and when night came, he was unexpectedly pleased to find himself near another town. At·a distance, he heard the watchman crying out, "We are visited"; and soon the men of the village stood out to see the stranger. He was again told to enter the lodge of the chief, and his reception was, in every respect, the same as he met the previous night, only that the young woman was more beautiful, and received him very kindly. But although urged to stay, his mind was fixed on the object of his journey. Before daylight he asked the young woman what time the Red Swan passed, and to point out the way. She did so, and said it passed yesterday when the sun was between midday and *pungishemoo*—its falling place.

He again set out rather slowly, but when the sun had arisen he tried his speed by shooting an arrow ahead, and running after it; but it fell behind him. Nothing remarkable happened in the course of the day, and he went on leisurely. Toward night, he came to the lodge of an old man. Some time after dark he saw a light emitted from a small low lodge. He went up to it very slyly, and peeping through the door, saw an old man alone, warming his back before the fire, with his head down on his breast. He thought the old man did not know that he was standing near the door, but in this he was disappointed; for so soon as he looked in, "Walk in, Nosis—grandchild," he said, "take a seat opposite to me, and take off your things and dry them, for you must be fatigued; and I will prepare you something to eat." Odjibwa did as he was requested.

The old man, whom he perceived to be a magician, then said, "My kettle with water stands near the fire"; and immediately a small earthen or kind of metallic pot with legs appeared by the fire. He then took one grain of corn, also one whortleberry, and put them in the pot. As the young man was very hungry, he thought that his chance for a supper was but small. Not a word or a look, however, revealed his feelings. The pot soon boiled, when the old man spoke, commanding it to stand some distance from the fire.

"Nosis," said he, "feed yourself," and he handed him a dish and ladle made out of the same metal as the pot. The young man helped himself to all that was in the pot. He felt ashamed to think of his having done so, but before he could speak, the old man said, "Nosis, eat, eat"; and soon after he again said, "Help yourself from the pot." Odjibwa was surprised on looking into it to see it full; he kept on taking all out, and as soon as this was done, it was again filled, till he had amply satisfied his hunger. The magician then spoke, and the pot occupied its accustomed place in one part of the lodge.

The young man then leisurely reclined back, and listened to the predictions of his entertainer who told him to keep on, and he would obtain his object. "To tell you more," said he, "I am not permitted; but go on as you have commenced, and you will not be disappointed. Tomorrow you will again reach one of my fellow old men; but the one you will see after him will tell you all, and the manner in which you will proceed to accomplish your journey. Often has this Red Swan passed, and those who have followed it have never returned. But you must be firm in your resolution, and be prepared for all events." "So will it be," answered Odjibwa, and they both laid down to sleep. Early in the morning, the old man had his magic kettle prepared, so that his guest should eat before leaving. When leaving, the old man gave him his parting advice.

Odjibwa set out in better spirits than he had done since leaving home. Night again found him in company with an old man, who received him kindly, and directed him on his way in the morning. He traveled with a light heart, expecting to meet the one who was to give him directions how to proceed to get the Red Swan. Toward nightfall, he reached the third old man's lodge. Before coming to the door, he heard him saying, "Nosis, come in," and going in immediately, he felt quite at home. The old man prepared him something to eat, acting as the other magicians had done, and his kettle was of the same dimensions and material.

The old man waited till he had done eating, when he commenced addressing him. "Young man, the errand you are on is very difficult. Numbers of young men have passed with the same purpose, but never returned. Be careful, and if your guardian spirits are powerful, you may succeed. This Red Swan you are following is the daughter of a magician, who has plenty of everything, but he values his daughter but little less than wampum. He wore a cap of wampum, which was attached to his scalp; but powerful Indians—warriors of a distant chief—came and told him that their chief's daughter was on the brink of the grave, and she herself requested his scalp of wampum to effect a cure. 'If I can only see it, I will recover,' she said. And it was for this reason they came, and after long urging, the magician at last consented to part with it, only from the idea of restoring the young woman to health; although when he took it off, it left his head bare and bloody. Several years have passed since, and it has not healed. The warriors' coming for it was only a cheat, and they now are constantly making sport of it, dancing it about from village to village; and on every insult it receives, the old man groans from pain. Those Indians are too powerful for the magician, and numbers have sacrificed themselves to recover it for him, but without success. The Red Swan has enticed many a young man, as she has done you, in order to get them to procure it, and whoever is the fortunate one that succeeds will receive the Red Swan as his reward. In the morning you will proceed on your way, and toward evening you will come to the magician's lodge, but before you enter you will hear his groans. He will immediately ask you in, and you will see no one but himself. He will make inquiries of you, as regards your dreams, and the powers of your guardian spirits. He will then ask you to attempt the recovery of his scalp. He will show you the direction, and if you feel inclined, as I dare say you do, go forward, my son, with a strong heart, persevere, and I have a presentiment you will succeed." The young man answered, "I will try."

Early next morning, after having eaten from the magic kettle, he started off on his journey. Toward evening he came to the lodge as he was told, and soon heard the groans of the magician. "Come in," he said, even before the young man reached the door. On entering Odjibwa saw the magician's head all bloody, and he was groaning most terribly. "Sit down, sit down," he said, "while I prepare you something to eat," at the same time doing as the other magicians had done, in preparing food. "You see," he said, "how poor I am; I have to attend to all my wants." He said this to conceal the fact that the Red Swan was there, but Odjibwa perceived that the lodge was partitioned, and he heard a rustling noise, now and then, in that quarter, which satisfied him that it was occupied.

After having taken his leggings and moccasins off, and eaten, the old magician commenced telling him how he had lost his scalp and the insults it was receiving; the pain he was suffering in consequence and his wishes to regain it; the unsuccessful attempts that had already been made, and the numbers and power of those who detained it. He stated the best and most probable way of getting it, touching the young man on his pride and ambition, by the proposed adventure; and last, he spoke of such things as would make an Indian rich. He would interrupt his discourse by now and then groaning, and saying, "Oh, how shamefully they are treating it." Odjibwa listened with solemn attention. The old man then asked him about his dreams—what he saw when asleep—at the particular time he had fasted and blackened his face to procure guardian spirits.

The young man then told him one dream; the magician groaned. "No, that is not it," he said. The young man told him another. He groaned again. "That is not it," he said. The young man told him of two or three others. The magician groaned at each recital, and said rather peevishly, "No, those are not them." The young man then thought to himself, "Who are you? You may groan as much as you please; I am inclined not to tell you any more dreams."

The magician then spoke in rather a supplicating tone. "Have you no more dreams of another kind?" "Yes," said the young man, and told him one. "That is it, that is it," he cried. "You will cause me to live. That was what I was wishing you to say." And he rejoiced greatly. "Will you then go and see if you cannot procure my scalp?" "Yes," said the young man, "I will go;

and the day after tomorrow, when you hear the cries of the hawk, you will know, by this sign, that I am successful, and you must prepare your head, and lean it out through the door, so that the moment I arrive, I may place your scalp on." "Yes, yes," said the magician, "as you say, it will be done."

Early next morning, he set out on his perilous adventure, and about the time that the sun hangs toward home, he heard the shouts of a great many people. He was in a wood at the time, and saw, as he thought, only a few men; but the farther he went, the more numerous they appeared. On emerging into a plain, their heads appeared like the hanging leaves for number. In the center he perceived a post, and something waving on it, which was the scalp. Now and then the air was rent with the *Sau-sau-quan*, for they were dancing the war dance around it. Before he could be perceived, he turned himself into a *No-noskau-see*—hummingbird—and flew toward the scalp.

As he passed some of those who were standing by, he flew close to their ears, making the humming noise which this bird does when it flies. They jumped on one side, and asked each other what it could be. By this time he had nearly reached the scalp, but fearing he should be perceived while untying it, he changed himself into *Me-sau-be-wau-aun*—the down of anything that floats lightly on the air—and then floated slowly and lightly onto the scalp. He untied it, and moved off slowly, as the weight was almost too great. It was as much as he could do to keep it up, and prevent the Indians from snatching it away.

The moment they saw it was moving, they filled the air with their cries of "It is taken from us; it is taken from us." He continued moving a few feet above them. The rush and hum of the people was like the dead beating surges after a storm. He soon gained on them, and they gave up the pursuit. After going a little farther, he changed himself into a hawk, and flew off with his prize, making that peculiar noise which this bird makes.

In the meantime, the magician had followed his instructions, leaning his head outside of the lodge as soon as he heard the cry of the hawk, and soon after he heard the rustling of its wings. In a moment Odjibwa stood before him. He immediately gave the magician a severe blow on the head with the wampum scalp. His limbs extended and quivered in agony from the effects of the blow; the scalp adhered, and the young man walked in and

101

sat down, feeling perfectly at home. The magician was so long in recovering from the stunning blow that the young man feared he had killed him. He was, however, pleased to see him show signs of life; he first commenced moving, and soon sat up. But how surprised was Odjibwa to see, not an aged man, far in years and decrepitude, but one of the handsomest young men he ever saw stand up before him.

"Thank you, my friend," he said; "you see that your kindness and bravery have restored me to my former shape. It was so ordained, and you have now accomplished the victory." The young magician urged the stay of his deliverer for a few days, and they soon formed a warm attachment for each other. The magician never alluded to the Red Swan in their conversations.

At last the day arrived when Odjibwa made preparations to return. The young magician amply repaid him for his kindness and bravery by various kinds of wampum, robes, and all such things as he had need of to make him an influential man. Though the young man's curiosity was at its height about the Red Swan, he controlled his feelings, and never so much as even hinted of her, feeling that he would surrender a point of propriety in so doing; while the one he had rendered such service to, whose hospitality he was now enjoying, and who had richly rewarded him, had never so much as even mentioned anything about her, but studiously concealed her.

Odjibwa's pack for traveling was ready, and he was taking his farewell smoke, when the young magician thus addressed him, "Friend, you know for what cause you came thus far. You have accomplished your object, and conferred a lasting obligation on me. Your perseverance shall not go unrewarded; and if you undertake other things with the same spirit you have this, you will never fail to accomplish them. My duty renders it necessary for me to remain where I am, although I should feel happy to go with you. I have given you all you will need as long as you live; but I see you feel backward to speak about the Red Swan. I vowed that whoever procured my scalp should be rewarded by possessing the Red Swan." He then spoke, and knocked on the partition. The door immediately opened, and the Red Swan met Odjibwa's eager gaze. She was a most beautiful woman, and as she stood majestically before him, it would be impossible to describe her charms, for she looked as if she did not belong to earth.

"Take her," the young magician said; "she is my sister, treat her well;

she is worthy of you, and what you have done for me merits more. She is ready to go with you to your kindred and friends, and has been so ever since your arrival, and my good wishes go with you both." She then looked very kindly on her husband, who now bid farewell to his friend indeed, and accompanied by the object of his wishes, he commenced retracing his footsteps.

They traveled slowly, and after two or three days reached the lodge of the third old man, who had fed Odjibwa from his small magic pot. He was very kind, and said, "You see what your perseverance has procured you; do so always, and you will succeed in all things you undertake."

On the following morning when they were going to start, he pulled from the side of the lodge a bag, which he presented to the young man, saying, "Nosis, I give you this; it contains a present for you; and I hope you will live happily till old age." They then bid farewell to him and proceeded on.

They soon reached the second old man's lodge. Their reception there was the same as at the first; he also gave them a present, with the old man's wishes that they would be happy. They went on and reached the first town, which the young man had passed in his pursuit. The watchman gave notice, and he was shown into the chief's lodge. "Sit down there, son-in-law," said the chief, pointing to a place near his daughter. "And you also," he said to the Red Swan.

The young woman of the lodge was busy in making something, but she tried to show her indifference about what was taking place, for she did not even raise her head to see who had come. Soon the chief said, "Let someone bring in the bundle of our son-in-law." When it was brought in, the young man opened one of the bags, which he had received from one of the old men; it contained wampum, robes, and various other articles. He presented them to his father-in-law, and all expressed their surprise at the value and richness of the gift. The chief's daughter then only stole a glance at the present, then at Odjibwa and his beautiful wife; she stopped working, and remained silent and thoughtful all the evening. They conversed about his adventures. After this the chief told him that he should take his daughter along with him in the morning; the young man said, "Yes." The chief then spoke out, saying, "Daughter, be ready to go with him in the morning."

There was a Maujeekewis in the lodge, who thought to have got the young woman to wife; he jumped up, saying, "Who is he that he should take her for a few presents. I will kill him," and he raised a knife which he had in his hand. But he only waited till someone held him back, and then sat down, for he was too great a coward to do as he had threatened.

Early they took their departure, amid the greetings of their new friends, and toward evening reached the other town. The watchman gave the signal, and numbers of men, women, and children stood out to see them. They were again shown into the chief's lodge, who welcomed them by saying, "Son-in-law, you are welcome," and requested him to take a seat by his daughter; and the two women did the same.

After the usual formalities of smoking and eating, the chief requested the young man to relate his travels in the hearing of all the inmates of the lodge, and those who came to see. They looked with admiration and astonishment at the Red Swan, for she was so beautiful. Odjibwa gave them his whole history. The chief then told him that his brothers had been to their town in search of him, but had returned, and given up all hope of ever seeing him again. He concluded by saying that since he had been so fortunate and so manly, he should take his daughter with him. "For although your brothers," said he, "were here, they were too timid to enter any of the lodges, and merely inquired for you and returned. You will take my daughter, treat her well, and that will bind us more closely together."

It is always the case in towns, that someone there is foolish or clownish. It happened to be so here; for a Maujeekewis was in the lodge; and after the young man had given his father-in-law presents, as he did to the first, this Maujeekewis jumped up in a passion, saying, "Who is this stranger, that he should have her? I want her myself." The chief told him to be quiet, and not to disturb or quarrel with one who was enjoying their hospitality. "No, no," he boisterously cried, and made an attempt to strike the stranger. Odjibwa was above fearing his threats, and paid no attention to him. He cried the louder, "I will have her; I will have her." In an instant he was laid flat on the ground from a blow of a war club given by the chief. After he came to himself, the chief upbraided him for his foolishness, and told him to go out and tell stories to the old women.

Their arrangements were then made, and the stranger invited a number of families to visit his hunting grounds, as there was plenty of game. They consented, and in the morning a large party were assembled to accompany the young man; and the chief with a large party of warriors escorted them a long distance. When ready to return, the chief made a speech, and invoked the blessing of the Great Good Spirit on his son-in-law and party.

After a numbers of days' travel, Odjibwa and his party came in sight of his home. The party rested while he went alone in advance to see his brothers. When he entered the lodge, he found it all dirty and covered with ashes; on one side was his eldest brother, with his face blackened, and sitting amid ashes, crying aloud. On the other side was Maujeekewis, his other brother; his face was also blackened, but his head was covered with feathers and swan's-down. He looked so odd, that the young man could not keep from laughing, for he appeared and pretended to be so absorbed with grief that he did not notice his brother's arrival. The eldest jumped up and shook hands with him, and kissed him, and felt very happy to see him again.

Odjibwa, after seeing all things put to rights, told them that he had brought each of them a wife. When Maujeekewis heard about the wife, he jumped up and said, "Why is it just now that you have come?" and made for the door and peeped out to see the women. He then commenced jumping and laughing, saying, "Women! women!" That was the only reception he gave his brother.

Odjibwa then told them to wash themselves and prepare, for he would go and fetch them in. Maujeekewis jumped and washed himself, but would every now and then go and peep out to see the women. When they came near, he said, "I will have this one, and that one." He did not exactly know which; he would go and sit down for an instant, and then go and peep and laugh; he acted like a madman.

As soon as order was restored, and all seated, Odjibwa presented one of the women to his eldest brother, saying, "These women were given to me; I now give one to each; I intended so from the first." Maujeekewis spoke, and said, "I think three wives would have been enough for you." The young man led one to Maujeekewis, saying, "My brother, here is one for you, and live happily." Maujeekewis hung down his head as if he was ashamed, but would every now and then steal a glance at his wife, and also at the other women. By and by he turned toward his wife, and acted as if he had been married for years. "Wife," he said, "I will go and hunt," and off he started.

All lived peacefully for some time, and their town prospered, the inhabitants increased, and everything was abundant among them. One day dissatisfaction was manifested in the conduct of the two elder brothers, on account of Odjibwa's having taken their deceased father's magic arrows. They upbraided him and urged him to procure others if he could. Their object was to get him away, so that one of them might afterward get his wife. One day, after listening to them, he told them he would go. Mau-jeekewis and himself went together into a sweat lodge to purify themselves. Even there, although it was held sacred, Maujeekewis upbraided him for the arrows. He told him again he would go; and next day, true to his word, he left them.

After traveling a long way, he came to an opening in the earth, and descending, it led him to the abode of departed spirits. The country appeared beautiful, the extent of it was lost in the distance. He saw animals of various kinds in abundance. The first he came near to were buffalo; his surprise was great when these animals addressed him as human beings.

They asked him what he came for, how he descended, why he was so bold as to visit the abode of the dead. He told them he was in search of magic arrows to appease his brothers. "Very well," said the leader of the buffalo, whose whole form was nothing but bone. "Yes, we know it," and he and his followers moved off a little space as if they were afraid of him. "You have come," resumed the buffalo spirit, "to a place where a living man has never before been. You will return immediately to your tribe, for your brothers are trying to dishonor your wife; and you will live to a very old age, and live and die happily; you can go no farther in these abodes of ours."

Odjibwa looked, as he thought to the west, and saw a bright light, as if the sun was shining in its splendor, but he saw no sun. "What light is that I see yonder?" he asked. The all-bone buffalo answered, "It is the place where those who were good dwell." "And that dark cloud?" Odjibwa again asked. "*Mud-jee-izzhi-wabezewin*—Wickedness," answered the buffalo.

He asked no more questions, and with the aid of his guardian spirits, again stood on this earth and saw the sun giving light as usual, and breathed the pure air. All else he saw in the abodes of the dead, and his travels and actions previous to his return, are unknown. After wandering a long time in quest of information to make his people happy, he one evening drew near to his village or town; passing all the other lodges and coming to his own, he heard his brothers at high words with each other; they were quarreling for possession of his wife. She had, however, remained constant, and mourned the absence and probable loss of her husband; but she had mourned him with the dignity of virtue.

The noble youth listened till he was satisfied of the base principles of his brothers. He then entered the lodge with the stern air and conscious dignity of a brave and honest man. He spoke not a word, but placing the magic arrows to his bow, drew them to their length and laid the brothers dead at his feet. Thus ended the contest between the hermit's sons, and a firm and happy union was consummated between Odjibwa, he of the primitive or intonated voice, and the Red Swan.

THE DUN HORSE

MANY YEARS AGO, there lived in the Pawnee tribe an old woman and her grandson, a boy about sixteen years old. These people had no relations and were very poor. They were so poor that they were despised by the rest of the tribe. They had nothing of their own, and always, after the village started to move the camp from one place to another, these two would stay behind the rest, to look over the old camp, and pick up anything that the other Indians had thrown away, as worn-out or useless. In this way, they would sometimes get pieces of robes, worn-out moccasins with holes in them, and bits of meat.

Now, it happened one day, after the tribe had moved away from the camp, that this old woman and her boy were following along the trail behind the rest, when they came to a miserable old worn-out dun horse, which they supposed had been abandoned by some Indians. He was thin and exhausted, was blind of one eye, had a sore back, and one of his forelegs was very much swollen. In fact, he was so worthless that none of the Pawnees had been willing to take the trouble to try to drive him along with them. But when the old woman and her boy came along, the boy said, "Come now, we will take this old horse, for we can make him carry our pack." So the old woman put her pack on the horse, and drove him along, but he limped and could only go very slowly.

The tribe moved up on the North Platte, until they came to Court House

Rock. The two poor Indians followed them, and camped with the others. One day while they were here, the young men who had been sent out to look for buffalo, came hurrying into camp and told the chiefs that a large herd of buffalo was near, and that among them was a spotted calf.

The head chief of the Pawnees had a very beautiful daughter, and when he heard about the spotted calf, he ordered his old crier to go about through the village, and call out that the man who killed the spotted calf should have his daughter for his wife. For a spotted robe is *ti-war-uks-ti*—big medicine.

The buffalo were feeding about four miles from the village, and the chiefs decided that the charge should be made from there. In this way, the man who had the fastest horse would be the most likely to kill the calf. Then all the warriors and the young men picked out their best and fastest horses, and made ready to start. Among those who prepared for the charge was the poor boy on the old dun horse. But when they saw him, all the rich young braves on their fast horses pointed at him, and said, "Oh, see! There is the horse that is going to catch the spotted calf." And they laughed at him, so that the poor boy was ashamed, and rode off to one side of the crowd, where he could not hear their jokes and laughter.

When he had ridden off some little way, the horse stopped, and turned his head round, and spoke to the boy. He said, "Take me down to the creek, and plaster me all over with mud. Cover my head and neck and body and legs." When the boy heard the horse speak, he was afraid; but he did as he was told. Then the horse said, "Now mount, but do not ride back to the warriors, who laugh at you because you have such a poor horse. Stay right here, until the word is given to charge." So the boy stayed there.

And presently all the fine horses were drawn up in line, and pranced about, and were so eager to go that their riders could hardly hold them in. At last the old crier gave the word, "*Loo-ah*—Go!" Then the Pawnees all leaned forward on their horses and yelled, and away they went. Suddenly, away off to the right was seen the old dun horse. He did not seem to run. He seemed to sail along like a bird. He passed all the fastest horses, and in a moment he was among the buffalo. First he picked out the spotted calf, and charging up alongside of it, *U-ra-rish!* straight flew the arrow. The calf fell. The boy drew another arrow, and killed a fat cow that was running by. Then he dismounted and began to skin the calf, before any of the other warriors had come up. But when the rider got off the old dun horse, how changed he was! He pranced about and would hardly stand still near the dead buffalo. His back was all right again; his legs were well and fine; and both his eyes were clear and bright.

The boy skinned the calf and the cow that he had killed; then he packed all the meat on the horse, put the spotted robe on top of the load, and started back to the camp on foot, leading the dun horse. But even with this heavy load the horse pranced all the time, and was scared at everything he saw. On the way to camp, one of the rich young chiefs of the tribe rode up to the boy, and offered him twelve good horses for the spotted robe, so that he could marry the head chief's beautiful daughter; but the boy laughed at him and would not sell the robe.

Now, while the boy walked to the camp leading the dun horse, most of the warriors rode back, and one of those that came first to the village went to the old woman and said to her, "Your grandson has killed the spotted calf." The old woman said, "Why do you come to tell me this? You ought to be ashamed to make fun of my boy, because he is poor." The warrior said, "What I have told you is true," and then he rode away. After a little while another brave rode up to the old woman and said to her, "Your grandson has killed the spotted calf." Then the old woman began to cry, she felt so badly because everyone made fun of her boy because he was poor.

Pretty soon the boy came along, leading the horse up to the lodge where he and his grandmother lived. It was a little lodge, just big enough for two, and was made up of old pieces of skin that the old woman had picked up, and was tied together with strings of rawhide and sinew. It was the meanest and worst lodge in the village. When the old woman saw her boy leading the dun horse with the load of meat and the robes on it, she was much surprised. The boy said to her, "Here, I have brought you plenty of meat to eat, and here is a robe that you may have for yourself. Take the meat off the horse." Then the old woman laughed, for her heart was glad. But when she went to take the meat from the horse's back, he snorted and jumped about, and acted like a wild horse. The old woman looked at him in wonder, and could hardly believe that it was the same horse. So the boy had to take off the meat, for the horse would not let the old woman come near him.

That night the horse spoke again to the boy and said, "*Wa-ti-hes Chah-ra-rat wa-ta*. Tomorrow the Sioux are coming—a large war party. They will attack the village, and you will have a great battle. Now, when the Sioux are drawn up in line of battle, and are all ready to fight, you jump on me. Ride as hard as you can right into the middle of the Sioux and up to their head chief, their greatest warrior, and count coup* on him and kill him, and then ride back. Do this four times, and count coup on four of the bravest Sioux and kill them, but don't go again. If you go the fifth time, maybe you will be killed, or else you will lose me. *La-ku-ta-chix*—remember." So the boy promised.

The next day it happened as the horse had said, and the Sioux came down and formed a line of battle. Then the boy took his bow and arrows, and jumped on the dun horse, and charged into the midst of them. When the Sioux saw that he was going to strike their head chief, they all shot their arrows at him, and the arrows flew so thickly across each other that the sky became dark, but none of them hit the boy. He counted coup on the chief and killed him, and then rode back. After that he charged again among the Sioux, where they were gathered thickest, and counted coup on their bravest warrior and killed him. Then twice more he charged until he had gone four times, as the horse had told him.

But the Sioux and the Pawnees kept on fighting, and the boy stood around and watched the battle. At last he said to himself, "I have been four times and have killed four Sioux, and I am all right. I am not hurt anywhere. Why may I not go again?" So he jumped on the dun horse and charged again. But when he got among the Sioux, one Sioux warrior drew an arrow and shot. The arrow struck the dun horse behind the forelegs and pierced him through, and the horse fell down dead. But the boy jumped off, and fought his way through the Sioux, and ran away as fast as he could to the Pawnees. Now, as soon as the horse was killed, the Sioux said to each other, "This horse was like a man. He was brave. He was not like a horse." And they took their knives and hatchets, and hacked the dun horse and gashed his flesh, and cut him into small pieces.

*Among some Plains tribes of North American Indians, the act of striking or touching an enemy in warfare with the hand or at close quarters, as with a short stick, in such a manner as by custom counts as an act of bravery.

The Pawnees and Sioux fought all day long, but toward night the Sioux broke and fled.

The boy felt very badly that he had lost his horse; and after the fight was over, he went out from the village to where it had taken place, to mourn for his horse. He went to the spot where the horse lay, and gathered up all the pieces of flesh, which the Sioux had cut off, and the legs and the hoofs, and put them all together in a pile. Then he went to the top of a hill near by, and sat down and drew his robe over his head, and began to mourn for his horse.

As he sat there, he heard a great windstorm coming up; it passed over him with a loud rushing sound, and after the wind came rain. The boy looked down, from where he sat, to the pile of flesh and bones, which was all that was left of his horse, and he could just see it through the rain. The rain passed by, but his heart was heavy, and he kept on mourning.

Pretty soon came another rushing wind and, after it, rain. As he looked through the driving rain toward the spot where the pieces lay, he thought that they seemed to come together and take shape, and that the pile looked like a horse lying down, but he could not see well for the thick rain.

After this came a third storm like the others. Now when he looked toward the horse he thought he saw its tail move from side to side two or three times, and that it lifted its head from the ground. The boy was afraid and wanted to run away, but he stayed.

As he waited there came another storm. And through the rain, the boy saw the horse raise himself up on his forelegs and look about. Then the dun horse stood up.

The boy left the hilltop, and went down to the horse. When the boy came near to him, the horse spoke and said, "You have seen how it has been this day, and you may know how it will be after this. But Ti-ra-wa has been good, and has let me come back to you. After this, do what I tell you, not any more, not any less. Now lead me off, far away from the camp, behind that big hill. Leave me there tonight, and in the morning come for me." And the boy did as he was told.

When the boy went for the horse in the morning, he found with him a beautiful white gelding, much more handsome than any horse in the tribe. That night the dun horse told the boy to take him again to the place behind the big hill, and to come for him the next morning. When the boy went again, he found with him a beautiful black gelding. So for ten nights he left the horse among the hills, and each morning he found a different horse —a bay, a roan, a gray, a blue, a spotted horse—all of them finer than any horses that the Pawnees had ever had in their tribe before.

Now the boy was rich, and he married the beautiful daughter of the head chief, and when he became older, he was made head chief himself. He had many children by his beautiful wife, and one day when his oldest boy died, he wrapped him in the spotted-calf robe and buried him in it. He always took good care of his old grandmother, and kept her in his own lodge until she died. The dun horse was never ridden except at feasts, and when they were going to have a doctors' dance, but he was always led about with the chief, wherever he went. The horse lived in the village for many years, until he became very old. And at last he died.

THE STORY OF A HEYOKA MAN

IT IS SAID that the people of the olden times knew when they were about to die, and they used to dream about their deaths and how they would be when the time drew near. One of those men said, "When the first thunder is heard next spring, I and my horse shall die." For that reason his kindred were weeping from time to time. This man who had dreamed of his death decorated the legs of his horse by moistening light gray clay and drawing zigzag lines down the legs. In like manner he decorated the neck and back of the horse, and he made similar lines on his own arms. Then he would walk about the prairie near the camp, singing and holding a pipe with the stem pointing toward the sky.

When the leaves opened out in the following spring, the first thunder-cloud was seen. Then the man said, "Ho, this is the day on which I am to die!" So he tied up his horse's tail in a rounded form, put a piece of scarlet blanket around the animal's neck, and spread a fine blanket over his back, as a saddlecloth, with the ends trailing along the ground. He painted him-

113

self and his horse just as he had been doing formerly, and taking the pipe he walked round and round at some distance from the camp, pointing the pipestem toward the clouds as he sang the Heyoka songs.

The following is given as a song of the human Heyoka man, but it is said to have been sung originally by the mysterious and superhuman Heyoka in the thundercloud.

Ko-la, o-ya-te kin, ko-la, wan-ni-yang u-pe e-ye he!
Ko-la, o-ya-te kin, ko-la, wan-ni-yang u-pe e-ye he!
Ko-la, lo-wan hi-bu we!
Ko-la, ee-ya hi-bu we!
O-ya-te wan-ma-ya-ka-pi ye.
He-he-he!
Ta-mun-ka sni kun e-ye-ye he!

In this song, *oyate* means the Thunder beings; *kola*, the Heyoka men here on earth, whom the Thunder beings threatened to kill; *oyate wan-mayakapi*, ordinary Indians who are not *wakan*—sacred. *He-he-he! ta-munka sni kun*—Alas! I hate to leave them (living Indians)—means that the singer expects to be killed by the Thunder beings. The whole song may be rendered freely thus:

My friends, the people are coming to see you!
My friends, the people are coming to see you!
My friends, he sings as he comes hither!
My friends, he cries as he comes hither!
You people on earth behold me while you may!
Alas! alas! alas!
I hate to leave my own people!

On the day referred to, the Heyoka man had not been absent very long from the camp when a high wind arose, and the rain was so plentiful that a person could not see very far. Then the Thunder beings looked (this was the lightning) and they roared; but still the man and his horse continued walking about over there in sight of the camp. By and by there was a very

sudden sound as if the trees had been struck. All the people were much frightened, and they thought that the Thunder beings had killed them. Some of the women and children fainted from fear, and the men sat holding them up. Some of the people thought that they saw many stars, and there seemed to be the sound, *"Tun!"* in the ears of each person.

When the storm had lasted a long time, the Thunder beings were departing slowly, amid considerable loud roaring. When it was all over the people ventured forth from their lodges. Behold, the man and his horse had been killed by the Thunder beings, so his relations were crying ere they reached the scene of the disaster.

The horse had been burned in the very places where the man had decorated him, and his sinews had been shriveled by the heat, so he lay with each limb stretched out stiff. The man, too, had been burned in the very places where he had painted himself. The grass all around appeared as if the Thunder beings had dragged each body along, for it was pushed partly down on all sides. So the people reached there and beheld the bodies.

As the men in former days used to know events beforehand, as has just been told, it has long been the rule for no one to reveal his personal mystery, which he regards as *wakan*.

BOKWEWA, OR THE HUMPBACK MAGICIAN

Bokwewa and his brother lived in a secluded part of the country. They were considered as Manitoes, who had assumed mortal shapes. Bokwewa was the most gifted in supernatural endowments, although he was deformed in person. His brother partook more of the nature of the present race of beings. They lived retired from the world, and undisturbed by its cares, and passed their time in contentment and happiness.

Bokwewa, owing to his deformity, was very domestic in his habits, and gave his attention to household affairs. He instructed his brother in the manner of pursuing game, and made him acquainted with all the accomplishments of a sagacious and expert hunter. His brother possessed a fine form, and an active and robust constitution, and felt a disposition to show himself off among men. He was restive in his seclusion, and showed a fondness for visiting remote places.

One day he told his brother that he was going to leave him, that he wished to visit the habitations of men and procure a wife. Bokwewa objected to his going, but his brother overruled all that he said, and he finally departed on his travels. He traveled a long time. At length he fell in with the footsteps of men. They were moving by encampments, for he saw several places where they had encamped. It was in the winter. He came to a place where one of their number had died. They had placed the corpse on a scaffold. He went to it and took it down. He saw that it was the corpse of a beautiful young woman. "She shall be my wife!" he exclaimed.

He took her up, and placing her on his back, returned to his brother. "Brother," he said, "cannot you restore her to life? Oh, do me that favor!" Bokwewa said he would try. He performed numerous ceremonies, and at last succeeded in restoring her to life. They lived very happily for some time. Bokwewa was extremely kind to his brother, and did everything to render his life happy. Being deformed and crippled, he always remained at home, while his brother went out to hunt. And it was by following his directions, which were those of a skillful hunter, that he always succeeded in returning with a good store of meat.

One day he had gone out as usual, and Bokwewa was sitting in his lodge, on the opposite side of his brother's wife, when a tall, fine young man entered, and immediately took the woman by the hand and drew her to the door. She resisted and called on Bokwewa, who jumped up to her assistance. But their joint resistance was unavailing; the man succeeded in carrying her away. In the scuffle, Bokwewa had his humpback much bruised on the stones near the door. He crawled into the lodge and wept very sorely, for he knew that it was a powerful Manito who had taken the woman.

When his brother returned, he related all to him exactly as it happened. He would not taste food for several days. Sometimes he would fall to weeping for a long time, and appeared almost beside himself. At last he said he would go in search of her. Bokwewa tried to dissuade him from it, but he insisted.

"Well!" said he, "since you are bent on going, listen to my advice. You will have to go south. It is a long distance to the residence of your captive wife, and there are so many charms and temptations in the way, I am afraid you will be led astray by them, and forget your errand. For the people you will see in that country do nothing but amuse themselves. They are very idle, gay, and effeminate, and I am fearful they will lead you astray. Your journey is beset with difficulties. I will mention one or two things, which you must be on your guard against. In the course of your journey, you will come to a large grapevine lying across your way. You must not even taste its fruit, for it is poisonous. Step over it. It is a snake. You will next come to something that looks like bear's fat, transparent and tremulous. Don't taste it, or you will be overcome by the pleasures of those people. It is frog's eggs. These are snares laid by the way for you."

He said he would follow the advice, and bid farewell to his brother. After traveling a long time, he came to the enchanted grapevine. It looked so tempting, he forgot his brother's advice and tasted the fruit. He went on till he came to the frog's eggs. The substance so much resembled bear's fat that he tasted it. He still went on. At length he came to a very extensive plain. As he emerged from the forest the sun was setting, and cast its scarlet and golden shades over all the plain. The air was perfectly calm, and the whole prospect had the air of an enchanted land. The most inviting fruits and flowers spread out before the eye. At a distance he beheld a large village, filled with people without number, and as he drew near he saw women beating corn in silver mortars. When they saw him approaching, they cried out, "Bokwewa's brother has come to see us." Throngs of men and women, gaily dressed, came out to meet him. He was soon overcome by their flatteries and pleasures, and he was not long afterward seen beating corn with their women—the strongest proof of effeminacy—although his wife, for whom he had mourned so much, was in that Indian metropolis.

Meantime, Bokwewa waited patiently for the return of his brother. At length, after the lapse of several years, he set out in search of him, and arrived in safety among the luxuriant people of the south. He met with the same allurements on the road, and the same flattering reception that his brother did. But he was above all temptations. The pleasures he saw had no other effect upon him than to make him regret the weakness of mind of those who were led away by them. He shed tears of pity to see that his

118

brother had laid aside the arms of a hunter, and was seen beating corn with the women.

He ascertained where his brother's wife remained. After deliberating some time, he went to the river where she usually came to draw water. He there changed himself into one of those hair snakes which are sometimes seen in running water. When she came down, he spoke to her, saying, "Take me up; I am Bokwewa." She then scooped him out and went home. In a short time the Manito who had taken her away asked her for water to drink. The lodge in which they lived was partitioned. He occupied a secret place, and was never seen by anyone but the woman. She handed him the water containing the hair snake, which he drank, with the snake, and soon after was a dead Manito.

Bokwewa then resumed his former shape. He went to his brother, and used every means to reclaim him. But he would not listen. He was so much taken up with the pleasures and dissipations into which he had fallen that he refused to give them up, although Bokwewa, with tears, tried to convince him of his foolishness, and to show him that those pleasures could not endure for a long time. Finding that he was past reclaiming, Bokwewa left him, and disappeared forever.

TI-KE-WA-KUSH, THE MAN WHO CALLED THE BUFFALO

THIS HAPPENED in the olden time before we had met the white people. Then the different bands lived in separate villages. The lodges were made of dirt. The Kit-ke-hahk-i band went off on a winter hunt, roaming over the country, as they used to do, after buffalo. At this time they did not find the buffalo near. They scouted in all directions, but could discover no signs of them. It was a hard time of starvation. The children cried and the women cried; they had nothing at all to eat.

There was a person who looked at the children crying for something to eat, and it touched his heart. They were very poor, and he felt sorry for them. He said to the head chief, "Tell the chiefs and other head men to do what I tell them. My heart is sick on account of the suffering of the people. It may be that I can help them. Let a new lodge be set up outside the village for us to meet in. I will see if I can do anything to relieve the tribe." The chief said that it was well to do this, and he gave orders for it.

While they were preparing to build this lodge they would miss this man in the night. He would disappear like a wind, and go off a long way, and just as daylight came, he would be there again. Sometimes, while sitting in his own lodge during the day, he would reach behind him, and bring out a small piece of buffalo meat, fat and lean, and would give it to someone, saying, "When you have had enough, save what is left, and give it to someone else." When he would give this small piece of meat to anyone, the person would think, "This is not enough to satisfy my hunger"; but after eating until he was full, there was always enough left to give to some other person.

In those days it was the custom for the head chief of the tribe, once in a while, to mount his horse, and ride about through the village, talking to the people, and giving them good advice, and telling them that they ought to do what was right by each other. At this time the chief spoke to the people, and explained that this man was going to try to benefit the tribe. So the people made him many fine presents, otter skins and eagle feathers, and when they gave him these things each one said, "I give you this. It is for yourself. Try to help us." He thanked them for these presents, and when they were all gathered together he said, "Now you chiefs and head men of the tribe, and you people, you have done well to give me these things. I shall give them to that person who gives me that power, and who has taken pity on me. I shall let you starve yet four days. Then help will come."

During these four days, every day and night he disappeared, but would come back the same night. He would say to the people that he had been far off, where it would take a person three or four days to go, but he was always back the same night. When he got back on the fourth night, he told the people that the buffalo were near, that the next morning they would be but a little way off. He went up on the hill near the camp, and sacrificed some eagle feathers, and some blue beads, and some Indian tobacco, and then returned to the camp. Then he said to the people, "When that object comes to that place of sacrifice, do not interfere with it; do not turn it back. Let it go by. Just watch and see."

The next morning at daylight, all the people came out of their lodges to watch this hill, and the place where he had sacrificed. While they were looking they saw a great buffalo bull come up over the hill to the place. He stood there for a short time and looked about, and then he walked on down the hill, and went galloping off past the village. Then this man spoke to the people, and said, "There. That is what I meant. That is the leader of the buffalo; where he went the whole herd will follow."

He sent his servant to the chiefs to tell them to choose four boys, and let them go to the top of the hill where the bull had come over, and to look beyond it. The boys were sent, and ran to the top of the hill, and when they looked over beyond it they stopped, and then turned, and came back, running. They went to the chiefs' lodge, and said to the chiefs sitting there, "Beyond that place of sacrifice there is coming a whole herd of buffalo; many, many, crowding and pushing each other."

Then, as it used to be in the old times, as soon as the young men had told the chief that the buffalo were coming, the chief rode about the village, and told everyone to get ready to chase them. He said to them besides, "Do not leave anything on the killing ground. Bring into the camp not only the meat and hides, but the heads and legs and all parts. Bring the best portions in first, and take them over to the new lodge, so that we may have a feast there." For so the man had directed.

Presently the buffalo came over the hill, and the people were ready, and they made a surround, and killed all that they could, and brought them home. Each man brought in his ribs and his young buffalo, and left them there at that lodge. The other parts they brought into the village, as he had directed. After they had brought in this meat, they went to the lodge, and stayed there four days and four nights, and had a great feast, roasting these ribs.

The man told them that they would make four surrounds like this, and to get all the meat that they could. "But," he said, "in surrounding these buffalo you must see that all the meat is saved. Ti-ra-wa does not like the people to waste the buffalo, and for that reason I advise you to make good use of all you kill." During the four nights they feasted this man used to disappear each night.

On the night of the fourth day he said to the people, "Tomorrow the buffalo will come again, and you will make another surround. Be careful not to kill a yellow calf—a little one—that you will see with the herd, nor its mother." This was in winter, and yet the calf was the same color as a young calf born in the spring. They made the surround, and let the yellow calf and its mother go.

A good many men in the tribe saw that this man was great, and that he had done great things for the tribe, and they made him many presents, the best horses that they had. He thanked them, but he did not want to accept the presents. The tribe believed that he had done this wonderful thing— had brought them buffalo—and all the people wanted to do just what he told them to.

In the first two surrounds, they killed many buffalo, and made much dried meat. All their sacks were full, and the dried meat was piled up out of doors. After the second surround, they feasted as before.

After four days, as they were going out to surround the buffalo the third time, the wind changed, and before the people got near them, the buffalo smelt them, and stampeded. While they were galloping away, the man ran up onto the top of the hill, to the place of sacrifice, carrying a pole, on which was tied the skin of a kit fox; and when he saw the buffalo running, and that the people could not catch them, he waved his pole, and called out "*Ska-a-a-a!*" and the buffalo turned rightabout, and charged back right through the people, and they killed many of them. He wished to show the people that he had the power over the buffalo.

After the third surround, they had a great deal of meat, and he called the chiefs together and said, "Now, my chiefs, are you satisfied?" They said, "Yes, we are satisfied, and we are thankful to you for taking pity on us and helping us. It is through your power that the tribe has been saved from starving to death." He said, "You are to make one more surround, and that will be the end. I want you to get all you can. Kill as many as possible, for this will be the last of the buffalo this winter. Those presents that you have made to me, and that I did not wish to take, I give them back to you."

Some of the people would not take back the presents, but insisted that he should keep them, and at last he said he would do so.

The fourth surround was made, and the people killed many buffalo, and saved the meat. The night after this last surround, he disappeared and drove the buffalo back. The next morning he told the people to look about, and tell him if they saw anything. They did so, but they could not see any buffalo.

The next day they moved camp, and went east toward their home. They had so much dried meat that they could not take it all at once, but had to come back and make two trips for it. When they moved below, going east, they had no fresh meat, only dried meat; but sometimes when this man would come in from his journeys, he would bring a piece of meat—a little piece—and he would divide it up among the people, and they would put it into the kettles and boil it, and everybody would eat, but they could not eat it all up. There would always be some left over. This man was so wonderful that he could change even the buffalo chips that you see on the prairie into meat. He would cover them up with his robe, and when he would take it off again, you would see there pounded buffalo meat and pemmican, *tup-o-har-ash.*

The man was not married; he was a young man, and by this time the people thought that he was one of the greatest men in the tribe, and they wanted him to marry. They went to one of the chiefs and told him that they wanted him to be this man's father-in-law, for they wanted him to raise children, thinking that they might do something to benefit the tribe. They did not want that race to die out. The old people say that it would have been good if he had had children, but he had none. If he had, perhaps they would have had the same power as their father.

That person called the buffalo twice, and twice saved the tribe from a famine. The second time the suffering was great, and they held a council to ask him to help the tribe. They filled up the pipe and held it out to him, asking him to take pity on the tribe. He took the pipe, and lighted it, and smoked. He did it in the same way as the first time, and they made four surrounds, and got much meat.

When this man died, all the people mourned for him a long time. The chief would ride around the village and call out, "Now I am poor in mind

123

on account of the death of this man, because he took pity on us and saved the tribe. Now he is gone and there is no one left like him."

This is a true and sacred story that belongs to the Kit-ke-hahk-i band. It happened once long ago, and has been handed down from father to son in this band. The Skidi had a man who once called the buffalo, causing them to return when stampeded, as was done in this story.

V

ROMANCE, ADVENTURE,
AND ENCHANTMENT

THE PRINCESS
WHO REJECTED HER COUSIN

THERE WAS A CUSTOM among our people that the nephew of the chief had to marry the chief's daughter, because the tribe of the chief wanted the chief's nephew to be the heir of his uncle and to inherit his place after his death. This custom has gone on, generation after generation, all along until now, and the places of the head men have thus been inherited. So it is with this story.

A very long time ago there was a great village with many people. They had only one chief. There was also his sister. They were the only two chiefs in the large town. The chief also had a beautiful daughter, and the chief's sister had a fine son. All the people of the village were glad to see the young prince and the young princess growing up, and they expected that these two would soon marry. Therefore the relatives of the prince went and talked with the father of the princess, and they also went to the uncles of the princess and talked with them.

Now, the relatives of the girl accepted, but the girl rejected the proposal and said that she would not marry him; but the young prince loved her very much, and still she refused him. The young man loved her still more, and he was always true to her. Moreover, he was very anxious to speak to her, but the young woman rejected him.

Now, the princess wanted to make a fool of her cousin. One day she dressed herself up and went to the end of the village to take some fresh air. The young man saw her pass by his door, and he went after her. Soon he saw her sitting under a large tree, and went up to her, and the girl was very kind to him. She smiled when she saw him coming. Then the young man sat down by her side under the tree as gently as he could. He asked her if she did not want to marry him. The girl said, "If you make a deep cut in your cheek, then you may marry me." Therefore the handsome young man took his knife and cut down his right cheek. The girl laughed at him, and they went home.

When the cheek of the young man was healed, the princess put on her finest dress, passed the door of her cousin, and the young man saw her pass by. He followed her, and saw her sit at the same place where he had met her before. He went to her, and she stretched out her hands to greet him, put her arms around him, and kissed him once, since her cousin wanted to marry her. Then the young man loved her still more because she had kissed him the first time ever since he had loved her; and when the young man was overflowing with love, she said, "If you love me so much, show your love and make a cut down your left cheek; then I shall know that you really love me." The young man did not like to do it. However, he wanted to marry her, and so he took his knife and made a cut down his left cheek. They went home, and the young man was always thinking of her.

Soon his wounded cheek was healed. He did not mind his foolish acts. On the following day he saw her passing his door. The young man followed her, and she was sitting under the tree. She smiled at him when he was coming to her, and said, "Do you come to me again, my beloved one?" and he replied, "Yes, I come to marry you." Then he put his arms around her, and she kissed him again. He asked her, "Do you love me, my dear cousin?" and she replied, "Yes, you know how much I love you," and the princess asked him, "Do you also love me, cousin?" and he replied, "Indeed, I love you very much." Thus said the young man, for he wanted to marry her. Then the princess said to him, "Now, show me your love. Cut off your hair; then you may marry me." So the young prince took his knife and cut off his beautiful yellow hair. (In those days the young men and the old men wore their hair as long as women's hair, and it was considered dishonorable to cut a man's hair as we do it now.)

They went home, and on the following day the young man sent someone to her, saying that he wanted to marry her now. Therefore the messenger went to her and told her what her cousin had said; but the woman replied, "Tell him that I do not want to marry a bad-looking person like him, ugly as he is"; and she gave him the nickname Mountain With Two Rock Slides, as he had a scar down each cheek. She laughed at him and scorned him, saying, "I do not want to marry a man who cut his hair like a slave."

The young man's messenger came back to him and told him what she had said. Therefore the youth was very much ashamed. He remembered that he also was a prince, and he cried because his own cousin had mocked him.

Now, he decided to leave his father's house and his uncle's house, for he was ashamed before his fellows of the scars which he had made on his own cheeks by order of his loved one. He went about, not knowing which way to go. Day by day he went, and he came to a narrow trail. He walked along it, and saw a small hut away off. He went toward it. Before it was evening he reached there; and when he was near, he walked up to it quietly. He stood outside and looked through a small hole. Behold! a woman was sitting there by the side of a fireplace. She said, "Come in, dear prince, if it is you who was rejected by his own cousin!" So the young man went in, and the woman made him sit down on the other side of the fire. She gave him to eat. When he started from home, four young men, his own friends, had accompanied him on his way; but three of them had gone back home, and only one, his dearest friend, followed him all along the way until they came to the little hut.

After the old woman had given them to eat, she said to the young man, "Soon you will arrive at the large house of Chief Pestilence, which is just across the little brook yonder. Leave your companion at this side of the brook, and you yourself go to the large house. When you get there, push open the large door, then say this, 'I come to be made beautiful in the house of Pestilence!' Shout this as loud as you can. Then you will see that the house on both sides is full of maimed persons. They will call you to come to their sides; but do not go there, because they will make you like one of them. When they stop calling you, then Chief Pestilence will call you to the rear of the house. Follow his calling. He will make you beautiful." Thus said the old woman to him. On the following day, after they had had their breakfast, they started. As soon as they crossed the brook, the prince said to his companion, "Stay here, and I will go on alone. Wait until I come back to you!" So the companion stayed there.

Now he went on alone. Soon he saw a large house in the distance, and went as quickly as he could. He pushed open the door, ran in, and shouted at the top of his voice, "I came to be made beautiful, Chief Pestilence!" Then all the maimed people on both sides of the house beckoned to him and shouted. Those on one side would say, "Come this way, come this way!"

and those on the other side said, "Come, come, come!" The prince remained standing in the doorway. There were many good-looking women among these maimed persons. They shouted and called him; but he stood still, waiting until Chief Pestilence should come forth from his room in the rear of the large house.

Soon the noise of the maimed people ceased. Then the door of the chief's room was opened, and, behold! Chief Pestilence came forth with his beautiful daughter. He said, "Dear prince, come this way!" Then the young man went to him and sat down on his right side.

Then Chief Pestilence ordered his attendants to bring his bathtub. They brought him a large tub full of water. Then the chief took the young man, put him into this tub, and, as soon as he was in the tub, the water began to boil, and the water boiled over the tub, boiling of its own accord. When the dross was all off, the chief took the bare bones of the young man, put them on a wide board, joining them together. After he had done so, he called to his young daughter, who leaped over the bones. Then the young man was alive again. His features were changed, and his body was as white as snow.

Then the chief said, "Bring me a nice comb!" and his attendants brought him a comb of crystal. The chief took it and combed the prince's hair down to his loins. His hair was red, like tongues of fire. He was the most beautiful of all.

The chief did not want to let him go at once, but kept him in his house for two days. The young man thought he had been there two days, but in reality two years had passed. Then the young man remembered his friend whom he had left by the brook before he entered the house of Chief Pestilence. The prince told the young woman that he had left his friend by the brook; therefore the young woman said, "Let us go to see him!" They went together; and when they came to the place, they found the man's bare bones heaped up there. Therefore the young prince wept, but the young woman commanded him to take the bare bones to her father's house. The young man did what the young woman had told him, and took the bare bones to the chief. The chief ordered his attendants to bring his bathtub. They brought it to him, and he put the bare bones into the tub. Then the water began to boil, and the dross of the bare bones boiled over the tub. Thus the young man saw what Chief Pestilence had done to him.

Then the chief took out the bones and placed them on a wide board and joined them together; and the young woman leaped over them four times, and the young man was alive again.

Next the chief asked for his own comb. They brought it to him, and the chief asked what color of hair he wanted. The man said, "Dark-yellow hair." He also asked him how long he wanted it, and the man said, "Right down to the knee." So the chief combed his hair down to his knees; and this man was lighter color than the other. Now they started for home. It was not many days before they arrived at their home. The prince looked like a supernatural being, and his friend too was handsomer than any of the other people. They came and visited them; and all the people talked about these two men who had just come back from the house of Chief Pestilence, who had transformed them and given them great beauty.

The young people coveted their beauty, and they questioned them one day to know how far the house of Chief Pestilence was from their village. Then the prince's friend told them that it was not very far away.

Now, let us go back to the princess who years ago had refused to marry her own cousin. She was very anxious to see her cousin who had just come home from the house of Chief Pestilence. People were talking about it, that he was more beautiful than any other person in the village; and she heard the people say that he looked like a supernatural being. Therefore the young woman tried hard to see him.

One day the chief, the father of the princess, invited his nephew to his house. The prince went with some of the chief's head men; and as soon as the prince entered his uncle's house, the young princess looked at him. Oh, how fine he looked! and more beautiful than any of the people. Then she tried to make her rejected cousin turn and look at her, but the young man took no notice of her courting. His hair was like fire, and his face shone like the rays of the sun.

Now, the young woman came down from her room, and walked to and fro behind the guests, laughing and talking, trying to make the beautiful prince look at her; but he took no notice of her. As soon as the feasting was over, he arose and went home, and the young princess felt full of sorrow.

The following day she sent her maid to call the beautiful prince. When the girl came to him and told him what her mistress had said, he did not

131

answer a word; and the maid went back to her mistress and told her that the prince would not answer her a word. She sent to him again; and when the girl came to him, she told him that her mistress wanted him to come and see her. But he said to the girl, "Go and tell her that she rejected me then, so I will not go to her now." Then the girl went and told her mistress what the prince had said. The princess sent her girl again. "Go and tell him that I will do whatever he desires me to do." She went and told him what her mistress had said. "My mistress says that whatever you desire her to do she will do." Then the prince said to the girl, "Go and tell her that I desire her to cut down her right cheek, and I will come and be her guest." Therefore the girl went and told her mistress what the prince had said. So the princess took her knife and cut down her right cheek. She said to her maid, "Go and tell him that I will do whatever he wants me to do." She went and told the prince what her mistress had done.

Again the beautiful prince said, "Just tell her to cut down her other cheek, and then I will come and see her." So she went and told her mistress, and thereupon the princess cut her left cheek. Again she sent her maid, who went to him and told him. This time he said, "Let her cut her hair, then I will go to her." She went and told her, and the princess took her knife and shaved off her hair, and she sent her hair to him. The maid took it to the prince, but when the prince saw the hair, he refused to accept it. "Don't bring it near me! It is too nasty! Take it back to your mistress and tell her that I don't want to see the ugly scars on her cheeks and her ugly shaved hair. It is too nasty for me." Then he left, and laughed louder and louder, mocking her; and the girl returned to her mistress very sad.

She came slowly, and her mistress asked her, "My dear, what tidings do you bring?" Then she told her mistress how scornfully he had spoken of the ugly scars on her cheeks, and of her shaving her hair, and that everybody had been laughing at her, and that everyone had heard him mocking her. Then the young princess was very much ashamed. She set out with her maid, and walked along crying. She wanted to hang herself, but her maid talked to her and comforted her all the way. They went on and on, trying to go to the house of Chief Pestilence. Her heart took courage, for she hoped to get there and ask Chief Pestilence to make her beautiful. They went on and on, and passed many mountains and rivers and valleys, and reached the edge of a large plain. There they met a man, who asked them which way they intended to go; and the princess told him that they intended to go to the house of Chief Pestilence. She passed by him, and did not look at him, for she was ashamed to let anyone look at her.

Soon they saw a large house in the distance. They went toward it; and when they reached the door, they went right in and shouted as they stood in the doorway, "We come to the house of Chief Pestilence to be made beautiful!" Then all the maimed people on both sides of the house called to them, "Come, come, come!" And those on the other side shouted, "This way, this way, this way!" And the princess went to those who called her to come; and the other one went to those who shouted, "This way!"

Then the maimed people fell on the princess, broke her backbone, and made her lame. They turned her head to one side, and broke one of her arms; and those on the other side plucked out one of the eyes of her maid, tore up one side of her mouth, and scratched the two women all over their bodies, and then threw them outside. There they lay wounded, and nobody came to help them. The princess was more severely injured than her maid.

When the maid felt a little better, she saw her mistress lying there with wounds all over her body. She went to her, and saw how she was bruised. They were both in great distress, and the princess was groaning. So her maid helped her up and led her home. They spent many days coming down, and finally arrived at their home. Then she lay in bed, and finally died.

SCARFACE, OR THE ORIGIN OF THE MEDICINE LODGE

IN THE EARLIEST TIMES there was no war. All the tribes were at peace. In those days there was a man who had a daughter, a very beautiful girl. Many young men wanted to marry her, but every time she was asked, she only shook her head and said she did not want a husband.

"How is this?" asked her father. "Some of these young men are rich, handsome, and brave."

"Why should I marry?" replied the girl. "I have a rich father and mother. Our lodge is good. The parfleches are never empty. There are plenty of tanned robes and soft furs for winter. Why worry me, then?"

The Raven Bearers held a dance; they all dressed carefully and wore their ornaments, and each one tried to dance the best. Afterward some of them asked for this girl, but still she said no. Then the Bulls, the Kit-foxes, and others of the *I-kun-uh-kah-tsi* held their dances, and all those who were rich, many great warriors, asked this man for his daughter, but to every one of them she said no. Then her father was angry, and said, "Why, now, this way? All the best men have asked for you, and still you say no. I believe you have a secret lover."

"Ah!" said her mother. "What shame for us should a child be born and our daughter still unmarried!" "Father! mother!" replied the girl, "pity me. I have no secret lover, but now hear the truth. That Above Person, the Sun, told me, 'Do not marry any of those men, for you are mine; thus you shall be happy, and live to great age'; and again he said, 'Take heed. You must not marry. You are mine.'"

"Ah!" replied her father. "It must always be as he says." And they talked no more about it.

There was a poor young man, very poor. His father, mother, all his relations, had gone to the Sand Hills. He had no lodge, no wife to tan his robes or sew his moccasins. He stopped in one lodge today, and tomorrow he ate and slept in another; thus he lived. He was a good-looking young man, except that on his cheek he had a scar, and his clothes were always old and poor.

After those dances, some of the young men met this poor Scarface, and they laughed at him, and said, "Why don't you ask that girl to marry you? You are so rich and handsome!" Scarface did not laugh; he replied, "Ah! I will do as you say. I will go and ask her." All the young men thought this was funny. They laughed a great deal. But Scarface went down by the river. He waited by the river, where the women came to get water, and by and by the girl came along. "Girl," he said, "wait. I want to speak with you. Not as a designing person do I ask you, but openly where the Sun looks down, and all may see."

"Speak then," said the girl.

"I have seen the days," continued the young man. "You have refused those who are young, and rich, and brave. Now, today, they laughed and said to me, 'Why do you not ask her?' I am poor, very poor. I have no lodge, no food, no clothes, no robes, and warm furs. I have no relations; all have gone to the Sand Hills; yet now, today, I ask you, take pity, be my wife.'"

The girl hid her face in her robe and brushed the ground with the point of her moccasin, back and forth, back and forth, for she was thinking. After a time she said, "True. I have refused all those rich young men, yet now the poor one asks me, and I am glad. I will be your wife, and my people will be happy. You are poor, but it does not matter. My father will give you dogs. My mother will make us a lodge. My people will give us robes and furs. You will be poor no longer."

Then the young man was happy, and he started to kiss her, but she held him back, and said, "Wait! The Sun has spoken to me. He says I may not marry, that I belong to him. He says if I listen to him, I shall live to great age. But now I say, 'Go to the Sun.' Tell him, 'She whom you spoke with heeds your words. She has never done wrong, but now she wants to marry. I want her for my wife.' Ask him to take that scar from your face. That will be his sign. I will know he is pleased. But if he refuses, or if you fail to find his lodge, then do not return to me."

"Oh!" cried the young man, "at first your words were good. I was glad. But now it is dark. My heart is dead. Where is that far-off lodge? Where the trail, which no one yet has traveled?"

"Take courage, take courage!" said the girl, and she went to her lodge.

Scarface was very sad. He sat down and covered his head with his robe and tried to think what to do. After a while he got up, and went to an old woman who had been kind to him. "Pity me," he said. "I am very poor. I am going away now on a long journey. Make me some moccasins."

"Where are you going?" asked the old woman. "There is no war; we are very peaceful here."

"I do not know where I shall go," replied Scarface. "I am in trouble, but I cannot tell you now what it is."

So the old woman made him some moccasins, seven pairs, with parfleche

soles, and also she gave him a sack of food—pemmican of berries, pounded meat, and dried back fat—for this old woman had a good heart. She liked the young man.

All alone, and with a sad heart, he climbed the bluffs and stopped to take a last look at the camp. He wondered if he would ever see his sweetheart and the people again. *"Hai-yu!* Pity me, O Sun," he prayed, and turning, he started to find the trail.

For many days he traveled on, over great prairies, along timbered rivers and among the mountains, and every day his sack of food grew lighter; but he saved it as much as he could, and ate berries, and roots, and sometimes he killed an animal of some kind. One night he stopped by the home of a wolf. *"Hai-yah!"* said that one, "what is my brother doing so far from home?"

"Ah!" replied Scarface, "I seek the place where the Sun lives; I am sent to speak with him."

"I have traveled far," said the wolf. "I know all the prairies, the valleys, and the mountains, but I have never seen the Sun's home. Wait; I know one who is very wise. Ask the bear. He may tell you."

The next day the man traveled on again, stopping now and then to pick a few berries, and when night came he arrived at the bear's lodge.

"Where is your home?" asked the bear. "Why are you traveling alone, my brother?"

"Help me! Pity me!" replied the young man; "because of her words I seek the Sun. I go to ask him for her."

"I know not where he stops," replied the bear. "I have traveled by many rivers, and I know the mountains, yet I have never seen his lodge. There is someone beyond, that striped-face, who is very smart. Go and ask him."

The badger was in his hole. Stooping over, the young man shouted, "Oh, cunning striped-face! Oh, generous animal! I wish to speak with you."

"What do you want?" said the badger, poking his head out of the hole.

"I want to find the Sun's home," replied Scarface. "I want to speak with him."

"I do not know where he lives," replied the badger. "I never travel very far. Over there in the timber is a wolverine. He is always traveling around, and is of much knowledge. Maybe he can tell you."

Then Scarface went to the woods and looked all around for the wolverine, but could not find him. So he sat down to rest. *"Hai-yu! Hai-yu!"* he cried. "Wolverine, take pity on me. My food is gone, my moccasins worn-out. Now I must die."

"What is it, my brother?" he heard, and looking around, he saw the animal sitting near.

"She whom I would marry," said Scarface, "belongs to the Sun; I am trying to find where he lives, to ask him for her."

"Ah!" said the wolverine. "I know where he lives. Wait; it is nearly night. Tomorrow I will show you the trail to the big water. He lives on the other side of it."

Early in the morning, the wolverine showed him the trail, and Scarface followed it until he came to the water's edge. He looked out over it, and his heart almost stopped. Never before had anyone seen such a big water. The other side could not be seen, and there was no end to it. Scarface sat down on the shore. His food was all gone, his moccasins worn-out. His heart was sick. "I cannot cross this big water," he said. "I cannot return to the people. Here, by this water, I shall die."

Not so. His helpers were there. Two swans came swimming up to the shore. "Why have you come here?" they asked him. "What are you doing? It is very far to the place where your people live."

"I am here," replied Scarface, "to die. Far away, in my country, is a beautiful girl. I want to marry her, but she belongs to the Sun. So I started to find him and ask for her. I have traveled many days. My food is gone. I cannot go back. I cannot cross this big water, so I am going to die."

"No," said the swans; "it shall not be so. Across this water is the home of that Above Person. Get on our backs, and we will take you there."

Scarface quickly rose. He felt strong again. He waded out into the water and lay down on the swans' backs, and they started off. Very deep and black is that fearful water. Strange people live there, mighty animals which often seize and drown a person. The swans carried him safely, and took him to the other side. Here was a broad hard trail leading back from the water's edge.

"Kyi," said the swans. "You are now close to the Sun's lodge. Follow that trail, and you will soon see it."

Scarface started up the trail, and pretty soon he came to some beautiful things, lying in it. There was a war shirt, a shield, and a bow and arrows. He had never seen such pretty weapons; but he did not touch them. He walked carefully around them, and traveled on. A little way farther on, he met a young man, the handsomest person he had ever seen. His hair was very long, and he wore clothing made of strange skins. His moccasins were sewed with bright colored feathers. The young man said to him, "Did you see some weapons lying on the trail?"

"Yes," replied Scarface, "I saw them."

"But did you not touch them?" asked the young man.

"No, I thought someone had left them there, so I did not take them."

"You are not a thief," said the young man. "What is your name?"

"Scarface."

"Where are you going?"

"To the Sun."

"My name," said the young man, "is A-pi-su-ahts, Morning Star. The Sun is my father; come, I will take you to our lodge. My father is not now at home, but he will come in at night."

Soon they came to the lodge. It was very large and handsome; strange medicine animals were painted on it. Behind, on a tripod, were strange weapons and beautiful clothes—the Sun's. Scarface was ashamed to go in, but Morning Star said, "Do not be afraid, my friend; we are glad you have come."

They entered. One person was sitting there, Ko-ko-mik-e-is, the Moon, the Sun's wife, Morning Star's mother. She spoke to Scarface kindly, and gave him something to eat. "Why have you come so far from your people?" she asked.

Then Scarface told her about the beautiful girl he wanted to marry. "She belongs to the Sun," he said. "I have come to ask him for her."

When it was time for the Sun to come home, the Moon hid Scarface under a pile of robes. As soon as the Sun got to the doorway, he stopped and said, "I smell a person."

"Yes, father," said Morning Star, "a good young man has come to see you. I know he is good, for he found some of my things on the trail and did not touch them."

Then Scarface came out from under the robes, and the Sun entered and sat down. "I am glad you have come to our lodge," he said. "Stay with us as long as you think best. My son is lonesome sometimes; be his friend."

The next day the Moon called Scarface out of the lodge, and said to him, "Go with Morning Star where you please, but never hunt near that big water; do not let him go there. It is the home of great birds which have long sharp bills; they kill people. I have had many sons, but these birds have killed them all. Morning Star is the only one left."

So Scarface stayed there a long time and hunted with Morning Star. One day they came near the water, and saw the big birds.

"Come," said Morning Star, "let us go and kill those birds."

"No, no!" replied Scarface; "we must not go there. Those are very terrible birds; they will kill us."

Morning Star would not listen. He ran toward the water, and Scarface followed. He knew that he must kill the birds and save the boy. If not, the Sun would be angry and might kill him. He ran ahead and met the birds, which were coming toward him to fight, and killed every one of them with his spear: not one was left. Then the young men cut off their heads, and carried them home. Morning Star's mother was glad when they told her what they had done, and showed her the birds' heads. She cried, and called Scarface "my son." When the Sun came home at night, she told him about it, and he too was glad. "My son," he said to Scarface, "I will not forget what you have this day done for me. Tell me now, what can I do for you?"

"*Hai-yu*," replied Scarface. "*Hai-yu*, pity me. I am here to ask you for that girl. I want to marry her. I asked her, and she was glad; but she says you own her, that you told her not to marry."

"What you say is true," said the Sun. "I have watched the days, so I know it. Now, then, I give her to you; she is yours. I am glad she has been wise. I know she has never done wrong. The Sun pities good women. They shall live a long time. So shall their husbands and children. Now you will soon go home. Let me tell you something. Be wise and listen: I am the only chief. Everything is mine. I made the earth, the mountains, prairies, rivers, and forests. I made the people and all the animals. This is why I say I alone am the chief. I can never die. True, the winter makes me old and weak, but every summer I grow young again."

Then said the Sun, "What one of all animals is smartest? The raven is, for he always finds food. He is never hungry. Which one of all the animals is most sacred? The buffalo is. Of all animals, I like him best. He is for the people. He is your food and your shelter. What part of his body is sacred? The tongue is. That is mine. What else is sacred? Berries are. They are mine too. Come with me and see the world." He took Scarface to the edge of the sky, and they looked down and saw it. It is round and flat, and all around the edge is the jumping-off place.

Then said the Sun, "When any man is sick or in danger, his wife may promise to build me a lodge, if he recovers. If the woman is pure and true, then I will be pleased and help the man. But if she is bad, if she lies, then I will be angry. You shall build the lodge like the world, round, with walls, but first you must build a sweat lodge of a hundred sticks. It shall be like the sky, and half of it shall be painted red. That is me. The other half you will paint black. That is the night."

Further said the Sun, "Which is the best, the heart or the brain? The brain is. The heart often lies, the brain never." Then he told Scarface everything about making the medicine lodge, and when he had finished, he rubbed a powerful medicine on his face, and the scar disappeared. Then he gave him two raven feathers, saying, "These are the sign for the girl that I give her to you. They must always be worn by the husband of the woman who builds a medicine lodge."

The young man was now ready to return home. Morning Star and the Sun gave him many beautiful presents. The Moon cried and kissed him, and called him "my son." Then the Sun showed him the short trail. It was the Wolf Road, the Milky Way. He followed it, and soon reached the ground.

It was a very hot day. All the lodge skins were raised, and the people sat in the shade. There was a chief, a very generous man, and all day long people kept coming to his lodge to feast and smoke with him. Early in the morning this chief saw a person sitting out on a butte near by, close wrapped in his robe. The chief's friends came and went, the sun reached the middle, and passed on, down toward the mountains. Still this person did not move. When it was almost night, the chief said, "Why does that person sit there so long? The heat has been strong, but he has never eaten nor drunk. He may be a stranger; go and ask him in."

So some young men went up to him, and said, "Why do you sit here in the great heat all day? Come to the shade of the lodges. The chief asks you to feast with him."

Then the person arose and threw off his robe, and they were surprised. He wore beautiful clothes. His bow, shield, and other weapons were of strange make. But they knew his face, although the scar was gone, and they ran ahead, shouting, "The scarface poor young man has come. He is poor no longer. The scar on his face is gone."

All the people rushed out to see him. "Where have you been?" they asked. "Where did you get all these pretty things?" He did not answer. There in the crowd stood that young woman; and taking the two raven feathers from his head, he gave them to her, and said, "The trail was very long, and I nearly died, but by those helpers, I found his lodge. He is glad. He sends these feathers to you. They are the sign."

Great was her gladness then. They were married, and made the first medicine lodge, as the Sun had said. The Sun was glad. He gave them great age. They were never sick. When they were very old, one morning, their children said, "Awake! Rise and eat." They did not move. In the night, in sleep, without pain, their shadows had departed for the Sand Hills.

THE HUNTER AND HIS WOODEN WIFE

A HUNTER married a young woman. He loved her very much because the young woman knew how to make dancing-blankets, which were very dear to the people in olden times.

Not many days after their marriage, the hunter made ready to go up the mountains for fall and winter hunting. One day they started, and he went with his young wife, taking all his woodworker's tools and his traps and snares. They went on and on until they arrived at his camping ground, and there they went into the hut.

In the autumn the young man first hunted mountain sheep, whose wool the young wife needed for making dancing-garments. Therefore the man killed many. He took off the good wool, and the young woman took all the wool and washed it. When it was dry enough, she spun it into yarn, and after she had spun it all, she dyed some. When she was ready, she began to weave; but when half of her weaving was finished, she became sick while her husband was away. When he came home, he found his young wife very ill.

When she was dying, she called her young husband to her side, and said, "My dear husband, keep your love for me after I am dead. Don't go home too soon! Watch over my grave!" Then she died.

The young man was in deep sorrow for her sake. He kept her dead body many days. Now the winter was nearly passed, and he still kept the body until it was decayed. Then he buried it. He carved an image of his wife out of red cedar.

This man never touched anything that his wife had made, and so it was with her dancing-garment which she was making when she died. It was still hanging there where it had been when she was working on it. When he made the image of his late wife, he seated it in front of her unfinished dancing-garment, and he made the fingers move as though they were weaving a dancing-garment. He made it turn when he opened the door, and he pretended that the image could speak.

Then he began to hunt again; and whenever he came home from hunting, he threw down his bear meat and fat outside the house. Then he would speak to his wife-image, "Come out and look at this!" Then he spoke to himself as though his image-wife were speaking: "Oh, I cannot, because my yarn is twisted around my fingers! Therefore I won't come out." Then he went in and embraced his wooden wife. He talked to his wooden wife, and would say, "You are very handsome."

Now many hunters were passing by. They looked into the house and saw a woman weaving a dancing-garment. Then someone said that the hunter's wife was made of wood. He told about it in the village.

There were two sisters among some young men. One night their mother was angry with them. Therefore they ran away from their mother and crossed the mountains. They crossed the mountains, valleys, and rivers, and one day they arrived at the camp of the wooden wife. They looked in through a knothole, and there was a woman seated by the side of a dancing-garment, which she was weaving. They wanted to ask her if she could give them food, so they opened the door, and the woman that was weaving turned her head to look at them. They stood there and asked her to give them a little food, but she did not pay any attention; and the yarn was twisted around her fingers, and she just moved her fingers. Therefore the elder sister said to her younger sister, "That is not a living being! I will go near and look." So she went near and touched her shoulder, and said, "Will you give us a little food, elder sister?" However, she felt that it was not a human being, but wood. She called her younger sister, and they were surprised. Then they laughed at her, and they remembered what they had heard about the hunter's wooden wife. They hid in a corner of the house among the dried meat and fat.

Soon they heard the hunter come down to his camp. He whistled, for he was very tired because his load was heavy. He said to his wooden wife, "Come out, my dear, and look at this!" Then he said to himself, "Not so, my dear, for my yarn is twisted around my fingers." Then he came in, ran to his wooden wife, and embraced her and kissed her, and the two young women laughed at him secretly. The man heard them laughing secretly. He got up and looked around, and found the two young women who were hiding among the dried meat. He called them and spread a large grizzly-bear skin on one side of the house. The two young women sat down on the large grizzly-bear skin, and he cooked for them rich meat, tallow, and fat. They ate many things that night, but the younger sister was afraid to eat much. She ate only a little of each kind of food. The elder sister ate a great deal. She overate. At midnight they went to bed.

The man spread another grizzly-bear skin for their bed, and he gave them fur garments. They slept soundly that night; but the elder sister, who had overeaten, soiled her bed early in the morning. The hunter arose and made a fire. He cooked a meal for the two women, and then called them. The younger one arose, but the elder one was ashamed to get up. The man said, "Wake up, my dear, we are waiting with breakfast!" But she cried because she was very much ashamed. Then the hunter made fun of her.

He wanted to marry the younger one. She replied, "You may marry me if you promise to destroy your wooden wife." He promised to destroy it, and she asked him to promise not to tell anyone what had happened to her elder sister. He also said that he would never do so, and he also said to her, "Don't tell anyone what I have done to the wooden figure!" And she promised not to do so. Then they were married.

The young woman was better than his former wife. He taught her to weave dancing-garments, and she learned the art quickly, and she made them better than his first wife. The hunter came to be richer than ever. He sent his sister-in-law back to the village; and at the end of the next autumn they moved back to the village. He gave a great feast to all the people, and built a large house, and became a head chief in his generation. His new wife was a wise woman and kind to all the people. That is the end.

THE ENCHANTED MOCCASINS

THERE ONCE LIVED a little boy, all alone with his sister, in a very wild un-inhabitable country. They saw nothing but beasts, and birds, the sky above them, and the earth beneath them. But there were no human beings besides themselves. The boy often retired to think, in lone places, and the opinion was formed that he had supernatural powers. It was supposed that he would perform some extraordinary exploits, and he was called Onwe Bahmondoong—He Who Carries a Ball on His Back. As he grew up he was impatient to know whether there were other beings near them. His sister replied that there were, but they lived at a remote distance. There was a large village of hunters and warriors.

Being now well grown, he determined to seek his fortune, and asked her to make him several pairs of moccasins to last him on the journey. With this request she complied. Then taking his bow and arrows, and his war club, and a little sack containing his *nawappo*, traveling victuals, he immediately set out on his journey. He traveled on, not knowing exactly where he went. Hills, plains, trees, rocks, forests, meadows, spread before him. Sometimes he killed an animal, sometimes a bird. The deer often started in his path. He saw the fox, the bear, and the ground hog. The eagles screamed above him. The ducks chattered in the ponds and lakes. He lay down and slept when he was tired; he rose up when he was refreshed. At last he came to a small wigwam, and on looking into it, discovered a very old woman sitting alone by the fire. As soon as she saw the stranger, she invited him in, and thus addressed him, "My poor grandchild, I suppose you are one of those who seek for the distant village, from which no person has ever yet returned. Unless your guardian is more powerful than the guardian of your predecessors, you too will share a similar fate of theirs. Be careful to provide yourself with the *Ozhebahguhnun*—the bones they use in the medicine dance—without which you cannot succeed."

After she had thus spoken, she gave him the following directions for his journey. "When you come near to the village which you seek, you will see in the center a large lodge, in which the chief of the village, who has two daughters, resides. Before the door you will see a great tree, which is smooth and destitute of bark. On this tree, about the height of a man from the ground, a small lodge is suspended, in which these two daughters dwell. It is here so many have been destroyed. Be wise, my grandchild, and abide strictly by my directions." The old woman then gave him the *Ozhebahguhnun*, which would cause his success.

Placing them in his bosom, he continued his journey, till at length he arrived at the sought-for village; and as he was gazing around him, he saw both the tree and the lodge which the old woman had mentioned. Immediately he bent his steps toward the tree, and approaching, he endeavored to reach the suspended lodge. But all his efforts were vain; for as often as he attempted to reach it, the tree began to tremble, and soon shot up so that the lodge could hardly be seen. Foiled as he was in all his attempts, he thought of his guardian and changed himself into a small squirrel, that he might more easily accomplish his design. He then mounted the tree in quest of the lodge.

After climbing for some time, he became fatigued, and panted for breath; but remembering the instructions which the old woman had given him, he took from his bosom one of the bones, and thrust it into the trunk of the tree, on which he sat. In this way he quickly found relief; and as often as he became fatigued, he repeated this; but whenever he came near the lodge

146

and attempted to touch it, the tree would shoot up as before, and place the lodge beyond his reach. At length, the bones being exhausted, he began to despair, for the earth had long since vanished from his sight. Summoning all resolution, he determined to make another effort to reach the object of his wishes. On he went; yet as soon as he came near the lodge and attempted to touch it, the tree again shook, but it had reached the arch of heaven, and could go no higher.

So now he entered the lodge, and beheld the two sisters sitting opposite each other. He asked their names. The one on his left hand called herself Azhabee—She Who Sits Behind—and the one on the right Negahnahbee —She Who Sits in Front. Whenever he addressed the one on his left hand, the tree would tremble as before, and settle down to its former position. But when he addressed the one on his right hand, it would again shoot upward. When he thus discovered that, by addressing the one on his left hand, the tree would descend, he continued to do so until it had resumed its former position. Then seizing his war club, he thus addressed the sisters, "You, who have caused the death of so many of my brothers, I will now put an end to, and thus have revenge for the numbers you have destroyed." As he said this he raised the club and laid them dead at his feet. He then descended, and learning that these sisters had a brother living with their father, who would pursue him for the deed he had done, he set off at random, not knowing whither he went.

Soon after, the father and mother of the young women visited their lodge and found their remains. They immediately told their son Mudjikewis that his sisters had been slain. He replied, "The person who has done this must be the Boy Who Carries the Ball on His Back. I will pursue him, and have revenge for the blood of my sisters." "It is well, my son," replied the father. "The spirit of your life grant you success. I counsel you to be wary in the pursuit. It is a strong spirit who has done this injury to us, and he will try to deceive you in every way. Above all, avoid tasting food till you succeed; for if you break your fast before you see his blood, your power will be destroyed." So saying, they parted.

His son instantly set out in search of the murderer, who, seeing he was closely pursued by the brother of the slain, climbed up into one of the tallest trees and shot forth his magic arrows. Finding that his pursuer was not turned back by his arrows, he renewed his flight. When he found himself hard-pressed, and his enemy close behind him, he transformed himself into the skeleton of a moose that had been killed, whose flesh had come off his bones. He then remembered the moccasins his sister had given him, which were enchanted. Taking a pair of them, he placed them near the skeleton. "Go," said he to them, "to the end of the earth."

The moccasins then left him, and their tracks remained. Mudjikewis at length came to the skeleton of the moose, when he perceived that the track he had long been pursuing did not end there, so he continued to follow it, till he came to the end of the earth, where he found only a pair of moccasins. Mortified that he had been outwitted by following a pair of moccasins instead of the object of his revenge, he bitterly complained, resolving not to give up the pursuit, and to be more wary and wise in scrutinizing signs. He then called to mind the skeleton he met on his way, and concluded that it must be the object of his search. He retraced his steps toward the skeleton, but found, to his surprise, that it had disappeared, and that the tracks of Onwe Bahmondoong were in another direction. He now became faint with hunger, and resolved to give up the pursuit; but when he remembered the blood of his sisters, he determined again to pursue.

The other, finding he was closely pursued, now changed himself into a very old man, with two daughters, who lived in a large lodge in the center of a beautiful garden, which was filled with everything that could delight the eye or was pleasant to the taste. He made himself appear so very old as to be unable to leave his lodge, and had his daughters to bring him food and wait on him. The garden also had the appearance of ancient occupancy, and was highly cultivated.

His pursuer continued on till he was nearly starved and ready to fall. He exclaimed, "Oh! I will forget the blood of my sisters, for I am starving"; but again he thought of the blood of his sisters, and again he resolved to pursue, and be satisfied with nothing but the attainment of his right to revenge.

He went on till he came to the beautiful garden. He approached the lodge. As soon as the daughters of the owner perceived him, they ran and told their father that a stranger approached the lodge. Their father replied, "Invite him in, my children, invite him in." They quickly did so, and by the command of their father, they boiled some corn and prepared other savory food.

Mudjikewis had no suspicion of the deception. He was faint and weary with travel, and felt that he could endure fasting no longer. Without hesitancy, he partook heartily of the meal, and in so doing was overcome. All at once he seemed to forget the blood of his sisters, and even the village of his nativity. He ate so heartily as to produce drowsiness, and soon fell into a profound sleep. Onwe Bahmondoong watched his opportunity, and as soon as he found the slumbers sound, resumed his youthful form. He then drew the magic ball from his back, which turned out to be a heavy war club, with one blow of which he put an end to his pursuer, and thus vindicated his title as the Wearer of the Ball.

THE STORY OF
MIMKUDAWOGOOSK, MOOSEWOOD MAN

AWAY IN THE WOODS dwelt a young woman alone. As she had no comrade, she was obliged to depend upon her own exertions for everything; she procured her own fuel, hunted and prepared her own food; she was often lonely and sad. One day, when gathering fuel, she cut and prepared a *noosagun* —poker for the fire—of *mimkudawok*, and brought it home with her; she did not bring it into the wigwam, but stuck it up in the ground outside. Some time in the evening she heard a sound, as of a human voice outside complaining of the cold, "*Numees kaooche*—My sister, I am cold." "Come in and warm yourself, then," was the answer. "I cannot come in; I am naked," was the reply. "Wait, then, and I will put you out some clothes," she replied. This was soon done.

He donned the robes tossed out to him, and walked in—a fine-looking fellow, who took his seat as the girl's younger brother; the poker which she left standing outside the door had been thus metamorphosed, and proved a very beneficial acquisition. He was very affable and kind, and withal an expert hunter; so that all the wants of the house were bountifully supplied. He was named Mimkudawogoosk, from the moosewood tree from which he sprang.

After a time his female friend hinted to him that it would be well for him to seek a companion. "I am lonely," said she, "when you are away; I want you to fetch me a sister-in-law." To this reasonable suggestion he consented; and they talked the matter over and made arrangements for carrying their plans into execution. His sister told him where to go, and how to pass certain dangers.

"You will have to pass several nests of serpents; but you must not fight them nor meddle with them. Clap one end of your bow on the ground, and use it as a pole to assist you in jumping, and leap right straight across them."

Having received these instructions, he started on his journey. After a while his sister became lonely from the loss of his company, and resolved to follow him. To give him warning, she sang; he heard, and answered her in the same style, instructing her to go back and not come after him. She did so.

He went on till he came to a large Indian village. He followed his sister's instruction, and entered one of the meanest wigwams. There, as he expected, he found quite a bevy of pretty girls. The youngest of the group excelled in beauty; he walked up and took his seat by her side. As she remained seated, and the parents showed their acquiescence by their silence, this settled the matter and consummated the marriage. The beauty of his countenance and his manly bearing had won the heart of the maiden and the esteem of the father. But the young men of the village were indignant. The young lady had had many suitors, who had all been rejected; and now to have her so easily won by a stranger was outrageous. They determined to kill him.

Meanwhile his father-in-law told him to go out and try his hand at hunting, and when he returned successful they would prepare a festival in honor of the marriage. So he took his wife with him in his father-in-law's canoe, and following the directions given by the old man, pushed up the river to the hunting grounds, where he landed and constructed a temporary hut. He went into the hunting business in earnest. He was at home in that occupation; and before many days he had collected a large amount of fur and venison, and was prepared to return.

But a conspiracy had been formed to cut him off and rob him of his prize. A band of young men of the village, who were skilled in magical arts, had followed him and reached the place where he had pitched his hut. But now the trouble was how to proceed; they dared not attack him openly, and in wiles he might be able to outdo them. But they adopted this plan. One of them was to transform himself into a mouse, and insinuate himself under the blanket while the man was asleep, and then give him a fatal stab. But our hero was wide-awake. When the mouse approached, he quietly clapped his knee on him, all unconsciously, as he pretended, and squeezed the little fellow most lovingly.

The poor little mouse could not stand the pressure, and sang out most lustily. This aroused the wife, who, perceiving that her husband was resting his leg heavily upon some poor fellow, jogged him and tried to make him understand what was going on. But he was wonderfully dull of apprehension, and could not understand what she was saying, and managed by what seemed an all-unconscious movement to squeeze the wily foe, the small mouse, more affectionately. He did not design to kill him, however, but to frighten him and send him off. Finally he released him, and never did poor mouse make greater speed to escape. He carried the warning to his companions, and they concluded to beat a hasty retreat.

Mimkudawogoosk now prepared to return. He asked his wife if she was willing to take the canoe, with its load, back to the village alone, and allow him to go and fetch his sister; she said she was willing, and he saw her safely off. She arrived in due time, and made report to her father. All were amazed at the amount of fur and food collected in so short a time. They conveyed it all safely up to the village, and then awaited the return of the husband. After a few days he came, bringing his sister, and the feasts and sports began.

After racing and other sports, he was challenged to dive and see who could remain the longer under water. He accepted the challenge, and went out with his antagonist. "What are you?" said Mimkudawogoosk. "I am a loon," answered the other proudly; "but you—what are you?" "I am a Chigumooeech." "Ah!" Down went the divers; and after a long time the poor loon floated up to the top, and drifted dead down the river. The spectators waited a long while; and finally the Chigumooeech came up, flapped his wings exultingly, and came to land in triumph.

"Let us try a game of growing," said another. "What will you choose to be?" said Mimkudawogoosk. "I will be a pine tree," answered the other. "Very well, I am the elm," answered his rival. So at it they went. The one rose as a large white pine, encumbered with branches, which exposed him to the blasts of the hurricane. The other rose high, and naked of limbs; and when the blast came he swayed and bent, but retained his hold on the earth, while his rival was overturned and killed.

The stranger came off victorious in all the contests, and returned exulting to camp. The father-in-law was pleased and proud of him; but his other daughters—and especially the oldest—were dying of envy and rage, and the young men of the village were indignant.

Meanwhile our hero was presented by his wife with a fine little boy, and the oldest sister pretended to be very friendly, and asked permission to nurse the child. But the mother declined the proffered assistance; she was suspicious of the ill-suppressed jealousy of her sister. "I can take care of my babe myself," she told her.

After a while the father-in-law advised Mimkudawogoosk to move back to his native place. The jealousy of the hunters was deepening. They were enraged to find themselves outdone, and their glory eclipsed in everything; they determined soon to make an attempt to rid themselves of him. He took the advice, and departed. His father-in-law furnished him with a canoe and weapons, and bade him defend himself if attacked. He went, taking with him his wife, child, and sister. He had not gone far before he was pursued and overtaken. But he was found to be as good in battle as in the chase; his foes were soon killed or dispersed, and he and his family pursued the even tenor of their way to their own land.

HATONDAS, THE LISTENER, FINDS A WIFE

HATONDAS was a poor orphan boy who lived with his uncle, an old man who was very wrinkled. They lived in a lodge far removed from any settlement, so that the boy grew up not knowing how other people acted.

The old uncle became more and more abusive and threw hot coals on Hatondas seeking to mutilate him. The boy never lifted his hand to strike his uncle but received his wounds without murmuring.

After a time the uncle said, "Now is the time when you must go up the hill and listen to all kinds of sounds. When you hear one that you never heard before, return to me."

Soon Hatondas returned and imitated the notes of a chickadee. "No, no, that is not anything different!" exclaimed the old man, and straightway fell to abusing the boy.

Day by day Hatondas listened, hearing an owl, a hawk, a woodpecker, a deer, and a bear. With each report, his uncle threw coals of fire down his shirt or beat him on the face with a paddle.

One morning he heard a song, and listening, heard his own name called out.

Listening with strained ears, he caught the words, "Hatondas, Hatondas, I am coming to marry you now. You hear this song, so make ready."

Quickly Hatondas ran to his uncle and reported what he had heard. The uncle now became greatly enraged and threw all manner of filth at Hatondas, then fell to beating his face with brands from the fire. When he had finished scolding the boy, the uncle washed his own face and put on his best clothing. Then he greased his hair and tied his cheeks back with a string, tying the string behind his head under his braid, to give the appearance of smooth cheeks.

Hatondas could not sleep that night, for his bed was infested with vermin his uncle had put into it, and it was foul with refuse that his uncle customarily threw there to make Hatondas an unsavory person.

Morning came, and all kinds of birds began to sing. Hatondas listened as before, and at sunrise he arose and went up the hill where he was accustomed to wait listening for the sounds which his uncle ordered him to report.

Again he heard the sound of distant singing, and it was a woman's voice. Now Hatondas began to feel very sad, for his appearance bothered him. He was dirty beyond all measure, and his hair was encrusted with dried refuse. So he felt very lonely and without friends.

Soon again he heard the song and saw a woman a long way off. She seemed calling his name, so he listened more intently. Then he saw a fine-looking young woman running toward him. As she neared him, he saw that she had a basket of marriage bread. She looked at him in great pity and asked him to lead her to his lodge.

When they entered the lodge, the young woman greeted the uncle, and said, "I have been sent by my mother to find a man here."

"Oh, I am the man you are looking for," said the uncle, at the same time ordering Hatondas to leave the lodge. "I am so sorry my nephew is filthy," said the uncle, in his most gracious language. "He is very dirty and utterly no good."

"He is the man I have come to marry," said the young woman.

Then the young woman took out a pot of oil and heated it, and calling Hatondas to her, cleaned his head, lifting off a great mass of filthy crusts. At this the uncle was furious, and demanded that the young woman leave the boy alone. She continued her work until she had cleansed him, when she said, "Oh, he will make a good husband when I clean him!"

"You must marry me," cried the uncle. "I have been waiting for you many years. See, my side of the lodge is very clean, and you could never sleep where Hatondas is accustomed to lie." But the young woman repulsed him, and went out into the woods with Hatondas, whereupon the old man burst into great rage, breaking his cheek strings and making himself look hideous. "Oh, I knew it would come," he screeched, "but I did not think so soon."

When the young woman had found a hollow log, she required Hatondas to crawl into it, and then through to the other end. When he emerged, he was clean and healed of his scars.

That night they were married, but at midnight a queer sound awoke Hatondas. He rose up and listened. Then the young wife spoke.

"He is upon us!" she cried, and leaping up, she called Hatondas to flee with her.

Jumping upon the fireplace, she scattered the glowing embers about the room, and in a moment the lodge was in flames.

Together the two ran to the top of the hill to the rear of the lodge. The young wife drew from her garment a small bundle and dropped it on the ground. Taking the whip she struck the bundle a smart blow. A tiny growl issued from the skin wrappings and grew louder as she continued to ply her switch. Presently a dog burst from the bundle and stood wagging his tail at her feet. She continued to lash it, and with each stroke the dog grew larger, and finally so large that both she and Hatondas were able to mount its back and send it dashing onward at great speed.

After some time they arrived on the shores of a vast expanse of water. The wife patted the dog back into the bundle and dropped it in her pouch, and with her husband leaped into a large canoe that lay moored to the shore. Untying the line, each grasped a paddle and swept the canoe out into the lake. They had gone but a short distance when a loud snort caused them to look back, and there on the shore was a gigantic bear in the act of casting a long fishline, and even as they looked it fell, wrapping around the stern of the canoe. The craft stopped in its course with a sudden jerk and then began to speed backward to the shore.

"Quick, Hatondas," exclaimed his wife, "empty your pipe on the line," and Hatondas obeyed with surprising alacrity. The line snapped and with a sweep of the paddle his wife sent the canoe back into its track.

Foiled in his attempt to capture the pair, the enraged monster pawed up the sand and pebbles. Swelling to an enormous size, he thrust his mouth into the water and gulped it down in such immense quantities that the lake changed its current and flowed toward the mouth of the monster. Death seemed certain to the young couple, for the canoe was drawn with great rapidity toward the beast. But ever resourceful, the young woman steadied herself, aimed and threw a round white stone directly at the creature's belly. It struck him with great force causing him to jerk up his head with a roar of pain and then belch the waters back into the lake. In the swiftly outflowing stream, spurred on by the paddles, the canoe shot back to its former course.

The great bear was furious with disappointment and roared, "You cannot escape me; soon I will catch you. I am Nia-gwa-he!" and then began to blow his icy breath upon the water. Ice commenced to form, and when he judged it sufficiently thick, he galloped out over the surface of the lake. "You cannot escape me!" he bellowed, "I am Nia-gwa-he!"

The canoe stood fast in the ice, and doom seemed certain to its inmates.

"Don't be downcast, Hatondas," said the wife, "only trust me."

The wife knelt in the bottom of the canoe where she had a little fire burning and a pot of water. She was apparently resigned to the fate from which there seemed no escape. Then when the bear was almost upon them, she stood upright and flung a kettle of steaming water at his feet. The beast stopped with a sudden jerk, as the clay pot broke into fragments, and the water splashed upon the ice. This momentary halt was fatal, for the water softened the ice, and the monster sank beneath the waters and disappeared. The ice vanished, and the canoe sped on once again.

Late in the day the canoe grated against the base of a high cliff that rose perpendicularly from the water. The wife called up to the top. A woman leaned over the edge far above, and seeing the couple below, dropped down two pairs of claw mittens. These Hatondas and his wife fastened to their hands, and with their aid, made their way slowly and cautiously to the summit.

The wife's sister greeted the bridal pair, and lead the way to a spacious lodge where a savory supper awaited them.

ORE-KA-RAHR, THE DEER GUARDIAN

A LONG TIME AGO, as the tribe were on their summer hunt, a man and his wife got to quarreling. They had a child, a boy about ten months old. It was while they were traveling along, going from one camp to another, that they began to quarrel. At length the wife became very angry, and threw the baby to the man, saying, "You take that baby. It belongs to you, for it is a man child. I am not going to nurse it for you any longer." Then she went away.

The man took the child and carried it along with him. He felt very bad-ly, on his own account and on account of his child. He was so unhappy that he almost wanted to kill himself. He was so poor-minded because it was a disgrace that he, being a man, should be obliged to take care of his child until it was grown up, and he had no female relatives to whom he could turn it over to be reared. So he was very unhappy, and determined to leave the tribe and wander off alone, far from his people.

He did so. He carried the child on his back, as a woman does. When it cried for its mother's milk, he had none to give it. He could only cry with it. He hated to kill the child, or to leave it behind to die on the prairie. He wandered off to the south. He traveled on for a time, until he came near to where the buffalo were. By this time, the child had changed from a very fat baby to a very thin one, because it had not been nursed. When he got to the buffalo, he killed a cow, and took its udder, and while it was fresh he let the child suck it, until it became sour. Then he killed another cow, and did the same thing.

In every way, he did the best he could to nourish the child. Sometimes he would get a slice of meat, and half cook it, and let the child suck the juice. The child began to improve, and to get a little stronger. In this way he supported it for quite a long time, and it did pretty well, and at last it got used to this food, and became strong and well. By this time he had gone a long way.

At length he found that the child could sit up alone. Then he began to give it all sorts of playthings, so that it could amuse itself. First he made for it a little bow and some arrows, and taught it how to use them. He made other things for the child to play with, and at last it got to be contented playing alone. Then the father would leave the child for a few minutes, and go off a little way, perhaps to the top of a hill near by, to look off over the country; but he would look back at the child every few steps to see that it was all right. When he would come back, he would find the child safe, playing, well contented. After a while, he got so that he would leave it for about an hour, and when he came back, find it safe and contented, playing. By this time the child had begun to walk. Finally the father went off once for half a day, and when he came back, he found the child playing about safe. It did not seem to mind much about the father's being absent. About this time he killed a buffalo cow, and made some dried meat, and put it in a certain place, and told the child when it was hungry to go there and get a piece.

He now went off and was gone a whole day, and when he came back at

night the child was safe. Finally he made his preparations and went off to stay overnight, and be gone two days. He did so, and when he came back, the boy was asleep. A second time he went away and was absent for two days, going quite a long distance. When he came back he found that the child was painted with white clay. The father thought this was strange. He said to himself, "Something must have come and talked to my child, and is taking care of him while I am gone."

When he came back the third time after a two days' journey, he found that the child had about his neck a string of *pahut*, wild currants. The fourth long journey he took lasted three days, and when he returned, he found his boy still wearing this same string of beads, and with a feather tied on his head. Now the father knew that something was looking after his child while he was away, and when he went off, he would pray for the child. He would say, "*No-a*, whatever it is that is taking pity on my child, also take pity on me."

The child had now grown so large that it could talk with him, and one day it said, "Father, you go away, and you be gone for four days; I will be all right here. When you come back you will find me safe."

The man went. He started to go way down south, to be gone for four days. After he had been gone two days and two nights, he saw a signal smoke and went toward it. As he raised his head and peeped over a hill before crossing it, he saw, far off, a lot of people and horses coming toward the river which lay between him and them. He lay on the hill a long time, watching to see where they would camp. When they had made camp, he went into a ravine, and crept down close to the camp, until he could see that it was just one lodge, and that about it was a whole herd of horses. He waited until evening, and then went over to the lodge. It was after dark when he went. The lodge was all surrounded by horses; everywhere nothing but horses, there were so many. He crept close to the lodge, and looked in through an opening by the door, and saw lying down opposite the door a great big man, and on either side a woman, only three persons in all. As he looked at these persons, he thought he recognized one of the women. He kept looking at her, and at last he remembered who she was, and that she had been captured long ago from the Pawnees. Her people were still living. The man was a Comanche.

While the Pawnee was watching the man inside the lodge asked for something, and the captive woman stood up to go out of the lodge, and the Pawnee stepped to one side, out of sight. The woman came out into the darkness, and went out among the horses. The Pawnee stepped up behind her very softly, and put his hand on her shoulder, and said to her in Pawnee, "Friend, do you belong to my tribe?" The woman started to scream, but he put his hand on her mouth, and said to her, "Be quiet. Keep still. Do not call out." She answered him, "Yes, I belong to your tribe." Then she said in a very low voice that shook, for she was afraid, "Do you belong to my tribe?" The man said, "Yes." Then he asked her, "Who is that other woman that I see in the lodge?" She answered him, "She also belongs to our tribe, and is a prisoner." Then the man said, "You just wait and keep still. I am going to kill that man." The woman said, "That is good That is good. This man is the biggest man of all the Comanches. He has come first to this place, and all the rest of the Comanches are coming here to meet him. I am glad that my people are living, and that I am going back to see them once more. Do not fail to kill him. I will tell the other woman to be ready, that our friend is here, and we will wait and watch."

When the woman went into the lodge, she whispered to the other woman, and said, "Be ready. A friend who belongs to our tribe is here. Take your hatchet, and be prepared to kill our husband."

The two women waited, and the Pawnee made ready to shoot the Comanche with his bow and arrow. The woman had said to him, "Push aside the door a little and be ready." He made a little bit of an opening by the door, just big enough to let an arrow pass through, and when the time came he let it go. *U-ra-rish!* the arrow flew straight, and pierced the Comanche through the heart. So he died, and the Pawnee counted coup on him and took his scalp.

The women felt so glad to meet a friend that they put their arms around the man and patted him. They were going back home to see their relations. They asked him, "How many of you are here?" He answered, "I am alone." They were surprised.

They took down the lodge, and packed everything on the horses, and drove off the herd, leaving the dead body of the enemy in the camp. All night they traveled, and all the next day; and as they were going, he told them how it came about that he was alone. They told him that there were about three hundred head of horses in the herd that they had with them. When they had come pretty close to where he had left the child, he told them about the boy being there all alone; and the women just ran their horses to get to the boy; whichever got there first, he should be hers. When they came to the boy, they took him in their arms and petted him, and took him as their own.

Now the father was no longer sad. He had recovered two captured women, had killed his enemy, and had taken a lot of horses.

They went on, and traveled far, and at length, one night, they came to the Pawnee tribe, and camped with them. The horses surrounded the lodge, you could just see the top of it over their backs. The next morning all the people wondered who these strangers could be. They found out that the man and child, who were lost, had returned, and with them two women, captured long ago by the Comanches. So there was great joy in the tribe. Then the man gave his relations many horses. In those days the Pawnees had not many horses, and it seems that this man brought good luck in horses to the tribe. Ever since that time they have had many horses. The mother of the child came to see it, she was so glad it was alive, but she was whipped out of the lodge.

The child grew to be a man, and was wealthy. After he had grown up, he told his father that ever since he could remember anything, a buck deer had talked to him, and taken care of him; that it had saved them, and brought them good fortune. In order that Ore-ka-rahr might be remembered, he established a dance, called the deer dance, which has been kept up to this day.

Many wonderful things happened to this same young man. Once he went on a war party against the Cheyennes, and stole some horses from them. The Cheyennes followed and overtook them, and they had a great fight. The first man killed was this young man. He was very brave, and the Cheyennes cut him up into small pieces, but that night it lightninged and thundered and rained, and soon after the storm was over, the young man came walking into the camp alive. He was all scarred over, where he had been cut up, but he had come to life because the deer had looked after him. He lived long to show the scars of the battles he had been through.

CAUGHT BY A HAIR-STRING

AWAY IN THE WOODS there was a large Indian town on the outskirts of which resided two old people who had but two children, and they were daughters. Both were very fair and beautiful, but they were shy and coy, and did not allow themselves to be seen by everybody. They rejected all offers of marriage.

The chief of the village had a fine son who was expected to take the office when his father should abdicate or die. This young man knew of the two belles of the village, and sought the hand of one of them in marriage.

He interested his father and some of his friends in the matter, and in due time they repaired to the lodge where the girls resided, to enter upon negotiations. The girls kept themselves out of sight behind a screen. The evening passed pleasantly away. They ate, drank, and engaged in games; in due time the old chief asked of the father the hand of one of his daughters for his son.

He replied that he would give an answer the next day.

In the meantime the young women, who had, of course, heard all that had passed, were questioned as to their wishes in the matter. They decided in the negative; and word to that effect was sent to the old chief, the father himself carrying the message.

Now it happened that there resided in the village a fellow who was ill-looking and stupid, a poor hand at every kind of work. He, hearing of the ill success of the young chief, said jocosely, "I could get one of these girls, if I chose." Forthwith some of his companions proposed to accompany him, and suggested that they should go that very evening, go in suddenly upon them, just as they were beginning their evening meal. This plan was carried out, and the girls had no time to jump behind their screen, so that the boys had a fair opportunity to look into their beautiful faces. They were invited to eat; they said they had eaten their suppers, but yielded to the invitation of the old people.

After supper they engaged in various games, one of which was called the *Mimgwodokadijik*. This was played by hiding in the ashes a small ring which was fished for by the parties, who had hidden their faces when the ring was secreted. First, one would plunge a pointed stick in the ashes, and

163

if he missed it, the other would take the stick and try. The one who found
the ring won the game.

Thus the evening passed, but not a word was hinted respecting matri-
mony, nor did the young women speak a single word to anyone. When it
grew late, the visitors went home, and the young man who had boasted
jestingly about his confidence of success was somewhat rallied by his comrades upon his failure.

Time passed, and the same young man went into the woods hunting with
a companion from whom he was separated during the course of the day.
He met an old woman wrinkled and bent down, whose hair was adorned
with a great display of hair-strings (*sagulobe*), which hung down over her
shoulders, binding up her hair and then trailing down to her feet. "Where
are you going?" she asked the young man. "Nowhere in particular," he replied. "Where are you from, grandmother?" he asked in return. "I have
not come far," she replied. "But look you here, are you anxious to marry
one of those beauties?" "Oh, by no means!" he replied. "But I can assist you,
and tell you how you can gain her affections and obtain her for your wife,
if you say the word," she continued. He inquired how he was to proceed.
"Take this," said she, handing him one of the hair-strings that hung in profusion over her shoulders, "roll it up and carry it in your pouch for a while,
and then watch your opportunity and toss it on her back. But take care that
she does not see you, and that no one knows of the matter but yourself."

So he took the *sagulobe*, and did as directed. Selecting a few of his comrades, he called on the parties, taking care to bolt in suddenly upon them
just as they were about to begin their supper. The girls had not time to hide.
The parents treated the visitors with great kindness and attention, and soon
an opportunity occurred to toss the *sagulobe* on the back of one of the girls.
Soon after this the young men retired to their homes.

A day or two later, as the young man was walking alone in the woods,
he saw coming toward him the girl to whom he had made love by tossing
at her the *sagulobe*. The old woman who had given him the string was a
witch, and the string was a magical snare that had caught the heart of the
girl, and she had gone out to meet the object of her affections. She first addressed him. "*Tame aleen?*—Whither are you going?" "I am going hunting," he answered. "But whence have you come, and what are you doing out

here alone? Are you lost?". "Oh, no, I am not lost," she answered. "You would better return home," he said, "and I will go with you and tell your parents that I have found you wandering in the woods, not knowing the way home."

To this proposal she agreed. When they arrived, he said to her parents, "I found your daughter lost in the woods, and have brought her home to you." Whereupon the father inquired of the young man if he would like to take her to be his wife. He answered in the affirmative, and without any ceremony save a festival, the matter was settled.

Some time after this the husband inquired of his wife, "Where did you get that pretty *sagulobe*?" "I found it in my *ntuboonk*, the place where I was accustomed to sit in the wigwam."

This man now felt disposed to assist the young chief in obtaining the other girl. So he went and inquired if he was still desirous of marrying her. Learning that this was the case, he told him how he could succeed. So they went into the woods together, and soon met the friendly fairy, who questioned the chief as she had questioned the other, gave him a *sagulobe*, and told him what to do with it. He proceeded according to directions, visited the lodge, bolting in suddenly at the evening meal. Watching his opportunity, he tossed the magic string on the back of the girl. It dropped down on the boughs, and was picked up in due time and exercised its magical influence over the heart of the finder, leading her to fall desperately in love with the young chief. He in the meantime had gone home and kept himself very close for a few days.

When he went out hunting, he met the object of his search, as the other had done, escorted her home, and told her parents that she was lost; though in answer to his inquiries on that point when they met, she had assured him that she was not lost. Her father inquired if he would like to take her home with him. He replied in the affirmative, and led her away to his father's lodge. A great festival followed, and the young men prepared for their young chief a large and spacious wigwam. The two men whose wives were sisters were on the best of terms and were much together.

One day the young chief asked his friend if he would like to learn to be a swift runner. He said, "I would." "I will tell you how you can do it," said the other. "Go, gather some feathers, and let them fly when the wind blows hard, and run after them. You will soon be able to outstrip the wind, and the art once acquired will be permanent. You will be able to run swiftly ever after." He went and tried it, and found that it was even so.

Having thus by the aid of magic and practice acquired the power of fleet running, he made further progress. The young chief showed him how he could become strong, and improve his eyesight and his skill in discovering animals in hunting. "Dress yourself up in the ugliest-looking clothes you can find, putting them on outside your ordinary dress. Fight the first man you can provoke to attack you. When he seizes you, slip out of your rags and run. Then you can escape after that from any man or beast that may get you in his grasp."

This was done, and he soon met a crazy man, whom he insulted and provoked. As soon as he was attacked, he slipped out from his harlequin dress, which he left in his assailant's hands, who imagined the wearer to be in it. So he beat it furiously and left it for dead, the other looking on and laughing the while, but at a safe distance.

"Take a handful of moose's hair," the young chief said to his friend, "clasp it in a roll firmly between your thumb and fingers, then hold it up in the wind and blow the hair away. You will be able to see all the moose that are about you for a long distance around. Take the hair of any other animal and do the same thing with it, the effect will be the same: you will see these animals, wherever they are." He took his lesson and put it in practice, and the result was as predicted.

Some time after this, in his rambles he entered a house. The man of the house was away, but the mistress was at home. He inquired where her husband was. She pointed to a field, and told him that he was out there. He looked, but could see nothing except a flock of geese.

He now asked the young chief how he could learn to see fishes. He was directed to gather all kinds of fishbones, to burn them, pound them to dust, and blow them up into the wind. This he did; he could now see the fish and call them to him.

He was specially interested in the whales. They are strong, and he desired to acquire physical strength. So he burned a piece of *bootupawigun*, whalebone, pounded it fine, and then, taking his stand on a rock that juts out into the sea, blew the dust away seaward. He immediately saw an immense number of whales in the distance. Again he blew his whalebone dust toward them, and they moved toward him. The young chief assured him that whales never die unless they are killed, and that with their assistance he could obtain a long life that should border on immortality.

Seven times he repeated the process, and one large, powerful monster came and placed himself alongside the rock on which he stood, and inquired what was wanted. "I want you to make me strong," said the man. "Very well," the whale answered, "put your hand in my mouth, and you will find what you want." So he thrust his hand in the monster's mouth, and feeling around found a golden key. "Take that, and you can accomplish whatever you desire. It will defend you against the attacks of enemies, wild beasts, sickness, or any other calamity." So he took the key and went home.

Everything prospered in the place. The inhabitants were well supplied with food; the animals multiplied and could be called right up to their dwellings. They were protected from the attacks of hostile Indians, and so increased and multiplied.

By and by the father-in-law became old and feeble, and the young chief told his brother-in-law that the old man was ill, and asked if he could not be made well and young again. But the other objected to this, and thought that they would better let Nature take her course.

After a while the old chief died, and his son succeeded him. He offered to abdicate in favor of Wechoosul, his wife's brother-in-law. The latter declined the offer, but he rendered his friend all due assistance as long as he lived.

VI

SPIRITS AND THE SUPERNATURAL

THE BOY WHO SAW A-TI-US

MANY YEARS AGO the Pawnees started on their winter hunt. The buffalo were scarce, and the people could get hardly any meat. It was very cold, and the snow lay deep on the ground. The tribe traveled southward, and crossed the Republican, but still found no buffalo. They had eaten all the dried meat and all the corn that they had brought with them, and now they were starving. The sufferings of the people were great, and the little ones began to die of hunger. Now they began to eat their robes, and parfleches, and moccasins.

There was in the tribe a boy about sixteen years old, who was all alone and was very poor. He had no relations who could take care of him, and he lived with a woman whose husband had been killed by the Sioux. She had two children, a boy and a girl; and she had a good heart, and was sorry for the poor boy. In this time of famine, these people had scarcely anything to eat, and whenever the boy got hold of any food, he gave it to the woman, who divided it among them all.

The tribe kept traveling southward looking for buffalo, but they had to go very slowly, because they were all so weak. Still they found no buffalo, and each day the young men that were sent out to look for them climbed the highest hills, and came back at night, and reported that they could only see the white prairie covered with snow. All this time little ones were dying of hunger, and the men and women were growing weaker every day.

The poor boy suffered with the rest, and at last he became so weak that he hardly could keep up with the camp, even though it moved very slowly. One morning he was hardly able to help the old woman pack the lodge, and after it had been packed, he went back to the fire, and sat down beside it, and watched the camp move slowly off across the valley, and up over the bluffs. He thought to himself, "Why should I go on? I can't keep up for more than a day or two longer anyhow. I may as well stay here and die." So he gathered together the ends of the sticks that lay by the fire, and put them on the coals, and spread his hands over the blaze, and rubbed them together and got warm, and then lay down by the fire. Pretty soon he went to sleep.

When he came to himself, it was about the middle of the day, and as he looked toward the sky he saw two spots there between him and the sun, and he wondered what they were. As he looked at them, they became larger and larger, and at last he could see that they were birds; and by and by, as they came still nearer, he saw that they were two swans. The swans kept coming lower and lower, and at last they alighted on the ground right by the fire, and walked up to where the boy lay. He was so weak he could not get up, and they came to him, one on each side, and stooped down, and pushed their shoulders under him, and raised him up and put him on their backs, and then spread their broad wings, and flew away upward. Then the boy went to sleep again.

When he awoke he was lying on the ground before a very big lodge. It was large and high, and on it were painted pictures of many strange animals, in beautiful colors. The boy had never seen such a fine lodge. The air was warm here, and he felt stronger than before. He tried to raise himself up, and after trying once or twice he got on his feet, and walked to the door of the lodge, and went in. Opposite the door sat A-ti-us. He was very large and very handsome, and his face was kind and gentle. He was dressed in beautiful clothes, and wore a white buffalo robe. Behind him, from the lodge poles, hung many strange weapons. Around the lodge on one side sat many chiefs, and doctors, and warriors. They all wore fine clothes of white buckskin, embroidered with beautifully colored quills. Their robes were all of beaver skin, very beautiful.

When the boy entered the lodge, A-ti-us said to him, "*Looah, pi-rau, we-tus suks-pit*—Welcome, my son, and sit down." And he said to one of the warriors, "Give him something to eat." The warrior took down a beautifully painted sack of parfleche, and took his knife from its sheath, and cut off a piece of dried meat about as big as one's two fingers, and a piece of fat about the same size, and gave them to the boy. The boy, who was so hungry, thought that this was not very much to give to one who was starving, but took it, and began to eat. He put the fat on the lean, and cut the pieces off, and ate for a long time. But after he had eaten for a long time, the pieces of meat remained the same size; and he ate all that he wanted, and then put the pieces down, still the same size.

After the boy had finished eating, A-ti-us spoke to him. He told him that he had seen the sufferings of his people, and had been sorry for them; and then he told the boy what to do. So he kept the boy there for a little while longer, and gave him some fine new clothing and weapons. And then he told one of the warriors to send the boy back; and the warrior led him out of the lodge to where the swans were standing near the entrance, and the boy got onto their backs. Then the warrior put his hand on his face, and pressed his eyelids together, and the boy went to sleep. And by and by the boy awoke, and found himself alone by the fire. The fire had gone out, but the ground was still covered with snow, and it was very cold.

Now the boy felt strong, and he stood up, and started running along the trail which the camp had taken. That night after dark he overtook the camp, for they traveled very slowly, and he walked through the village till he came to the lodge where the woman was, and went in. She was surprised to see him in his new clothes, and looking so well and strong, and told him to sit down. There was a little fire in the lodge, and the boy could see that the woman was cutting up something into small pieces with her knife.

The boy said to her, "What are you doing?"

She answered, "I am going to boil our last piece of robe. After we have eaten this, there will be nothing left, and we can then only die."

The boy said nothing, but watched her for a little while, and then stood up and went out of the lodge. The door had hardly fallen behind him, when the woman heard a buffalo coughing, and then the breaking of the crisp snow, as if a heavy weight was settling on it. In a moment the boy lifted the lodge door, and came in, and sat down by the fire, and said to the woman, "Go out and bring in some meat." The woman looked at him, for she was astonished, but he said nothing; so she went out, and there in the snow by the side of the lodge was a fat buffalo cow. Then the woman's heart was glad. She skinned the cow, and brought some of the meat into the lodge and cooked it, and they all ate and were satisfied. The woman was good, so she sent her son to the lodges of all her relations, and all her friends, and told them all to come next morning to her lodge to a feast, "for," she said, "I have plenty of meat."

So the next morning all her relations and all her friends came, so many that they could not all get into the lodge; some had to stand outside, but they ate with her. She cooked the meat of the cow for them, and they ate until it was all gone, and they were satisfied. And after they had done eating, they lighted their pipes and prayed, saying, "*A-ti-us, we-tus kittah-we*—Father, you are the ruler."

While they were smoking, the poor boy called the woman's son to him, and pointed to a high hill near the camp, and said, "*Looah, suks-kus-sis-pah ti-rah hah-tur*—Run hard to the top of that hill, and tell me what you see." So the boy threw off his robe, and smoothed back his hair, and started, and ran as hard as he could over the snow to the top of the hill. When he got there, he shaded his eyes with his hand, for the sun shone bright on the snow and blinded him, and he looked east, and west, and north, and south, but he could see nothing but the shining white snow on the prairie. After he had looked all ways, he ran back as hard as he could to the village. When he came to the lodge, he went to the poor boy, and said to him, "I don't see anything but the snow." The poor boy said, "You don't look good. Go again." So the boy started again, and ran as hard as he could to the hilltop, and when he got there, panting, he looked all ways, long and carefully, but still he could see nothing but the snow. So he turned and ran back to the village, and told the poor boy again that he saw nothing. The boy said, "You don't look good."

Then he took his bow in his hand, and put his quiver on his back, and drew his robe up under his arm so that he could run well, and started himself, and ran as hard as he could to the top of the hill. When he got there he looked off to the south, and there, as far as he could see, the plain was black with buffalo struggling in the deep snow. And he turned to the village, and signaled them with his robe that buffalo were in sight. In a few minutes all the Pawnees had seized their bows and arrows, and were running toward him, and the women fixed the travois, and took their knives, and followed.

The boy waited on the hilltop until the warriors came up, and then they went down to the buffalo, running on the snow. The buffalo could not get away on account of the deep snow, and the Pawnees made a great killing. Plenty of fat meat they got, enough to last them until the summer hunt, and plenty of warm winter robes. They did not have to move any farther, but stayed right there, killing meat and drying it until they were all fat and strong again.

And the poor boy became a great doctor in the tribe, and got rich.

Before this the Pawnees had always had a woman chief, but when the woman who was chief died, she named the poor boy as her successor, and the people made him head chief of the tribe.

THE STAR FAMILY, OR THE CELESTIAL SISTERS

WAUPEE, the White Hawk, lived in a remote part of the forest, where animals and birds were abundant. Every day he returned from the chase with the reward of his toil, for he was one of the most skillful and celebrated hunters of his tribe. With a tall, manly form, and the fire of youth beaming from his eye, there was no forest too gloomy for him to penetrate, and no track made by the numerous kinds of birds and beasts which he could not follow.

One day he penetrated beyond any point which he had before visited. He traveled through an open forest, which enabled him to see a great distance. At length he beheld a light breaking through the foliage, which made him sure that he was on the borders of a prairie. It was a wide plain covered with grass and flowers. After walking some time without a path, he suddenly came to a ring worn through the sod, as if it had been made by footsteps following a circle. But what excited his surprise was that there was no path leading to or from it. Not the least trace of footsteps could be found, even in a crushed leaf or broken twig.

He thought he would hide himself, and lie in wait to see what this circle meant. Presently he heard the faint sounds of music in the air. He looked up in the direction they came from, and saw a small object descending from above. At first it looked like a mere speck, but rapidly increased, and as it came down, the music became plainer and sweeter. It assumed the form of a basket, and was filled with twelve sisters of the most lovely forms and enchanting beauty. As soon as the basket touched the ground, they leaped out, and began to dance round the magic ring, striking, as they did so, a shining ball as we strike the drum.

Waupee gazed upon their graceful forms and motions from his place of concealment. He admired them all, but was most pleased with the youngest. Unable longer to restrain his admiration, he rushed out and endeavored to seize her. But the sisters, with the quickness of birds, the moment they descried the form of a man, leaped back into the basket and were drawn up into the sky.

Regretting his ill luck and indiscretion, he gazed till he saw them disappear, and then said, "They are gone, and I shall see them no more." He returned to his solitary lodge, but found no relief to his mind. Next day he went back to the prairie, and took his station near the ring; but in order to deceive the sisters, he assumed the form of an opossum.

He had not waited long, when he saw the wicker car descend, and heard the same sweet music. They commenced the same sportive dance, and seemed even more beautiful and graceful than before. He crept slowly toward the ring, but the instant the sisters saw him they were startled, and sprang into their car. It rose but a short distance, when one of the elder sisters spoke. "Perhaps," said she, "it is come to show us how the game is played by mortals." "Oh, no!" the youngest replied. "Quick, let us ascend." And all joining in a chant, they rose out of sight.

Waupee returned to his own form again, and walked sorrowfully back to his lodge. But the night seemed a very long one, and he went back betimes the next day. He reflected upon the sort of plan to follow to secure success. He found an old stump near by, in which there were a number of mice. He thought their small form would not create alarm, and accordingly assumed it. He brought the stump and set it up near the ring. The sisters came down and resumed their sport. "But see," cried the youngest sister, "that stump was not there before." She ran affrighted toward the car. They only smiled, and gathering round the stump, struck it in jest, when out ran the mice, and Waupee among the rest. They killed them all but one, which was pursued by the youngest sister; but just as she had raised her stick to kill it, the form of Waupee arose, and he clasped his prize in his arms. The other eleven sprang to their basket and were drawn up to the skies.

He exerted all his skill to please his bride and win her affections. He wiped the tears from her eyes. He related his adventures in the chase. He dwelt upon the charms of life on the earth. He was incessant in his attentions, and picked out the way for her to walk as he led her gently toward his lodge. He felt his heart glow with joy as she entered it, and from that moment he was one of the happiest of men.

Winter and summer passed rapidly away, and their happiness was increased by the addition of a beautiful boy to their lodge. She was a daughter of one of the stars, and as the scenes of earth began to pall, she sighed to revisit her father. But she was obliged to hide these feelings from her husband. She remembered the charm that would carry her up, and took occasion, while Waupee was engaged in the chase, to construct a wicker basket, which she kept concealed. In the meantime, she collected such rarities from the earth as she thought would please her father, as well as the most dainty kinds of food. When all was in readiness, she went out one day, while Waupee was absent, to the charmed ring, taking her little son with her. As soon as they got into the car, she commenced her song and the basket rose.

As the song was wafted by the wind, it caught her husband's ear. It was a voice which he well knew, and he instantly ran to the prairie. But he could not reach the ring before he saw his wife and child ascend. He lifted up his voice in loud appeals, but they were unavailing. The basket still went up. He watched it till it became a small speck, and finally it vanished in the sky. He then bent his head down to the ground, and was miserable.

Waupee bewailed his loss through a long winter and a long summer. But he found no relief. He mourned his wife's loss sorely, but his son's still more. In the meantime, his wife had reached her home in the stars, and almost forgot, in the blissful employments there, that she had left a husband on the earth. She was reminded of this by the presence of her son, who, as he grew up, became anxious to visit the scene of his birth.

His grandfather said to his daughter one day, "Go, my child, and take your son down to his father, and ask him to come up and live with us. But tell him to bring along a specimen of each kind of bird and animal he kills in the chase." She accordingly took the boy and descended. Waupee, who was ever near the enchanted spot, heard her voice as she came down the sky. His heart beat with impatience as he saw her form and that of his son, and they were soon clasped in his arms.

He heard the message of the Star Chief, and began to hunt with the greatest activity, that he might collect the present. He spent whole nights, as well as days, in searching for every curious and beautiful bird or animal. He only preserved a tail, foot, or wing of each, to identify the species; and, when all was ready, they went to the circle and were carried up.

Great joy was manifested on their arrival at the starry plains. The Star Chief invited all his people to a feast, and, when they had assembled, he proclaimed aloud that each one might take of the earthly gifts such as he liked best. A very strange confusion immediately arose. Some chose a foot, some a wing, some a tail, and some a claw. Those who selected tails or claws were changed into animals, and ran off; the others assumed the form of birds, and flew away.

Waupee chose a white hawk's feather. His wife and son followed his example, and each one became a white hawk. Pleased with his transformation and new vitality, the chief spread out gracefully his white wings, and followed by his wife and son, descended to the earth, where the species are still to be found.

WEENG, THE SPIRIT OF SLEEP

SLEEP IS PERSONIFIED by the Ojibwas under the name of Weeng. The power of sound sleep is executed by a peculiar class of gnome-like beings called *Weengs*. These subordinate creations, although invisible to the human eye, are each armed with a tiny war club, a *puggamaugun*, with which they nimbly climb up the forehead and knock the drowsy person on the head, on which sleepiness is immediately produced. If the first blow is insufficient, another is given, until the eyelids close, and a sound sleep is produced.

It is the constant duty of these little agents to put everyone to sleep whom they encounter—men, women, and children. And they are found secreted around the bed, or on small protuberances of the bark of the Indian lodges. They hide themselves in the *Gushkeepitaugun*, the smoking pouch of the hunter, and when he sits down to light his pipe in the woods are ready to fly out and exert their sleep-compelling power. If they succeed, the game is suffered to pass, and the hunter obliged to return to his lodge without a reward.

In general, however, they are represented to possess friendly dispositions, seeking constantly to restore vigor and elasticity to the exhausted body. But being without judgment, their power is sometimes exerted at the hazard of reputation, or even life. Sleep may be induced in a person carelessly floating in his canoe, above a falls; or in a war party, on the borders of an enemy country; or in a female, without the protection of the lodge circle. Although their peculiar season of action is in the night, they are also alert during the day.

While the forms of these gnomes are believed to be those of *ininees*, little fairy men, the figure of Weeng himself is unknown, and it is not certain that he has ever been seen. Most of what is known on this subject is derived from Iagoo, who related that, going out one day with his dogs to hunt, he passed through a wide range of thicket, where he lost his dogs. He became much alarmed, for they were faithful animals, and he was greatly attached to them. He called out, and made every exertion to recover them in vain. At length he came to a spot where he found them asleep, having incautiously run near the residence of Weeng. After great exertion he aroused them, but not without having felt the power of sleep himself.

As he cast his eyes up from the place where the dogs were lying, he saw the spirit of sleep sitting on the branch of a tree. He was in the shape of a giant insect, or *monetos*, with many wings on his back, which made a low deep murmuring sound, like distant falling water. But Iagoo himself, being a very great liar and braggart, little credit was given to his story.

Weeng is not only the giver of sleep, but it seems he is also the author of dullness, which gives the word an ironical use. If an orator fails, he is said

179

to be struck by Weeng. If a warrior lingers, he has ventured too near the sleepy god. If children begin to nod or yawn, the Indian mother looks up smilingly, and says, "They have been struck by Weeng," and puts them to bed.

THE GHOST BRIDE

IN A PLACE where we used to have a village, a young woman died just before the tribe started on the hunt. When she died, they dressed her in her finest clothes, and buried her, and soon after this the tribe started on the hunt.

A party of young men had gone off to visit another tribe, and they did not get back until after this girl had died and the tribe had left the village. Most of this party did not go back to the village, but met the tribe and went with them on the hunt. Among the young men who had been away was one who had loved this girl who had died. He went back alone to the village. It was empty and silent, but before he reached it, he could see, far off, someone sitting on top of a lodge. When he came near, he saw it was the girl he loved.

He did not know that she had died, and he wondered to see her there alone, for the time was coming when he would be her husband and she his wife. When she saw him coming, she came down from the top of the lodge and went inside. When he came close to her, he spoke and said, "Why are you here alone in the village?" She answered him, "They have gone off on the hunt. I was sulky with my relations, and they went off and left me behind." The man wanted her now to be his wife, but the girl said to him, "No, not yet, but later we will be married." She said to him, "You must not be afraid. Tonight there will be dances here; the ghosts will dance."

This is an old custom of the Pawnees. When they danced, they used to go from one lodge to another, singing, dancing and hallooing. So now, when the tribe had gone and the village was deserted, the ghosts did this. He could hear them coming along the empty streets, and going from one lodge to another. They came into the lodge where he was, and danced about, and whooped and sang, and sometimes they almost touched him, and he came pretty near being scared.

The next day, the young man persuaded the girl to go on with him, and follow the tribe, to join it on the hunt. They started to travel together, and she promised him that she would surely be his wife, but not until the time came. They overtook the tribe; but before they got to the camp, the girl stopped. She said, "Now we have arrived, but you must go first to the village, and prepare a place for me. Where I sleep, let it be behind a curtain.

For four days and four nights, I must remain behind this curtain. Do not speak of me. Do not mention my name to anyone."

The young man left her there and went into the camp. When he got to his lodge, he told a woman, one of his relations, to go out to a certain place and bring in a woman, who was waiting there for him. His relative asked him, "Who is the woman?" And to avoid speaking her name, he told who were her father and mother. His relation, in surprise, said, "It cannot be that girl, for she died some days before we started on the hunt."

When the woman went to look for the girl, she could not find her. The girl had disappeared. The young man had disobeyed her, and had told who she was. She had told him that she must stay behind a curtain for four days, and that no one must know who she was. Instead of doing what she had said, he told who she was, and the girl disappeared because she was a ghost. If he had obeyed the girl, she would have lived a second time on earth. That same night this young man died in sleep.

Then the people were convinced that there must be a life after this one.

IOSCO, OR THE PRAIRIE BOYS' VISIT TO THE SUN AND MOON

ONE PLEASANT MORNING, five young men and a boy about ten years of age, called Iosco, went out a-shooting with their bows and arrows. They left their lodges with the first appearance of daylight, and having passed through a long reach of woods, had ascended a high hill before the sun arose. While standing there in a group, the sun suddenly burst forth in all its glory. The air was so clear that it appeared to be at no great distance. "How very near it is," they all said. "It cannot be far," said the eldest, "and if you will accompany me, we will see if we cannot reach it." A loud assent burst from every lip. Even the boy, Iosco, said he would go. They told him he was too young, but he replied, "If you do not permit me to go with you, I will tell your plan to each of your parents." They then said to him, "You shall also go with us, so be quiet."

They then fell upon the following arrangement. It was resolved that each one should obtain from his parents as many pairs of moccasins as he could, and also new clothing of leather. They fixed on a spot where they would conceal all their articles, until they were ready to start on their journey, and which would serve, in the meantime, as a place of rendezvous, where they might secretly meet and consult. This being arranged, they returned home.

A long time passed before they could put their plan into execution. But they kept it a profound secret, even to the boy. They frequently met at the appointed place, and discussed the subject. At length everything was in readiness, and they decided on a day to set out. That morning the boy shed tears for a pair of new leather leggings. "Don't you see," said he to his parents, "how my companions are dressed?" This appeal to their pride and envy prevailed. He obtained the leggings.

Artifices were also resorted to by the others, under the plea of going out on a special hunt. They said to one another, but in a tone that they might be overheard, "We will see who will bring in the most game." They went out in different directions, but soon met at the appointed place, where they had hid the articles for their journey, with as many arrows as they had time to make. Each one took something on his back, and they began their march.

They traveled day after day, through a thick forest, but the sun was always at the same distance. "We must," said they, "travel toward *Waubunong*, the east, and we shall get to the object, some time or other." No one was discouraged, although winter overtook them. They built a lodge and hunted till they obtained as much dried meat as they could carry, and then continued on. This they did several times; season followed season. More than one winter overtook them. Yet none of them became discouraged, or expressed dissatisfaction.

One day the travelers came to the banks of a river, whose waters ran toward the east. They followed it down many days. As they were walking one day, they came to rising ground, from which they saw something white or clear through the trees. They encamped on this elevation. Next morning they came, suddenly, in view of an immense body of water. No land could be seen as far as the eye could reach. One or two of them lay down on the beach to drink. As soon as they got the water in their mouths, they spit it out, and exclaimed, with surprise, "*Shewetagon awbo!*"—salt water. It was the sea.

While looking on the water, the sun arose as if from the deep, and went on its steady course through the heavens, enlivening the scene with his cheering and animating beams. They stood in admiration, but the object appeared to be as distant from them as ever. They thought it best to encamp, and consult whether it were advisable to go on, or return. "We see," said the leader, "that the sun is still on the opposite side of this great water, but let us not be disheartened. We can walk around the shore." To this they all assented.

Next morning they took the northerly shore, to walk around it, but had only gone a short distance when they came to a large river. They again encamped, and while sitting before the fire, the question was put, whether anyone of them had ever dreamed of water, or of walking on it. After a long silence, the eldest said he had. Soon after, they lay down to sleep.

When they arose the following morning, the eldest addressed them: "We have done wrong in coming north. Last night my spirit appeared to me, and told me to go south, and that but a short distance beyond the spot we left yesterday, we should come to a river with high banks. That by looking off its mouth, we should see an island, which would approach to us. He directed that we should all get on it. He then told me to cast my eyes toward the water. I did so, and I saw all he had declared. He then informed me that we must return south, and wait at the river until the day after tomorrow. I believe all that was revealed to me in this dream, and that we shall do well to follow it."

The party immediately retraced their footsteps in exact obedience to this dream. Toward the evening they came to the borders of the indicated river. It had high banks, behind which they encamped, and here they patiently awaited the fulfillment of the dream. The appointed day arrived. They said, "We will see if that which has been said will be seen. Midday is the promised time." Early in the morning two had gone to the shore to keep a lookout. They waited anxiously for the middle of the day, straining their eyes to see if they could discover anything. Suddenly they raised a shout, "*Ewaddee suh neen!*—There it is! There it is!"

On rushing to the spot they beheld something like an island steadily advancing toward the shore. As it approached, they could discover that something was moving on it in various directions. They said, "It is a Manito, let us be off into the woods." "No, no," cried the eldest, "let us stay and watch." It now became stationary, and lost much of its imagined height. They could only see three trees, as they thought, resembling trees in a pinery that had been burned. The wind, which had been off the sea, now died away into a perfect calm. They saw something leaving the fancied island and approaching the shore, throwing and flapping its wings, like a loon when he attempts to fly in calm weather. It entered the mouth of the river.

They were on the point of running away, but the eldest dissuaded them. "Let us hide in this hollow," he said, "and we will see what it can be." They did so. They soon heard the sounds of chopping, and quickly after they heard the falling of trees. Suddenly a man came up to the place of their concealment. He stood still and gazed at them. They did the same in utter amazement. After looking at them for some time, the person advanced and extended his hand toward them. The eldest took it, and they shook hands. He then spoke, but they could not understand each other. He then cried out for his comrades. They came, and examined very minutely the dress of the travelers.

They again tried to converse. Finding it impossible, the strangers then motioned to the *Naubequon*, a small boat, wishing them to embark. They consulted with each other for a short time. The eldest then motioned that they should go on board. They embarked on board the boat, which they found to be loaded with wood. When they reached the side of the supposed island, they were surprised to see a great number of people, who all came to the side and looked at them with open mouths. One spoke out, above the others, and appeared to be the leader. He motioned them to get on board. He looked at and examined them, and took them down into the cabin, and set things before them to eat. He treated them very kindly.

When they came on deck again, all the sails were spread, and they were fast losing sight of land. In the course of the night and the following day, they were sick at the stomach, but soon recovered. When they had been out at sea ten days, they became sorrowful, as they could not converse with the strangers—those who had hats on.

The following night Iosco dreamed that his spirit appeared to him. He told him not to be discouraged, that he would open his ears, so as to be able to understand the people with hats. "I will not permit you to understand much," said he, "only sufficient to reveal your wants, and to know what is said to you." Iosco repeated this dream to his friends, and they were satisfied and encouraged by it. When they had been out about thirty days, the master of the ship motioned them to change their dresses of leather for such as his people wore; for if they did not, his master would be displeased. It was on this occasion that the elder first understood a few words of the language. The first phrase he understood was *La que notte*, and from one word to another he was soon able to speak it.

One day the men cried out, "Land!" and soon after they heard a noise resembling thunder, in repeated peals. When they had got over their fears, they were shown the large guns which made this noise. Soon after, they saw a vessel smaller than their own, sailing out of a bay, in the direction toward them. She had flags on her masts, and when she came near she fired a gun. The large vessel also hoisted her flags, and the boat came alongside. The master told the person who came in it to tell his master or king that he had six travelers on board, such as had never been seen before, and that they were coming to visit him. It was some time after the departure of this messenger before the vessel got up to the town. It was then dark, but they could see people, and horses, and vehicles ashore. They were landed and placed in a covered vehicle, and driven off. When they stopped, they were taken into a large and splendid room. They were here told that the great chief wished to see them. They were shown into another large room, filled with men and women. All the room was of massive silver.

The chief asked them their business, and the object of their journey. They told him where they were from, and where they were going, and the nature of the enterprise which they had undertaken. He tried to dissuade them from its execution, telling them of the many trials and difficulties they would have to undergo; that so many days' march from his country dwelt a bad spirit, or Manito, who foreknew and foretold the existence and arrival of all who entered his country. It is impossible, he said, my children, for you ever to arrive at the object you are in search of.

Iosco replied, "Nosa," and they could see the chief blush in being called father, "we have come so far on our way, and we will continue it; we have resolved firmly that we will do so. We think our lives are of no value, for we have given them up for this object. Nosa," he repeated, "do not then prevent us from going on our journey." The chief then dismissed them with valuable presents, after having appointed the next day to speak to them again, and provided everything that they needed or wished for.

Next day they were again summoned to appear before the king. He again tried to dissuade them. He said he would send them back to their country in one of his vessels; but all he said had no effect. "Well," said he, "if you will go, I will furnish you all that is needed for your journey." He had everything provided accordingly. He told them that three days before they reached the bad spirit he had warned them of, they would hear his rattle. He cautioned them to be wise, for he felt that he should never see them all again.

They resumed their journey, and traveled sometimes through villages, but they soon left them behind and passed over a region of forests and plains, without inhabitants. They found that all the productions of the new country, trees, animals, birds, were entirely different from those they were accustomed to, on the other side of the great waters. They traveled and traveled, till they wore out all of the clothing that had been given to them, and had to take to their leather clothing again.

The three days the chief spoke of meant three years, for it was only at the end of the third year that they came within the sound of the spirit's rattle. The sound appeared to be near, but they continued walking on, day after day, without apparently getting any nearer to it. Suddenly they came to a very extensive plain. They could see the blue ridges of distant mountains rising on the horizon beyond it. They pushed on, thinking to get over the plain before night, but they were overtaken by darkness. They were now on a stony part of the plain, covered by about a foot's depth of water. They were weary and fatigued. Some of them said, "Let us lie down." "No, no," said the others, "let us push on."

Soon they stood on firm ground, but it was as much as they could do to stand, for they were very weary. They, however, made an effort to encamp, lighted a fire, and refreshed themselves by eating. They then began conversing about the sound of the spirit's rattle, which they had heard for several days. Suddenly the noise began again; it sounded as if it was sub-terraneous, and it shook the ground. They tied up their bundles and went toward the spot. They soon came to a large building, which was illuminated. As soon as they came to the door, they were met by a rather elderly man. "How do ye do," said he, "my grandsons? Walk in, walk in; I am glad to see you; I knew when you started; I saw you encamp this evening. Sit down, and tell me the news of the country you left, for I am interested in it."

They complied with his wishes, and when they had concluded, each one presented him with a piece of tobacco. He then revealed to them things that would happen in their journey, and predicted its successful accomplishment. "I do not say that all of you," said he, "will successfully go through it. You have passed over three-fourths of your way, and I will tell you how to proceed after you get to the edge of the earth. Soon after you leave this place, you will hear a deafening sound. It is the sky descending on the edge, but it keeps moving up and down. You will watch, and when it moves up, you will see a vacant space between it and the earth. You must not be afraid. A chasm of awful depth is there, which separates the unknown from this earth, and a veil of darkness conceals it. Fear not. You must leap through; and if you succeed, you will find yourselves on a beautiful plain, and in a soft and mild light emitted by the moon." They thanked him for his advice. A pause ensued.

"I have told you the way," he said. "Now tell me again of the country you have left, for I committed dreadful ravages while I was there. Does not the country show marks of it? And do not the inhabitants tell of me to their children? I came to this place to mourn over my bad actions, and am trying, by my present course of life, to relieve my mind of the load that is on it." They told him that their fathers spoke often of a celebrated personage called Manabozho, who performed great exploits. "I am he," said the spirit. They gazed with astonishment and fear. "Do you see this pointed house?" said he, pointing to one that resembled a sugar loaf. "You can now each speak your wishes, and will be answered from that house. Speak out, and ask what each wants, and it shall be granted."

One of them, who was vain, asked with presumption that he might live forever, and never be in want. He was answered, "Your wish shall be granted." The second made the same request, and received the same answer. The third asked to live longer than common people, and to be always successful in his war excursions, never losing any of his young men. He was told, "Your wishes are granted." The fourth joined in the same request, and received the same reply. The fifth made a humble request, asking to live as long as men generally do, and that he might be crowned with such success in hunting as to be able to provide for his parents and relatives. The sixth made the same request, and it was granted to both, in pleasing tones, from the pointed house.

After hearing these responses they prepared to depart. They were told by Manabozho that they had been with him but one day, but they afterward found that they had remained there upward of a year. When they were on the point of setting out, Manabozho exclaimed, "Stop! you two, who asked me for eternal life, will receive the boon you wish immediately." He spoke, and one was turned into a stone called *Shin-gauba-wossin,* and the other into a cedar tree. "Now," said he to the others, "you can go." They left him in fear, saying, "We were fortunate to escape so, for the king told us he was wicked, and that we should not probably escape from him."

They had not proceeded far when they began to hear the sound of the beating sky. It appeared to be near at hand, but they had a long interval to travel before they came near, and the sound was then stunning to their senses; for when the sky came down, its pressure would force gusts of wind from the opening, so strong that it was with difficulty they could keep their feet, and the sun passed but a short distance above their heads. They, however, approached boldly, but had to wait some time before they could muster courage enough to leap through the dark veil that covered the passage. The sky would come down with violence, but it would rise slowly and gradually.

The two who had made the humble request stood near the edge, and with no little exertion succeeded, one after the other, in leaping through, and gaining a firm foothold. The remaining two were fearful and undecided. The others spoke to them through the darkness, saying, "Leap! leap! the sky is on its way down." These two looked up and saw it descending, but fear paralyzed their efforts; they made but a feeble attempt, so as to reach the opposite side with their hands. But the sky at the same time struck the earth with great violence and a terrible sound, and forced them into the dreadful black chasm.

The two successful adventurers, of whom Iosco now was chief, found themselves in a beautiful country, lighted by the moon, which shed around a mild and pleasant light. They could see the moon approaching as if it were from behind a hill. They advanced, and an aged woman spoke to them; she had a white face and pleasing air, and looked rather old, though she spoke to them very kindly. They knew from her first appearance that she was the Moon. She asked them several questions; she told them that she knew of their coming, and was happy to see them; she informed them that they were halfway to her brother's, and that from the earth to her abode was half the distance.

"I will, by and by, have leisure," said she, "and will go and conduct you to my brother, for he is now absent on his daily course. You will succeed in your object, and return in safety to your country and friends, with the good wishes, I am sure, of my brother." While the travelers were with her, they received every attention. When the proper time arrived, she said to them, "My brother is now rising from below, and we shall see his light as he comes over the distant edge. Come," said she, "I will lead you up." They went forward, but in some mysterious way they hardly knew how; they rose almost directly up, as if they had ascended steps. They then came upon an immense plain, declining in the direction of the Sun's approach. When he came near, the Moon spoke, "I have brought you these persons, whom we knew were coming," and with this she disappeared. The Sun motioned with his hand for them to follow him. They did so, but found it rather difficult, as the way was steep. They found it particularly so from the edge of the earth till they got halfway between that point and midday.

When they reached this spot the Sun stopped and sat down to rest. "What, my children," said he, "has brought you here? I could not speak to you before. I could not stop at any place but this, for this is my first resting place; then at the center, which is at midday, and then halfway from that to the western edge. Tell me," he continued, "the object of your undertaking this journey and all the circumstances which have happened to you on the way."

They complied. Iosco told him their main object was to see him. They had lost four of their friends on the way, and they wished to know whether they could return in safety to the earth, that they might inform their friends and relatives of all that had befallen them. They concluded by requesting him to grant their wishes. He replied, "Yes, you shall certainly return in safety; but your companions were vain and presumptuous in their demands. They were Foolish Ones. They aspired to what Manitoes only could enjoy. But you two, as I said, shall get back to your country and become as happy as the hunter's life can make you. You shall never be in want of the necessaries of life as long as you are permitted to live; and you will have the satisfaction of relating your journey to your friends, and also of telling them of me. Follow me, follow me," he said, commencing his course again.

The ascent was now gradual, and they soon came to a level plain. After traveling some time he again sat down to rest, for he had arrived at the halfway line. "You see," said he, "it is level at this place, but a short distance onward, my way descends gradually to my last resting place, from which there is an abrupt descent." He repeated his assurance that they should be shielded from danger if they relied firmly on his power. "Come here quickly," he said, placing something before them on which they could descend. "Keep firm," said he, as they resumed the descent. They went downward as if they had been let down by ropes.

In the meantime, the parents of these two young men dreamed that their sons were returning, and that they should soon see them. They placed the fullest confidence in their dreams. Early in the morning they left their lodges for a remote point in the forest, where they expected to meet them. They were not long at the place before they saw the adventurers returning, for they had descended not far from that place. The young men knew they were their fathers. They met, and were happy. They related all that had befallen them. They did not conceal anything; and they expressed their gratitude to the different Manitoes who had preserved them, by feasting and gifts, and particularly to the Sun and Moon, who had received them as their children.

THE WHITE STONE CANOE

THERE WAS ONCE a very beautiful girl, who died suddenly on the day she was to have been married to a handsome young man. He was also brave, but his heart was not proof against this loss. From the hour she was buried, there was no more joy or peace for him. He went often to visit the spot where the women had buried her, and sat musing there, when it was ·thought by some of his friends he would have done better to try to amuse himself in the chase, or by diverting his thoughts on the warpath. But war and hunting had both lost their charms for him. His heart was already dead within him. He pushed aside both his war club and his bow and arrows.

He heard the old people say that there was a path that led to the land of souls, and he determined to follow it. He accordingly set out one morning, after having completed his preparations for the journey. At first he hardly knew which way to go. He was only guided by the tradition that he must go south.

For a while he could see no change in the face of the country. Forests, and hills, and valleys, and streams had the same look they wore in his native place. There was snow on the ground when he set out, and it was sometimes seen to be piled and matted on the thick trees and bushes. At length it began to diminish, and finally disappeared. The forest assumed a more cheerful appearance, and the leaves put forth their buds, and before he was aware of the completeness of the change, he found himself surrounded by spring. He had left behind him the land of snow and ice.

The air became mild; the dark clouds of winter had rolled away from the sky. A pure field of blue was above him, and as he went he saw flowers beside his path, and heard the songs of birds. By these signs he knew that he was going the right way, for they agreed with the traditions of his tribe. At length he spied a path. It led him through a grove, then up a long and elevated ridge, on the very top of which he came to a lodge. At the door stood an old man with white hair, whose eyes, though deeply sunk, had a fiery brilliancy. He had a long robe of skins thrown loosely around his shoulders and a staff in his hands. It was Chebiabos.

The young Chippewa began to tell his story, but the venerable chief stopped him before he had spoken ten words. "I have expected you," he replied, "and had just risen to bid you welcome to my abode. She whom you seek passed here but a few days since, and being fatigued with her journey, rested herself here. Enter my lodge and be seated, and I will then satisfy your inquiries, and give you directions for your journey from this point." Having done this, they both went to the lodge door. "You see yonder gulf," said he, "and the wide stretching blue plains beyond. It is the land of souls. You stand upon its borders, and my lodge is the gate of entrance. But you cannot take your body along. Leave it here with your bow and arrows, your bundle, and your dog. You will find them safe on your return."

So saying, he re-entered the lodge, and the freed traveler bounded forward, as if his feet had suddenly been given wings. But all things retained their natural colors and shapes. The woods and leaves, and streams and lakes, were only brighter and more beautiful than he had ever seen. Animals bounded across his path, with a freedom and a confidence which seemed to tell him there was no bloodshed here. Birds of beautiful plumage inhabited the groves, and sported in the waters. There was but one thing in which he saw a very unusual effect. He noticed that his passage was not stopped by trees or other objects. He appeared to walk directly through them. They were, in fact, but the souls or shadows of material trees. He became sensible that he was in a land of shadows.

When he had traveled half a day's journey through a country which was continually becoming more attractive, he came to the banks of a broad lake, in the center of which was a large and beautiful island. He found a canoe of shining white stone tied to the shore. He was now sure that he had come the right path, for the aged man had told him of this. There were also shining paddles. He immediately entered the canoe, and took the paddles in his hands, when to his joy and surprise, on turning round, he beheld the object of his search in another canoe, exactly its counterpart in everything. She had exactly imitated his motions, and they were side by side.

They at once pushed out from shore and began to cross the lake. Its waves seemed to be rising, and at a distance looked ready to swallow them up; but just as they entered the whitened edge of them they seemed to melt away, as if they were but the images of waves. But no sooner was one wreath of foam passed, than another, more threatening still, rose up. Thus they were in perpetual fear; and what added to it, was the clearness of the water, through which they could see many beings who had perished before, and whose bones lay strewed on the bottom of the lake. The Master of Life had, however, decreed to let them pass, for the actions of neither of them had been bad. But they saw many others struggling and sinking in the waves. Old men and young men, males and females of all ages and ranks were there; some passed, and some sank. It was only the little children whose canoes seemed to meet no waves.

At length, every difficulty was gone, as in a moment, and they both leaped out on the happy island. They felt that the very air was food. It strengthened and nourished them. They wandered together over the blissful fields, where everything was formed to please the eye and the ear. There were no tempests—there was no ice, no chilly winds—no one shivered for the want of warm clothes; no one suffered hunger; no one mourned the dead. They saw no graves. They heard of no wars. There was no hunting of animals, for the air itself was their food.

Gladly would the young warrior have remained there forever, but he was obliged to go back for his body. He did not see the Master of Life, but he heard his voice in a soft breeze. "Go back," said this voice, "to the land from whence you come. Your time has not yet come. The duties for which I made you, and which you are to perform, are not yet finished. Return to your people and accomplish the duties of a good man. You will be the ruler of your tribe for many days. The rules you must observe will be told you by my messenger, who keeps the gate. When he surrenders back your body, he will tell you what to do. Listen to him, and you shall afterward rejoin the spirit which you must now leave behind. She is accepted, and will be ever here, as young and as happy as she was when I first called her from the land of snows."

When this voice ceased, the young man awoke. It was the fancywork of a dream, and he was still in the bitter land of snows, and hunger, and tears.

THE THUNDER BOY

THIS LEGEND happened long ago on an island in the St. Lawrence River. The island is called by the Akwesasne Mohawks, Jo-ka-ta-ren-re, and lies opposite St. Regis Point on the St. Regis Reservation. A man and his wife and daughter lived alone on this island. They had a garden where they raised corn, beans and squashes. One day, as the three were working in their garden, the sky became very dark. Glancing up at the dark clouds, the father said that they had better run quickly for their house, or they would be caught in the rain.

The mother shouted to her daughter, who was working at the other end of the field, telling her to cease her work and run for the house. The man and his wife then quickly ran for the house. Before they were halfway there, the storm had reached them. Heavy bursts of rain fell all about them. Flashes of lightning lit up the sky, and thunder roared above them. Inside the house, the man and his wife waited for their daughter, whom they supposed was following them. "Probably when the storm overtook her, she sought shelter in the forest," said the mother. In vain, the parents waited for the daughter.

After the storm the parents returned to the field. They searched the island, but they could find no trace of the daughter. They called to the girl, but they received no answer. Sadly they returned to their house. "The Thunder People have taken her away," said the mother, and she wept bitter tears.

The young daughter had been busy working in the garden when the storm was approaching. When she saw the fast-thickening clouds and heard her parents calling her to the cabin, she had dropped her hoe and started to follow them. Suddenly she was entirely surrounded by what seemed to be a heavy mist. Her head felt strangely dizzy, and before she knew what was happening, she felt herself lifted up into the sky. In a dazed condition, she was carried swiftly above the earth.

After a while the girl found herself in a strange land. Never before had she seen anything like it. He who carried her was a little man. He led her through this country until they came to a long council house. Upon entering this house, the girl saw many other strange little men, all of whom stared at her. At one end of the house stood a man who seemed to be the chief of these little people.

This little chief seemed very angry when he saw the girl and her escort. "My son," said he, "why did you bring this earth person to our country?" The son answered, "Father, I saw her working in the field, and I fell in love with her. I wanted her, so I took her away."

The chief said, "You should have left her upon the earth. Her ways are not our ways. She cannot eat snails, bugs, and worms, which is the kind of food that we live on." Again he spoke, "If you insist upon keeping her here, you, yourself, must return to earth and secure earth food for her. The ways of Ra-ti-we-ras, the Thunder People, are different from the ways of the Earth People."

The son agreed to do this. Every day he would travel to earth to secure food for his earth wife. For one year this earth girl lived in the country of the Thunder People. Her husband granted her every wish, and she became very happy. Though she sometimes thought of her parents, she did not become lonesome.

One day the chief of the Thunder People said, "My daughter, you are soon to give birth to a son. It would not do to have the child born in this land. You must return to your old home on the island, Jo-ka-ta-ren-re. But there is one thing I want to warn you about. After your boy is born, guard him carefully. You must warn everyone who goes near the boy never to strike him. If anyone ever strikes the boy, you will lose him."

Suddenly, without warning, the girl was again surrounded by the heavy mist. Her mind became dazed. Once again she found herself traveling at a great speed through space. After what seemed a little while, she opened her eyes, and to her surprise, found herself in front of her mother's cabin back at the island. The parents of the girl were happy to see her. They had long given her up for lost. The girl told her strange story and said that soon she was to give birth to a son.

What the Thunder Chief had said came true. In time a little son was born to the girl. This boy was smaller than an earth child, and in many ways his habits differed from the habits of an ordinary boy. Whenever a thunderstorm would approach the island, the boy would become very excited. He would run out into the storm and laugh and play about. At such times the thunder would seem to roar more often. Great flashes of lightning would light the heavens.

The old grandmother did not like to have the boy run out into the storm. Whenever a storm approached, she would try to shut the child up in the cabin, but the boy always managed to escape in spite of all she could do.

One day, at the approach of a storm, the old grandmother locked the boy in the cabin. She scolded him and forbade him to go out into the storm. The boy became very angry. He ran about the cabin throwing to the floor everything he could get his hands on. He was in a terrible temper. The grandmother told him to cease his mischief and to sit down, but the boy only stamped around more. When the boy became angry, faint sounds as of distant thunder seemed to come from his body. The more angry he became, the louder the thunder sounded. His grandmother told him to cease his noise. In his rage, he continued to wreck everything he could get his hands on.

The old woman lost her temper. Taking up a stick, she gave the boy a sharp blow across his legs. Instantly, there was a blinding flash of lightning, followed by a loud roar of thunder! The room became filled with a heavy mist. Trembling with fear, the old woman huddled in a corner of the cabin. When the mist cleared, the boy had vanished. Far away she could hear a rumble of thunder that sounded fainter and fainter in the distance.

When the boy's mother returned to the cabin she said, "You have struck my son. His father has taken him to live with him in the land of the Thunder People. We will never see him again."

Because the Thunder Boy is half Indian, the Thunder People are friends of the Indian and will never strike one of that race. In the early spring, at the coming of the first thunder, it is said to please the Thunder People if you throw real tobacco on the fire.

TAU-WAU-CHEE-HEZKAW, OR THE WHITE FEATHER

THERE WAS AN OLD MAN living in the center of a forest with his grandson, whom he had taken when quite an infant. The child had no parents, brothers, or sisters; they had all been destroyed by six giants, and he had been informed that he had no other relative living besides his grandfather. The band to whom he belonged had wagered their children in a race against those of the giants, and had thus lost them. There was an old tradition in the band that it would produce a great man, who would wear a white feather, and who would astonish everyone with his skill and feats of bravery.

The grandfather, as soon as the child could play about, gave him a bow and arrows to amuse himself. He went into the edge of the woods one day and saw a rabbit, but not knowing what it was, he ran home and described it to his grandfather. He told him what it was, that its flesh was good to eat, and that if he would shoot one of his arrows into its body, he would kill it. He did so, and brought the little animal home, which he asked his grandfather to boil, that they might feast on it. He humored the boy in this, and encouraged him to go on in acquiring the knowledge of hunting, until he could kill deer and larger animals; and he became, as he grew up, an expert hunter.

As they lived alone, and away from other Indians, his curiosity was excited to know what was passing in the world. One day he came to the edge of a prairie, where he saw ashes like those at his grandfather's lodge, and lodgepoles left standing. He returned and inquired whether his grandfather put up the poles and made the fire. He was answered, "No," nor did the grandfather believe that he had seen anything of the kind. It was all imagination.

Another day he went out to discover anything that was curious, and on entering the woods, he heard a voice calling out to him, "Come here, you destined wearer of the White Feather. You do not yet wear it, but you are worthy of it. Return home and take a short nap. You will dream of hearing a voice, which will tell you to rise and smoke. You will see in your dream a pipe, a smoking sack, and a large white feather. When you awake you will find these articles. Put the feather on your head, and you will become a great hunter, a great warrior, and a great man, capable of doing anything. As a proof that you will become a great hunter, when you smoke the smoke will turn into pigeons."

The voice then informed him who he was, and disclosed the true character of his grandfather, who had deceived him. The voice spirit then gave him a vine, and told him he was of an age to avenge the injuries of his relations. "When you meet your enemy," continued the spirit, "you will run a race with him. He will not see the vine, because it is enchanted. While you are running, you will throw it over his head and entangle him, so that you will win the race."

Long ere this speech was ended, he had turned to the quarter from which the voice proceeded, and was astonished to behold a man, for as yet he had never seen any man besides his grandfather, whose object it was to keep him in ignorance. But the circumstance that gave him the most surprise was that this man, who had the look of great age, was composed of wood from his breast downward, and appeared to be fixed in the earth.

He returned home, slept, heard the voice, awoke, and found the promised articles. His grandfather was greatly surprised to find him with a white feather on his forehead, and to see flocks of pigeons flying out of his lodge. He then recollected what had been predicted, and began to weep at the prospect of losing his charge.

Invested with these honors, the young man departed the next morning to seek his enemies and gratify his revenge. The giants lived in a very high lodge in the middle of a wood. He traveled on till he came to this lodge, where he found that his coming had been made known by the little spirits who carry the news. The giants came out, and gave a cry of joy as they saw him coming. When he approached nearer, they began to make sport of him, saying, "Here comes the little man with the white feather, who is to achieve such wonders." They, however, spoke very fair to him when he came up, saying he was a brave man, and would do brave things. This they said to encourage and the more surely to deceive him. He, however, understood the object.

He went fearlessly up to the lodge. They told him to commence the race with the smallest of their number. The point to which they were to run was a peeled tree toward the rising sun, and then back to the starting place, which was marked by a *Chaunkahpee*, a war club made of iron. This club was the stake, and whoever won it was to use it in beating the other's brains out. If he beat the first giant, he was to try the second, and so on until they had all measured speed with him. He won the first race by a dexterous use of the vine, and immediately despatched his competitor, and cut off his head. Next morning he ran with the second giant, whom he also outran, killed, and decapitated. He proceeded in this way for five successive mornings, always conquering by the use of his vine, cutting off the heads of the vanquished.

The survivor acknowledged his power, but prepared secretly to deceive him. He wished him to leave the heads he had cut off, as he believed he could again reunite them with the bodies by means of one of their medicines. White Feather insisted, however, on carrying all the heads to his grandfather.

One more contest was to be tried, which would decide the victory; but before going to the giant's lodge on the sixth morning, he met his old counselor who had seemed fixed in the earth. The old man told him that he was about to be deceived. That he had never known any other sex but his own, but that, as he went on his way to the lodge, he would meet the most beautiful woman in the world. He must pay no attention to her, but on meeting her, he must wish himself changed into a male elk. The transformation would take place immediately, but he must start feeding and not regard her.

He proceeded toward the lodge, met the female, and became an elk. She reproached him for having turned himself into an elk on seeing her, said she had traveled a great distance for the purpose of seeing him and becoming his wife. Now this woman was the sixth giant, who had assumed this disguise; but Tau-Wau-Chee-Hezkaw remained in ignorance of it. Her reproaches and her beauty affected him so much, that he wished himself a man again, and he at once resumed his natural shape. They sat down together, and he began to caress her and make love to her. He finally ventured to lay his head on her lap, and went to sleep. She pushed his head aside at first to test if he was really asleep, and when she was satisfied he was, she took her axe and broke his back. She then assumed her natural shape, which was in the form of the sixth giant, and afterward changed him into a dog, in which degraded form he followed his enemy to the lodge. The giant took the white feather, and wore it as a trophy on his own head.

There was an Indian village at some distance, in which there lived two girls, who were rival sisters, the daughters of a chief. They were fasting to acquire power for the purpose of enticing the wearer of the white feather to visit their village. They each secretly hoped to engage his affections. Each one built herself a lodge at a short distance from the village.

The giant, knowing this, and having now obtained the valued plume, went immediately to visit them. As he approached, the girls saw and recognized the feather. The elder sister prepared her lodge with great care and show, to attract the eye. The younger, supposing that he was a man of sense and would not be enticed by mere show, touched nothing in her lodge, but left it as it ordinarily was. The elder went out to meet the giant and invited him in. He accepted her invitation, and made her his wife. The younger invited the enchanted dog into her lodge, and made him a good bed, and treated him with as much attention as if he were her husband.

The giant, supposing that whoever possessed the white feather possessed also all its virtues, went out on the prairie to hunt, but returned unsuccessful. The dog went out the same day a-hunting on the banks of a river. He drew a stone out of the water, which immediately became a beaver. The next day the giant followed the dog, and hiding behind a tree, saw the manner in which the dog went into the river and drew out a stone, which at once turned into a beaver.

As soon as the dog left the place, the giant went to the river, and observing the same manner, drew out a stone, and had the satisfaction of seeing it transformed into a beaver. Tying it to his belt, he carried it home, and as is customary, threw it down at the door of the lodge before he entered. After being seated a short time, he told his wife to bring in his belt, or hunting girdle. She did so, and returned with it, with nothing tied to it but a stone.

The next day, the dog, finding his method of catching beavers had been discovered, went to a wood at some distance, and broke off a charred limb from a burned tree, which instantly became a bear. The giant, who had again watched him, did the same, and carried a bear home; but his wife, when she came to go out for it, found nothing but a black stick tied to his belt.

The giant's wife determined to go to her father and tell him what a valuable husband her sister had, who furnished her lodge with abundance. She set out while her husband went to hunt. As soon as they had departed, the dog made signs to his mistress to sweat him after the manner of the Indians. She accordingly made a lodge just large enough for him to creep into. She then put in heated stones, and poured on water. After this had been continued the usual time, he came out a very handsome young man, but had not the power of speech.

Meantime, the elder daughter had reached her father's, and told him of the manner in which her sister supported a dog, treating him as her husband, and of the singular skill this animal had in hunting. The old man, suspecting there was some magic in it, sent a deputation of young men and women to ask her to come to him, and bring her dog along. When this deputation arrived, they were surprised to find, in the place of the dog, so fine a young man. They both accompanied the messengers to the father, who was no less astonished. He assembled all the old and wise men of the nation to see the exploits which, it was reported, the young man could perform. The giant was among the number.

The father took his pipe and filled it, and passed it to the husbands, to see if anything would happen when they smoked. It was passed to the young man who had been a dog, who made a sign to hand it to the giant first, which was done, but nothing happened. He then took it himself. He made a sign to them to put the white feather upon his head. This was done, and immediately he regained his speech. He then commenced smoking, and behold! immense flocks of white and blue pigeons rushed from the smoke.

The chief demanded of him his history, which he faithfully recounted. When it was finished, the chief ordered that the giant should be transformed into a dog, and turned into the middle of the village, where the boys should pelt him to death with clubs. This sentence was executed.

The chief then ordered, on the request of the White Feather, that all the young men should employ themselves four days in making arrows. He also asked for a buffalo robe. This robe he cut into thin shreds and sowed in the prairie. At the end of the four days, he invited them to gather together all their arrows, and accompany him on a buffalo hunt. They found that these shreds of skin had grown into a very large herd of buffalo. They killed as many as they pleased, and enjoyed a grand festival, in honor of the triumph over the giants.

Having accomplished their labor, the White Feather got his wife to ask her father's permission to go with him on a visit to his grandfather. He replied to this request that a woman must follow her husband into whatever quarter of the world he may choose to go.

The young men then placed the white feather in his frontlet, and taking his war club in his hand, White Feather led the way into the forest, followed by his faithful wife.

VII

SORCERY AND WITCHCRAFT

THE BOY WHO OVERCAME ALL MAGIC
BY LAUGHTER

THE WORLD was once visited by a demon of enchantment who scattered all the people and bewitched all the animals, all the trees, all the lakes, all the rivers, all the boys and girls, and all the older people. Strange to say, nobody knew that they had been enchanted; they only knew that all their wishes were thwarted, and that there was misery everywhere.

Now, Gajihsondis did not know that he had been placed under an evil spell. He was a boy and was filled with all the ambitions of a boy, but all his desires were curbed by his queer-looking old grandfather. The boy did not even know that it was strange to live in a hole in the ground under his grandfather's bed or to be whipped with burning switches. He only knew that he wanted to do things—to play down by the spring and to go hunting. After a while he grew curious to know the reason of things and so asked many questions.

One day when he had grown to the age of twelve years he asked, "My grandfather, where are my parents? Why have you never taken me to my father and my mother?"

His grandfather eyed him curiously and refused to give Gajihsondis any satisfaction. But the boy kept questioning until the old man growled like a bear and said, "My grandson, you should not ask questions. You have forced me to speak, and you must not blame me for the trouble that you have now brought upon the world. You shall now die because I am about to answer you. There is a spring near the path that leads from this lodge into the deep forest. I have never let you go there because in that spring is a terrible monster that is filled with great magic. His *orenda*—magical power—is more powerful than anything else in the world. If you go far from this lodge, the beast will reach out with his long claws and devour you. You have never been allowed to stray from the doorway because of this. But now that you know this circumstance, you must learn to use a bow and arrow. You must become a hunter, for what I have told you has made me very old, and I shall soon be unable to hunt."

The old man, looking more ugly than ever, went to his hunting pouch and took out a small bow and a quiver of arrows. "Now, take these, my grandson. Go and hunt. Find your first prey on a tree."

Gajihsondis went out of the lodge very happy. "I am now a hunter," thought he. "I shall soon bring in all the meat." He watched carefully for signs of game. Then he spied what he thought a great bird upon the trunk of a tree. He lifted up his bow and shot, but missed his quarry. Thereupon he ran back to the lodge and cried, "Oh, grandfather, I have been unable to kill my prey." Then he wept with disappointment.

"I thought you would fail," said the grandfather. "You have never had practice. I will hang up the foot of a raccoon, and you must shoot this wherever I hang it. When you hit it every time without missing once, you may go on a hunt again." He then hung the coon's foot by a cord to the roof pole and allowed it to dangle over the fire. "I am going on a hunt now, but it will be my last. If you are unable to hit the raccoon's foot by the time I return, we are lost."

Thereupon the grandfather took his hunting equipment and departed. This gave Gajihsondis his chance. After many failures, he hit the foot, and when he became proficient he tried other things.

After many days the grandfather returned. "We are lost now," said he. "The beast is coming to devour us. Only four days remain for us to live." "I'll shoot it," exclaimed Gajihsondis. "I am a good marksman now!"

The old man laughed. "Oh, no," said he, "I gave you an arrow that can never hit its mark. You cannot shoot." "But, my grandfather," contradicted the boy, "I never miss the mark." The grandfather grunted, "*Wha-a-aah.*"

Gajihsondis then shot the raccoon's foot. This made the old man look up. "It is only a chance," he said. "You had power with you but for a moment. Nevermore can you do it. I will place the foot elsewhere." Thereupon he threw it to the top of a tall tree. "Now you cannot hit it," he said.

Gajihsondis took easy aim and hit the foot, knocking it from its hanging to another tree much higher, and with a second arrow he knocked it again, bringing it to the ground.

Instead of being pleased, the old man was very angry and said, "Who has been here to guide you? There is some evil thing lurking about. Well, never mind this, you cannot kill real game. You have no arrows to hit anything."

Gajihsondis then went out and saw the bird he first had aimed at. Again he shot, and killed it this time. Taking it up, he ran in great glee to his grandfather. "Oh, contempt!" exclaimed the old man. "You have killed nothing but a chickadee." But even so, the old man worried, for he knew that his grandson had killed the first creature which by custom a child is permitted to kill when he learns to hunt.

Again the boy went out and soon returned with a raccoon. It was a fine fat animal and made a good meal for the two, but the grandfather ridiculed the boy and said it was only temporary luck, for the boy possessed no *orenda*. Again the boy tried his skill and killed a fine turkey, which the old man dressed and cooked, at the same time sneering as before. On his fourth excursion, Gajihsondis killed a deer and brought it in. This time the old man angrily exclaimed, "It is not right that you should become proficient as a hunter, but it seems that you have. Oh, now we shall all die, for you will consider yourself able to leave this lodge and to follow the path."

Now, this is just what Gajihsondis wanted to do. He had only one desire: to overcome the monster that barred him from his father and mother. "Now I am going," said he, without further ado. "I shall slay the monster."

The old man scolded and wept, but Gajihsondis was soon out of sight down the well-beaten path that led from the lodge into the deep forest. After a day's journey, he found a gigantic frog crying out terrible threats. "Whoso comes near this spring," he croaked, "shall die. I eat whoever comes near this spring."

Gajihsondis was not a bit frightened; he simply drew his bow and shot the frog, and though it was larger than he, he tied its feet together, hung it to his carrying frame, and returned to his grandfather's lodge. The old man was very angry, but the boy only laughed. Now he had learned a new trick, that of laughing. He had never done this before, and to have him laugh made his grandfather even more angry.

The grandson went out a second time and found a gigantic duck guarding the spring. It cried out threats and proclaimed its great power. This did not daunt Gajihsondis, who merely fixed his bow and shot it. Again he returned to his grandfather, who became even more angry. "How could you do this?" he asked. "By magic the path was changed, but you found the spring again. You shall not find it again."

For a third time, the boy went out on his hunt for the spring and easily found it, for as plain as day he could see a path leading directly to it. (Now this was strange for it was not a path that ordinary eyes could see, which made the grandfather believe that it could not be discovered.) When he neared the spring, he heard the cries of a great beaver threatening to gnaw anyone in twain who approached the pool. It was a very terrifying beaver, but Gajihsondis found it an easy mark for his arrows. He laughed as he trussed it in his carrying frame, and laughed as three days later he flung it down at his grandfather's doorway. The old man roused himself in furious anger and flung his charm bundles in the fire. He pawed the earth like a beast and shouted until his throat bled, but Gajihsondis only laughed again and went away, saying, "Oh, it is very easy!"

Now when he went down the path, Gajihsondis knew that it had been changed. First he had gone north, then west, then south, and now he was going east over the path that, while invisible to common eyes, was visible to him, yet he did not know how he could see it. For if he tried to look, he could see nothing, and when he did not try, he could see everything. He also knew something that he would not tell.

For a fourth time he drew near to the mysterious pool. It was most beautiful, and the trees about it were very tall. There were rocks looking like enchanted beasts asleep about it. The water, itself, was very clear and sparkled as if the sun were upon it, even when it was night. Gajihsondis went right up to the spring and flung in a fishing line. In an instant he had a bite, and some terrifying thing began to pull him into the water. Though he was sore pressed and saw himself falling over the edge of the pool, he laughed, and when he did he gave a great pull, staggered backward, and pulled out a lizard four times his own length. It was the blue *Dagwenigoge*. Though he had hooked it, the creature was not dead; but as Gajihsondis looked at it, it sprang toward him with a cry and bit off both his legs. This made Gajihsondis laugh with all his might, and he laughed so hard that the beast grew weak. The creature then, despairing of killing the boy, stabbed him in the breast with its tail, crying, "Put me back in the spring."

Again the boy laughed. "Oh, how can I put you back in the spring," said he, "seeing that I have no legs wherewith to walk? Replace my legs, and I will put you back." Then he laughed again.

Now the lizard was a creature of great magic, and it conjured a man and a woman who came forth from the water and made Gajihsondis's legs whole again and smoothed up the wound where the incision had been. The boy laughed and instead of thanking them caught them with his fishline and cut off the heads of each. "I know you," said he. "You are the evil servants of the lizard." So saying, he cast them in a fire and burned them to ashes. When the heads were consumed, they burst with a loud explosion, and out flew a great flock of screech owls. He then threw the lizard back into the pool, saying, "I despise you for your lack of magic."

Laughing as he went, Gajihsondis followed the path until he came to a clearing. Though he greatly wondered what was in the clearing, for he heard human voices, he could not proceed, for there, hovering over the path, were many white owls, screaming at him and swooping down to pluck out his eyes.

Gajihsondis now thought of a plan to overcome the owls. It seemed best to be truthful, he thought, and so he determined what to say. So he called out, "I claim this land. It is mine, and I shall possess it, but I am willing to make one of you owls chief with me." The owls then began to quarrel among themselves as to who would be chief. They made a great noise and soon had clawed each other to death. None remained to rule with Gajihsondis, so he went forward. As he proceeded, he found that the path had changed, and that instead of entering the clearing from the north he was entering from the west. Soon he paused, for the path was guarded by powerful panthers.

Again he resolved to declare his intentions. "I claim this land," he cried. "It is mine, I shall possess it, but am willing to make one of you panthers chief to govern with me." The two panthers then began to quarrel and soon were engaged in murderous combat. In a few moments both were dead. Gajihsondis then went on, but noticed that the path had changed and that he was entering the clearing from the south.

He paused as he was about to enter the clearing for there, guarding the

211

path with lowered antlers, were two elk. He saluted them calling out, "This is my land. I shall possess it, but I shall make one of you chief to help me govern." As before, the creatures fought themselves to death, each one desiring to be chief. Gajihsondis then journeyed on, finding as before that the path had changed. This time he approached from the east.

As he was about to enter the clearing, two enormous serpents rose up and hissed at him. As before, he loudly proclaimed, "I claim this land. It is mine, and I shall possess it, but I am willing to make one of you rattlesnakes chief with me." Then did the great serpents begin to fight, and after a fierce struggle both bit one another and both died.

Gajihsondis strode on into the clearing and found a great lodge within. It was strongly built and large enough to hold a great company of people. Entering the lodge, he found an old man cooking corn mush. The old man said nothing until the food was cooked, when he said, "Come eat, it is ready." The two finished the meal, for Gajihsondis was very hungry and was especially fond of corn pudding. "We will now sleep here," said the old man pointing to mats on the floor.

Both lay down on the mats instead of on the long shelflike beds that were on either side of the lodge. As the old man lay down with all his clothing, his pouch leaped from him and went to a peg on the center pole; his leggings drew from him and rolled up in a corner; his moccasins leaped to a bench, and his breechcloth came off and hung itself over a pole. Then all the supper dishes leaped about, the pot emptying itself and then jumping to the upper shelf of the lodge. After a while, the old man went to sleep, and as he did, a white deer emerged from his breast, leaped into the air and sailed away through the smoke hole. Gajihsondis watched far into the night. He could not sleep, for the utensils in the lodge moved about and talked to each other.

Gajihsondis conceived the idea of robbing the house of its magical objects, and finally decided it might be better to escape without a burden. Carefully he crawled out from his skin coverings and made haste to withdraw. He did this with entire success, and ran a long way into the night. Soon, however, he saw a white deer dart down from the sky and enter the smoke hole of the lodge. He knew then that the old man would awake and pursue him. Nor was he mistaken, for soon he could hear the old man running after him. On and on he came, until when just behind Gajihsondis he waved his war club and struck the boy on the head.

"I have killed another," shrieked the old man, as he sawed a knick in his war club with his flint knife. "No man escapes me."

The old man then went about the forest and restored all the animals slain or dead through the craft of Gajihsondis. At length he found the lizard in the pool and told it all concerning his work of restoration. "It must be Gajihsondis who has done all this," said the lizard, after he had been restored to his own magical power. "Only Gajihsondis could have slain all these helpers. I greatly fear that he has acquired sufficient magic to slay us all."

"But I have slain him, and he will trouble us no more," said the old man.

"Oh, no," replied the lizard. "Gajihsondis will revive. Then let us beware."

The old man returned to his lodge and passed the body of Gajihsondis, and to his great satisfaction saw the great crows picking at it. "He is dead," he thought, and went straightway to sleep.

The boy soon recovered consciousness and, completely restored, he crept into the old man's lodge. "I will now be truthful," he thought. "I will address the war club."

"War club," he commanded, "stand up," and the club stood erect. "Now war club, in you is power. I want you to be my friend and assist me in slaying my enemy. I am a man and will not be denied."

The war club then pointed to a bed far away from the door, and Gajihsondis went to the bed and saw a pile of soft tanned pelts. Removing these, he saw a sleeping maiden. He took a brand from the fire and held it over the girl. "I have now come for you," he said. "I am going to rob this house and take you with me. This is my land, and I shall rule it." The girl looked at Gajihsondis and was pleased. She liked the looks of Gajihsondis. "I will go," she said, "but first you must slay my uncle. It is because he fears you will find me that we are all bewitched."

The boy went over to the old man and awakened him. His clothing flew upon him, a white deer entered his body, and then he sat up. "What do you want?" he inquired.

"I want to fight with you," said Gajihsondis.

"Now just wait," said the old man. "I must get my war paint ready." So saying, he threw charcoal from the fire into the corn mortar and made a black paste. Then he took red paint from a box. He applied black to one side of his face and red to the other.

"Now I am ready," he announced. "Why do you wish to fight me?"

"I want all your things, and I am going to take your niece," said the boy.

At this, the old man became very angry and whooped. He then sang a magic song and grasped his war club, and rushed upon Gajihsondis. The young man grasped his war club, and then the two began to fight. In a short time the old man was overcome and exhausted. Gajihsondis bound up the old man and put him in his carrying frame. Then he took the girl by the hand and led her away to his own lodge.

Reaching his grandfather's lodge he noticed for the first time that it was identical with the one in which he had had his fight. His grandfather and the old man looked the same. There was no difference.

When the old man, his grandfather, saw that Gajihsondis had brought home the old man bound and also the girl, he was very angry but said nothing. He made up his mind to kill the boy and to marry the girl. Now when the boy slept, and the girl had crawled into her robes afar from the door, the old man grasped his war club and sang to it. Now the prisoner sat up and did likewise, and both did exactly as the other did. "I will kill the boy now," said the old man, and so saying, he shot three arrows into his back.

In a short time the boy awakened, being in great pain. He arose and went out of the lodge. Near the creek he found a sweat lodge, and as he stood near it a voice spoke, "Go in," it said, "I will help you." He looked and there saw another person exactly like himself, only very white and clear. "I have always known you were my friend," said Gajihsondis. "But this time I see you."

Gajihsondis went into the lodge and took a sweat, and when the arrows had come out he took an emetic. After a while he saw clearly in the dark. He saw his friend walk toward him and enter his body. The two became one. "This is the power that has guided me," he thought. "But I will never tell anyone I have seen him, until the day I am about to die."

Thereupon he returned to the lodge and awoke his grandfather. "Come and fight me, grandfather," he exclaimed. "I believe that you have done me a great wrong."

The old man sprang from his bed, and as he did so the prisoner became as a mist and floated into him. Then the grandfather grasped his war club, but it was no longer strong like good hickory, but soft like wet rawhide. He could not fight.

He began to whimper. "Oh, my grandson," he moaned, "do not kill your grandfather. My strength is gone. I will confess. I have been a great wizard and have created many evil monsters and slain many people by magic. Now I am undone. Oh, restore my nature, and make me human again. Do not kill me."

"Then tell me everything," demanded Gajihsondis, and the old man told him of his conjuring. The girl, he said, was foreordained as Gajihsondis's wife. His parents were in the ground back of the lodge in the clearing. He had exercised his magic in order to claim the girl. He and the old man in the house in the clearing were one and the same person, though dual by magic. The path was well-trodden because he had traveled over it so many times.

"I must now go out and kill all the monsters," said Gajihsondis. He did so and killed all the magically evil creatures. He dug up the ground back of the lodge in the clearing, and there found a bark house hidden by the roots of the trees. There he found his mother, his father, and his sister. All were very happy that Gajihsondis had released them, and together they made their journey back to the grandfather's lodge. When he saw them returning, he died and turned into a shriveled human skin. This Gajihsondis rolled into a bundle and hid it in the rafters. Then he called to the girl, and she came out of the blankets from the bed at the far side of the lodge. She was a beautiful young woman and dressed in fine garments.

"Who is this?" asked Gajihsondis's father and mother.

"This is my wife," he replied. "We shall all live in a new house."

So he took them all away, and he showed them a new lodge of bark he had built. So this is the story of Gajihsondis.

WOMEN ENTICED BY MAGIC SONG

MORNING GREEN, chief of Casa Grande, invited Chief Tcernatsing and his women to visit him. Tcernatsing lived in a great house situated near Gila Crossing, which is so far away from Casa Grande that he found it necessary to camp one night en route at the settlement on the Gila River opposite Sacaton. When the visitors arrived at Casa Grande, a dance was celebrated in the open space north of compound A, somewhere between it and the circular wall enclosing a reservoir, or well. Here the women who accompanied Tcernatsing danced with those of Casa Grande, singing the song:

> *Ta sai na wu wu*
> Sun shade sing with me
> My body will become a hummingbird.

When Tcernatsing came and witnessed the women dancing, he shook his rattle and sang a magic song, which enticed all the women of Casa Grande to follow him to another dance place, nearer the Gila. Morning Green, who also sang a magic song, found it powerless to prevent the departure of the women, and he went back to his house for a more powerful medicine, after which he returned to the dance and ordered his women back to their dwellings; but they were so much bewitched by the songs of Tcernatsing that they could not, or would not, obey him.

Farther and farther from their homes, Tcernatsing enticed the women, dancing first in one place and then in another until they came to his compound. Among the women who abandoned their home, was the wife of Morning Green, who refused to return even after he sent a special messenger to her.

The sequel of the legend is that Tcernatsing married Nactci, a daughter of Morning Green, making her father so angry that he sent a spider to bite his own grandson, offspring of the union. When the boy was sick unto death, Tcernatsing invited Morning Green to visit his grandson before the boy died. Morning Green relented and sent his daughter an herb (the name of which is lost) powerful enough to cure the spider's bite, and thus the child's life was spared.

THE WOULD-BE WITCH

A MAN, whose brother was very sick, suspected the witches of causing his illness. He tried to find out who they were and where they met, so he went to an old woman and told her he wanted to be a witch. She said, "If you are very much in earnest you may be, but when you begin, you must go to your sister and point at her. Then she will be taken sick, and after a time will die." So he went and told his sister, and they arranged a plan. She was to pretend to be ill after he came home, and let this be known.

When night came, he started for the place of meeting with the old woman, but as he went, he now and then broke off a leaf or a bit of under-brush. All at once the old woman sprang into a tree and clung to it, and as she turned around, she was a great panther, with sharp teeth, long claws, and glaring eyes. As she spat and snarled at him, he was terribly frightened, but pretended not to be afraid. So she came down as an old woman again, and said, "Didn't I frighten you?" "Oh, no," he replied, "I was not a bit afraid. I would like to be like that myself." So they went on, and as they went he broke the brush here and there.

After a time they came to an open place in the woods, where were gathered many old men and women, and some young women, too. He was surprised at those he found there. There was a little kettle over a fire in the midst of the place. It was very small indeed, not larger than a teacup. Over it hung a bunch of snakes, from which blood dripped into the kettle, and of this all drank a little from time to time. He pretended to drink, and after that looked carefully about to see who were there. They did many things and took many shapes, and often asked what he would like to be. He said, "A screech owl." So they gave him an owl's head, which he was to put on later.

They told him when he had this on he would be able to fly like a bird. He imitated the owl's cries and movements, and they said he would be a boss witch. When he put on the head, he seemed to lose control of himself, and it took him over the trees to his brother's house. At the same time the meeting broke up, and the witches went off in various shapes, as foxes, wolves, panthers, hawks, and owls.

217

When he came to his brother's, all in the house were scared at the noise of an owl on the roof, for he made sounds just like one. Then he took off the head and went into the house. He pointed at a dog instead of his sister, and the dog sickened and died. His sister pretended to be sick, as they had agreed, and the witches came to see her. They mourned for her, just as though they had not intended her death, and talked about her illness everywhere.

The next day the young man got the warriors together and told what he had seen. They consulted and armed themselves, agreeing to follow him that night. The band went through the bushes and trees, finding the way by the twigs and leaves he had broken. They knew the spot, which was on their reservation, and when they reached it the witches' meeting had begun. They had officers and speakers, and one of these was making a fine speech. They said if they killed any persons they would go to heaven, and the Great Spirit would reward the witches well. They might save their victims from much evil by killing them, for they might become bad or unfortunate. If they died now, they would go to the Good Spirit. While he was speaking, the young man gave a sign. The warriors rushed in and killed all the witches.

THE ADVENTURES OF KIVIUNG

AN OLD WOMAN lived with her grandson in a small hut. As she had no husband and no son to take care of her and the boy, they were very poor, the boy's clothing being made of skins of birds which they caught in snares. When the boy would come out of the hut and join his playfellows, the men would laugh at him and tear his outer garment. Only one man, whose name was Kiviung, was kind to the young boy, but he could not protect him from the others. Often the lad came to his grandmother crying and weeping, and she always consoled him and each time made him a new garment. She entreated the men to stop teasing the boy and tearing his clothing, but they would not listen to her prayer. At last she got angry and swore she would take revenge upon his abusers, and she could easily do so, as she was a great *angakoq* (a shaman or medicine man).

She commanded her grandson to step into a puddle which was on the floor of the hut, telling him what would happen and how he should behave. As soon as he stood in the water, the earth opened and he sank out of sight, but the next moment he rose near the beach as a yearling seal with a beautiful skin, and swam about lustily.

The men had barely seen the seal when they took to their kayaks, eager to secure the pretty animal. But the transformed boy quickly swam away, as his grandmother had told him, and the men continued in pursuit. Whenever he rose to breathe, he took care to come up behind the kayaks, where the men could not get at him with their harpoons; there, however, he splashed and dabbled in order to attract their attention and lure them on. But before anyone could turn his kayak, he had dived again and swam away. The men were so interested in the pursuit that they did not observe that they were being led far from the coast and that the land was now altogether invisible.

Suddenly a gale arose; the sea foamed and roared and the waves destroyed or upset their frail vessels. After all seemed to be drowned, the seal was again transformed into the lad, who went home without wetting his feet. There was nobody now to tear his clothing, all his abusers being dead.

Only Kiviung, who was a great *angakoq* and had never abused the boy, had escaped the wind and waves. Bravely he strove against the wild sea, but the storm did not abate. After he had drifted for many days on the wide sea, a dark mass loomed up through the mist. His hope revived and he worked hard to reach the supposed land. The nearer he came, however, the more agitated did the sea become, and he saw that he had mistaken a wild, black sea, with raging whirlpools, for land. Barely escaping, he drifted again for many days, but the storm did not abate, and he did not see any land. Again he saw a dark mass looming up through the mist, but he was once more deceived, for it was another whirlpool which made the sea rise in gigantic waves.

At last the storm moderated, the sea subsided, and at a great distance he saw land. Gradually he came nearer, and following the coast, he at length spied a stone house in which a light was burning. He landed and entered the house. Nobody was inside but an old woman whose name was Arnaitiang. She received him kindly, and at his request pulled off his boots, slippers, and stockings, and dried them on the frame hanging over the lamp. Then she went out to light a fire and cook a good meal.

When the stockings were dry, Kiviung tried to take them from the frame in order to put them on, but as soon as he extended his hand to touch them the frame rose out of his reach. Having tried several times in vain, he called Arnaitiang and asked her to give him back the stockings. She answered, "Take them yourself, there they are, there they are," and went out again. The fact is she was a very bad woman and wanted to eat Kiviung.

Then he tried once more to take hold of his stockings, but with no better result. He called again for Arnaitiang and asked her to give him the boots and stockings, whereupon she said, "Sit down where I sat when you entered my house, then you can get them." After that she left him again. Kiviung tried it once more, but the frame rose as before, and he could not reach it.

Now he understood that Arnaitiang meditated mischief; so he summoned his *tornaq*, a huge white bear, who arose roaring from under the floor of the house. At first Arnaitiang did not hear him, but as Kiviung kept on conjuring, the spirit came nearer and nearer to the surface. When she heard his loud roar, she rushed in trembling with fear and gave Kiviung what he had asked for. "Here are your boots," she cried, "here are your slippers, here are your stockings. I'll help you put them on." But Kiviung would not stay any longer with this horrid witch and did not even dare to put on his boots, but took them from Arnaitiang and rushed out of the door.

He had barely escaped when it clapped violently together and just caught the tail of his jacket, which was torn off. He hastened to his kayak without once stopping to look behind and paddled away. He had only gone a short distance before Arnaitiang, who had recovered from her fear, came out swinging her glittering woman's knife and threatening to kill him. He was nearly frightened to death and almost upset his kayak. However, he managed to balance it again and cried in answer, lifting up his spear, "I shall kill you with my spear." When Arnaitiang heard these words, she fell down terror-stricken and broke her knife. Kiviung then observed that it was made of a thin slab of fresh-water ice.

He traveled on for many days and nights, following the shore. At last he came to a hut, and again a lamp was burning inside. As his clothing was wet and he was hungry, he landed and entered the house. There he found a woman who lived all alone with her daughter. Her son-in-law was a log of driftwood which had four boughs. Every day, about the time of low water, they carried it to the beach, and when the tide came in, it swam away. When night came again, it returned with eight large seals, two being fastened to every bough. Thus the timber provided its wife, her mother, and Kiviung with an abundance of food. One day, however, after they had launched it as they had always done, it left and never returned.

After a short interval Kiviung married the young widow. Now he went sealing every day himself and was very successful. As he thought of leaving someday, he was anxious to get a good stock of mittens (that his hands might keep dry during the long journey). Every night after returning from hunting, he pretended to have lost his mittens. In reality he had concealed them in the hood of his jacket.

After a while the old woman became jealous of her daughter, for the new husband of the latter was a splendid hunter, and she wished to marry him herself. One day when he was away hunting, she murdered her daughter, and in order to deceive him she removed her daughter's skin and crept into it, thus changing her shape into that of the young woman. When Kiviung returned, she went to meet him, as had been her daughter's custom, and without exciting any suspicion. But when he entered the hut and saw the bones of his wife, he at once became aware of the cruel deed and of the deception that had been practiced and fled away.

He traveled on for many days and nights, always following the shore. At last he again came to a hut where a lamp was burning. As his clothing was wet and he was hungry, he landed and went up to the house. Before entering, it occurred to him that it would be best to find out first who was inside. He therefore climbed up to the window and looked through the peephole. On the bed sat an old woman, whose name was Aissivang —spider. When she saw the dark figure before the window, she believed it was a cloud passing the sun, and as the light was insufficient to enable her to go on with her work she got angry. With her knife she cut away her eyebrows, ate them, and did not mind the dripping blood, but sewed on. When Kiviung saw this, he thought that she must be a very bad woman and turned away.

Still he traveled on days and nights. At last he came to a land which seemed familiar to him and soon he recognized his own country. He was very glad when he saw some boats coming to meet him. They had been on a whaling excursion and were towing a great carcass to the village. In the bow of one of them stood a stout young man who had killed the whale. He was Kiviung's son, whom he had left a small boy, and who was now grown up and had become a great hunter. His wife had taken a new husband, but now she returned to Kiviung.

HEART SQUEEZING AND THE DANCE OF NAKED PERSONS

A WOMAN and her son lived together in a lodge situated not far from a small settlement. The boy began his career by hunting small game, but he soon killed such large game that everyone was astonished at his prowess. As he grew older, he went farther and farther into the woods. His mother, however, always warned him against going toward the northeast, saying that an evil woman lived there.

One day while hunting, the boy thought, "I do not believe there is anyone who can overcome me magically," whereupon he determined to go toward the northeast. Starting thither, he soon came to an opening, where he saw a woman who sang out, "I have caught you, my brother," and at that moment the boy, feeling her in his body squeezing his heart, screamed with pain. Then the woman stopped an instant, and then squeezed his heart harder than before, causing him intense pain.

Just then he heard a woman's voice say, "Hurry home, and as you go, sing, 'I am going to have a naked dance and a potlatch.'" The young man did this, and as he sang he felt easier. When he got home his mother said, "You have been toward the northeast, although I told you that you would get into trouble if you went there." The mother immediately sent a messenger to tell her uncle, her mother's brother, what had happened, and he inquired what the boy sang. The messenger told him, and he replied, "Tell his mother to notify everyone that she is going to have a dance of naked persons."

All the people were notified accordingly. The old man came, and one by one all the rest assembled. Then the old man asked whether all the guests were there who had been invited. The woman, the youth's mother, after looking around, said, "Yes." Telling the people to take off their garments, and to dance facing the wall, the old man, seating himself in the center of the room, began to sing. When he had finished the song, he said, "That will do." Thereupon the dance broke up, the people dressing themselves and going home.

The young man felt better, but he was angry with the woman who had tormented him. So he decided to go again and say to her, "I have caught you," before she had time to say it. The next morning he started off without telling his mother where he was going. When near the opening, halting, he called for a mole. In a short time the mole came, whereupon the boy said, "You must carry me to the spot where the woman is, but she must not see us."

Reducing his size until he was quite small, the young man entered the body of the mole, which went beneath the surface of the ground. After a while they peeped out, but the woman was still far off. They went on again, and when they looked out a second time, they were quite near the woman. She had large eyes, twice as large as those of anyone else, which were red as blood, and whenever she said, "I have caught you," nothing had power over her.

The boy told the mole to go underground, so as to come out just beneath her feet. The mole did so, and then the boy, exclaiming, "I have caught you!" at that instant going into her body, squeezed her heart. She cried out with pain, "Do not squeeze so hard." He answered, "I did not say, 'Do not squeeze so hard,' when you squeezed my heart." Thereupon the woman hurried home. When near home, she saw that her sisters were pounding corn for bread, and they noticed that she was crying, so one of them said, "I told you that that young man could not be beaten; you should not have touched him."

One of the sisters, going to the same old man who had cured the boy, said, "Uncle, our youngest sister is very sick; she is singing, 'I am going to have a dance of naked persons and a potlatch.'" The old man told her to invite the people to her pot. She did so, and when they were assembled the dance began. At the moment the old man said, "My song is finished," the young man squeezed the girl's heart so hard that she fell down dead. Coming out of her body, the young man went some distance before he became visible. He went home and was tormented no more. He could now hunt in any direction.

THE BOY AND HIS GRANDMOTHER

AN OLD WOMAN lived with her grandson in the wilderness. The boy amused himself by shooting with his bow and arrows, and was very happy. His grandmother cooked and cleaned. She talked much to him of the future and the time when he should go out into the world. "Never, my grandson," she would say, "never go west—go always to the east." And the boy wondered very much at this, because, he said, all other boys went west, and they found much game there. But he promised.

However, one day he asked his grandmother so often why she always forbade him to go west, that she told him. "Far away in the west," said she, "there lives one who waits to destroy us, and if he sees you he will injure you and me. I warn you do not go that way." But the boy questioned how and why, and thought to himself that on the first opportunity he would see for himself. So he struck out for the west, keeping a sharp lookout for the man, because his grandmother had taught him he should always bow first.

As he neared the lake he heard the man's voice, but although he looked all around, he could see no one. The voice said, "Ah! ah! my little fellow,

I see you." Still he could see no one. "What shall I do now?" thought he. Then the voice said, "What would you think if I sent a hurricane to tear your grandmother's cabin all up?" The boy replied, "Oh, I should like it. We have hard work to get wood. It would be a good thing." And the voice replied, "You had better run home and see." So he went home to his grandmother.

As he neared his cabin, he heard a great noise, and his grandmother called to him, "Come in, come in, we shall be blown away. You have disobeyed me. Now we shall be destroyed. The hurricane is upon us." But the boy only laughed and said, "We will turn the house into a rock." And he turned it into a rock, and when the hurricane was over, they were unharmed, and found plenty of wood to burn.

Then said the boy, "Grandmother, we are all right." But the old woman said, "Do not venture any more; next time he will destroy us." But the lad thought he would try again. In the morning he started off east as long as his grandmother could see him, then he turned to the west, and kept a sharp watch right and left as he neared the pond.

Then, all at once, he heard the man's voice again. "What," it asked, "would you say if a great hailstorm came down upon your grandmother's cabin, with spears as sharp as needles?" "Oh," replied the youngster, "I have always wanted some spears; I would be glad of some." "You had better go home and see," said the voice. So home he sped, hearing the gathering of a great storm.

The grandmother said, "We are going to be destroyed with a hailstorm of spears." But he laughed aloud and said, "I need spears for fishing; let them come. We will turn the house into a rock again." And he did, and when the storm was ended, he and his grandmother came out, and the ground was covered with spears. "No matter," said he, "I will get poles and fit them on for fishing"; but when he brought the pole he could not find any spears. "How is this?" he asked. And his grandmother said, "They are melted—they were ice."

The boy was very much disappointed and mourned aloud. "What can I do to punish the old fellow?" he cried. "Heed my warning," said his grandmother, "and leave him alone."

But the lad was determined. He started off once more, taking with him a stone round his neck as a charm. He watched the direction in which he had heard the voice, and all at once he saw in the middle of the lake a great head, with a face on every side of it. He cried out, "Ha! ha! uncle, I have you now. How should you like it if the lake dried up?" "That it will never do," said the voice. "Go home," mocked the lad, "and see!" And he threw the stone which he had. As it whirled through the air, it became very large and fell into the lake, when at once the water began to boil.

Then the boy returned to his grandmother's cabin and told her all about it. She said, "It has been tried again and again, but no one has ever seen him before or has been able to hunt him."

Next morning he went over to the lake and found it all dried up and all the animals dead, and only a large frog remained, into which the man had been turned. So the boy killed the frog, and no more trouble ever came to him or his grandmother.

VIII

TRICKSTER AND TRANSFORMER LEGENDS

THE DOG AND THE STICK

THIS HAPPENED LONG AGO. In those days the people were hungry. No buffalo nor antelope were seen on the prairie. The deer and the elk trails were covered with grass and leaves; not even a rabbit could be found in the brush. Then the people prayed, saying, "Oh, Old Man, help us now, or we shall die. The buffalo and deer are gone. Uselessly we kindle the morning fires; useless are our arrows; our knives stick fast in the sheaths."

Then Old Man started out to find the game, and he took with him a young man, the son of a chief. For many days they traveled the prairies and ate nothing but berries and roots. One day they climbed a high ridge, and when they had reached the top, they saw, far off by a stream, a single lodge.

"What kind of person can it be," said the young man, "who camps there all alone, far from friends?"

"That," said Old Man, "is the one who has hidden all the buffalo and deer from the people. He has a wife and a little son."

Then they went close to the lodge, and Old Man changed himself into a little dog, and he said, "That is I." Then the young man changed himself into a root-digger, and he said, "That is I."

Now the little boy, playing about, found the dog, and he carried it to his father, saying, "Look! See what a pretty little dog I have found."

"Throw it away," said his father; "it is not a dog." And the little boy cried, but his father made him carry the dog away. Then the boy found the root-digger; and again picking up the dog, he carried them both to the lodge, saying, "Look, mother! see the pretty root-digger I have found!"

"Throw them both away," said his father; "that is not a stick, that is not a dog."

"I want that stick," said the woman; "let our son have the little dog."

"Very well," said her husband, "but remember, if trouble comes, you bring it on yourself and on our son." Then he sent his wife and son off to pick berries; and when they were out of sight, he went out and killed a buffalo cow, and brought the meat into the lodge and covered it up, and the bones, skin, and offal he threw in the creek. When his wife returned, he gave her some of the meat to roast; and while they were eating, the little boy fed the dog three times. When he gave it more, his father took the meat away, saying, "That is not a dog, you shall not feed it more."

In the night, when all were asleep, Old Man and the young man arose in their right shapes, and ate of the meat. "You were right," said the young man; "this is surely the person who has hidden the buffalo from us." "Wait," said Old Man; and when they had finished eating, they changed themselves back into the stick and the dog.

In the morning the man sent his wife and son to dig roots, and the woman took the stick with her. The dog followed the little boy. Now, as they traveled along in search of roots, they came near a cave, and at its mouth stood a buffalo cow. Then the dog ran into the cave, and the stick, slipping from the woman's hand, followed, gliding along like a snake. In this cave they found all the buffalo and other game, and they began to drive them out; and soon the prairie was covered with buffalo and deer. Never before were seen so many.

Pretty soon the man came running up, and he said to his wife, "Who now drives out my animals?" and she replied, "The dog and the stick are now in there." "Did I not tell you," said he, "that those were not what they looked like? See now the trouble you have brought upon us." And he put an arrow on his bow and waited for them to come out. But they were cunning, for when the last animal—a big bull—was about to go out, the stick grasped him by the hair under his neck, and coiled up in it, and the dog held on by the hair beneath, until they were far out on the prairie, when they changed into their true shapes, and drove the buffalo toward camp.

When the people saw the buffalo coming, they drove a big band of them to the *piskun*; but just as the leaders were about to jump off, a raven came and flapped its wings in front of them and croaked, and they turned off another way. Every time a band of buffalo was driven near the *piskun*, this raven frightened them away. Then Old Man knew that the raven was the one who had kept the buffalo cached.

So he went and changed himself into a beaver, and lay stretched out on the bank of the river, as if dead; and the raven, which was very hungry, flew down and began to pick at him. Then Old Man caught it by the legs and ran with it to camp, and all the chiefs came together to decide what should be done with it. Some said to kill it, but Old Man said, "No! I will punish it," and he tied it over the lodge, right in the smoke hole.

As the days went by, the raven grew poor and weak, and his eyes were blurred with the thick smoke, and he cried continually to Old Man to pity him. One day Old Man untied him, and told him to take his right shape, saying, "Why have you tried to fool Old Man? Look at me! I cannot die. Look at me! Of all peoples and tribes I am the chief. I cannot die. I made the mountains. They are standing yet. I made the prairies and the rocks. You see them yet. Go home, then, to your wife and your child, and when you are hungry, hunt like anyone else, or you shall die."

THE RABBIT GOES DUCK HUNTING

THE RABBIT was so boastful that he would claim to do whatever he saw anyone else do, and so tricky that he could usually make the other animals believe it all. Once he pretended that he could swim in the water and eat fish just as the Otter did, and when the others told him to prove it, he fixed up a plan so that the Otter himself was deceived.

Soon afterward they met again and the Otter said, "I eat ducks sometimes." Said the Rabbit, "Well, I eat ducks too." The Otter challenged him to try it; so they went up along the river until they saw several ducks in the water and managed to get near without being seen. The Rabbit told the Otter to go first. The Otter never hesitated, but dived from the bank and swam under water until he reached the ducks, when he pulled one down without being noticed by the others, and came back in the same way.

While the Otter had been under the water, the Rabbit had peeled some bark from a sapling and made himself a noose. "Now," he said, "just watch me." And he dived in and swam a little way under the water until he was nearly choking and had to come up to the top to breathe. He went under again and came up again a little nearer to the ducks. He took another breath and dived under, and this time he came up among the ducks and threw the noose over the head of one and caught it. The duck struggled hard and finally spread its wings and flew up from the water with the Rabbit hanging onto the noose.

It flew on and on until at last the Rabbit could not hold on any longer, but had to let go and drop. As it happened, he fell into a tall, hollow sycamore stump without any hole at the bottom to get out from, and there he stayed until he was so hungry that he had to eat his own fur, as the rabbit does ever since when he is starving. After several days, when he was very weak with hunger, he heard children playing outside around the trees. He began to sing:

> Cut a door and look at me;
> I'm the prettiest thing you ever did see.

The children ran home and told their father, who came and began to cut a hole in the tree. As he chopped away, the Rabbit inside kept singing, "Cut it larger, so you can see me better; I'm so pretty." They made the hole larger, and then the Rabbit told them to stand back so that they could take a good look as he came out. They stood away back, and the Rabbit watched his chance and jumped out and got away.

PÁUP-PUK-KEEWIS

THE VERNAL EQUINOX in the north generally takes place while the ground is covered with snow, and winter still wears a polar aspect. Storms of wind and light drifting snow, expressively called *poudre* by the French, and *peewun* by the Indians, fill the atmosphere, and render it impossible to distinguish objects at a short distance. The fine powdery flakes of snow are driven into the smallest crannies of buildings and fixtures, and seem to be endowed with a subtle power of insinuation, which renders northern join-

erwork but a poor defense. It is not uncommon for the sleeper, on waking up in the morning, to find heaps of snow, where he had supposed himself quite secure on lying down.

Such seasons are, almost invariably, times of scarcity and hunger with the Indians, for the light snows have buried the traps of the hunters, and the fishermen are deterred from exercising their customary skill in decoying fish through openings cut in the ice. They are often reduced to the greatest straits, and compelled to exercise their utmost ingenuity to keep their children from starving. Abstinence, on the part of the elder members of the family, is regarded both as a duty and a merit. Every effort is made to satisfy the need of the little ones for food, and if there is a storyteller in the lodge, he is sure to draw upon his cabin lore, to amuse their minds, and beguile the time.

In these storms, when each inmate of the lodge has his *conaus*, his wrapper, tightly drawn around him, and all are quivering around the cabin fire, should some sudden puff of wind drive a volume of light snow into the lodge, it would scarcely happen but that someone of the group would cry out, "Ah, Paup-Puk-Keewis is now gathering his harvest," an expression which has the effect of putting them all in good humor.

Paup-Puk-Keewis was a crazy-brain, who played many queer tricks, but took care, nevertheless, to supply his family and children with food. But, in this, he was not always successful. Many winters have passed since he was overtaken, at this very season of the year, with great want, and he, with his whole family, was on the point of starvation. Every resource seemed to have failed. The snow was so deep, and the storm continued so long, that he could not even find a partridge or a hare. And his usual resource of fish had entirely failed. His lodge stood in a point of woods, not far back from the shores of the Gitchiguma, the great water, where the autumnal storms had piled up the ice into high pinnacles, resembling castles.

"I will go," said he to his family one morning, "to these castles, and solicit the pity of the spirits who inhabit them, for I know that they are the residence of some of the spirits of Kabiboonoka." He did so, and found that his petition was not disregarded. They told him to fill his *mushkemoot*, his sack, with the ice and snow, and pass on toward his lodge, without looking back, until he came to a certain hill. He must then drop it and leave it till morning, when he would find it filled with fish.

They cautioned him that he must by no means look back, although he would hear a great many voices crying out to him, in abusive terms, for these voices were nothing but the wind playing through the branches of the trees. He faithfully obeyed the injunction, although he found it hard to avoid turning round, to see who was calling out to him. And when he visited his sack in the morning, he found it filled with fish.

It chanced that Manabozho visited him on the morning that he brought home the sack of fish. He was invited to partake of a feast, which Paup-Puk-Keewis ordered to be prepared for him. While they were eating, Manabozho could not help asking him by what means he had procured such an abundance of food, at a time when they were all in a state of starvation.

Paup-Puk-Keewis frankly told him the secret, and repeated the precautions which were necessary to insure success. Manabozho determined to profit by his information, and as soon as he could, he set out to visit the icy castles. All things happened as he had been told. The spirits seemed propitious, and told him to fill and carry. He accordingly filled his sacks with ice and snow, and proceeded rapidly toward the hill of transmutation. But as he ran he heard voices calling out behind him. "Thief! thief! He has stolen fish from Kabiboonoka," cried one. *"Mukumik! mukumik!*—Take it away! Take it away!" cried another.

In fine, his ears were so assailed by all manner of opprobrious terms, that he could not avoid turning his head, to see who it was that thus abused him. But his curiosity dissolved the charm. When he came to visit his bags next morning, he found them filled with ice and snow. A high drifting snowstorm never fails to bring up this story about Paup-Puk-Keewis.

The origin of this queer character is as queer as his acts are fantastic. The myth says that a man of large stature, and great activity of mind and body, found himself standing alone on a prairie. He thought to himself, "How came I here? Are there no beings on this earth but myself? I must travel and see. I must walk till I find the lodges of men." As soon as his mind was made up, he set out, he knew not where, in search of habitations. No obstacles could divert him from his purpose. Neither prairies, rivers, woods, nor storms had the effect to daunt his courage or turn him back.

After traveling a long time, he came to a wood, in which he saw decayed stumps of trees, as if they had been cut in ancient times, but no other traces of men. Pursuing his journey, he found more recent marks of the same kind. And after this, he came to fresh traces of human beings, first their footsteps, and then the wood they had cut, lying in heaps. Continuing on, he emerged toward dusk from the forest, and beheld at a distance a large village of high lodges, standing on rising ground. He said to himself, "I will arrive there on a run." Off he started with all his speed. On coming to the first large lodge, he jumped over it. Those within saw something pass over the opening, and then heard a thump on the ground.

"What is that?" they all said.

One came out to see, and invited him in. He found himself in company with an old chief and several men, who were seated in the lodge. Meat was set before him, after which the chief asked him where he was going and what his name was. He answered that he was in search of adventures, and his name was Paup-Puk-Keewis. A stare followed.

"Paup-Puk-Keewis! Grasshopper!" said one to another, and a general titter went round.

He was not easy in his new position. The village was too small to give him full scope for his powers, and after a short stay he made up his mind to go farther, taking with him a young man who had formed a strong attachment for him, and might serve him as his pipe bearer. They set out together, and when his companion was fatigued with walking, he would show him a few tricks, such as leaping over trees, and turning round on one leg till he made the dust fly, by which he was mightily pleased, although it sometimes happened that the character of these tricks frightened the young man.

One day they came to a very large village, where they were well received. After staying in it some time, they were informed of a number of Manitoes who lived at a distance, and who made it a practice to kill all who came to their lodge. Attempts had been made to kill them, but the war parties who went out for this purpose were always unsuccessful. Paup-Puk-Keewis determined to visit them, although he was advised not to do so. The chief warned him of the danger of the visit. But, finding him resolved, "Well," said he, "if you will go, being my guest, I will send twenty warriors to serve you."

He thanked him for the offer. Twenty young men were ready at the instant, and they went forward, and in due time discovered the lodge of the Manitoes. He placed his friend and the warriors near enough to see all that passed, while he went alone to the lodge. As he entered he saw five horrid-looking Manitoes in the act of eating. It was the father and his four sons. They looked hideous; their eyes were swimming low in their heads, as if half starved. They offered him something to eat, which he refused.

"What have you come for?" said the old one.

"Nothing," Paup-Puk-Keewis answered.

They all stared at him.

"Do you not wish to wrestle?" they all asked.

"Yes," he replied.

A hideous smile came over their faces.

"You go," they said to the eldest brother.

They got ready, and were soon clinched in each other's arms for a deadly throw. He knew their object—his death—his flesh was all they wanted, but he was prepared for them.

"*Haw! haw!*" they cried, and soon the dust and dry leaves flew about as if driven by a strong wind.

The Manito was strong, but Paup-Puk-Keewis soon found that he could master him; and, giving him a trip, he threw him with a giant's force head foremost on a stone, and he fell like a puffed thing.

The brothers stepped up in quick succession, but he put a number of tricks in force, and soon the whole four lay bleeding on the ground. The old Manito got frightened and ran for his life. Paup-Puk-Keewis pursued him for sport; sometimes he was before him, sometimes flying over his head. He would now give him a kick, then a push or a trip, till he was almost exhausted. Meantime his friend and the warriors cried out, "*Ha! ha! a! ha! ha! a!* Paup-Puk-Keewis is driving him before him." The Manito only turned his head now and then to look back; at last, Paup-Puk-Keewis gave him a kick on his back, and broke his backbone; down he fell, and the blood gushing out of his mouth prevented him from saying a word. The warriors

239

piled all the bodies together in the lodge, and then took fire and burned them. They all looked with deep interest at the quantity of human bones scattered around.

Paup-Puk-Keewis then took three arrows, and after having performed a ceremony to the Great Spirit, he shot one into the air, crying, with a loud voice, "You who are lying down, rise up, or you will be hit!" The bones all moved to one place. He shot the second arrow, repeating the same words, when each bone drew toward its fellow bone; the third arrow brought forth to life the whole multitude of people who had been killed by the Manitoes. Paup-Puk-Keewis then led them to the chief of the village who had proved his friend, and gave them up to him. Soon after the chief came with his counselors. "Who is more worthy," said he, "to rule than you? You alone can defend them."

Paup-Puk-Keewis thanked him, and told him he was in search of more adventures. The chief insisted. Paup-Puk-Keewis told him to confer the chieftainship on his friend, who, he said, would remain while he went on his travels. He told them that he would, some time or other, come back and see them.

"Ho! ho! ho!" they all cried, "come back again and see us," insisting on it. He promised them he would, and then set out alone.

After traveling some time he came to a large lake; on looking about, he discovered a very large otter on an island. He thought to himself, "His skin will make me a fine pouch," and immediately drew up, at long shot, and drove an arrow into his side. He waded into the lake, and with some difficulty dragged him ashore. He took out the entrails, and even then the carcass was so heavy that it was as much as he could do to drag it up a hill overlooking the lake. As soon as he got him up into the sunshine, where it was warm, he skinned him, and threw the carcass some distance, thinking the war eagle would come, and he should have a chance to get his skin and feathers as head ornaments.

He soon heard a rushing noise in the air, but could see nothing; by and by, a large eagle dropped, as if from the air, on the otter's carcass. He drew his bow, and the arrow passed through under both his wings. The bird made a convulsive flight upward with such force, that the heavy carcass (which was nearly as big as a moose) was borne up several feet. Fortunately, both claws were fastened deeply into the meat, the weight of which soon brought the bird down. He skinned him, crowned his head with the trophy, and next day was on his way, on the lookout for something new.

After walking a while, he came to a lake, which flooded the trees on its banks; he found it was only a lake made by beavers. He took his station on the elevated dam, where the stream escaped, to see whether any of the beavers would show themselves. He soon saw the head of one peeping out of the water to see who disturbed them.

"My friend," said Paup-Puk-Keewis, "could you not turn me into a beaver like yourself?" for he thought, if he could become a beaver, he would see and know how these animals lived.

"I do not know," replied the beaver; "I will go and ask the others."

Soon all the beavers showed their heads above the water, and looked to see if he was armed; but he had left his bow and arrows in a hollow tree at a short distance. When they were satisfied, they all came near.

"Can you not, with all your united power," said he, "turn me into a beaver? I wish to live among you."

"Yes," answered their chief, "lie down," and he soon found himself changed into one of them.

"You must make me large," said he, "larger than any of you."

"Yes, yes!" said they. "By and by, when we get into the lodge, it shall be done."

In they all dove into the lake; and, in passing large heaps of limbs and logs at the bottom, he asked the use of them. They answered, "It is for our winter's provisions." When they all got into the lodge, their number was about one hundred. The lodge was large and warm.

"Now we will make you large," said they. "Will that do?" exerting their power.

"Yes," he answered, for he found he was ten times the size of the largest.

"You need not go out," said they. "We will bring your food into the lodge, and you will be our chief."

"Very well," Paup-Puk-Keewis answered. He thought, "I will stay here and grow fat at their expense." But, soon after, one ran into the lodge out of breath, saying, "We are visited by Indians." All huddled together in great fear. The water began to lower, for the hunters had broken down the dam, and they soon heard them on the roof of the lodge breaking it up. Out jumped all the beavers into the water, and so escaped. Paup-Puk-Keewis tried to follow them; but, alas! they had made him so large that he could not creep out of the hole. He tried to call them back, but to no effect; he worried himself so much in trying to escape that he looked like a bladder. He could not turn himself back into a man, although he heard and understood all the hunters said. One of them put his head in at the top of the lodge.

"*Ty-au!*" cried he, "*Tut Ty-au!* Me-shau-mik, king of the beavers is in." They all got at him, and knocked his skull till it was as soft as his brains. He thought as well as ever he did, although he was a beaver. Seven or eight of them then placed his body on poles and carried him home. As they went, he reflected in this manner, "What will become of me? My ghost or shadow will not die after they get me to their lodges." Invitations were immediately sent out for a grand feast. The women took him out into the snow to skin him; but as soon as his flesh got cold, his *Jee-bi*, his spirit, went off.

Paup-Puk-Keewis found himself standing near a prairie, having reassumed his mortal shape. After walking a distance, he saw a herd of elk feeding. He admired the apparent ease and enjoyment of their life, and thought there could be nothing pleasanter than the liberty of running about and feeding on the prairies. He asked them if they could not turn him into their shape.

"Yes," they answered, after a pause. "Get down on your hands and feet." And soon he found himself an elk.

"I want big horns, big feet," said he. "I wish to be very large."

"Yes! yes!" they said.

"There!" exerting their power. "Are you big enough?"

"Yes!" he answered, for he saw that he was very large. They spent a good time in grazing and running. Being rather cold one day, he went into a thick wood for shelter, and was followed by most of the herd. They had not been long there before some elks from behind passed the others like a strong wind. All took the alarm, and off they ran, he with the rest.

"Keep out on the plains," they said.

But he found it was too late, as they had already got entangled in the thick woods. Paup-Puk-Keewis soon smelled the hunters, who were closely following his trail, for they had left all the others and followed him. He jumped furiously, and broke down saplings in his flight, but it only served to retard his progress. He soon felt an arrow in his side. He jumped over trees in his agony, but the arrows clattered thicker and thicker upon his sides, and at last one entered his heart. He fell to the ground, and heard the whoop of triumph sounded by the hunters.

On coming up, they looked on the carcass with astonishment, and with their hands up to their mouths exclaimed, *"Ty-au! Ty-au!"* There were about sixty in the party, who had come out on a special hunt, as one of their number had, the day before, observed his large tracks on the plains. After skinning him and his flesh getting cold, his *Jee-bi* took its flight from the carcass, and he again found himself in human shape, with a bow and arrows.

But his passion for adventure was not yet cooled; for on coming to a large lake with a sandy beach, he saw a large flock of brant, and speaking to them, asked them to turn him into a brant.

"Yes," they replied.

"But I want to be very large," he said.

"Very well," they answered; and he soon found himself a large brant, all the others gazing in astonishment at his large size.

"You must fly as leader," they said.

"No," answered Paup-Puk-Keewis, "I will fly behind."

"Very well," they said. "One thing more we have to say to you. You must be careful, in flying, not to look down, for something may happen to you."

"Well! it is so," said he; and soon the flock rose up into the air, for they were bound north. They flew very fast, he behind. One day, while going with a strong wind, and as swift as their wings could flap, while passing over a large village, the Indians raised a great shout on seeing them, particularly on Paup-Puk-Keewis's account, for his wings were broader than two large mats. They made such a noise that he forgot what had been told him about looking down.

They were now going as swift as arrows; and as soon as he brought his neck in and stretched it down to look at the shouters, his tail was caught by the wind, and over and over he was blown. He tried to right himself, but without success. Down, down he went, making more turns than he wished, from a height of several miles. The first thing he knew was that he was jammed into a large hollow tree. To get back or forward was out of the question, and there he remained till his brant life was ended by starvation. His *Jee-bi* again left the carcass, and he once more found himself in the shape of a human being.

Traveling was still his passion; and while traveling, he came to a lodge in which were two old men with heads white from age. They treated him well, and he told them that he was going back to his village to see his friends and people. They said they would aid him, and pointed out the direction he should go; but they were deceivers.

After walking all day, he came to a lodge looking very much like the first, with two old men in it with white heads. It was, in fact, the very same lodge, and he had been walking in a circle; but they did not undeceive him, pretending to be strangers, and saying, in a kind voice, "We will show you the way." After walking the third day, and coming back to the same place, he found out their tricks, for he had cut a notch on the doorpost.

"Who are you," said he to them, "to treat me so?" And he gave one a kick and the other a slap, which killed them. Their blood flew against the rocks near the lodge, and this is the reason there are red streaks in them to this day. He then burned their lodge down, and freed the earth of two pretended good men, who were Manitoes.

He then continued his journey, not knowing exactly which way to go. At last he came to a big lake. He got on the highest hill to try and see the opposite side, but he could not. He then made a canoe, and took a sail into the lake. On looking into the water, which was very clear, before he got to the abrupt depth, he saw the bottom covered with dark fishes, numbers of which he caught. This inspired him with a wish to return to his village and to bring his people to live near this lake. He went on, and toward evening came to a large island, where he encamped and ate the fish he had speared.

Next day he returned to the mainland, and in wandering along the shore, he encountered a more powerful Manito than himself, called Manabozho. He thought best, after playing him a trick, to keep out of his way. He again thought of returning to his village; and transforming himself into a partridge, took his flight toward it. In a short time he reached it, and his return was welcomed with feastings and songs. He told them of the lake and the fish, and persuaded them all to remove to it, as it would be easier for them to live there. He immediately began to remove them by short encampments, and all things turned out as he had said. They caught abundance of fish.

After this, a messenger came for him in the shape of a bear, who said that their king wished to see him immediately at his village. Paup-Puk-Keewis was ready in an instant, and getting on to the messenger's back, off he rode. Toward evening they went up a high mountain, and came to a cave where the bear king lived. He was a very large person, and made him welcome by inviting him into his lodge. As soon as propriety allowed, he spoke, and said that he had sent for him on hearing that he was the chief who was moving a large party toward his hunting grounds.

"You must know," said he, "that you have no right there. And I wish you would leave the country with your party, or else the strongest force will take possession."

"Very well," replied Paup-Puk-Keewis. "So be it." He did not wish to do anything without consulting his people; and besides, he saw that the bear king was raising a war party. He then told him he would go back that night. The bear king left him to do as he wished, but told him that one of his young men was ready at his command; and immediately jumping on his back, Paup-Puk-Keewis rode home. He assembled the village, and told the young men to kill the bear, make a feast of it, and hang the head outside the village, for he knew the bear spies would soon see it, and carry the news to their chief.

Next morning Paup-Puk-Keewis got all his young warriors ready for a fight. After waiting one day, the bear war party came in sight, making a tremendous noise. The bear chief advanced, and said that he did not wish to shed the blood of the young warriors, but that if he, Paup-Puk-Keewis, consented, they two would have a race, and the winner should kill the losing chief, and all his young men should be slaves to the other.

Paup-Puk-Keewis agreed, and they ran before all the warriors. He was victor, and came in first; but not to terminate the race too soon, he gave the bear chief some specimens of his skill and swiftness by forming eddies and whirlwinds with the sand, as he leaped and turned about him. As the bear chief came up, he drove an arrow through him, and a great chief fell.

Having done this, he told his young men to take all those blackfish (meaning the bears), and tie them at the door of each lodge, that they might remain in future to serve as servants.

After seeing that all was quiet and prosperous in the village, Paup-Puk-Keewis felt his desire for adventure returning. He took a kind leave of his friends and people, and started off again. After wandering a long time, he came to the lodge of Manabozho, who was absent. He thought he would play him a trick, and so turned everything in the lodge upside down, and killed his chickens. Now Manabozho calls all the fowls of the air his chickens; and among the number was a raven, the meanest of birds, which Paup-Puk-Keewis killed and hung up by the neck to insult him. He then went on till he came to a very high point of rocks running out into the lake, from the top of which he could see the country back as far as the eye could reach.

While sitting there, Manabozho's mountain chickens flew round and past him in great numbers. So, out of spite, he shot them in great numbers, for his arrows were sure and the birds very plentiful, and he amused himself by throwing the birds down the rocky precipice. At length a wary bird cried out, "Paup-Puk-Keewis is killing us. Go and tell our father." Away flew a delegation of them, and Manabozho soon made his appearance on the plain below. Paup-Puk-Keewis made his escape on the opposite side. Manabozho cried out from the mountain, "The earth is not so large but I can get up to you."

Off Paup-Puk-Keewis ran, and Manabozho after him. He ran over hills and prairies with all his speed, but still saw his pursuer hard after him. He then thought of this expedient: He stopped and climbed a large pine tree, stripped it of all its green foliage, and threw it to the winds, and then went on. When Manabozho reached the spot, the tree addressed him.

"Great chief," said the tree, "will you give me my life again? Paup-Puk-Keewis has killed me."

"Yes," replied Manabozho; but it took him some time to gather the scattered foliage. Then he renewed the pursuit. Paup-Puk-Keewis repeated the same thing with the hemlock, and with various other trees, for Manabozho would always stop to restore what he had destroyed. By this means he kept in advance, but Manabozho persevered, and was fast overtaking him, when Paup-Puk-Keewis happened to see an elk. He asked him to take him on his back, which the elk did, and for some time he made great progress, but still Manabozho was in sight. Paup-Puk-Keewis dismounted, and coming to a large sandstone rock, he broke it in pieces and scattered the grains. Manabozho was so close upon him at this place that he had almost caught him; but the foundation of the rock cried out, "*Haye!* Nemesho, Paup-Puk-Keewis has spoiled me. Will you not restore me to life?"

"Yes," replied Manabozho; and he restored the rock to its previous shape. He then pushed on in pursuit of Paup-Puk-Keewis, and had got so near as to put out his arm to seize him. But Paup-Puk-Keewis dodged him, and immediately raised such a dust and commotion by whirlwinds as made the trees break, and the sand and leaves dance in the air. Again Manabozho's hand was put out to catch him; but he dodged him at every turn, and kept up such a tumult of dust that in the thickest of it he dashed into a hollow tree which had been blown down, and changed himself into a snake, and crept out at the roots. Well that he did; for at the moment he had crept out, Manabozho, using his lightning power, struck the tree and it was in fragments.

Paup-Puk-Keewis was again in human shape; again Manabozho pressed him hard. At a distance he saw a very high bluff of rock jutting out into the lake, and ran for the foot of the precipice, which was abrupt and elevated. As he came near, the local Manito of the rock opened his door and told him to come in. The door was no sooner closed than Manabozho knocked.

"Open it!" he cried with a loud voice.

The Manito was afraid of him, but he said to his guest, "Since I have sheltered you, I would sooner die with you than open the door."

"Open it!" Manabozho again cried.

The Manito kept silent. Manabozho, however, made no attempt to open it by force. He waited a few moments. "Very well," he said, "I give you only till night to live." The Manito trembled, for he knew he would be shut up under the earth.

Night came. The clouds hung low and black, and every moment the forked lightning would flash from them. The black clouds advanced slowly, and threw their dark shadows afar, and behind there was heard the rumbling noise of the coming thunder. As they came near to the precipice, the thunder roared, the lightning flashed, the ground shook, and the solid rocks split, tottered, and fell. And under their ruins were crushed the mortal bodies of Paup-Puk-Keewis and the Manito.

It was only then that Paup-Puk-Keewis found he was really dead. He had been killed in different animal shapes; but now his body, in human shape, was crushed. Manabozho came and took their *Jee-bi-ug*, their spirits.

"You," said he to Paup-Puk-Keewis, "shall not be again permitted to live on the earth. I will give you the shape of the war eagle, and you will be the chief of all fowls, and your duty shall be to watch over their destinies."

RAVEN PRETENDS TO BUILD A CANOE

AFTER RAVEN* HAD VISITED every country, he found a little hut in which were two women—a widow and her daughter; and the widow was very kind to him, and fed him with many kinds of food. After Raven had eaten, he said to the widow, "I will marry your daughter," and the widow agreed. Then Raven was glad that the widow's daughter was to marry him, for the widow's house was full of all kinds of food. The young woman who was the wife of Raven was very beautiful.

After a while Raven said to his young wife, "Now, my dear, you know that I love you very much, and therefore I shall build a nice little canoe for your mother. I shall go away tomorrow to look for red cedar. Then I will build a canoe for her. I want you to get ready, for I want to start early in the morning." The young woman repeated this to her mother.

Early the next morning the mother-in-law arose and prepared breakfast for her son-in-law. When it was ready she called her son-in-law. Raven arose and ate his breakfast. Then he went off to search for red cedar. He came back before it was evening, went to his wife, and told her that he had found a very good red cedar of proper size. He said, "I will cut it down tomorrow. Then I will cut it the right length for a canoe." His mother-in-law prepared supper for him, and she cooked all the food she had. After he had

*There are many legends about the transformer-trickster, who at birth was called Giant. In the Tsimshian language, Raven is Txamsem (pronounced *Tchem-sem*)—the name by which he was known to the tribes of the Northwest Coast.

eaten his meal, he lay down; and while he was lying there, he whispered to his wife, "When the canoe is finished, I will go around the island. You shall sit in the stern, your mother shall sit in the middle of the canoe, and I will sit in the bow. Then we shall have a happy time." Thus spoke Raven to his wife. Next morning he arose, while his mother-in-law prepared his breakfast.

After he had taken his meal, he took his mother-in-law's stone tools and went; and his mother-in-law and his wife heard him cut the tree with his stone axe. They also heard the large cedar tree fall, and after a while they heard also how he was working with the stone axe. He came home before it was evening, weary and sore on account of the hard work that he had been doing all day long. When he came home, he said to his wife, "Just tell your mother that I want her to boil for me a good dried salmon every evening, for I like the soup of dried salmon. It is very good for a man who is building a canoe." She did so every evening. When the fourth day came, Raven told his wife that the canoe was almost finished. By this time his mother-in-law's provisions were nearly spent, and some of her food boxes were empty.

A few days later Raven started again, and on the following morning he went to take along some food for his dinner. Now, the widow said to her daughter, "Go, my dear daughter, and see how long it may take until your husband has finished the canoe that he is building, but go secretly." Then the daughter went to the place where her husband was working. Unseen she arrived at the place where he was, and saw him standing at the end of an old rotten cedar tree beating it with a stone axe to make a noise like a man who is working with an axe. His wife saw that there was a large hole in the rotten cedar tree, and therefore it made much noise when Raven was striking it. His wife left.

When she came to her mother, she told her all about her husband. Therefore they took the canoe and moved to their tribe. They took away all the provisions that were left. Raven went back before it was evening. Before he reached his mother-in-law's hut he was glad and whistled, because he thought his mother-in-law had prepared his supper for him. But when he went in, he saw that everything was gone. Nothing remained except empty boxes and a little fire. Then he was hungry again.

RAVEN FINDS A BEAUTIFUL BLANKET

Now, RAVEN took a dancing-garment of one of the chiefs and wore it. He threw away his raven blanket which his father had given him, and went on, not knowing where he went. He went along, and tore his dancing-blanket, and was very poor; but he remembered his raven blanket which

he had thrown away. He turned back and searched for his raven blanket a long time. At last he found it, took it up, and put it on; then he was glad to have it back. He went on, and saw a very nice dancing-blanket like the one he had worn before.

At once he tore his raven blanket which his father had given him, and took the dancing-blanket that hung before him. He went on, dressed like a young prince; but when he was walking, behold! it was no dancing-garment; but he had on only lichens. He sat there weeping, turned back, and searched for his raven blanket, tied it together, and walked on, hungry and weeping.

As he went along, behold! there were a marten blanket and a dancing-blanket hanging there. So he went toward them, took off his raven blanket, and wore the marten blanket below, and the dancing-blanket over it. He went on, dressed like a young chief. Then he saw a village before him, and his heart rose in pride; but, behold! his garments were only common moss and lichens. He stood there again weeping, and turned back to search for his raven blanket which his father had given him. He found it, put it on, and flew toward the town.

MANABOZHO

A RED MOON rode the windy sky. A great, dark, batlike shadow screened it for the length of a heartbeat. An owl hooted eerily in the depth of the dark forest; then the shrill shrieks of a newborn man-child filled the air. All night noises ceased. Black clouds veiled the moon, and the sky was filled with the wings of many birds in wild flight. Forest animals fled in terror. Manabozho, transformer and trickster, had been born. Very little is told of his early boyhood. We take him up in the following legend at a period of advanced youth, when we find him living with his grandmother. And at this time he possessed, although he had not yet exercised, all the anomalous and contradictory powers of body and mind, of manship and divinity, which he afterward evinced.

The timidity and rawness of the boy quickly gave way in the courageous developments of the man. He soon evinced the sagacity, cunning, perseverance, and heroic courage which constitute the admiration of the Indians. And he relied largely upon these in the gratification of an ambitious, vainglorious, and mischief-loving disposition. In wisdom and energy he was superior to anyone who had ever lived before. Yet he was simple when circumstances required it, and was ever the object of tricks and ridicule in others. He could transform himself into any animal he pleased, being man or Manito, as circumstances rendered necessary. He often conversed with animals, fowls, reptiles, and fishes. He deemed himself related to them, and invariably addressed them by the term "my brother"; and one of his greatest resources, when hard-pressed, was to change himself into their shapes.

Manitoes constitute the great power and absorbing topic of Indian lore. Their agency is at once the groundwork of their mythology and demonology. They supply the machinery of their poetic inventions, and the belief in their multitudinous existence exerts a powerful influence upon the lives and character of individuals. As their Manitoes are of all imaginary kinds, grades, and powers, benign and malicious, it seems a grand conception among the Indians to create a personage strong enough in his necromantic and spiritual powers to baffle the most malicious, beat the stoutest, and overreach the most cunning. In carrying out this conception in the following myth, they have, however, rather exhibited an incarnation of the power of evil than of the genius of benevolence.

Manabozho was living with his grandmother near the edge of a wide prairie. On this prairie he first saw animals and birds of every kind. He there also saw exhibitions of divine power in the sweeping tempests, in the thunder and lightning, and the various shades of light and darkness, which form a never-ending scene of observation. Every new sight he beheld in the heavens was a subject of remark; every new animal or bird an object of deep interest; and every sound uttered by the animal creation a new lesson, which he was expected to learn. He often trembled at what he heard and saw.

To this scene his grandmother sent him at an early age to watch. The first sound he heard was that of the owl, at which he was greatly terrified, and quickly descending the tree he had climbed, he ran with alarm to the lodge, "Noko! Noko!" he cried, "I have heard a *monedo*." She laughed at his fears, and asked him what kind of noise it made. He answered, "It makes a noise like this, *Ko-ko-ko-ho*." She told him that he was young and foolish, that what he had heard was only a bird, deriving its name from the noise it made.

He went back and continued his watch. While there, he thought to himself, "It is singular that I am so simple, and my grandmother so wise, and that I have neither father nor mother. I have never heard a word about them. I must ask and find out." He went home and sat down silent and dejected. At length his grandmother asked him, "Manabozho, what is the matter with you?" He answered, "I wish you would tell me whether I have any parents living, and who my relatives are." Knowing that he was of a wicked and revengeful disposition, she dreaded telling him the story of his parentage, but he insisted on her compliance.

"Yes," she said, "you have a father and three brothers living. Your mother is dead. She was taken without the consent of her parents by your father, the West. Your brothers are the North, East, and South, and being older than yourself, your father has given them great power with the winds, according to their names. You are the youngest of his children. I have nourished you from your infancy, for your mother died in giving you birth, owing to the ill treatment of your father. I have no relations besides you this side of the planet in which I was born, and from which I was precipitated by female jealousy. Your mother was my only child, and you are my only hope."

He appeared to be rejoiced to hear that his father was living, for he had already thought in his heart to try and kill him. He told his grandmother he should set out in the morning to visit him. She said it was a long distance to the place where Ningabiun, Wind of the West, lived. But that did not stop him, for he had now attained manhood, possessed a giant's height, and was endowed by nature with a giant's strength and power. He set out and soon reached the place, for every step he took covered a large surface of ground. The meeting took place on a high mountain in the west. His father was very happy to see him. He also appeared pleased. They spent some days in talking with each other.

One evening Manabozho asked his father what he was most afraid of on earth. He replied, "Nothing." "But is there not something you dread here? Tell me." At last his father said, yielding, "Yes, there is a black stone found in such a place. It is the only thing earthly I am afraid of; for if it should hit me or any part of my body, it would injure me very much."

He said this as a secret, and in return asked his son the same question. Knowing each other's power, although the son's was limited, the father feared him on account of his great strength. Manabozho answered, "Nothing!" intending to avoid the question, or to refer to some harmless object as the one of which he was afraid. He was asked again and again, and answered, "Nothing!" But the West said, "There must be something you are afraid of." "Well! I will tell you," said Manabozho, "what it is."

But before he would pronounce the word, he affected great pain. "*Ie-ee—Ie-ee*—it is—it is," said he, "*yeo! yeo!* I cannot name it; I am seized with a dread." The West told him to banish his fears. He commenced again, in a strain of mock sensitiveness, repeating the same words. At last he cried out, "It is the root of the bulrush." He appeared to be exhausted by the effort of pronouncing the word, in all this skillfully acting a studied part.

Some time after he observed, "I will get some of the black rock." The West said, "Far be it from you; do not do so, my son." He still persisted. "Well," said the father, "I will also get the *apukwa* root." Manabozho immediately cried out, "No! no!" affecting, as before, to be in great dread of it, but really wishing, by this course, to urge on the West to procure it, that he might draw him into combat. He went out and got a large piece of the black rock and brought it home. The West also took care to bring the dreaded root.

In the course of conversation, he asked his father whether he had been the cause of his mother's death. The answer was, "Yes!" He then took up the rock and struck him. Blow led to blow, and here commenced an obstinate and furious combat, which continued several days. Fragments of the rock, broken off under Manabozho's blows, can be seen in various places to this day. The root did not prove as mortal a weapon as his well-acted fears had led his father to expect, although he suffered severely from the blows. This battle commenced on the mountains. The West was forced to give ground. Manabozho drove him across rivers, and over mountains and lakes, and at last he came to the brink of this world.

"Hold!" cried he, "my son; you know my power, and that it is impossible to kill me. Desist, and I will also portion you out with as much power as your brothers. The four quarters of the globe are already occupied; but you can go forth and do a great deal of good to the people of this earth, which is infested with large serpents, beasts, and monsters, who make great havoc among the inhabitants. Go and do good. You have the power now to do so, and your fame with the beings of this earth will last forever. When you have finished your work, I will have a place provided for you. You will then go and sit with your brother Kabibboonocca in the north."

Manabozho was pacified. He returned to his lodge, where he was confined by the wounds he had received. But from his grandmother's skill in medicines he was soon recovered. She told him that his grandfather, who had come to the earth in search of her, had been killed by Megissogwon, the Pearl Feather, who lived on the opposite side of the great lake. "When he was alive," she continued, "I was never without oil to put on my head, but now my hair is fast falling off for the want of it." "Well!" said he, "Noko, get cedar bark and make me a line, whilst I make a canoe."

When all was ready, he went out to the middle of the lake to fish. He put his line down, saying, "Me-she-nah-ma-gwai, kingfish, take hold of my bait." He kept repeating this for some time. At last the king of the fishes said, "Manabozho troubles me. Here trout, take hold of his line." The trout did so. He then commenced drawing up his line, which was very heavy, so that his canoe stood nearly perpendicular; but he kept crying out, "Wha-ee-he! wha-ee-he!" till he could see the trout. As soon as he saw him, he spoke to him. "Why did you take hold of my hook? Esa! Shame! You ugly fish." The trout, being thus rebuked, let go.

Manabozho put his line again in the water, saying, "King of fishes, take hold of my line." But the king of the fishes told a monstrous sunfish to take hold of it; for Manabozho was tiring him with his incessant calls. He again drew up his line with difficulty, saying as before, "Wha-ee-he! wha-ee-he!" while his canoe was turning in swift circles. When he saw the sunfish, he cried, "Esa! Esa! you odious fish! Why did you dirty my hook by taking it in your mouth? Let go, I say, let go." The sunfish did so, and told the king of fishes what Manabozho said.

Just at that moment the bait came near the king, and hearing Manabozho continually crying out, "Me-she-nah-ma-gwai, take hold of my hook," at last he did so, and allowed himself to be drawn up to the surface, which he had no sooner reached than, at one mouthful, he took Manabozho and his canoe down. When he came to himself, he found that he was in the fish's belly, and also his canoe. He now turned his thoughts to the way of making his escape.

Looking in his canoe, he saw his war club, with which he immediately struck the heart of the fish. He then felt a sudden motion, as if he were moving with great speed. The fish observed to the others, "I am sick at stomach for having swallowed this dirty fellow Manabozho." Just at this moment he received another severe blow on the heart. Manabozho thought, "If I am thrown up in the middle of the lake, I shall be drowned; so I must prevent it." He drew his canoe and placed it across the fish's throat, and just as he had finished, the fish commenced vomiting, but to no effect. In this he was aided by a squirrel, who had accompanied him unperceived until that moment. This animal had taken an active part in helping him to place his canoe across the fish's throat. For this act he named him, saying, "For the future, boys shall always call you Ajidaumo."

He then renewed his attack upon the fish's heart, and succeeded, by repeated blows, in killing him, which he first knew by the loss of motion, and by the sound of the beating of the body against the shore. He waited a day longer to see what would happen. He heard birds scratching on the body, and all at once the rays of light broke in. He could see the heads of gulls, who were looking in by the opening they had made. "Oh!" cried Manabozho, "my younger brothers, make the opening larger, so that I can get out." They told each other that their brother Manabozho was inside the fish. They immediately set about enlarging the opening, and in a short time liberated him. After he got out he said to the gulls, "For the future you shall be called Kayoshk—nobles who scratch—for your kindness to me."

The spot where the fish happened to be driven ashore was near his lodge.

He went and told his grandmother to go and prepare as much oil as she wanted. All else, he informed her, he should keep for himself.

Some time after this, he commenced making preparations for a war excursion against the Pearl Feather, the Manito who lived on the opposite side of the great lake, who had killed his grandfather. The abode of this spirit was defended, first, by fiery serpents, who hissed fire so that no one could pass them; and, second, by a large mass of gummy matter lying on the water, so soft and adhesive that whoever attempted to pass, or whatever came in contact with it, was sure to stick there.

He continued making bows and arrows without number, but he had no heads for his arrows. At last Noko told him that an old man who lived at some distance could make them. He sent her to get some. She soon returned with her *conaus*, her wrapper, full. Still he told her he had not enough, and sent her again. She returned with as much more. He thought to himself, "I must find out the way of making these heads." Cunning and curiosity prompted him to make the discovery. But he deemed it necessary to deceive his grandmother in so doing. "Noko," said he, "while I take my drum and rattle, and sing my war songs, go and try to get me some larger heads for my arrows, for those you brought me are all of the same size. Go and see whether the old man cannot make some a little larger."

He followed her as she went, keeping at a distance, and saw the old artificer at work, and so discovered his process. He also beheld the old man's daughter, and perceived that she was very beautiful. He felt his breast beat with a new emotion, but said nothing. He took care to get home before his grandmother, and commenced singing as if he had never left his lodge. When the old woman came near, she heard his drum and rattle, without any suspicion that he had followed her. She delivered him the arrowheads.

One evening the old woman said, "My son, you ought to fast before you go to war, as your brothers frequently do, to find out whether you will be successful." He said he had no objection, and immediately commenced a fast for several days. He would retire every day from the lodge so far as to be out of reach of his grandmother's voice. It seems she had indicated this spot, and was very anxious he should fast there, and not at another place. She had a secret motive, which she carefully hid from him. Deception always begets suspicion. After a while he thought to himself, "I must find out why my grandmother is so anxious for me to fast at this spot."

Next evening he went but a short distance. She cried out, "A little farther off"; but he came nearer to the lodge, and called in a low voice, to make it appear that he was distant. She then replied, "That is far enough." He had got so near that he could see all that passed in the lodge. He had not been long in his place of concealment, when a man in the shape of a bear entered the lodge. He had very long hair. They commenced talking about him, and appeared to be improperly familiar. At that time people lived to a very great age, and he perceived, from the marked attentions of this visitor, that he did not think a grandmother too old to be pleased with such attentions.

He listened to their conversation some time. At last he determined to play the visitor a trick. He took some fire, and when the bear had turned his back, touched his long hair. When the animal felt the flame, he jumped out, but the open air only made it burn the fiercer, and he was seen running off in a full blaze.

Manabozho ran to his customary place of fasting, and assuming a tone of simplicity, began to cry out, "Noko! Noko! Is it time for me to come home?" "Yes," she cried. When he came in, she told him what had taken place, at which he appeared to be very much surprised.

After having finished his term of fasting and sung his war song—from which the Indians of the present day derive the custom—he embarked in his canoe, fully prepared for war. In addition to the usual implements, he had a plentiful supply of oil. He traveled rapidly night and day, for he had only to will or speak, and the canoe went. At length he arrived in sight of the fiery serpents. He stopped to view them. He saw they were some distance apart, and that only the flame which issued from them reached across the water. He commenced talking as a friend to them; but they answered, "We know you, Manabozho, you cannot pass."

He then thought of some expedient to deceive them, and hit upon this. He pushed his canoe as near as possible. All at once he cried out, with a loud and terrified voice, "What is that behind you?" The serpents instantly turned their heads, when, at a single word, he passed them. "Well!" said he, placidly, after he had got by, "how do you like my exploit?" He then took up his bow and arrows, and with deliberate aim shot them, which was easily done, for the serpents were stationary, and could not move beyond a certain spot. They were of enormous length and of a bright color.

Having overcome the sentinel serpents, he went on in his magic canoe till he came to a soft gummy portion of the lake, called Pigiu-wagumee, Pitchwater. He took the oil and rubbed it on his canoe, and then pushed into it. The oil softened the surface and enabled him to slip through it with ease, although it required frequent rubbing, and a constant reapplication of the oil. Just as his oil failed, he extricated himself, and was the first person who ever succeeded in overcoming it.

He now came in view of land, on which he debarked in safety, and could see the lodge of the Shining Manito, situated on a hill. He commenced preparing for the fight, putting his arrows and clubs in order, and just at the dawn of day began his attack, yelling and shouting, and crying with triple voices, "Surround him! Surround him! Run up! Run up!" making it appear that he had many followers. He advanced crying out, "It was you that killed my grandfather," and with this shot his arrows.

The combat continued all day. Manabozho's arrows had no effect, for his antagonist was clothed with pure wampum. He was now reduced to three arrows, and it was only by extraordinary agility that he could escape the blows which the Manito kept making at him. At that moment a large woodpecker, the *ma-ma*, flew past, and lit on a tree. "Manabozho," he cried, "your adversary has a vulnerable point; shoot at the lock of hair on the crown of his head." He shot his first arrow so as only to draw blood from that part. The Manito made one or two unsteady steps, but recovered himself. He began to parley, but in the act, received a second arrow, which brought him to his knees. But he again recovered. In so doing, however, he exposed his head, and gave his adversary a chance to fire his third arrow, which penetrated deep, and brought him, a lifeless corpse, to the ground.

Manabozho uttered his *saw-saw-quan*, his war cry, and taking the scalp as a trophy, he called the woodpecker to come and receive a reward for his information. He took the blood of the Manito and rubbed it on the woodpecker's head, the feathers of which are red to this day.

After this victory he returned home, singing songs of triumph and beating his drum. When his grandmother heard him, she came to the shore and welcomed him with songs and dancing. Glory fired his mind. He displayed the trophies he had brought in the most conspicuous manner, and felt an unconquerable desire for other adventures. He felt himself urged by the consciousness of his power to new trials of bravery, skill, and necromantic prowess. He had destroyed the Manito of Wealth, and killed his guardian serpents, and eluded all his charms.

He did not long remain inactive. His next adventure was upon the water, and proved him the prince of fishermen. He captured a fish of such monstrous size that the fat and oil he obtained from it formed a small lake. He therefore invited all the animals and fowls to a banquet, and he made the order in which they partook of this repast the measure of their fatness. As fast as they arrived, he told them to plunge in. The bear came first, and was followed by the deer, opossum, and such other animals as are noted for their peculiar fatness at certain seasons. The moose and bison came tardily. The partridge looked on till the reservoir was nearly exhausted. The hare and marten came last, and these animals have, consequently, no fat.

When this ceremony was over, he told the assembled animals and birds to dance, taking up his drum and crying, "New songs from the south, come, brothers, dance." He directed them to pass in a circle around him, and to shut their eyes. They did so. When he saw a fat fowl pass by him, he adroitly wrung off its head, at the same time beating his drum and singing with greater vehemence, to drown the noise of the fluttering, and crying out, in a tone of admiration:

"That's the way, my brothers, that's the way."

At last a small duck, the diver, thinking there was something wrong, opened one eye and saw what he was doing. Giving a spring, and crying, "*Ha-ha-a!* Manabozho is killing us," he made for the water. Manabozho followed him, and just as the duck was getting into the water, gave him a kick, which is the cause of his back being flattened and his legs being straightened out backward, so that when he gets on land he cannot walk, and his tail feathers are few. Meantime the other birds flew off, and the animals ran into the woods.

After this Manabozho set out to travel. He wished to outdo all others, and to see new countries. But after walking over America and encountering many adventures, he became satisfied as well as fatigued. He had heard

260

of great feats in hunting, and felt a desire to try his power in that way. One evening, as he was walking along the shores of a great lake, weary and hungry, he encountered a great magician in the form of an old wolf, with six young ones, coming toward him.

The wolf, as soon as he saw him, told his whelps to keep out of the way of Manabozho. "For I know that it is he that we see yonder." The young wolves were in the act of running off, when Manabozho cried out, "My grandchildren, where are you going? Stop, and I will go with you." He appeared rejoiced to see the old wolf, and asked him whither he was journeying. Being told that they were looking out for a place where they could find most game, to pass the winter, he said he should like to go with them, and addressed the old wolf in the following words, "Brother, I have a passion for the chase. Are you willing to change me into a wolf?" He was answered favorably, and his transformation immediately effected.

Manabozho was fond of novelty. He found himself a wolf corresponding in size with the others, but he was not quite satisfied with the change, crying out, "Oh, make me a little larger." They did so. "A little larger still," he exclaimed. They said, "Let us humor him," and granted his request. "Well," said he, "that will do." He looked at his tail. "Oh!" cried he, "do make my tail a little longer and more bushy." They did so.

They then all started off in company, dashing up a ravine. After getting into the woods some distance, they fell in with the tracks of moose. The young ones went after them, Manabozho and the old wolf following at their leisure. "Well," said the wolf, "who do you think is the fastest of the boys? Can you tell by the jumps they take?" "Why," he replied, "that one that takes such long jumps, he is the fastest, to be sure." "Ha! ha! you are mistaken," said the old wolf. "He makes a good start, but he will be the first to tire out. This one, who appears to be behind, will be the one to kill the game."

They then came to the place where the boys had started in chase. One had dropped his small bundle. "Take that, Manabozho," said the old wolf. "*Esa!*" he replied, "what will I do with a dirty dogskin?" The wolf took it up; it was a beautiful robe. "Oh, I will carry it now," said Manabozho. "Oh, no," replied the wolf, who at the moment exerted his magic power, "it is a robe of pearls!" And from this moment he omitted no occasion to display his superiority, both in the hunter's and magician's art, above his conceited companion.

Coming to a place where the moose had lain down, they saw that the young wolves had made a fresh start after their prey. "Why," said the wolf, "this moose is poor. I know by the tracks, for I can always tell whether they are fat or not." They next came to a place where one of the wolves had bit at the moose, and had broken one of his teeth on a tree. "Manabozho," said the wolf, "one of your grandchildren has shot at the game. Take his arrow; there it is." "No," he replied, "what will I do with a dirty dog's tooth!" The old wolf took it up, and behold! it was a beautiful silver arrow.

When they overtook the youngsters, they had killed a very fat moose. Manabozho was very hungry; but, alas! such is the power of enchantment, he saw nothing but the bones picked quite clean. He thought to himself, "Just as I expected, dirty, greedy fellows!" However, he sat down without saying a word. At length the old wolf spoke to one of the young ones, saying, "Give some meat to your grandfather." One of them obeyed, and coming near to Manabozho, opened his mouth as if he was about to vomit. He jumped up, saying, "You filthy dog, you have eaten so much that your stomach refuses to hold it. Get you gone into some other place."

The old wolf, hearing the abuse, went a little to one side to see, and behold! a heap of fresh ruddy meat, with the fat, was lying all ready prepared. He was followed by Manabozho, who, having the enchantment instantly removed, put on a smiling face. "Amazing!" said he. "How fine the meat is." "Yes," replied the wolf, "it is always so with us; we know our work, and always get the best. It is not a long tail that makes a hunter." Manabozho bit his lip.

They then commenced fixing their winter quarters, while the youngsters went out in search of game, and soon brought in a large supply. One day, during the absence of the young wolves, the old one amused himself in cracking the large bones of a moose. "Manabozho," said he, "cover your head with the robe, and do not look at me while I am at these bones, for a piece may fly in your eye." He did as he was told, but looking through a rent that was in the robe, he saw what the other was about. Just at that moment a piece flew off and hit him on the eye. He cried out, "*Tyau*, why do you strike me, you old dog?" The wolf said, "You must have been looking at me." But deception commonly leads to falsehood. "No, no," he said, "why should I want to look at you?" "Manabozho," said the wolf, "you must have been looking, or you would not have got hurt." "No, no," he replied again, "I was not."

Thought he to himself, "I will repay the saucy wolf this." So next day, taking up a bone to obtain the marrow, he said to the wolf, "Cover your head and don't look at me, for I fear a piece may fly in your eye." The wolf did so. He then took the leg bone of the moose, and looking first to see if the wolf was well covered, he hit him a blow with all his might. The wolf jumped up, cried out, and fell prostrate from the effects of the blow. "Why," said he, "do you strike me so?" "Strike you!" he replied. "No, you must have been looking at me." "No," answered the wolf, "I say I have not." But he persisted in the assertion, and the poor magician had to give up.

Manabozho was an expert hunter when he earnestly undertook it. He went out one day and killed a fat moose. He was very hungry, and sat down to eat. But immediately he fell into great doubts as to the proper point to begin. "Well," said he, "I do not know where to commence. At the head? No! People will laugh, and say, 'He ate him backward.'" He went to the side. "No!" said he, "they will say I ate sideways." He then went to the hindquarter. "No!" said he, "they will say I ate him forward. I will commence here, say what they will."

He took a delicate piece from the rump, and was just ready to put it in his mouth, when a tree close by made a creaking noise, caused by the rubbing of one large branch against another. This annoyed him. "Why!" he exclaimed, "I cannot eat when I hear such a noise. Stop! stop!" said he to the tree. He was putting the morsel again to his mouth, when the noise was repeated. He put it down, exclaiming, "I cannot eat with such a noise," and immediately left the meat, although very hungry, to go and put a stop to the noise. He climbed the tree and was pulling at the limb, when his arm was caught between the two branches so that he could not extricate himself. While thus held fast, he saw a pack of wolves coming in the direction toward his meat. "Go that way! go that way!" he cried out. "What would you come to get here?"

The wolves talked among themselves and said, "Manabozho must have something there, or he would not tell us to go another way." "I begin to know him," said an old wolf, "and all his tricks. Let us go forward and see." They came on, and finding the moose, soon made way with the whole carcass. Manabozho looked on wishfully to see them eat till they were fully satisfied, and they left him nothing but the bare bones. The next heavy blast of wind opened the branches and liberated him. He went home, thinking to himself, "See the effect of meddling with frivolous things when I had certain good in my possession."

Next day the old wolf addressed him thus, "My brother, I am going to separate from you, but I will leave behind me one of the young wolves to be your hunter." He then departed. In the act Manabozho was disenchanted, and again resumed his mortal shape. He was sorrowful and dejected, but soon resumed his wonted air of cheerfulness. The young wolf who was left with him was a good hunter, and never failed to keep the lodge well supplied with meat. One day Manabozho addressed him as follows, "My grandson, I had a dream last night, and it does not portend good. It is of the large lake which lies in that direction. You must be careful never to cross it, even if the ice should appear good. If you should come to it at night weary or hungry, you must make the circuit of it."

Spring commenced, and the snow was melting fast under the rays of the sun, when one evening the wolf came to this lake, weary with the day's chase. He disliked to go so far to make the circuit of it. "*Hwooh!*" he exclaimed, "there can be no great harm in trying the ice, as it appears to be sound. Nesho, my grandfather, is over cautious on this point." But he had not got halfway across when the ice gave way and he fell in, and was immediately seized by the serpents, who knew it was Manabozho's grandson, and were thirsting for revenge upon him. Manabozho sat pensively in his lodge.

Night came on, but no grandson returned. The second and third night passed, but he did not appear. He became very desolate and sorrowful. "Ah!" said he, "he must have disobeyed me, and has lost his life in that lake I told him of. Well!" said he at last, "I must mourn for him." So he took coal and blackened his face. But he was much perplexed as to the right mode. "I wonder," said he, "how I must do it. I will cry 'Oh! my grandson! Oh! my grandson!'" He burst out laughing. "No! no! that won't do. I will try 'Oh! my heart! Oh! my heart! ha! ha! ha!' That won't do either. I will cry, 'Oh my grandson *obiquadj*!'" This satisfied him, and he remained in his lodge and fasted till his days of mourning were over.

"Now," said he, "I will go in search of him." He set out and traveled some time. At last he came to a great lake. He then raised the same cries of lamentation for his grandson which had pleased him. He sat down near a small brook that emptied itself into the lake, and repeated his cries. Soon a bird called *Ke-ske-mun-i-see*, the kingfisher, came near him. The bird inquired, "What are you doing here?" "Nothing," he replied; "but can you tell me whether anyone lives in this lake, and what brings you here yourself?" "Yes," responded the bird; "the prince of serpents lives here, and I am watching to see whether the *obiquadj* of Manabozho's grandson will not drift ashore, for he was killed by the serpents last spring. But are you not Manabozho himself?"

"No," he answered, with his usual deceit; "how do you think he could get to this place? But tell me, do the serpents ever appear? When? And where? Tell me all about their habits." "Do you see that beautiful white sandy beach?" said the bird. "Yes," he answered. "It is there," continued the kingfisher, "that they bask in the sun. Before they come out, the lake will appear perfectly calm; not even a ripple will appear. After midday, *na-wi-qua*, you will see them."

"Thank you. I am Manabozho himself. I have come in search of the body of my son, and to seek my revenge. Come near me that I may put a medal round your neck as a reward for your information." The bird unsuspectingly came near, and received a white medal, which can be seen to this day. While bestowing the medal, he attempted slyly to wring the bird's head off, but it escaped him, with only a disturbance of the crown feathers of its head, which are rumpled backward. He had found out all he wanted to know, and then desired to conceal the knowledge of his purposes by killing his informant.

He went to the sandy beach indicated, and transformed himself into an oak stump. He had not been there long before he saw the lake perfectly calm. Soon hundreds of monstrous serpents came crawling on the beach. One of the number was beautifully white. He was the prince. The others were red and yellow. The prince said to those about him, "I never saw that black stump standing there before. It may be Manabozho. There is no knowing but he may be somewhere about here. He has the power of an evil genius, and we should be on our guard against his wiles." One of the large serpents immediately went and twisted himself around it to the top, and pressed it very hard. The greatest pressure happened to be on his throat; he was just ready to cry out when the serpent let go. Eight of them went in succession and did the like, but always let go at the moment he was ready to cry out. "It cannot be him," they said. "He is too great a coward for that."

They then coiled themselves in a circle about their prince. It was a long time before they fell asleep. When they did so, Manabozho took his bow and arrows, and cautiously stepping over the serpents till he came to the prince, drew up his arrow with the full strength of his arm, and shot him in the left side. He then gave a war cry and ran off at full speed. The sound uttered by the snakes on seeing their prince mortally wounded was horrible. They cried, "Manabozho has killed our prince; go in chase of him." Meantime he ran over hill and valley, to gain the interior of the country, with all his strength and speed, treading a mile at a step. But his pursuers were also spirits, and he could hear that something was approaching him fast.

He made for the highest mountain, and climbed the highest tree on its summit, when, dreadful to behold, the whole lower country was seen to be overflowed, and the water was gaining rapidly on the highlands. He saw it reach to the foot of the mountain, and at length it came up to the foot of the tree, but there was no abatement. The flood rose steadily. He soon felt the lower part of his body to be immersed in it. He addressed the tree, "Grandfather, stretch yourself." The tree did so. But the waters still rose. He repeated his request, and was again obeyed. He asked a third time, and was again obeyed. But the tree replied, "It is the last time; I cannot get any higher." The waters continued to rise till they reached up to his chin, at which point they stood, and soon began to abate.

Hope revived in his heart. He then cast his eyes around and spied a loon. "Dive down, my brother," he said to him, "and fetch up some earth, so that I can make a new earth." The bird obeyed, but rose up to the surface a lifeless form. He then saw a muskrat. "Dive!" said he, "and if you succeed, you may hereafter live either on land or water, as you please; or I will give you a chain of beautiful little lakes, surrounded with rushes, to inhabit." He dove down, but floated up senseless.

Manabozho took the body and breathed in his nostrils, which restored him to life. "Try again," said he. The muskrat did so. He came up senseless the second time, but clutched a little earth in one of his paws, from which, together with the carcass of the dead loon, Manabozho created a new earth as large as the former had been, with all living animals, fowls, and plants.

As he was walking to survey the new earth, he heard someone singing. He went to the place, and found a female spirit, in the disguise of an old woman, singing these words, and crying at every pause:

> *Ma nau bo sho, O do zheem un,*
> *Ogeem au wun, Onis sa waun,*
> *Hee-Ub bub ub bub.*

> Dread Manabozho in revenge,
> For his grandson lost—
> Has killed the chief—the king.

"Noko," said he, "what is the matter?" "Matter!" said she, "where have you been, not to have heard how Manabozho shot my son, the prince of serpents, in revenge for the loss of his grandson, and how the earth was overflowed and created anew? So I brought my son here, that he might kill and destroy the inhabitants, as he did on the former earth. But," she continued, casting a scrutinizing glance, *"N'yau! indego* Manabozho! *hub! ub! ub! ub!*—Oh, I am afraid you are Manabozho!" He burst into a laugh to quiet her fears. "Ha! ha! ha! how can that be? Has not the old earth perished, and all that was in it?" "Impossible! Impossible!"

"But, Noko," he continued, "what do you intend doing with all that cedar cord on your back?" "Why," said she, "I am fixing a snare for Manabozho, if he should be on this earth; and in the meantime, I am looking for herbs to heal my son. I am the only person that can do him any good. He always gets better when I sing."

> *Manabozho a ne we guawk,*
> *Koan dan mau wah, ne we guawk,*
> *Koan dan mau wah, ne we guawk.*

It is Manabozho's dart,
I try my magic power to withdraw.

Having found out, by conversation with her, all he wished, he put her to death. He then took off her skin, and assuming this disguise, took the cedar cord on his back, and limped away singing her songs. He completely aped the gait and voice of the old woman. He was met by one who told him to make haste, that the prince was worse. At the lodge, limping and muttering, he took notice that they had his grandson's hide to hang over the door. "Oh dogs!" said he, "the evil dogs!" He sat down near the door, and commenced sobbing like an aged woman. One observed, "Why don't you attend the sick, and not sit there making such a noise?"

He took up the poker and laid it on them, mimicking the voice of the old woman. "Dogs that you are! Why do you laugh at me? You know very well that I am so sad that I am nearly out of my head." With that he approached the prince, singing the songs of the old woman, without exciting any suspicion. He saw that his arrow had gone in about half its length. He pretended to make preparations for extracting it, but only made ready to finish his victim, and giving the dart a sudden thrust, he put an end to the prince's life.

He performed this act with the power of a giant, bursting the old woman's skin, and at the same moment rushing through the door. The serpents followed him, hissing and crying out, "Perfidy! murder! vengeance! It is Manabozho." He immediately transformed himself into a wolf, and ran over the plain with all his speed, aided by his father the West Wind. When he got to the mountains he saw a badger. "Brother," said he, "make a hole quick, for the serpents are after me." The badger obeyed. They both went in, and the badger threw all the earth backward, so that it filled up the way behind.

The serpents came to the badger's burrow and decided to watch. "We will starve him out," said they, so they continued watching. Manabozho told the badger to make an opening on the other side of the mountain, from which he could go out and hunt, and bring meat in. Thus they lived some time.

One day the badger came in his way and displeased him. He immediately put him to death, and threw out his carcass, saying, "I don't like you to be getting in my way so often."

After living in this confinement for some time alone, he decided to go out. He immediately did so; and after making the circuit of the mountain, came to the corpse of the prince, who had been deserted by the serpents to pursue his destroyer. He went to work and skinned him. He then drew on his skin, in which there were great virtues, took up his war club, and set out for the place where he first went in the ground. He found the serpents still watching. When they saw the form of their dead prince advancing toward them, fear and dread took hold of them. Some fled. Those who remained Manabozho killed. Those who fled went toward the south.

Having accomplished the victory over the reptiles, Manabozho returned to his former place of dwelling, and married the arrow maker's daughter.

After Manabozho had killed the prince of serpents, he was living in a state of great want, completely deserted by his powers as a deity, and not able to procure the ordinary means of subsistence. He was at this time living with his wife and children, in a remote part of the country, where he could get no game. He was miserably poor. It was winter, and he had not the common Indian comforts.

He said to his wife one day, "I will go out walking, and see if I cannot find some lodges." After walking some time, he saw a lodge at a distance. The children were playing at the door. When they saw him approaching, they ran into the lodge, and told their parents that Manabozho was coming. It was the lodge of the large redheaded Woodpecker. He came to the door and asked Manabozho to enter. He did so. After some time, the Woodpecker, who was a magician, said to his wife, "Have you nothing to give Manabozho? He must be hungry." She answered, "No."

In the center of the lodge stood a large white tamarack tree. The Woodpecker flew onto it, and commenced going up, turning his head on each side of the tree, and every now and then driving in his bill. At last he drew something out of the tree, and threw it down, when, behold! a fine, fat raccoon was on the ground. He drew out six or seven more. He then descended, and told his wife to prepare them. "Manabozho," he said, "this is the only thing we eat. What else can we give you?" "It is very good," replied Manabozho. They smoked their pipes and conversed with each other.

After eating, the great spirit chief got ready to go home. The Woodpecker said to his wife, "Give him what remains of the raccoons to take home for his children." In the act of leaving the lodge, he dropped intentionally one of his *minjekawun*, mittens, which was soon after observed. "Run," said the Woodpecker to his eldest son, "and give it to him. But don't give it into his hand; throw it at him, for there is no knowing him, he acts so curiously." The boy did as he was bid. "Nemesho, my grandfather," said he, as he came up to him, "you have left one of your mittens—here it is." "Yes," said he, affecting to be ignorant of the circumstance, "it is so. But don't throw it, you will soil it on the snow." The lad, however, threw it, and was about to return. "List," said Manabozho, "is that all you eat—do you eat nothing else with the raccoon?" "No," replied the young woodpecker.

"Then tell your father," he answered, "to come and visit me, and let him bring a sack. I will give him what he shall eat with his raccoon meat." When the young one reported this to his father, the old man turned up his nose at the invitation. "What does the old fellow think he has got!" exclaimed he.

Some time after, the Woodpecker went to pay a visit to Manabozho. He was received with the usual attention. It had been the boast of Manabozho, in former days, that he could do what any other being in creation could, whether man or animals. He affected to have the sagacity of all animals, to understand their language, and to be capable of exactly imitating it. And in his visits to men, it was his custom to return, exactly, the treatment he had received. He was very ceremonious in following the very voice and manner of his entertainers.

The Woodpecker had no sooner entered his lodge, therefore, than he commenced playing the mimic. He had previously directed his wife to change his lodge, so as to enclose a large dry tamarack tree. "What can I give you?" said he to the Woodpecker; "but as we eat, so shall you eat." He then put a long piece of bone in his nose, in imitation of the bill of this bird, and jumping on the tamarack tree, attempted to climb it, doing as he had seen the Woodpecker do. He turned his head first on one side, then on the other. He made awkward efforts to ascend, but continually slipped down. He struck the tree with the bone in his nose, until at last he drove it so far up his nostrils that the blood began to flow, and he fell down senseless at the foot of the tree.

The Woodpecker started after his drum and rattle to restore him, and having got them, succeeded in bringing him to. As soon as he came to his senses, he began to lay the blame of his failure to his wife, saying to his guest, "Nemesho, it is this woman relation of yours—she is the cause of my not succeeding. She has rendered me a worthless fellow. Before I took her I could also get raccoons." The Woodpecker said nothing, but flying on the tree, drew out several fine raccoons. "Here," said he, "this is the way we do," and left him with apparent contempt.

Severe weather continued, and Manabozho still suffered for the want of food. One day he walked out, and came to a lodge, which was occupied by Moz, the Moose. The young Mozonsug saw him and told their father Manabozho was at the door. He told them to invite him in. Being seated, they entered into conversation. At last the Moose, who was a *Meeta*, said, "What shall we give Manabozho to eat? We have nothing." His wife was seated with her back toward him, making garters. He walked up to her, and untying the covering of the armlet from her back, cut off a large piece of flesh from the square of her shoulder. He then put some medicine on it, which immediately healed the wound. The skin did not even appear to have been broken, and his wife was so little affected by it that she did not so much as leave off her work till he told her to prepare the flesh for eating. "Manabozho," said he, "this is all we eat, and it is all we can give you."

After they had finished eating, Manabozho set out for home, but intentionally, as before, dropped one of his mittens. One of the young moose took it to him, telling him that his father had sent him with it. He had been cautioned not to hand it to him, but to throw it at him. Having done so, contrary to the remonstrance of Manabozho, he was going back, when the latter cried out, "Stop! Stop! Is that the only kind of meat you eat? Tell me." "Yes," answered the young man, "that is all; we have nothing else." "Tell your father," he replied, "to come and visit me, and I will give him what you shall eat with your meat." The old Moose listened to this message indignantly. "I wonder what he thinks he has got, poor fellow!"

He was bound, however, to obey the invitation, and went accordingly, taking along a cedar sack, for he had been told to bring one. Manabozho received him in the same manner he had himself been received—repeating the same remarks, and attempting to supply the lack of food in the same manner. To this end he had requested his wife to busy herself in making garters. He arose and untied the covering of her back as he had seen the Moose do. He then cut her back shockingly, paying no attention to her cries or resistance, until he saw her fall down from the loss of blood.

"Manabozho," said the Moose, "you are killing your wife." He immediately ran for his drum and rattle, and restored her to life by his skill. He had no sooner done this than Manabozho began to lay the blame of his ill success on his wife. "Why, Nemesho," said he, "this woman, this relation of yours—she is making me a most worthless fellow. Formerly, I procured my meat in this way. But now I can accomplish nothing."

The Moose then cut large pieces of flesh off his own thighs, without the least injury to himself, and gave them to Manabozho, saying, with a contemptuous air, "This is the way we do." He then left the lodge.

After these visits, Manabozho was sitting pensively in his lodge one day, with his head down. He heard the wind whistling around it, and thought, by attentively listening, he could hear the voice of someone speaking to him. It seemed to say to him, "Great chief, why are you sorrowful? Am not I your friend—your guardian spirit?" He immediately took up his rattle, and without leaving his sitting posture, began to sing the chant which at the close of every stanza has the chorus, *"Whaw Lay Le Aw."* When he had devoted a long time to this chant, he laid his rattle aside, and determined to fast. For this purpose he went to a cave, and built a very small fire, near which he lay down, first telling his wife that neither she nor the children must come near him till he had finished his fast.

At the end of seven days he came back to the lodge, pale and emaciated. His wife in the meantime had dug through the snow, and got a small quantity of the root called truffles. These she boiled and set before him. When he had finished his repast, he took his large bow and bent it. Then placing a strong arrow to the string, he drew it back, and sent the arrow, with the strength of a giant, through the side of his bark lodge. "There," said he to his wife, "go to the outside, and you will find a large bear, shot through the heart." She did so, and found one as he had predicted.

He then sent the children out to get red willow sticks. Of these he cut off as many pieces, of equal length, as would serve to invite his friends to a feast. A red stick was sent to each one, not forgetting the Moose and the Woodpecker.

When they arrived, they were astonished to see such a profusion of meat cooked for them, at such a time of scarcity. Manabozho understood their glances, and felt a conscious pride in making such a display. "Akewazi," said he, to one of the oldest of the party, "the weather is very cold, and the snow lasts a long time. We can kill nothing now but small squirrels. And I have sent for you to help me eat some of them." The Woodpecker was the first to put the bear's meat to his mouth, but he had no sooner begun to taste it than it changed into a dry powder, and set him coughing. It appeared as bitter as ashes. The Moose felt the same effect, and began to cough.

Each one, in turn, was added to the number of coughers. But they had too much sense of decorum, and respect for their entertainer, to say anything. The meat looked very fine. They thought they would try more of it. But the more they ate, the faster they coughed, and the louder became the uproar, until Manabozho, exerting his former power, which he now felt to be renewed, transformed them each into an *Adjidamo*, a squirrel, an animal which is still found to have the habit of barking, or coughing, whenever it sees anyone approach its nest.

RAVEN VISITS CHIEF ECHO

RAVEN WAS SITTING THERE, thinking quietly how many hard things he had done among men; still his needs were not satisfied. At last he made up his mind to try to go again to the people in order to get something to eat, for he was a great eater. He went to a lonely place, and was very anxious to find some people in the woods. Soon he came to a great plain. No trees were to be seen, just grass and flowers. At a distance he beheld a large house, and inside the large house with carved front he heard many people singing. He saw sparks flying up from the smoke hole, and he knew that it must be the house of a great chief.

When he came near the house, he heard something saying with a loud voice, "A stranger is coming, a chief is coming!" and he knew that they meant him. So he went in, but he saw nobody. Still he heard the voices. He saw a great fire in the center, and a good new mat was spread out for him alongside the fire. Then he heard a voice which called to him, "Sit down on the mat! This way, great chief! This way, great chief! This way!" He walked proudly toward the mat. Then Raven sat down on it.

This was the house of Chief Echo. Then Raven heard the chief speak to his slaves and tell them to roast a dried salmon; and he saw a carved box open itself and dried salmon come out of it. Then he saw a nice dish walk toward the fire all by itself. Raven was scared and astonished to see these things. When the dried salmon was roasted and cut into pieces of the right length, the pieces went into the dish all by themselves. The dish laid itself down in front of Raven, and he thought, while he was eating, what strange things he was seeing now. When he had finished, a horn dipper came forward filled with water. He took it by its handle and drank.

Then he saw a large dish full of crabapples mixed with grease, and a black horn spoon, come forward by themselves. Raven took the handle and ate all he could. Before he emptied his dish, he looked around, and, behold! mountain-goat fat was hanging on one side of the house. He thought, "I will take down one of these large pieces of fat." Thus Raven thought while he was eating. Then he heard many women laughing in one corner of the house, "Ha, ha! Raven thinks he will take down one of those large pieces of mountain-goat fat!" Then Raven was ashamed on account of what the women were saying.

He ate all the crabapples, and another dish came forward filled with cranberries mixed with grease and with water. Raven ate again, and, behold! he saw dried mountain-sheep fat hanging in one corner of the large house. He thought again, "I will take down one of these pieces of mountain-sheep fat, and I will run out with it." Again he heard many women laughing, "Ha, ha! Raven is thinking he will take down a piece of the mountain-sheep fat and will run out with it."

Raven was much troubled on account of what he heard the women saying, and when he heard them laughing in the corner of the house. He arose, ran out, snatching one of the pieces of mountain-goat meat and of mountain-sheep fat; but when he came to the door, a large stone hammer beat him on the ankle, and he fell to the ground badly hurt. He lost the meat and fat, and someone dragged him along and cast him out. He lay there a while and began to cry, for he was very hungry, and his foot very sore. On the following day, when he was a little better, he took a stick and tried to walk away.

RAVEN KILLS LITTLE PITCH

RAVEN WENT ON, not knowing which way to go. He was very weak and hungry, and sore of foot. He went on and on in the woods until he saw a house far off. He went toward it, came near, and entered. There were a man and his wife, a very pretty young woman, there. They permitted him to come in, for they had pity on the poor man who had come to their house. They asked him if he wanted something to eat, and they gave him to eat. Then the young woman tried to cure his ankle, which was hurt by the stone in the house of Chief Echo.

He was now in the house of Little Pitch. He came in, and the people were very kind to him. The wife of Little Pitch put pitch on his sore ankle. After two days he was quite well, and he was very glad. The young woman gave him to eat every day. The house of Little Pitch was full of dried halibut and of all kinds of provisions. Raven made up his mind to kill his friend who had treated him so kindly.

On the following evening, after he had eaten his supper, he said to his friend that they would go out the next morning to catch halibut. Little Pitch was willing, and said to Raven, "It is not good for me if I go out fishing in the sun, because I am so weak. I must return home while it is still chilly." Raven replied, "I will do whatever you say, sir. I think we shall have plenty of time." Thus spoke Raven. They started for the fishing ground, and fished all night until daybreak.

When the sun rose, Little Pitch wanted to go home; but Raven said, "I enjoy fishing. Lie down there in the bow of the canoe, and cover yourself with a mat." Little Pitch lay down, and Raven called him, "Little Pitch!" "Hey!" he replied. After a while Raven called him again, "Little Pitch!" "Hey!" he answered again with a loud voice. Raven called him once more, "Little Pitch!" Then he answered, "Hey!" in a low voice. Raven called him still again. He answered, "Hey, hey!" with a very weak voice. "Now I will pull up my fishing lines," said Raven; and after he had hauled his lines into the canoe, he paddled away home.

Raven paddled very hard. He called again, "Little Pitch!" but there was no answer; so he went to see what had happened to Little Pitch. As soon as he touched the mat that covered Little Pitch, behold! pitch was running out all over the halibut. Little Pitch was dead, and melted pitch ran all over the halibut. Therefore the halibut is black on one side.

Raven was very glad. He paddled along until he reached the shore in front of Little Pitch's house, expecting to get a good supper from Little Pitch's wife. He took the line, tied up his canoe, and went up, glad in his heart. He went on and on, but could not find any house. He searched everywhere, but could not find it. Only a little green spruce tree was standing there, with a drop of pitch upon one side. Finally Raven remembered that his canoe was full of halibut. So he went down to the beach, being very hungry, but he could not find his canoe. Only a spruce log with roots was there. Then Raven felt very badly.

RAVEN INVITES THE MONSTERS

RAVEN HAD BEEN AWAY from this country for a long time, many years; and when he came back from the north, wearing the old raven garment, he gave a great feast to all the monsters on one of the outer islands. When his guests came into the bay on the outer side of that island, Raven went out to meet them. The water was full in front of the new carved house that Raven had built.

This was the first potlatch to which he invited all kinds of monsters; and when they came into the bay, Raven stood in front of his house and began to address his guests. "O chiefs! I am so glad to see that you have come to my potlatch. I have been away from this country for a long time, therefore I am glad to see you again. I want to say something else. I wish you would stay there and become rocks." Then all the monsters became rocks. He continued, "And I will also become a rock." As soon as Raven said this, the devilfish went down quickly. Therefore the devilfish stays now at the bottom of the sea.

The people were much pleased because all the monsters had been turned into stone; and Raven himself became a stone shaped like a raven, and only

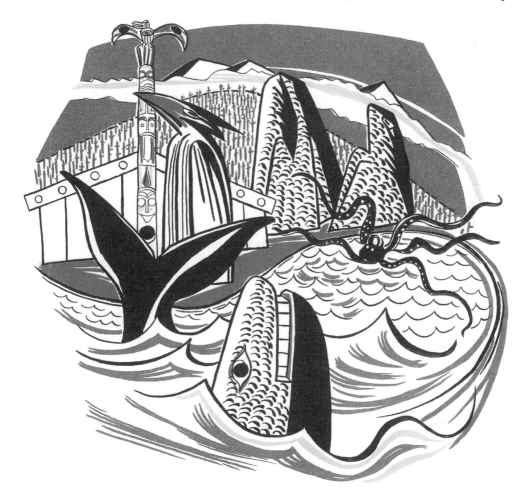

the devilfish remains alive. The people say that nowadays, when a devilfish comes out of the water, the people cry, "Caw, caw, caw!" like a raven, and the devilfish dies when he hears the raven cry. That island is full of stones shaped like all kinds of monsters—whales, killer whales, sharks, and so on—and the raven stands in front of his carved house even now.

THE THEFT FROM THE SUN

ONCE Old Man was traveling around, when he came to the Sun's lodge, and the Sun asked him to stay a while. Old Man was very glad to do so.

One day the meat was all gone, and the Sun said, "*Kyi!* Old Man, what say you if we go and kill some deer?"

"You speak well," replied Old Man. "I like deer meat."

The Sun took down a bag and pulled out a beautiful pair of leggings. They were embroidered with porcupine quills and bright feathers. "These," said the Sun, "are my hunting leggings. They are great medicine. All I have to do is to put them on and walk around a patch of brush, when the leggings set it on fire and drive the deer out so that I can shoot them."

"*Hai-yah!*" exclaimed Old Man. "How wonderful!" He made up his mind he would have those leggings, if he had to steal them.

They went out to hunt, and the first patch of brush they came to, the Sun set on fire with his hunting leggings. A lot of white-tail deer ran out, and they each shot one.

That night, when they went to bed, the Sun pulled off his leggings and placed them to one side. Old Man saw where he put them, and in the middle of the night, when everyone was asleep, he stole them and went off. He traveled a long time, until he had gone far and was very tired, and then, making a pillow of the leggings, lay down and slept. In the morning, he heard someone talking. The Sun was saying, "Old Man, why are my leggings under your head?" He looked around, and saw he was in the Sun's lodge, and thought he must have wandered around and got lost, and returned there. Again the Sun spoke and said, "What are you doing with my leggings?" "Oh," replied Old Man, "I couldn't find anything for a pillow, so I just put these under my head."

Night came again, and again Old Man stole the leggings and ran off. This time he did not walk at all; he kept running until pretty near morning, and then lay down and slept. You see what a fool he was. He did not know that the whole world is the Sun's lodge. He did not know that, no matter how far he ran, he could not get out of the Sun's sight. When morning came, he found himself still in the Sun's lodge. But this time the Sun said, "Old Man, since you like my leggings so much, I will give them to you. Keep them." Then Old Man was very glad and went away.

One day his food was all gone, so he put on the medicine leggings and set fire to a piece of brush. He was just going to kill some deer that were running out, when he saw that the fire was getting close to him. He ran away as fast as he could, but the fire gained on him and began to burn his legs. His leggings were all on fire. He came to a river and jumped in, and pulled off the leggings as soon as he could. They were burned to pieces.

Perhaps the Sun did this to him because he tried to steal the leggings.

IX

LEGENDS OF ANIMALS AND BIRDS, AND BIRD-AND-ANIMAL PEOPLE

THE MOUSE'S CHILDREN

ONCE, a long time ago, when the Cheyennes lived in earth houses, their village was on a stream, and the houses stood in a row along the bank. The camp was short of food and everyone was hungry, and all the people were going out to hunt buffalo. They started, but one young man did not leave with the others; he stayed in the camp for some time after they had gone. He had determined that he would be the last person to start.

At length he set out, and as he passed the houses, he heard in one of them a woman crying. He wondered who this could be, for everyone had left the village, and he stopped and listened. After he had listened for a little while, he determined that he would go over and see who it was that was crying. As he drew near the house, the mourning grew lower and lower, and when he reached the house the woman had stopped crying. He went to the door and looked in, and saw a woman sitting at the foot of a bed, and a man at the head of the bed. When he looked in the door the man spoke to him, greeting him, and said to the woman, "Get him something to eat." The young man sat down, and presently the woman put before him some dried meat and some marrow fat, and he ate.

After he had finished eating, the man said to the guest, "This woman, Mouse Woman, is crying and mourning because she has lost her children. They have been taken prisoner. She had her children in the arrow lodge, and they are there now and cannot get out." The man and the woman begged this young man to help get her children back. "For," said the man, "this woman has been crying ever since she lost her children."

The young man listened to all that they said, and at length he promised to try to do all he could to get her children back for her.

At last the sun began to get low in the west, and the young man stood up and said to these people, "Now I must go on and follow up the camp." The man said again to him, "The woman's children are in the medicine bundle in the lodge that you will find in the center of the camp. Do what you can to help her."

The young man said, "I will try in every way I can to get these children. If I can get them out tonight, I will come back at once, tonight."

He started on the trail of the camp, and traveled fast, but it was after night when he reached the camp. He had been thinking hard all the time as he traveled along, to see what he could do to get this woman's children. As he went along, he prepared presents, and as he came near to the arrow lodge, he began to mourn and to cry.

The arrow keeper in his lodge heard the sound of his mourning, and as it drew nearer he said to his wife, "Someone is coming with gifts; get all things ready and then go out." The woman got things ready, and when the young man came to the door of the lodge, she went out. The medicine man spoke, asking the young man to come in. He went in, and the host asked him to come over and sit by him at the back of the lodge.

"Why have you come to see me?" said the arrow keeper; and the young man told him that he had come to make these offerings. The medicine man took them and prayed over them, performing the needed ceremonies. Then he gave them back to the young man and told him to take them out in front of the lodge and spread them over the arrow bundle where it hung over the door.

When he went out to spread his gifts over the arrow bundle, he thrust his hand into the bundle, and found there a mouse's nest with four little mice in it. After he had got the mice and put them in a fold of his robe, and had spread the gifts over the arrow bundle, he started back to the old village. When he had come within hearing distance of it, he could hear the woman still crying for her children. He kept on, and as he drew nearer the lodge, the mourning grew lower, and when he had come to the door it stopped.

He entered and said, "Well, I have brought you your children," and he handed her the little mice, and she and the man both kissed the children. Then the man said to the young man, "You see how foolish my wife was to keep her children in the arrow lodge. They were lost, and she might never have seen them again, but you have helped her and brought them back to her. Now I will give you a name which shall become great, and which everyone shall hear of. You shall become a leading man, and always when people are talking of wars and fights your name shall be mentioned first. Your name shall be Mouse's Road."

After the man had talked in this way for a little time, the young man happened to look out of the door, and as he did so he heard the sound of mice squeaking and running, and looking back, he saw that the man and the woman had turned into mice and had run under the bed, and that he was there alone.

Now the young man returned to the camp, and as he followed the trail he was continually praying, for he remembered what the mouse person had told him. When he reached the camp, he went to his mother's lodge. She said to him, "Where have you been? I thought you would have been here long ago."

"No," he said, "I only just got in." Then said his mother, "A war party left while you were away. They sent for you to come with them." The young man said nothing, but the next morning he started and followed up the trail of the war party, and overtook them and went on with them.

In the first fight that they had, he, first of all, killed an enemy, and when he told what he had done, the people learned that his name was Mouse's Road. When the party got back, some old man cried out through the camp that Mouse's Road had killed the first enemy. In all fights after that, he was always the first to do some great thing, and his name was always mentioned first.

After this war party had returned, they counted many coups and had many scalp dances. Also, on the hunt they got many buffalo and dried much meat, and then they returned to their village.

MANSTIN, THE RABBIT

MANSTIN was an adventurous brave, but very kindhearted. Stamping a moccasined foot as he drew on his buckskin leggings, he said, "Grandmother, beware of Iktomi! Do not let him lure you into some cunning trap. I am going to the North country on a long hunt."

With these words of caution to the bent old rabbit grandmother with whom he had lived since he was a tiny babe, Manstin started off toward the north. He was scarce over the great high hills when he heard the shrieking of a human child.

"*Wan!*" he said, pointing his long ears toward the direction of the sound; "*Wan!* That is the work of cruel Double-Face. Shameless coward! He delights in torturing helpless creatures!"

Muttering indistinct words, Manstin ran up the last hill and lo! in the ravine beyond stood the terrible monster with a face in front and one in the back of his head!

This brown giant was without clothes save for a wild-cat skin about his loins. With a wicked gleaming eye, he watched the little black-haired baby he held in his strong arm. In a laughing voice he hummed an Indian mother's lullaby, "*A-boo! Aboo!*" and at the same time he switched the naked baby with a thorny wild-rose bush.

Quickly Manstin jumped behind a large sage bush on the brow of the hill. He bent his bow, and the sinewy string twanged. Now an arrow stuck above the ear of Double-Face. It was a poisoned arrow, and the giant fell dead. Then Manstin took the little brown baby and hurried away from the ravine. Soon he came to a teepee from whence loud wailing voices broke. It was the teepee of the stolen baby, and the mourners were its heartbroken parents.

When gallant Manstin returned the child to the eager arms of the mother, there came a sudden terror into the eyes of both the Dakotas. They feared lest it was Double-Face come in a new guise to torture them. The rabbit understood their fear and said, "I am Manstin, the kindhearted—Manstin, the noted huntsman. I am your friend. Do not fear."

That night a strange thing happened. While the father and mother slept, Manstin took the wee baby. With his feet placed gently yet firmly upon the tiny toes of the little child, he drew upward by each small hand the sleeping child till he was a full-grown man. With a forefinger he traced a slit in the upper lip, and when on the morrow the man and woman awoke, they could not distinguish their own son from Manstin, so much alike were the braves.

"Henceforth we are friends, to help each other," said Manstin, shaking a right hand in farewell. "The earth is our common ear, to carry from its uttermost extremes one's slightest wish for the other!"

"*Ho!* Be it so!" answered the newly made man.

Upon leaving his friend, Manstin hurried away toward the North country whither he was bound for a long hunt. Suddenly he came upon the edge of a wide brook. His alert eye caught sight of a rawhide rope staked to the water's brink, which led away toward a small round hut in the distance. The ground was trodden into a deep groove beneath the loosely drawn rawhide rope.

"*Hun-he!*" exclaimed Manstin, bending over the freshly made footprints in the moist bank of the brook. "A man's footprints!" he said to himself. "A blind man lives in yonder hut! This rope is his guide by which he comes for his daily water!" surmised Manstin, who knew all the peculiar contrivances of the people. At once his eyes became fixed upon the solitary dwelling, and hither he followed his curiosity—a real blind man's rope.

Quietly he lifted the door-flap and entered. An old toothless grandfather, blind and shaky with age, sat upon the ground. He was not deaf, however. He heard the entrance and felt the presence of some stranger.

"*How!* grandchild," he mumbled, for he was old enough to be grandparent to every living thing, "*how!* I cannot see you. Pray, speak your name!"

"Grandfather, I am Manstin," answered the rabbit, all the while looking with curious eyes about the wigwam.

"Grandfather, what is it so tightly packed in all these buckskin bags placed against the tent poles?" he asked.

"My grandchild, those are dried buffalo meat and venison. These are magic bags which never grow empty. I am blind and cannot go on a hunt. Hence a kind Maker has given me these magic bags of choicest foods."

Then the old, bent man pulled at a rope which lay by his right hand.

"This leads me to the brook where I drink! And this," said he, turning to the one on his left, "and this takes me into the forest, where I feel about for dry sticks for my fire."

"Grandfather, I wish I lived in such sure luxury! I would lean back against a tent pole, and with crossed feet I would smoke sweet-willow bark the rest of my days," sighed Manstin.

"My grandchild, your eyes are your luxury! You would be unhappy without them!" the old man replied.

"Grandfather, I would give you my two eyes for your place!" cried Manstin.

"*How!* you have said it. Arise. Take out your eyes and give them to me. Henceforth you are at home here in my stead."

At once Manstin took out both his eyes, and the old man put them on! Rejoicing, the old man started away with his young eyes while the blind rabbit filled his dream pipe, leaning lazily against the tent pole. For a short time it was a most pleasant pastime to smoke willow bark and to eat from the magic bags.

Manstin grew thirsty, but there was no water in the small dwelling. Taking one of the rawhide ropes, he started toward the brook to quench his thirst. He was young and unwilling to trudge slowly in the old man's footpath. He was full of glee, for it had been many long moons since he had tasted such good food. Thus he skipped confidently along, jerking the old weather-beaten rawhide spasmodically, till all of a sudden it gave way and Manstin fell headlong into the water.

"*En! En!*" he grunted, kicking frantically amidstream. All along the slippery bank he vainly tried to climb, till at last he chanced upon the old stake and the deeply worn footpath. Exhausted and inwardly disgusted with his mishaps, he crawled more cautiously on all fours to his wigwam door.

Dripping with his recent plunge, he sat with chattering teeth within his unfired wigwam.

The sun had set and the night air was chilly, but there was no firewood in the dwelling. "*Hin!*" murmured Manstin and bravely tried the other rope. "I go for some firewood!" he said, following the rawhide rope which led into the forest. Soon he stumbled upon thickly strewn dry willow sticks.

Eagerly with both hands he gathered the wood into his outspread blanket. Manstin was naturally an energetic fellow.

When he had a large heap, he tied two opposite ends of the blanket together and lifted the bundle of wood upon his back, but alas! he had unconsciously dropped the end of the rope, and now he was lost in the wood!

"*Hin! hin!*" he groaned. Then pausing a moment, he set his fanlike ears to catch any sound of approaching footsteps. There was none. Not even a night bird twittered to help him out of his predicament.

With a bold face, he made a start at random. He fell into some tangled wood where he was held fast. Manstin let go his bundle and began to lament having given away his two eyes.

"Friend, my friend, I have need of you! The old oak-tree grandfather has gone off with my eyes, and I am lost in the woods!" he cried with his lips close to the earth.

Scarcely had he spoken when the sound of voices was audible on the outer edge of the forest. Nearer and louder grew the voices: one was the clear flute notes of a young brave, and the other the tremulous squeaks of an old grandfather.

It was Manstin's friend with the Earth Ear and the old grandfather. "Here, Manstin, take back your eyes," said the old man, "I knew you would not be content in my stead, but I wanted you to learn your lesson. I have had pleasure seeing with your eyes and trying your bow and arrows, but since I am old and feeble I much prefer my own teepee and my magic bags!"

Thus talking, the three returned to the hut. The old grandfather crept into his wigwam, which is often mistaken for a mere oak tree by little Indian boys and girls.

Manstin, with his own bright eyes fitted into his head again, went on happily to hunt in the North country.

THE COYOTE AND HIS GUESTS

THE BLACK BEAR invited the Coyote to her underground lodge. He went the next morning, and on arriving was kindly treated by the Bear. She gave him berries and other food to eat, which was very acceptable to him, as he was almost famishing. Before long, the Black Bear put more wood on the fire, and placed a dish down by the side of the fire. Then she held her hands, fingers turned downward, in front of the blaze. Before long melted fat commenced to drip from her fingertips into the dish below, which in a short time became quite full. She took the dish and placed it in front of the Coyote, asking him to partake of the fat, which he did, eating as much as he was able. After finishing his repast, the Coyote said that he would now go home. At the same time he invited the Black Bear to his house on the morrow, when he said he would return her dish, which in the meantime he would borrow so as to take home the rest of the fat for his wife.

In due course, the Black Bear arrived at the Coyote's house, where she was treated to some offal which the Coyote had found, but which he told her was fresh, as he had been out hunting and had just brought it in. After a while the Coyote told his wife to stir the fire, because he wanted to get some fat to give to his guest. He then set the dish down close to the fire, and holding up his paws in front of the blaze, exactly as the Black Bear had done, he awaited results. As there was no sign of any fat coming, he placed his paws still nearer to the flame, and held them there until they commenced to shrivel and curl up with the heat, and still there were no signs of any grease dripping down. His paws had now almost shrunk up into a ball. He was unable to endure the pain any longer, withdrew his hands from the fire, and ran around the house, howling with pain. The Black Bear then said to him, "What a fool you are! Poor fellow! Watch me how I do it." She then held up her paws in front of the fire, as she had done on the previous day, and before long the dish was full of grease. She then made the Coyote a present of the grease, and told him never to try and do what was beyond his power.

Some time afterward the Coyote felt hungry and thought he would pay a visit to Tsalas, who lived in an underground lodge some little distance away. Upon entering, Tsalas treated him kindly, telling him that he would go and get some fresh fish for him to eat. He went outside, took a withe from some neighboring bushes, and went down to the river, where he made a small hole in the ice, and commenced to dive for fish. The Coyote, meanwhile, watched all his movements from the top of the ladder. Before long, Tsalas had caught a goodly number of fish, which he strung on the withe, and returning home, cooked some of them for the Coyote, who soon ate his fill.

On leaving, the Coyote invited Tsalas to visit him at his house on the morrow. Accordingly, the next day, Tsalas repaired to the Coyote's house, where he was offered old meat; but unlike the Black Bear, he was not fond of such food. Therefore the Coyote proposed to go and get some fresh fish for him. The Coyote left the house, took a withe, and after making a hole in the ice, put his head down the hole in order to look for the fish before diving. But in trying to get his head out again, he found that he could not. Wondering at this long absence, Tsalas went to look for his friend, and found him with his head stuck down in the ice hole. He pulled him out, more dead than alive, and addressing him, said, "Poor fellow! Why should you make yourself worse off than you already are? You are very foolish to try to do things that are beyond your powers. Now look at me!" Tsalas then put his head down in the hole and soon commenced to toss plenty of fish out on the ice. He made a present of them to the Coyote, and went home, leaving the Coyote in anything but a pleasant mood.

Some time afterward the Coyote went to the mountains to watch the Magpie and learn his methods of hunting. The latter had set a net snare close by his underground lodge. He went up the mountains, singled out a large buck deer, which he teased, and called names, such as "big posterior," "hairy posterior," and "short-tail." The buck at last grew angry and charged the Magpie, who ran away. He just kept a little ahead of the buck, so as to encourage him, and led him right into the snare, in which his antlers stuck fast, while the Magpie jumped over it, and turning round, stabbed the entangled buck to death.

The Coyote made up his mind that he would do as the Magpie had done. So he placed a net snare close by his house, and, going up the mountains, soon fell in with a buck deer, whom he commenced to belittle and slander, calling him all kinds of nasty names, just as the Magpie had done. The buck grew angry, charged the Coyote, who made for home, where his snare was, with the buck close after him. On reaching the net, the Coyote tried to jump over it, but failed to do so. He fell into the net and became entangled in it. Then the buck began to prod him with his antlers, and would have killed him if the people had not run out and prevented it by killing the buck.

THE RACCOON AND THE BLIND MEN

THERE WAS a large settlement on the shore of a lake, and among its people were two very old blind men. It was decided to remove these men to the opposite side of the lake, where they might live in safety, as the settlement was exposed to the attack of enemies, when they might easily be captured and killed. So the relations of the old men got a canoe, some food, a kettle, and a bowl and started across the lake, where they built for them a wigwam in a grove some distance from the water. A line was stretched from the door of the wigwam to a post in the water, so that they would have no difficulty in helping themselves. The food and vessels were put into the wigwam, and after the relations of the old men promised them that they would call often and keep them provided with everything that was needful, they returned to their settlement.

The two old blind men now began to take care of themselves. On one day one of them would do the cooking while the other went for water, and on the next day they would change about in their work, so that their labors were evenly divided. As they knew just how much food they required for each meal, the quantity prepared was equally divided, but was eaten out of the one bowl which they had.

Here they lived in contentment for several years; but one day a Raccoon, which was following the water's edge looking for crawfish, came to the line which had been stretched from the lake to the wigwam. The Raccoon thought it rather curious to find a cord where he had not before observed one, and wondered to himself, "What is this? I think I shall follow this cord to see where it leads." So he followed the path along which the cord was stretched until he came to the wigwam. Approaching very cautiously, he went up to the entrance, where he saw the two old men asleep on the ground, their heads at the door and their feet directed toward the heap of hot coals within. The Raccoon sniffed about and soon found there was something good to eat within the wigwam. But he decided not to enter at once for fear of waking the old men, so he retired a short distance to hide himself and to see what they would do.

Presently the old men awoke, and one said to the other, "My friend, I am getting hungry; let us prepare some food." "Very well," replied his companion, "you go down to the lake and fetch some water while I get the fire started."

The Raccoon heard this conversation, and wishing to deceive the old man, immediately ran to the water, untied the cord from the post, and carried it to a clump of bushes, where he tied it. When the old man came along with his kettle to get water, he stumbled around the bush until he found the end of the cord; then he began to dip his kettle down upon the ground for water. Not finding any, he slowly returned and said to his companion, "We shall surely die, because the lake is dried up and the brush is grown where we used to get water. What shall we do?"

"That cannot be," responded his companion, "for we have not been asleep long enough for the brush to grow upon the lake bed. Let me go out to try if I cannot get some water." So taking the kettle from his friend he started off.

So, soon as the first old man had returned to the wigwam, the Raccoon took the cord back and tied it where he had found it, then waited to see the result.

The second old man now came along, entered the lake, and getting his kettle full of water returned to the wigwam, saying as he entered, "My friend, you told me what was not true. There is water enough, for here, you see, I have our kettle full." The other could not understand this at all, and wondered what had caused the deception.

The Raccoon approached the wigwam and entered to await the cooking of the food. When it was ready, the pieces of meat, for there were eight of them, were put into the bowl, and the old men sat down on the ground

facing each other, with the bowl between them. Each took a piece of meat, and they began to talk of various things and were enjoying themselves.

The Raccoon now quietly removed four pieces of meat from the bowl and began to eat them, enjoying the feast even more than the old blind men. Presently one of them reached into the bowl to get another piece of meat, and finding that only two pieces remained, said, "My friend, you must be very hungry to eat so rapidly. I have had but one piece, and there are but two pieces left."

The other replied, "I have not taken them, but suspect you have eaten them yourself"; whereupon the other replied more angrily than before. Thus they argued, and the Raccoon, desiring to have more sport, tapped each of them on the face. The old men, each believing the other had struck him, began to fight, rolling over the floor of the wigwam, upsetting the bowl and the kettle, and causing the fire to be scattered. The Raccoon then took the two remaining pieces of meat and made his exit from the wigwam, laughing ha, ha, ha, ha; whereupon the old men instantly ceased their strife, for they now knew they had been deceived. The Raccoon then remarked to them, "I have played a nice trick on you; you should not find fault with each other so easily." Then the Raccoon continued his crawfish hunting along the lake shore.

THE PRINCESS AND THE MOUSE

IT WAS SOON AFTER the Deluge. A new town was built in the same place where the old town had been before the Deluge, and the people grew up and became numerous in the same town at Prairie Town. They had a great chief who had a beautiful daughter. Her mother and her father loved her very much. The girl grew up, and many princes wanted to marry her; but her parents refused them, for the chief wanted his daughter to marry a high prince. The chief watched her in the night, lest someone visit her. Her father made her bed above his own bed. She went up early every evening, and woke up late every morning, as her parents ordered her to do. When she wanted to take a walk in her father's village, she invited some young women to walk with her. She did so once every year. The name of this girl's mother was Gúndax, and her own name was Sudal.

Thus many years passed. One night the princess felt that someone came to her, and she saw a young man by her side. Before daybreak the young man went out, and the princess stayed in bed until very late. The following night the young man came again, and she loved him very much. Every night he came to her.

One night it occurred to the young princess that she wanted to know who the young man was who came to her every night. Therefore she watched him early in the morning; and when the young man arose, he was transformed into a mouse, which went through the knothole above her bed. Then she felt very much troubled.

She was with child; and when her time came, her father asked his wife the name of the man who had been with his daughter. Her mother asked the young woman, but she did not tell her. Therefore her father invited all the best woodworkers and told them to make a box. They did so, and calked it with gum. When they had finished it, they brought it to the chief. The chief ordered his attendants to take it down to the bank of the river.

Then the great chief told his men to bring down all his wealth; and they brought down ten costly coppers* and many elk skins, marten blankets, and all kinds of expensive garments. They put the costly coppers in the bottom of the box, and spread over them elk skins and marten garments, and skins of many other animals. Then they put the princess into the box and tied it up, by order of the great chief, and they threw her into the river, and the strong current took the box down the river. The great chief was very much ashamed on account of what his only daughter had done. Then the whole village mourned for the young princess.

Now the box drifted down the river to the sea. The young woman was still alive in the box. For many days she floated on the water. One day the young woman felt that her box was being moved by great waves. She felt it going up and down the great waves on a sandy beach, and soon she felt that her box struck the ground.

*Large pieces of sheet copper used among the Indians of the northwestern coast of North America as a symbol of wealth or distinction.

Now another noble family was encamped on this sand bar on Queen Charlotte Islands. This family had lost their young daughter not many days before, and the great chieftainess was mourning for her day by day. Early in the morning the chieftainess went out walking along the beach; and when she came round the sandy point, she sat down there, weeping. And while she was sitting there weeping, when she opened her eyes, she beheld a large object just under high-water mark. She stopped crying and went down to the place where the large object lay; and when she came to it, she recognized a large bundle of goods. She went back to her husband without touching the large bundle, and she said that she had found a large bundle on the beach.

They ran down together; and when they came to the place, they saw elk skins around it. They took their knives and cut the thongs with which it was tied. Then something moved inside. They opened the skins one by one; and as soon as the last one was off, many mice ran out of the bundle to the shore.

Then the chief and his wife ran back full of fear; but as soon as all the mice were out they saw a lovely princess lying in there. She smiled when she saw the two people standing over her. Therefore they said, "This is our daughter that was dead. She has come back to life." So they took her to their camp and carried up the costly things. They found costly coppers in the bottom of the box.

Now the noble family was very happy because they had found again their beloved daughter. They loved her very much. The chief invited all the chiefs on Queen Charlotte Islands, and he gave his newly found daughter the name of his late daughter. The chief had a nephew, a very excellent young man. Therefore the chief's nephew wanted to marry his uncle's daughter.

Now we will turn to the mice. The many mice were the children of the young woman, which she had from her sweetheart in her father's house at the head of Skeena River.

Now her cousin married her on Queen Charlotte Islands, and she had a son, whom she called Yoihetk; and another son was born to her, whom she called Gamalukt; and still another son was born to her, whom she called Gayaa. Then the chief who had found her on the sand beach died; and after the chief had died, another son was born to her, and she called him Bax-gwan.

Not very long after this, the wife of the chief also died, when she was very old. Then another child was born to the young mother, whom she called Sudal. Now these children were growing up together. The youngest children were playing about in the house, while the mother of these children's father was sitting by the fire. Then one of the little children fell against her grandmother's back, so that she fell to the ground by the fire. As soon as she opened her eyes, she scolded her grandchildren, and said, "Nobody knows your family. You come from a country far away, you foolish, common people!"

All these children were of a noble family, therefore their mother had given them noble names. The children cried, and their mother asked them what had happened. Then the elder girl told her mother what their grandmother had said to them, and the young woman went out and cried in the woods behind the house late in the evening. The young mother came in again when her eldest son came home from hunting. He asked her what made her so sad, and his mother told him what his grandmother had said to his younger sisters. Then the young man questioned her further, and his mother told her story. She said to him, "This is not our tribe. Our people live far away at the head of a great river. Our family is a noble family in a large town, where there are many people, and your grandfather's house is in the center of the town. It is a large carved house, and my uncle's houses are on each side of my father's house. I want you to go back to my country and to my people. Take all your brothers and your two sisters with you!"

The eldest son agreed to do what his mother said. Therefore he asked his father to make for him a good-sized canoe. His father did as his son had requested. He made a very good canoe for him; and after the canoe was finished, they made ready to go. The father of the children was very sorry to know that all his children were going to leave him. Before they set out, their mother took them to the sand bar at Rose Point. She pointed with her finger a little south of sunrise, and said, "Keep the head of your canoe in this direction; and when you reach the mouth of a great river, make a pole with which to punt up the river; and after you have passed a great canyon upriver, you will reach a great town. That is the town of your relatives."

Soon after she had given them this advice, the children started across the sea. For two days they paddled across the strait. Then they came to a passage between two large islands. They still kept the head of the canoe a little south of sunrise, and then they arrived at the mouth of a great river which had been unknown to them before. They did as their mother had commanded them; and when they camped in a certain place, they prepared a pole to use on the river. On the following morning they started again, going up the river. Their father had loaded their canoe with meat of seals, sea lions, halibut, and all kinds of sea animals, also with shellfish. They went up the river day after day. Now they arrived at a large canyon, as their mother had told them, and after four days they had passed through the canyon. Another day passed, and they saw a large town before them. Toward evening they arrived below the large town and camped there; and before they walked up on the trail that led to the town, they turned their good canoe upside down, and it was transformed into a little hill, and all the animals were changed into stones, which are there to this day.

In the evening they walked up to the village, at the time when all the young people of the village were walking on the street. Then this noble family walked up and down, and nobody knew who these strangers were. They saw a large house in the center of the town, and their mother had told them that this was their grandfather's house. They met a young man, whom they asked, "To whom does this large house belong?" The young man told them that it was a great chief's house. The eldest son understood the language of his mother, while the rest used the Haida language. Then the young man ran into the chief's house and told him that some strangers were standing outside—four young men and two young women. Therefore the chief sent four of his young men to call them in. The messenger went out on the street and told them that the chief invited them to come in. Then the chief ordered his men to spread a good mat by the side of his large fire, and they sat down there. Then the eldest son inquired if a chief of this town had cast out his daughter years ago on the river, and the new chief remembered that his uncle had cast out his only daughter on the river years ago. Therefore they said, "Yes, we do remember it." Then the eldest son said, "We are her children."

The whole village was astir that night, and the new chief invited all the old men, and he told them that these four princes and two princesses were the grandchildren of his late uncle. The wise men asked the princes for their names, and the eldest one told them his own name, Yoihetk; the second brother's name, Gamalukt; the third brother's name, Gayaa; the fourth one's, Bax-gwan; the elder girl's name, Gundax; and the younger girl's name, Sudal. He told them that their mother had given them these names. Then all the wise men received them gladly. They lived in their grandfather's house, and all the people loved them very much.

Now we will turn again to the mother of the young princes and of the princesses on Queen Charlotte Islands. As soon as her children had gone away, she went into the woods weeping. She wandered away. While she was walking in the woods, she came upon a narrow trail. There she met some young people, good-looking young people, who asked her, "Why are you so sad?" She told them what had happened to all her children. She said, "All my children have gone to our old home, and I am left alone in this strange land, without relatives. I have only my husband." Therefore these young people said, "We are your children, too. Don't be so sorrowful! Come with us to our house, and you shall see how many children you have with you in this strange country!"

Therefore the woman went with them. They came to a large town, and crowds of people assembled around her. When all the people had assembled, one of them spoke, "Now, my dear mother, we all are your children. Our old grandfather cast you into the river, and us too. Therefore we are here. We cannot go back to our own native country, therefore we built a town here. You shall stay with us here, for you brought us to this side. We will keep you as long as you live."

The woman, however, wanted to bring her husband with her, but they would not allow it. Then the woman agreed to their request. This town was the town of the many Mice—the children of the woman and her Mouse lover, who came to her in her father's house in her native land, when she was young. Now they had a dance in their house to comfort their mother, and they danced day by day. Soon after their meal every evening they would dance.

One day the husband of this woman went into the woods to search for his wife, but he could not find her. He went on day after day. One day the woman went back of her children's town to refresh herself, as she used to do every day. Then she thought that she heard a low moan a little distance away, that called her name. She recognized her husband's voice, and went toward the voice secretly. She heard him, and then she called him to come. He embraced her, but his wife told him her whole story, and said that her children were dancing. So the man was very anxious to see the dance. She hastened to go home. Her husband would not let her go, but asked her to come back to his own home, but she would not do so. She said, "Go away, for my children will kill you! They will soon come to look for me." The man, however, still held her in his arms.

At last four young men came to call their mother to the house. They saw the man with their mother, and they said that they must kill him. But their mother said, "Not so, my children! Be kind to him. He is my husband. He is like your father. He wishes very much to see your dance." Then they agreed to their mother's request. They said, "We will allow him four days in our midst. Then he must go away to his own house."

Evening came, and they began to dance until late at night. Thus the man learned their song and the dances they had. The whole village was asleep in the daytime; but before dusk they awoke, took their meal, and after they had eaten they began to dance. All the people of the village came to the house where their mother was, and danced there all night until daybreak.

At the end of four days, they sent the man back to his own home, and they said, "After four days more we shall send our mother back to you." And the Chief Mouse commanded him, "Don't mistreat any mouse when you human beings see one on your way or in your house, lest you be beset by dangers, for all the mice on this island are of noble blood. Therefore if any human being does something bad to a mouse, we shall kill him. I will give you a dancing feather, a neckband, and a skin drum. Then you shall teach your people how to dance."

As soon as the Chief Mouse had spoken, the man left and went to his own home. Then all his people came to him in his house, and the man taught them his song. When all his people knew how to sing this song, he put on his eagle feather and his necklace, then he began to dance; and all his people came to see him—men, women, and children—and everybody was delighted to see this dance.

At the end of four days the wife also came. She was a good singer; therefore all the women stood around her to learn her songs, and she taught them. Thus all the different villages on Queen Charlotte Islands learned how to dance, because the Mouse taught them. When the chiefs of all the tribes assembled at a dance in a chief's town, the singers assembled in his house. Thus the chief became the head of his people, and they had dances all the time. That is the end.

THE COYOTE

ONCE UPON A TIME, Too-whay-shur-wee-deh, the Little Blue Fox, was wandering near a pueblo, and chanced to come to the threshing floors, where a great many crows were hopping. Just then the Coyote passed, very hungry, and while yet far off, said, "*Ai!* how the stomach cries! I will just eat Little Blue Fox." And coming, he said, "Now, Little Blue Fox, you have troubled me enough! You are the cause of my being chased by the dogs and people, and now I will pay you. I am going to eat you up this very now!"

"No, Coyote friend," answered the Little Blue Fox, "don't eat me up! I am here guarding these chickens, for there is a wedding in yonder house, which is my master's, and these chickens are for the wedding dinner. Soon they will come for the chickens, and will invite me to the dinner—and you can come also."

"Well," said the Coyote, "if that is so, I will not eat you, but will help you watch the chickens." So he lay down beside him.

At this, Little Blue Fox was troubled, thinking how to get away; and at last he said, "Friend Coyote, I make strange that they have not before now come for the chickens. Perhaps they have forgotten. The best way is for me to go to the house and see what the servants are doing."

"It is well," said the Coyote. "Go, and I will guard the chickens for you."

So the Little Blue Fox started toward the house; but getting behind a small hill, he ran away with fast feet. When it was a good while, and he did not come back, the Coyote thought, "While he is gone, I will give myself some of the chickens." Crawling upon his belly to the threshing floor, he gave a great leap. But the chickens were only crows, and they flew away. Then he began to say evil of the Little Blue Fox for giving him a trick, and started on the trail, vowing, "I will eat him up wherever I catch him."

After many miles he overtook the Little Blue Fox, and with a bad face said, "Here! Now I am going to eat you up!"

The other made as if greatly excited, and answered, "No, friend Coyote! Do you not hear the *tombe*?" The Coyote listened, and heard a drum in the pueblo.

"Well," said the Little Blue Fox, "I am called for that dance, and very soon they will come for me. Won't you go too?"

"If that is so, I will not eat you, but we will go to the dance." And the Coyote sat down and began to comb his hair and to make himself pretty with face paint. When no one came, the Little Blue Fox said, "Friend Coyote, I make strange that the *alguazil*—officer—does not come. It is best for me to go up on this hill, whence I can see into the village. You wait here."

"He will not dare to give me another trick," thought the Coyote. So he replied, "It is well. But do not forget to call me."

So the Little Blue Fox went up the hill; and as soon as he was out of sight, he began to run for his life. Very long the Coyote waited; and at last, being tired, went up on the hill, but there was no one there. Then he was very angry, and said, "I will follow him, and eat him surely! Nothing shall save him!" And finding the trail, he began to follow as fast as a bird.

Just as the Little Blue Fox came to some high cliffs, he looked back and saw the Coyote coming over a hill. So he stood up on his hind feet and put his forepaws up against the cliff, and made many groans, and was as if much excited. In a moment came the Coyote, very angry, crying, "Now you shall not escape me! I am going to eat you up now—now!"

"Oh, no, friend Coyote!" said the other; "for I saw this cliff falling down, and ran to hold it up. If I let go, it will fall and kill us both. But come, help me to hold it."

Then the Coyote stood up and pushed against the cliff with his forepaws, very hard, and there they stood side by side.

Time passing so, the Little Blue Fox said, "Friend Coyote, it is long that I am holding up the cliff, and I am very tired and thirsty. You are fresher. So you hold up the cliff while I go and hunt water for us both, for soon you too will be thirsty. There is a lake somewhere on the other side of this mountain. I will find it and get a drink, and then come back and hold up the cliff while you go."

The Coyote agreed, and the Little Blue Fox ran away over the mountain till he came to the lake, just as the moon was rising.

But soon the Coyote was very tired and thirsty, for he held up the cliff with all his might. At last he said, "*Ai!* how hard it is! I am so thirsty that I will go to the lake, even if I die!"

So he began to let go of the cliff, slowly, slowly, until he held it only with his fingernails; and then he made a great jump away backward, and ran as hard as he could to a hill. But when he looked around and saw that the cliff did not fall, he was very angry, and swore to eat Too-whay-shur-wee-deh the very minute he should catch him.

Running on the trail, he came to the lake, and there the Little Blue Fox was lying on the bank, whining as if greatly excited. "Now I will eat you up this minute!" cried the Coyote. But the other said, "No, friend Coyote! Don't eat me up! I am waiting for someone who can swim as well as you can. I just bought a big cheese from a shepherd to share with you, but when I went to drink, it slipped out of my hands into the water. Come here, and I will show you." He took the Coyote to the edge of the high bank, and pointed to the moon in the water.

"M—m!" said the Coyote, who was fainting with hunger. "But how shall I get it? It is very deep in the water, and I shall float up before I can dive to it."

"That is true, friend," said the other. "There is but one way. We must tie some stones to your neck, to make you heavy, so you can go down to it."

So they hunted about until they found a buckskin thong and some large stones; and the Little Blue Fox tied the stones to the Coyote's neck, the Coyote holding his chin up to help.

"Now, friend Coyote, come here to the edge of the bank and stand ready.

I will take you by the back and count *weem, wee-si, pah-chu!* And when I say three, you must jump and I will push—for now you are very heavy."

So he took the Coyote by the back of the neck, swaying him back and forth as he counted. And at *"pah-chu!"* he pushed hard, and the Coyote jumped and went into deep water, and never came out again!

AGGODAGAUDA AND HIS DAUGHTER, OR THE MAN WITH HIS LEG TIED UP

THE PRAIRIE and forest tribes were once at war, and it required the keenest eyes to keep out of the way of danger. Aggodagauda lived on the borders, in the forests, but he was in a by-place not easy to find. He was a successful hunter and fisher, although he had, by some mischance, lost the use of one of his legs. So he had it tied, and looped up, and got over the ground by hopping.

Use had given him great power in the sound leg, and he could hop to a distance, which was surprising. There was nobody in the country who could outgo him on a hunt. Even Paup-Puk-Keewis, in his best days, could hardly excel him. But he had a great enemy in the chief or king of the buffalo, who frequently passed over the plains with the force of a tempest.

It was a peculiarity of Aggodagauda that he had an only child, a daughter, who was very beautiful, whom it was the aim of this enemy to carry off, and he had to exert his skill to guard her from the inroad of his great and wily opponent. To protect her the better, he had built a log house, and it was only on the roof of this that he could permit his daughter to take the open air, and disport herself. Now, her hair was so long, that when she untied it, the raven locks hung down to the ground.

One fine morning, the father had prepared himself to go out fishing, but before leaving the lodge, he put her on her guard against their archenemy. "The sun shines," said he, "and the buffalo chief will be apt to move this way before the sun gets to the middle point. You must be careful not to pass out of the house, for there is no knowing but he is always closely watching. If you go out at all, let it be on the roof, and even there keep a sharp lookout, lest he sweep by and catch you with his long horns."

With this advice he left his lodge. But he had scarcely got seated in his canoe, on his favorite fishing ground, when his ear caught insulting strains from his enemy. He listened again, and the sound was now clearer than before.

> Aggodagauda—one-legged man,
> Man with his leg tied up;
> What is he but a grasshopper,
> Hipped, and legged?

He immediately paddled his canoe ashore, and took his way home—hopping a hundred rods at a leap. But when he reached his house his daughter was gone. She had gone out on the top of the house, and sat, combing her long and beautiful hair, on the eaves of the lodge, when the buffalo king, coming suddenly by, caught her glossy hair, and winding it about his horns, tossed her onto his shoulders and swept off in an opposite direction to his village. He was followed by his whole troop, who made the plains shake under their tread. They soon reached and dashed across a river, and pursued their course to the chief's village, where she was received by all with great attention. His other wives did all they could to put the lodge in order, and the buffalo king himself was unremitting in his kindness and attention. He took down from the walls his *pibbegwun*, and began to play the softest strains, to please her ear. Ever and anon, as the chorus paused, could be heard the words:

> *Ne ne mo sha makow,*
> *Aghi saw ge naun.*
>
> My sweetheart—my bosom is true,
> You only—it is you that I love.

They brought her cold water in bark dishes from the spring. They set before her the choicest food. The king handed her nuts from the pecan tree, then he went out hunting to get her the finest meats and water fowl. But she remained pensive, and sat fasting in her lodge day after day, and gave him no hopes of forgiveness for his treachery.

In the meantime, Aggodagauda came home, and finding his daughter had been stolen, determined to get her back. For this purpose he immediately set out. He could easily track the king, until he came to the banks of the river, and saw that he had plunged in and swam over. But there had been a frosty night or two since, and the water was covered with thin ice, so that he could not walk on it. He determined to encamp till it became solid, and then crossed over and pursued the trail.

As he went along he saw branches broken off and strewed behind, for these had been purposely cast along by the daughter, that the way might be found. And the manner in which she had accomplished it was this. Her hair was all untied when she was caught up, and being very long, it caught on the branches as they darted along, and it was these twigs that she broke off for signs to her father.

When he came to the king's lodge it was evening. Carefully approaching it, he peeped through the sides and saw his daughter sitting disconsolately. She immediately caught his eye, and knowing that it was her father come for her, she all at once appeared to relent in her heart, and asking for the dipper, said to the king, "I will go and get you a drink of water." This token of submission delighted him, and he waited with impatience for her return.

At last he went out with his followers, but nothing could be seen or heard of the captive daughter. They sallied out in the plains, but had not gone far, by the light of the moon, when a party of hunters, headed by the father-in-law of Aggodaguada, set up their yells in their rear, and a shower of arrows was poured in upon them. Many of their numbers fell, but the king being stronger and swifter than the rest, fled toward the west, and never again appeared in that part of the country.

While all this was passing, Aggodagauda, who had met his daughter the moment she came out of the lodge, and being helped by his guardian spirit, took her on his shoulders and hopped off, a hundred steps in one, till he reached the stream, crossed it, and brought back his daughter in triumph to his lodge.

THE LOST BOY

A LONG TIME AGO, among the Onondaga Indians, were several families who went off to camp near the wildwood streams, where fish, deer, otter, beaver and other like game could be caught for winter use. These Onondagas, or People of the Hill, journeyed several days, and finally came to the hunting grounds. The hunting ground where they stopped was a very beautiful place, with its little hills and the river with high banks. Not far from their camp was a beautiful lake, with high, rocky banks, and with little islands full of cedar trees. When they came there it was in the moon of Chutho-wa-ah—month of October. Some of these Indians made their camps near the river, and some near the lake. As it was quite early in the season for hunting, some of the Indians amused themselves by making birchbark canoes. With these they could go up and down the river and on the lakes, fishing and trapping, or making dead falls for other small game.

In the party were five little boys who had their own bows and arrows, and would go hunting, imitating their fathers and uncles. Among them was one much smaller than the rest, who was greatly teased by the other and older boys. Sometimes they would run away from him and hide themselves in the woods, leaving him crying; then they would come back and show themselves, and have a great laugh over the little boy's distress. Sometimes they would run for the camp, and would tell him that a bear or a wolf was chasing them, leaving the little boy far behind, crying with all his might. Many a time he sought his father's camp all alone, when the other boys would leave him and hide themselves in the woods.

One day these little Indians found a great hollow log lying on the ground. One of them said, "Maybe there is a *Ta-hone-tah-na-ken* (rabbit) or a *Hi-sen* (red squirrel) in this hollow log. Let us shoot into it, and see if there is a *Ta-hone-tah-na-ken* in it." All agreed to this, and they began to take the little boy's arrows from him, and shoot them into the hole. Then the larger boys said to him, "Now go into the hollow log and get your arrows." The little boy said, "No, I am afraid something might catch me." Then he began to cry, and was not at all willing to go into the log. The others coaxed him to do so, and one said he would get his uncle to make

309

him a new bow and arrows if he would go into the log and get the arrows they had shot there.

At last this tempted the little boy. He stopped crying, got down on his hands and knees, and crawled into the log. When he had gone in a little way, he found one of his arrows, and handed it out. This gave him courage to go in a little farther. When he had advanced some distance in the log, one of the larger boys said, "Let's stop up the log and trap that boy in it, so that he can't get out." This was soon agreed to and the boys began to fetch old rotten wood and old limbs, stopping up the hollow log and trapping the little boy in it. When this mischief was done the four boys ran to their camp, saying not a word about the little boy who was trapped in the log.

It was two days before the mother and father began to notice the absence of their boy, for they thought he must have stayed overnight with one of the others, as very often he had done; but the second day a search was begun, and the other four boys were asked whereabouts they had left him. They all said that they did not know, and that the last time they were out the little boy did not go with them. Then the entire camp turned out to join in the search, as now they knew that the boy must be lost. After they had hunted a long time he could not be found, and they ceased to look for him. They thought he must have been killed and eaten by a wolf or bear.

When he was first shut up in the log the little boy tried to get out, but could not do it, as the chunks of rotten wood were too large for him to move. He could not kick or push them out. Then he cried for help, but no one came. There he was for three days and three nights, crying loudly for help, and now and then falling asleep. But on the fourth night, while he was in the hollow log, he thought he heard someone coming. He listened, and was sure he heard the crying of a very old woman, and the noise of the tramping of feet. The crying and the tramping came nearer to the log where he was. At last the crying came very close to him, and then he heard a noise as though someone sat down on the log. Now he heard the old woman cry in earnest, and now and then she would say, "Oh, how tired I am! How tired I am! And yet I may have come too late, for I do not hear my grandchild cry. He may be dead! He may be dead!" Then the old woman would cry in earnest again.

At last he heard a rap on the log and his own name called, "Ha-yah-noo! Ha-yah-noo! Are you still alive?" Ha-yah-noo, or Footprints under the Water—for this was the little boy's name—answered the old woman, and said that he still lived. The old woman said, "O, how glad I am to find my grandchild still alive!" Then she asked Ha-yah-noo if he could not get out; but he said he could not, for he had already tried. Then said the old woman, "I will try to get you out of this log." He heard her pull at the chunks of old wood, but at last she said she could not get him out, as she was too old and tired. She had heard him crying three days before, and had journeyed three days and nights to come and help her grandchild out of his trouble. Now this old woman was called O-ne-ha-tah, meaning Full of Quills, or porcupine. She lived in an old hemlock tree near the spot where the boy was shut up in the log.

When Grandmother O-ne-ha-tah had said that she had to journey three days and nights, and now she could not help Ha-yah-noo out of the log, she was very sorry and began to cry again. Finally she said she had three children who were very strong, and that she would get them to help her; so she went after them. It was almost daylight when they came, and then Ha-yah-noo heard them pull out the chunks which stopped up the log. At last Grandmother O-ne-ha-tah said to him, "Come out now. My children have got the chunks out of the log. You can come out."

When Ha-yah-noo came out he saw four wild animals around him. There was Grandmother O-ne-ha-tah and her three children, as she called them. They were Oo-kwa-e, the Bear; Sken-no-doh, the Deer; and Tah-you-ne, the Wolf. "Now," said O-ne-ha-tah, "I want one of you to take care of this boy, and love him as your own child. You all know that now I am very, very old. If I were younger I would take care of him myself."

Tah-you-ne, the Wolf, was the first one to speak, saying she could take care of the boy, as she lived on the same meat on which he fed. "No," said O-ne-ha-tah, "you are too greedy. You would eat up the boy as soon as he is left with you alone." The Wolf was very angry. She showed her teeth and snapped them at the boy, who was much afraid and wanted no such mother.

The next that spoke was Sken-no-doh, the Deer. She said that she and her husband would take care of the boy, as they lived on corn and other things which they knew the boy liked. Her husband would carry him on his back wherever they went. But Grandmother O-ne-ha-tah said, "No, you can't take care of the boy, for you are always traveling, and never stay in one place. The boy cannot do the traveling that you do, for you run very fast and make very long journeys. The boy cannot stand it, and you have no home for him for the winter. Boys like this have homes." Then the Deer ran away, very happy, as though she were glad to be rid of the boy.

Then Oo-kwa-e, the Bear, said she knew she could take care of him, as she lived in a large stone house and had plenty to eat. She lived on meats and fishes, and all kinds of nuts and berries, and even wild honey, all of which the boy would like. She had a good warm bed for him to sleep on through the winter, and she was a loving mother to her children. She would rather die than see them abused. Then O-ne-ha-tah said, "You are just the one to take care of this boy. Take him and carry him home." So the Bear, like a loving mother, took the boy and brought him to her home. When they got there, Oo-kwa-e said to her two children, Oo-tutch-ha, Young Bears, "Don't play with him roughly, and he will be your kind little brother." Then she gave him berries to eat, and they were all happy.

The stone house was a cave in the rocks, but to the boy it seemed to have rooms, like any other house, and the little bears seemed like human children. They did not tease him, but lived in the most friendly way, and the old Oo-kwa-e was a very kind mother to the boy. It was now quite late in the fall, and the days were short and dark. Then Mother Oo-kwa-e said, "It is late and dark now. We had better go to bed." The nights were cold, but the bed was warm, and they slept till the spring.

One evening it thundered. The bears do not wake up till the thunder is heard. It made such a noise that they thought the walls were coming down. Then the old Oo-kwa-e said, "Why! it's getting light. We had better get up." So they lived happily together for a very long time. She went out in the woods, going to and fro for food, and the children amused themselves at home.

Every now and then, through the summer, the bear people would come in and say, "In such a place are many berries." These would be strawberries, raspberries, or others, according to the season. Later they told of chestnuts and other nuts of which they were fond. Then they would say, "Let us go and gather them." So Mother Bear and Little Bears went, taking the little boy along, for they always expected a good time. The other bears knew nothing about the boy. When they came near the spot and he was seen, they would be frightened and say, "There is a human being! Let us run! let us run!" So they would scamper off as fast as bears can, leaving their heaps of nuts or berries behind them. Then the old Oo-kwa-e would gather these up, she and her children, and take them home, which was a very easy way of getting plenty of food. Thus the boy became very useful to Mother Bear.

The boy lived with them thus for about three years, and the same things happened every year. In the third year, Mother Bear said, "Someone is coming to kill us." Then all looked out and saw a man coming through the woods, with his bow and arrows in his hand, and his dog running all around, looking for game. Then Mother Bear said, "I must see what I can do." So she took a forked stick, and pointed the open fork toward the man. It seemed to come near him, and appeared to him like a line of thick brush that he did not wish to break through. So he turned aside and went another way, and they were safe that time.

Another day she again said, "Someone is coming toward us again, and we shall be killed." She put forth the forked stick; but the man did not mind it, and came straight toward her stone house. The stick itself split, and there was nothing in the way. Then she took a bag of feathers and threw these outside. They flew up and down, and around, and seemed like a flock of partridges. The dog ran after them, through the bushes and trees, supposing them to be birds, and so the second man went away.

The days went by, and for the third time Mother Bear saw a man coming. This time she said, "Now we certainly are all going to die." Then she said to the boy, "Your father is coming now, and he is too good a hunter to be fooled. There is his dog, with his four eyes, and he, too, is one of the best of hunters." Now when a dog has a light spot over each eye, the Indians say that he has four eyes. So the man came nearer. She tried the forked stick, but it split, and still the man and dog came on. She scattered the feathers, and they flew around as before, but the hunter and dog heeded them not, and still both came on. At last the dog reached the door and barked, and the man drew his bow, ready to shoot anything that came out.

313

When Mother Oo-kwa-e saw the man standing there, she said, "Now, children, we must all take our bundles and go." So each of the Little Bears took a small bundle and laid it on his back, but there was no bundle for the boy. When all were ready, she said, "I will go first, whatever may happen." So she opened the door, and as she went out the man shot, and she was killed. Then the oldest of the Oo-tutch-ha said, "I will go next," and as he went he also was killed.

The last Little Bear was afraid, and said to the boy, "You go first." But the little boy was also afraid, and said, "No, you go first. I have no bundle." For all the bears tried to get their bundles between them and the man. So Little Bear and the boy at last went out together; but though Little Bear tried to keep behind, the man shot at him first and he was killed. As the hunter was about to shoot again, the boy called out, "Don't shoot me! Don't shoot me! I am not a bear!" His father dropped his arrow, for he knew his voice at once, and said, "Why did you not call out before? Then I would not have killed the Oo-kwa-e and Oo-tutch-ha. I am very sorry for what I have done, for the bears have been good to you." But the boy said, "You did not kill them, though you thought so. You only shot the bundles. I saw them thrown down and the spirits of the bears run off from behind them." Still, the man was sorry that he had shot at the bears. He wished to be kind to them as they had been to his boy.

Then the father began to look at his boy more closely, to see how he had grown and how he had changed. Then he saw that long hairs were growing between his fingers, for, living so long with them, he had already begun to turn into a bear. He was very glad when he took the boy back to his home, and his friends, relatives, and the whole town rejoiced with him.

THE SIX HAWKS, OR BROKEN WING

THERE WERE six young falcons living in a nest, all but one of whom were still unable to fly, when it so happened that both the parents were shot by the hunters in one day. The young brood waited with impatience for their return; but night came, and they were left without their parents and without food. Meeji-geeg-wona, the Gray Eagle, the eldest, and the only one whose feathers had become full enough to enable him to leave the nest, assumed the duty of stilling their cries and providing them with food, in which he was very successful. But, after a short time had passed, he, by an unlucky mischance, got one of his wings broken in pouncing upon a swan. This was the more unlucky, because the season had arrived when they were soon to go off to a southern climate to pass the winter, and they were only waiting to become a little stronger and more expert for the journey. Finding that he did not return, they resolved to go in search of him, and found him sorely wounded and unable to fly.

"Brothers," he said, "an accident has befallen me, but let not this prevent your going to a warmer climate. Winter is rapidly approaching, and you cannot remain here. It is better that I alone should die than for you all to suffer miserably on my account." "No! no!" they replied, with one voice, "we will not forsake you; we will share your sufferings; we will abandon our journey, and take care of you, as you did of us, before we were able to take care of ourselves. If the climate kills you, it shall kill us. Do you think we can so soon forget your brotherly care, which has surpassed a father's and even a mother's kindness? Whether you live or die, we will live or die with you."

They sought out a hollow tree to winter in, and contrived to carry their wounded nest mate there; and before the rigors of winter set in, they had stored up food enough to carry them through its severities. To make it last the better, two of the number went off south, leaving the other three to watch over, feed, and protect the wounded bird. Meeji-geeg-wona in due time recovered from his wound, and he repaid their kindness by giving them such advice and instruction in the art of hunting as his experience had qualified him to impart.

As spring advanced, they began to venture out of their hiding place, and

315

were all successful in getting food to eke out their winter's stock, except the youngest, who was called Peepi-geewi-zains, the Pigeon Hawk. Being small and foolish, flying hither and yon, he always came back without anything. At last the Gray Eagle spoke to him, and demanded the cause of his ill luck. "It is not my smallness or weakness of body," said he, "that prevents my bringing home flesh as well as my brothers. I kill ducks and other birds every time I go out; but, just as I get to the woods, a large owl robs me of my prey."

"Well! don't despair, brother," said Meeji-geeg-wona. "I now feel my strength perfectly recovered, and I will go out with you tomorrow," for he was the most courageous and warlike of them all.

Next day they went forth in company, the eldest seating himself near the lake. Peepi-geewi-zains started out, and soon pounced upon a duck.

"Well done!" thought his brother, who saw his success; but just as he was getting to land with his prize, up came a large white owl from a tree, where he had been watching, and laid claim to it. He was about wresting it from him, when Meeji-geeg-wona came up, and fixing his talons in both sides of the owl, flew home with him.

The little Pigeon Hawk followed him closely and was rejoiced and happy to think he had brought home something at last. He then flew in the owl's face, and wanted to tear out his eyes, and vented his passion in abundance of reproachful terms. "Softly," said the Gray Eagle; "do not be in such a passion, or show so revengeful a disposition; for this will be a lesson to him not to tyrannize over anyone who is weaker than himself for the future." So, after giving him good advice, and telling him what kind of herbs would cure his wounds, they let the owl go.

While this act was taking place, and before the liberated owl had yet got out of view, two visitors appeared at the hollow tree. They were the two nest mates, who had just returned from the south after passing the winter there, and they were thus all happily reunited, and each one soon chose a mate and flew off to the woods. Spring had now revisited the north. The cold winds had ceased, the ice had melted, the streams were open, and the forest began rapidly to put on its vernal hue.

"But it is in vain," said the old man who related this story, "it is in vain that spring returns, if we are not thankful to the Master of Life who has preserved us through the winter. Nor does that man answer the end for which he was made who does not show a kind and charitable feeling to all who are in want or sickness, especially to his blood relations. These six birds only represent one of our impoverished northern families of children, who had been deprived of both their parents and the aid of their elder brother at nearly the same time."

THE MOQUI BOY AND THE EAGLE

THE EAGLE is Kah-bay-deh, commander of all that flies, and his feathers are strongest in medicine.

So long ago that no man can tell how long, there lived in Moqui an old man and an old woman, who had two children, a boy and a girl. The boy, whose name was Tai-oh, had a pet Eagle, of which he was very fond; and the Eagle loved its young master. Despite his youth, Tai-oh was an excellent hunter, and every day he brought home not only rabbits enough for the family but also to keep the Eagle well fed.

One day when he was about to start on a hunt, he asked his sister to look out for the Eagle during his absence. No sooner was he out of sight than the girl began to upbraid the bird bitterly, saying, "How I hate you, for my brother loves you so much. If it were not for you, he would give me many more rabbits, but now you eat them up."

The Eagle, feeling the injustice of this, was angry; so when she brought him a rabbit for breakfast the Eagle turned his head and looked at it sidewise, and would not touch it. At noon, when she brought him his dinner, he did the same thing; and at night, when Tai-oh returned, the Eagle told him all that had happened.

"Now," said the Eagle, "I am very tired of staying always here in Moqui, and I want to go home to visit my people a little. Come and go along with me, that you may see where the Eagle people live."

"It is well," replied Tai-oh. "Tomorrow morning we will go together."

In the morning they all went out into the fields, far down in the valley, to hoe their corn, leaving Tai-oh at home.

"Now," said the Eagle, "untie this thong from my leg, friend, and get astride my neck, and we will go."

The string was soon untied, and Tai-oh got astride the neck of the great

bird, which rose up into the air as though it carried no weight at all. It circled over the town a long time, and the people cried out with wonder and fear at seeing an Eagle with a boy on his back. Then they sailed out over the fields where Tai-oh's parents and his sister were at work; and all three began to cry, and went home in great sorrow.

The Eagle kept soaring up and up until they came to the very sky. There in the blue was a little door, through which the Eagle flew. Alighting on the floor of the sky, he let Tai-oh down from his back, and said, "Now, you wait here, friend, while I go and see my people," and off he flew.

Tai-oh waited three days, and still the Eagle did not return; so he became uneasy and started out to see what he could find. After wandering a long way, he met an old Spider woman.

"Where are you going, my son?" she asked.

"I am trying to find my friend, the Eagle."

"Very well, then, I will help you. Come into my house."

"But how can I come into so small a door?" objected Tai-oh.

"Just put your foot in, and it will open big enough for you to enter."

So Tai-oh put his foot in, and, sure enough, the door opened wide, and he went into the Spider's house and sat down.

"Now," said she, "you will have some trouble in getting to the house of your friend, the Eagle, for to get there you will have to climb a dreadful ladder. It is well that you came to me for help, for that ladder is set with sharp arrowheads and knives of flint, so that if you tried to go up it, it would cut your legs off. But I will give you this sack of sacred herbs to help you. When you come to the ladder, you must chew some of the herbs and spit the juice on the ladder, which will at once become smooth for you."

Tai-oh thanked the Spider woman and started off with the sack. After a while he came to the foot of a great ladder, which went away up out of sight. Its sides and rungs were bristling with keen arrowheads, so that no living thing could climb it; but when Tai-oh chewed some of the magic herb and spat upon the ladder, all the sharp points fell off, and it was so smooth that he climbed it without a single scratch.

After a long, long climb, he came to the top of the ladder, and stepped upon the roof of the Eagle's house. But when he came to the door he found it so bristling with arrow points that whoever might try to enter would be cut to pieces. Again he chewed some of the herb, and spat upon the door; and at once all the points fell off, and he entered safely, and inside he found his Eagle friend and all the Eagle people. His friend had fallen in love with an Eagle girl and married her, and that was the reason he had not returned sooner.

Tai-oh stayed there some time, being very nicely entertained, and enjoyed himself greatly in the strange sky country. At last one of the wise old Eagle men came to him and said, "Now, my son, it is well that you go home, for your parents are very sad, thinking you are dead. After this, whenever you see an Eagle caught and kept captive, you must let it go; for now you have been in our country, and know that when we come home we take off our feather coats and are people like your own."

So Tai-oh went to his Eagle friend and said he thought he must go home.

"Very well," said the Eagle; "get on my back and shut your eyes, and we will go."

So he got on, and they went down out of the sky, and down and down until at last they came to Moqui. There the Eagle let Tai-oh down among the wondering people, and bidding him an affectionate good-by, flew off to his young wife in the sky.

Tai-oh went to his home loaded down with dried meat and tanned buckskin, which the Eagle had given him; and there was great rejoicing, for all had given him up as dead. And this is why, to this very day, the Moquis will not keep an eagle captive, though nearly all the other Pueblo towns have all the eagle prisoners they can get.

THE MOOSE WIFE

A YOUNG MAN living with his mother concluded to go into the forest to hunt for a whole year, collecting and drying meat, and intending at the end of that period to return to visit his mother. So he traveled a long way into the forest to a region in which he thought there was plenty of deer and other game. There, having built a cabin, he began housekeeping by himself. His daily routine was to make a fire, get breakfast, and then start off to hunt. He would stay away hunting all day. Often when he got home at night he was so tired that he would not take the trouble to prepare supper, but throwing himself on his couch, he would go to sleep. He was collecting a great quantity of cured meat.

One evening when he was returning from a long tramp, he saw, as he neared his cabin, smoke issuing from the smoke hole in the roof. At this he became greatly troubled, for he thought that the fire may have spread and ignited his lodge. Running into the lodge as quickly as possible, what was his surprise to find a bright fire burning in the fire pit, and his kettle, which had been suffered to boil, hanging on the crook in such a way as to keep its contents hot. He wondered who had come to cook for him, for during the time he had lived there and during his journeys he had never found a cabin, nor had he seen a human being. He searched all around to see whether he could find a trace of a person's visit.

He saw that the deer he had brought home the evening before was dressed and hung up, that a pile of wood that he had cut had been brought in, that everything had been put in order, and that even corn bread had been made. On the way home he had thought of going to bed the moment he set foot in the cabin, so he was greatly rejoiced to find a warm supper awaiting him. He sat down and ate the supper, thinking to himself, "Surely the person who got this ready will come back," but no one came.

The next morning he started as usual to hunt. When he returned in the evening, he looked to see whether smoke was coming out of the smoke hole of his cabin. There was smoke issuing from it, and again he found supper ready for him. On discovering a partially finished braid of fibers of bark, he knew that a woman had been at work. He saw, moreover, that she had also put a large number of his green deerskins to soak, preparatory to making buckskin. Thereupon he thought how good she was, and he resolved to see her, whoever she might be, even if he had to give up hunting in order to do so.

In the morning he started off as though he were going to hunt, but went only a short way into the woods to a place whence he could watch the cabin. He had built no fire that morning, so that he might be able to tell the moment smoke began to rise from the lodge. Stealthily creeping back toward his home, he soon saw smoke rising from the cabin. As he drew nearer, he saw what to him was a woman come out of the lodge and take up an armful of wood.

When she went into the lodge, he followed her as quickly as possible. There he found a beautiful young woman, to whom he said, "You have been very kind to me, and I am very thankful to you." She said in reply, "I knew you were starving for lack of a woman's aid, so I came to see whether you would take me as your wife." He accepted her offer, for he was very happy that she was willing to remain. She never left him after that. Every day she tanned the deerskins and cooked for him, working hard all the time. His wife was beautiful, and he loved her dearly.

Before the end of a year, a boy was born to them, and they were perfectly happy. When the time was near to fulfill his promise to visit his mother, she said to him, "I know you promised to visit your mother, and the time is now here. I have everything ready for you. I have made moccasins for you and for your mother." He said in reply, "I wonder how I can carry her some meat, for she lives a long way off." "You have only to choose the meat you want," she replied; "I know how you can carry it." He decided to take some of every kind.

She warned him to be true and faithful to her while away, for many women when they saw what a good hunter he was would ask him of his mother. She said, "You must be true to me as I will be to you. You must never yield to temptation, for I shall know if you do, and you will never see me again." He promised her everything she asked. Early the next morning she asked him to go to the river with her; it was not far from the cabin. She knew how he came, and that he would reach his mother's home sooner by going on the river. When they reached the bank, she took out of her bosom a tiny canoe. He wondered what she was going to do with so little a plaything. She told him to take hold of one end and to pull away from her. On doing so, the canoe stretched out until it was a very large one.

Then they brought on their backs basketful after basketful of meat, which they packed away in the canoe. Giving him a package, she said, "I have made these moccasins for your mother. Here is another package for you. I wish you to put on a pair every morning, throwing away the old ones."

He promised to return in the fall, and then they parted. When he reached his mother's lodge, the news spread that a certain woman's son had returned after a year's hunting, and many came to see him and the great amount of meat he had brought. He did not tell even his mother that he was married, and many young girls asked for him as a husband. His mother had a beautiful girl in view for him, and continually urged him to marry her, but he would not consent. After a while he said to his mother, "I am going to the woods again. I have a cabin there, and sometime you will know why I do not wish to marry." So saying, he started off.

When he reached the river, he shook his boat as his wife had instructed him to do, whereupon it again stretched out. Getting aboard, he started up the river. When he neared his cabin, he saw his wife waiting for him and his little boy running around at play, and they were very happy again. She told him she loved him better than ever, for he had withstood temptation.

Another year passed. They had all the meat they could take care of, and another boy had been born to them. Again she got him ready to carry meat to his mother, just as she had done before. She seemed, however, to feel that this time he would yield to temptation, so she said to him, "If you marry another woman, you will never see me again; but if you love me and your children, you will be true to us and come back. If you are not true, I will not be surprised if your new wife will soon be sucking her moccasins from hunger, for your *orenda*, your magic power for hunting, will vanish." He promised her everything.

As before, on reaching home his fame as a hunter brought many beautiful girls to ask for him in marriage. Again his mother urged him to marry, and the temptation to yield then was far greater than the first time, but he resisted and was ready to start for his cabin, when one day a beautiful stranger, appearing in the village, came to his mother's lodge. The mother urged him to marry her, as she was so lovely, and he finally yielded.

The wife in the woods, knowing the conditions, said, "Now children, we must be getting ready to go away. Your father does not love us and will never come back to us." Though the children were troubled by their mother's tears, still they were full of play and fun, but the poor mother was always weeping while preparing to leave her home.

After the man had taken a second wife, the meat in his lodge began to fall away strangely. He could almost see it disappear, though there was a good supply when he married. In a few days but little was left. He went hunting but could kill nothing; he went day after day, but always had the same ill luck, for he had lost his magic power for hunting, as his wife had foretold. One day when he came home from hunting, he found his new wife sucking her moccasin, for she was famishing from hunger. He cried and sobbed, saying, "This is my punishment; she warned me that this would happen if I was untrue to her." Thereupon he decided to go back to his first wife and children at once and never to leave them again.

He set out without saying a word to the starving wife or to his anxious mother. When he reached his cabin not a single footprint was to be seen. He went in, but only to find it empty—wife and children were not there, nor any meat, but their worn moccasins were hanging up. The sight of these made him very sad. As he was nearly starved, he searched everywhere for food. On the hearth he found three small mounds of ashes, of different sizes, the third being very small. Sitting down, he wondered what this could mean, for he knew that it must have been left by his wife as a sign to him should he ever come to the cabin. At last he made up his mind that he had three children now, and he determined to find them even if he had to follow them to the end of the world.

He mused, "My boys are very playful, and as they followed their mother they must have hacked the trees as they went." Indeed, as the mother and the boys were starting away, the boys said, "We will make some sign, so that if our father ever thinks of us and comes back, he will be able to follow us." But the mother said, "No, children, you must not; he will never come, for he has another wife, and will never think of his children in the woods." Nevertheless, as they went on and played by the way, the boys hacked the trees and shot arrows in sport, so the father was soon able to trace them. He found that after a day's journey they had camped for the night, for he discovered the remains of a fire, and on a tree near by, four pairs of worn-out moccasins. Tying these in a bundle, he hung it on his arm.

Again he walked all day, finally coming to the remains of a fire, near which he saw four pairs of worn moccasins hanging up as before. He was very tired and hungry.

The next morning he traveled on, and as before, found the remains of a fire and four pairs of worn moccasins hanging on a tree. He always took these with him. Near noon the next day he saw smoke in the distance, seeming to rise from a cabin, and so it proved to be. He saw also two boys playing around, running, and shooting arrows; on seeing him they ran to tell their mother that a man was coming. On looking out, she recognized her husband, whereupon she told the boys to stay inside the lodge. He had not recognized the children as his sons, but supposed they belonged to the people living in the cabin.

As he was very hungry and tired, he thought he would go in and ask for food. The woman turned her back as he entered, but the eldest boy, recognizing his father, ran to him and put his hand on his knee. The father, however, not recognizing the child, gently pushed his hand away. At this moment the mother, turning around, saw this action. "There," she said, "I told you to keep away from him, for he does not love you."

Now the man, recognizing his wife, cried out, begging her to forgive him and to receive him home again. He seemed to be sorry, and begged so hard that she forgave him and brought him his little daughter, born after he had gone away. Ever afterward he was true to his Moose wife (for she was a Moose woman), and never again left his home in the woods. He and his little family were always very happy.

X

INDIAN "HOW," "WHY," AND ORIGIN LEGENDS

THE LOON'S NECKLACE

THE MEDICINE MAN was sad, and for good reason, as he sat facing the bright beams of the afternoon sun. A sky of shimmering turquoise crowned the fragrant forest. It was the Moon of Painted Leaves. The hardwoods were tinted with crimson, copper, orange-red, and tawny russet shades. The quivering leaves of the aspens shone like burnished gold, reflecting the mellow, golden light of the sun and the black spires of spruce and pine towered skyward, just beyond the village. Overhead, a golden eagle drifted in the cloudless sky, but the eyes of the medicine man did not follow the wonder of its effortless hovering. He felt the warm touch of autumn on his face. His keen ears heard the faintest rustle of the woodland wild folk, but he saw them not. Dark Night, the medicine man, was sorrowful because he was blind. As he sat in front of his lodge, he heard the voice of his scolding wife. She added to his troubles by her constant complaints.

"Why weave you not baskets or make arrows, like other men who live in the night shadows?" she grumbled. "If you did, we could trade such things for food and skins. Then we would not know hunger and cold, as we will when snow flies. People now pay you little for your counsel as a medicine man. They say that you only know things by fours and that four cannot be strong medicine, cannot cure their ills. All you can think of and say is 'four'. Our people laugh when you say, 'When the owl hoots four times, seek spruce sap for your cough'. Or, 'Place four white pebbles on the red rock by the lake shore on the fourth day', " she mocked cruelly.

Dark Night heard, but he was patient. "Four is my medicine sign," he told her. "I learned it in my dream when my secret totem and medicine animal were revealed."

"Why call you not on your totem to help us now?" demanded his wife.

"When the time comes, I will," he promised patiently.

Only when he heard the quavering laugh of a loon come from a near-by lake did the sad, resigned look leave his face. Then he would smile and listen, and his lips would move in unspoken answers to the wild, weird calls.

The "painted leaves" fell. A wild wind blew from the north. Winter came.

The fear of hunger flowed like mist in the hearts of the people. A black cloud of dread hung over the lodges of the tribe. Even before the Snow Moon, hunting had been bad. With the snow it became worse. Bands of hunters returned to the village with the same story: neither animals nor birds were to be found. Lone hunters, the best in the tribe, brought back no game, even after long, cold days on the trail. Then the chief sent his young men through the deep snow to neighboring tribes with beads and weapons to trade for food. They returned with the same trade goods which they had taken with them. Their friendly neighbors also sought food in vain. There was none to spare. Then, when the Hunger Moon shone in the sad sky, there was none at all.

One night of bitter cold, lying awake in his lodge, Dark Night heard, four times, the wild, wavering, warning cry of a loon directly overhead. Instantly he dozed and dreamed. In his troubled sleep his mind's eye saw a vision of sickness, sorrow, famine, danger, and death. Throughout his dream he heard always the unearthly, high-pitched, savage attack cry of wolves coming ever nearer. Four loud, haunting loon laughs awoke him. Sleep suddenly left him, but the dream stayed in his mind. The awful attack call of the wolf packs and the four warning notes of the loon were still with him when night left to let daybreak come.

When the sun shone, he groped his way to the council lodge. Inside, the chief of the band sat with the tribal medicine man and the wisest men of the tribe. Dark Night stood before them. "This is how it will be," he warned them as he told of his dream and the coming attack by wolf packs in four days' time. Those in council silently mocked him.

"Were the shadow of hunger not in my heart, I would laugh," the tribal medicine man declared. The Wise Ones smiled pityingly but were silent.

When they heard of Dark Night's warning, the people of the village made fun of him. They had ceased to respect or fear his powers as a medicine man. They pointed their fingers at him and tried to forget their hunger in their silent mockery.

At the end of the fourth day, as night spread its dark, star-studded blanket over the village, the mockers heard the savage cry of wolves. Fear spread like fire in the hearts of the people. They were scared, silent, stunned, for fierce, starving wolf packs came. That night the ravenous beasts raided the village. They cruelly injured men and women and carried away children before they could be driven off with fire and weapons. Each night the bloodthirsty wolves attacked and killed, and for days the bravest warriors feared to leave the village.

Then the chief sent his tribal medicine man to Dark Night and begged him to go to the council lodge. At once he obeyed his chief and followed the well-beaten trail through the deep snow to the meeting place. This time the chief and his counselors did not mock Dark Night.

"Help us," pleaded the chief as he guided the blind medicine man to the place of honor beside him. "Tell us what to do. It has been whispered by the Wise Ones that you have a magic bow. Arrows fired from that bow, they tell, cannot miss. Let our best hunter use it, should the wolves come again tonight."

"No one but I can bend the magic bow," declared Dark Night, "but tonight I will use it if your young men will bring me many hunting arrows."

"You will have all of our best arrows," promised the chief. He gave orders that the warriors and young men take their finest arrows to the lodge of Dark Night at once. The wife of the medicine man received them. She was now proud of the blind husband she had mocked before the snow came.

That night the wolves attacked again. Dark Night, dressed in his best buckskin hunting dress, circled the village. He held his magic bow and was guided by a great warrior who carried many arrows but no bow. When Dark Night heard the movement of a wolf he quickly placed an arrow on the bow thong, pointed the shaft in the direction of the sinister sound and pulled the bow taut. As the song of the bow thong whipped the darkness, the whistle of feathered shaft was followed each time by the death howl of a wolf. The snarls of famished beasts shattered the silence of the night. With blazing eyes and bristling hackles, the wolves fought each other with blood-flecked jaws that they might devour the bodies of their fellows which had fallen to Dark Night's bow. Arrows, fired by a tireless arm, flew from the magic bow until the pale fingers of morning groped among the trunks of the gray birches. Then the wolves fled, leaving many great, gray bodies stretched out in the crimson-stained snow. The hungry people feasted on the slain beasts and presents were piled high before the lodge of Dark Night. Often from that night until the snows left to let spring come, the blind medicine man's bow twanged to serve his people. Then the grass came back, deer returned to the forests, and the people were happy again.

Late one sun-filled evening, Dark Night sat outside his fine new lodge which the grateful people had made for him. A smile hovered about his lips and he seemed to be listening. Clearly, loudly, from the distant lake came the strange, soul-stirring cry of a loon. Four times did the quavering *wah-hoo-o-o-o-o-o* blend with the serene spring song of the fragrant forest. Once again Dark Night dressed himself in his finest buckskin. Around his neck he reverently placed his most prized possession, a necklace made of gleaming, snow-white shells. Refusing the help of many willing hands, he groped his way from tree to tree toward the loon call and the lake. When the cry sounded directly in front of him, the medicine man held onto the slim trunk of a paper-birch tree while he thrust the toe of his moccasin-clad foot forward. It touched soft, saffron sand at the edge of the lake. The setting sun, which he could not see, was sinking in a flaming curtain of splendor on the placid water of the silver-misted lake. Startlingly the loon call broke the silence. Never before had Dark Night heard the notes so loud and clear and near. Tremblingly the medicine man spoke, "O Father Loon, my totem bird, I have a wish which my heart prays may be granted."

"Speak, my son, that I may know your desire," replied a deep, musical voice.

The words came from a point so close to Dark Night's feet that he was startled. He managed to murmur, "For many, many moons I have lived in a darkness deeper than darkest night. I pray you, let my eyes see the wonders which I can only sense."

"Faith makes you believe. Faith will make you see, my son. You have been patient. Climb onto my back and hold tight to my wings."

Astonishment, fear, eagerness and hope were strong in Dark Night's heart as he did as he was bid. He grasped the loon's wings firmly and the great bird dived. In the space of an indrawn breath, the medicine man felt the cold waters of the lake flow beneath his sightless eyes.

The loon came to the surface when the distant shore was reached. "Has the light come to your eyes, my son?"

"No, Father Loon, all is still dark."

"Hold tightly," warned the loon.

Once again it dived smoothly beneath the surface and swam to the opposite shore. When they reached it, the loon asked the same question.

"Not yet, Father Loon, but I seem to see a grayness before me."

When the lake had been crossed for the third time, the loon again asked, "Has the light come?"

"Yes, Father Loon, I can now see, though but dimly."

Again the loon warned the medicine man to hold on. Then it dived. Again the water flowed swiftly against the open eyes of the medicine man.

When the loon asked the question for the fourth time, the medicine man stood on the spot from where he had first heard the loon's loud laugh. When he looked down, he clearly saw a great loon floating feather-light on the surface of the lake in front of him. Dark Night flung his arms upward, hands held high, in a heartfelt gesture of thanks.

"Father Loon," he gasped, and his voice was choked with joy and grateful tears, "I can see! How can I thank you? How can I ever repay you?" Then, swift as the swoop of a hawk, he knew. He would give the loon his greatest treasure, his sacred necklace. Fumbling fingers at last loosened the treasured collar. With both trembling hands outstretched, he dropped the band of glistening white shells over the loon's head. As it raised its neck, the glittering, snowy collar glided gently down its black feathers. Like a lovely necklace it shone on the bird's neck. Some shells fell from the collar and lay sparkling like snow crystals on the loon's dark back and wings. The bird raised its long black beak skyward. Four times its lilting laugh filled the luminous twilight with music of savage splendor.

The heart of the medicine man was glad when he saw that his lovely collar of shells had become a glistening feather necklace, white as feathery flakes of snow.

THE ORIGIN OF THE MEDICINE PIPE

THUNDER—you have heard him. He is everywhere. He roars in the mountains, he shouts far out on the prairie. He strikes the high rocks, and they fall to pieces. He hits a tree, and it is broken in slivers. He strikes the people, and they die. He is bad. He does not like the towering cliff, the standing tree, or living man. He likes to strike and crush them to the ground. Yes! yes! Of all he is most powerful; he is the one most strong. But I have not told you the worst: he sometimes steals women.

Long ago, almost in the beginning, a man and his wife were sitting in their lodge, when Thunder came and struck them. The man was not killed. At first he was as if dead, but after a while he lived again, and rising looked about him. His wife was not there. "Oh, well," he thought, "she has gone to get some water or wood," and he sat awhile; but when the sun had under-disappeared, he went out and inquired about her of the people. No one had seen her. He searched throughout the camp, but did not find her. Then he knew that Thunder had stolen her, and he went out on the hills alone and mourned.

When morning came, he rose and wandered far away, and he asked all the animals he met if they knew where Thunder lived. They laughed, and would not answer. The Wolf said, "Do you think we would seek the home of the only one we fear? He is our only danger. From all others we can run away, but from him there is no running. He strikes, and there we lie. Turn back! Go home! Do not look for the dwelling place of that dreadful one." But the man kept on, and traveled far away. Now he came to a lodge, a queer lodge, for it was made of stone—just like any other lodge, only it was made of stone. Here lived the Raven chief. The man entered.

"Welcome, my friend," said the chief of the Ravens. "Sit down, sit down." And food was placed before him.

Then, when he had finished eating, the Raven said, "Why have you come?"

"Thunder has stolen my wife," replied the man. "I seek his dwelling place that I may find her."

"Would you dare enter the lodge of that dreadful person?" asked the Raven. "He lives close by here. His lodge is of stone, like this; and hanging there, within, are eyes, the eyes of those he has killed or stolen. He has taken out their eyes and hung them in his lodge. Now, then, dare you enter there?"

"No," replied the man, "I am afraid. What man could look at such dreadful things and live?"

"No person can," said the Raven. "There is but one old Thunder fears. There is but one he cannot kill. It is I, it is the Raven. Now I will give you medicine, and he shall not harm you. You shall enter there, and seek among those eyes your wife's; and if you find them, tell that Thunder why you came, and make him give them to you. Here, now, is a raven's wing. Just point it at him, and he will start back quick; but if that fails, take this. It is an arrow, and the shaft is made of elk horn. Take this, I say, and shoot it through the lodge."

"Why make a fool of me?" the poor man asked. "My heart is sad. I am crying." And he covered his head with his robe, and wept.

"Oh," said the Raven, "you do not believe me. Come out, come out, and I will make you believe." When they stood outside, the Raven asked, "Is the home of your people far?"

"A great distance," said the man.

"Can you tell how many days you have traveled?"

"No," he replied, "my heart is sad. I did not count the days. The berries have grown and ripened since I left."

"Can you see your camp from here?" asked the Raven.

The man did not speak. Then the Raven rubbed some medicine on his eyes and said, "Look!" The man looked, and saw the camp. It was close. He saw the people. He saw the smoke rising from the lodges.

"Now you will believe," said the Raven. "Take now the arrow and the wing, and go and get your wife."

So the man took these things, and went to the Thunder's lodge. He entered and sat down by the doorway. The Thunder sat within and looked at him with awful eyes. But the man looked above, and saw many pairs of eyes. Among them were those of his wife.

"Why have you come?" said the Thunder in a fearful voice.

"I seek my wife," the man replied, "whom you have stolen. There hang her eyes."

"No man can enter my lodge and live," said the Thunder; and he rose to strike him. Then the man pointed the raven wing at the Thunder, and he fell back on his couch and shivered. But he soon recovered, and rose again. Then the man fitted the elk-horn arrow to his bow, and shot it through the lodge of rock; right through that lodge of rock it pierced a jagged hole, and let the sunlight in.

"Hold," said the Thunder. "Stop; you are the stronger. Yours the great medicine. You shall have your wife. Take down her eyes." Then the man cut the string that held them, and immediately his wife stood beside him.

"Now," said the Thunder, "you know me. I am of great power. I live here in summer, but when winter comes, I go far south. I go south with the birds. Here is my pipe. It is medicine. Take it, and keep it. Now, when I first come in the spring, you shall fill and light this pipe, and you shall pray to me, you and the people. For I bring the rain which makes the berries large and ripe. I bring the rain which makes all things grow, and for this you shall pray to me, you and all the people."

Thus the people got the first medicine pipe. It was long ago.

BROTHER BIRCH

OLD MAN, powerful magic-maker of the Blackfoot, did not always play mean tricks on the wild things and trees of the forest. Like most people, he could be kind and cruel, sensible and unwise, grateful and ungrateful, petty and noble. He knew that one did not need to be a magician to possess all of these mixed qualities.

Once Old Man pretended to play with a band of trusting little prairie dogs. It was good fun for the prairie dogs while the game lasted, but they all ended up under the hot ashes of the fire to become a tasty meal. It is too bad that the trustful little creatures did not know that the magician was hungry!

As Old Man wished to sleep while the dogs were baking, he ordered his nose to act as sentry and wake him up should any forest prowlers come close to his campfire. His nose was alert and snored loudly each time an animal came near the fire. Old Man then awoke and chased the intruder away. It was a different story when the silent lynx slunk up to the fire. He was attracted by the savory smell of the cooking prairie dogs. He raked them from the fire with his long, sharp claws and had eaten the last one before the magician woke up and caught him. Old Man punished the lynx terribly for having robbed him of his supper, and the lynx carry the marks to this day.

Old Man then decided to punish his nose also. This was not one of his wise moments. He took a blazing branch from the fire and held it to his nose. He burned it very thoroughly, but he felt the pain as much as his nose did, which he had not stopped to think about when he made up his mind to punish it. Old Man snatched the burning branch away quickly but a hot cinder still clung to his nose. He jumped up and down in pain. He burned his fingers when he tried to remove the smoldering spark. Even when the cinder ceased to glow, the magician's nose seemed to burn more and more. He hastily climbed a little hill in search of a cooling breeze.

"Help me, O Spirit of the Wind," he wailed. "Blow on my nose that it may be cool again."

The Wind Spirit was angry because Old Man had betrayed the little prairie dogs and been cruel to the lynx. At first it blew gently on the burned and burning nose.

"Harder, harder," begged the magician.

At these words the wind blew stronger and stronger. At last it blew so hard that it picked Old Man up and carried him along with it. The magician was bumped and bruised by the trees and bushes when the wind threw him against them. He grabbed at branches, bushes, and grass as he was blown swiftly along. None of them could stop him. The grass pulled out by the roots and the branches broke as soon as he laid hands on them. He became so tired and helpless that he feared he would be drowned in a great river which flowed a short distance in front of him.

"Stop me, stop me," he begged the bushes and grass as he seized them in passing. None of them would help to stop his rapid flight. Just as he neared the river, he managed to grasp an oak sapling.

337

"Now I am safe," thought the battered magician when the little tree arrested his wind-blown body.

He was not safe for long. Under the force of great wind puffs and the weight of the magician the strong sapling broke. Once more Old Man was being carried fast toward the river.

Only a bow length in front of the raging water, he was able to grasp the gleaming trunk of a canoe birch. The graceful tree bent and twisted under the forceful gusts of the angry wind. While the magician hung onto the slim trunk with all his might, he pleaded with the Wind Spirit.

"O Powerful One," he gasped, "I have been beaten, battered, bruised, bumped, and buffeted! Please blow me no more like a withered leaf. My heart is on the ground. Spare me. For the next moon I will do only good to the wild things. I promise."

The wind believed Old Man. Suddenly it ceased to blow. The tired magician lay on the ground for a long time. It was his turn to do the puffing and blowing. He still grasped the slender white trunk of the birch which had saved him.

When Old Man was able to speak he said, "Brother birch, kind and wonderful tree, you have saved my life. You are beautiful, but I will make you even more so, that all may know that I owe my life to you. I now give you fine markings such as no other tree has." Then he gently and lightly marked the bark of the birch all over with the dull side of his stone knife.

And that, O you who sit by the glowing council fire, is how the Blackfoot say the canoe birch got its lovely markings.

THE HUNTER AND SELU

A HUNTER had been tramping over the mountains all day long without finding any game, and when the sun went down, he built a fire in a hollow stump, swallowed a few mouthfuls of corn gruel and lay down to sleep, tired out and completely discouraged. About the middle of the night he dreamed, and seemed to hear the sound of beautiful singing, which con-

tinued until near daybreak, and then appeared to die away into the upper air.

All next day he hunted with the same poor success, and at night made his lonely camp again in the woods. He slept and the strange dream came to him again, but so vividly that it seemed to him like an actual happening. Rousing himself before daylight, he still heard the song, and feeling sure now that it was real, he went in the direction of the sound, and found that it came from a single green stalk of corn—*selu*.

The plant spoke to him, and told him to cut off some of its roots and take them to his home in the settlement, and the next morning to chew them and "go to water" (urinate) before anyone else was awake. Then he was to go out again into the woods, and he would kill many deer, and from that time on would always be successful in the hunt. The corn plant continued to talk, teaching him hunting secrets and telling him always to be generous with the game he took, until it was noon and the sun was high, when it suddenly took the form of a woman and rose gracefully into the air and was gone from sight, leaving the hunter alone in the woods.

He returned home and told his story, and all the people knew that he had seen Selu, the wife of Kanati. He did as the spirit had directed, and from that time was noted as the most successful of all the hunters in the settlement.

MON-DAW-MIN,
OR THE ORIGIN OF INDIAN CORN

IN TIMES PAST, a poor Indian was living with his wife and children in a beautiful part of the country. He was not only poor, but was not expert in procuring food for his family, and his children were all too young to give him assistance. Although poor, he was a man of a kind and contented disposition. He was always thankful to the Great Spirit for everything he received.

The same disposition was inherited by his eldest son, who had now arrived at the proper age to undertake the ceremony of the *Ke-ig-uish-im-o-win*, a fast to see what kind of spirit would be his guide and guardian through life. Wunzh, for this was his name, had been an obedient boy from his infancy, and was of a pensive, thoughtful, and mild disposition, so that he was beloved by the whole family. As soon as the first indications of spring appeared, they built him the customary little lodge at a retired spot, some distance from their own, where he would not be disturbed during this solemn rite. In the meantime he prepared himself, and immediately went into it, and commenced his fast.

The first few days, he amused himself in the mornings by walking in the woods and over the mountains, examining the early plants and flowers, and in this way prepared himself to enjoy his sleep, and at the same time stored his mind with pleasant ideas for his dreams. While he rambled through the woods, he felt a strong desire to know how the plants, herbs, and berries grew without any aid from man, and why it was that some species were good to eat and others possessed medicinal or poisonous juices. He recalled these thoughts to mind after he became too languid to walk about, and had confined himself strictly to the lodge. He wished he could dream of something that would prove a benefit to his father and family, and to all others.

"True!" he thought, "the Great Spirit made all things, and it is to him that we owe our lives. But could he not make it easier for us to get our food, than by hunting animals and taking fish? I must try to find out this in my visions."

On the third day he became weak and faint, and kept his bed. He fancied, while thus lying, that he saw a handsome young man coming down from the sky and advancing toward him. He was richly and gaily dressed, having on a great many garments of green and yellow colors, but differing in their deeper or lighter shades. He had a plume of waving feathers on his head, and all his motions were graceful.

"I am sent to you, my friend," said the celestial visitor, "by that Great Spirit who made all things in the sky and on the earth. He has seen and knows your motives in fasting. He sees that it is from a kind and benevolent wish to do good to your people, and to procure a benefit for them, and that you do not seek for strength in war or the praise of warriors. I am sent to instruct you, and show you how you can do your kindred good." He then told the young man to arise, and prepare to wrestle with him, as it was only by this means that he could hope to succeed in his wishes.

Wunzh knew he was weak from fasting, but he felt his courage rising in his heart, and immediately got up, determined to die rather than fail. He commenced the trial, and after a protracted effort, was almost exhausted, when the beautiful stranger said, "My friend, it is enough for once; I will come again to try you"; and smiling on him, he ascended in the air in the same direction from which he came.

The next day the celestial visitor reappeared at the same hour and renewed the trial. Wunzh felt that his strength was even less than the day before, but the courage of his mind seemed to increase in proportion as his body became weaker. Seeing this, the stranger again spoke to him in the same words he used before, adding, "Tomorrow will be your last trial. Be strong, my friend, for this is the only way you can overcome me, and obtain the boon you seek."

On the third day he again appeared at the same time and renewed the struggle. The poor youth was very faint in body, but grew stronger in mind at every contest, and was determined to prevail or perish in the attempt. He exerted his utmost powers, and after the contest had been continued the usual time, the stranger ceased his efforts and declared himself conquered. For the first time he entered the lodge, and sitting down beside the youth, he began to deliver his instructions to him, telling him in what manner he should proceed to take advantage of his victory.

"You have won your desires of the Great Spirit," said the stranger. "You have wrestled manfully. Tomorrow will be the seventh day of your fasting. Your father will give you food to strengthen you, and as it is the last day of trial, you will prevail. I know this, and now tell you what you must do to benefit your family and your tribe. Tomorrow," he repeated, "I shall meet you and wrestle with you for the last time; and as soon as you have prevailed against me, you will strip off my garments and throw me down, clean the earth of roots and weeds, make it soft, and bury me in the spot. When you have done this, leave my body in the earth, and do not disturb it, but come occasionally to visit the place to see whether I have come to life, and be careful never to let the grass or weeds grow on my grave. Once a month cover me with fresh earth. If you follow my instructions, you will accomplish your object of doing good to your fellow creatures by teaching them the knowledge I now teach you." He then shook him by the hand and disappeared.

In the morning the youth's father came with some light refreshments, saying, "My son, you have fasted long enough. If the Great Spirit will favor you, he will do it now. It is seven days since you have tasted food, and you must not sacrifice your life. The Master of Life does not require that."

"My father," replied the youth, "wait till the sun goes down. I have a particular reason for extending my fast to that hour."

"Very well," said the old man, "I shall wait till the hour arrives, and you feel inclined to eat."

At the usual hour of the day, the sky visitor returned, and the trial of strength was renewed. Although the youth had not availed himself of his father's offer of food, he felt that new strength had been given to him, and that exertion had renewed his strength and fortified his courage. He grasped his angelic antagonist with supernatural strength, threw him down, took from him his beautiful garments and plume, and finding him dead, immediately buried him on the spot, taking all the precautions he had been told of, and being very confident, at the same time, that his friend would again come to life.

He then returned to his father's lodge, and partook sparingly of the meal that had been prepared for him. But he never for a moment forgot the grave of his friend. He carefully visited it throughout the spring, and weeded out the grass, and kept the ground in a soft and pliant state. Very soon he saw the tops of the green plumes coming through the ground; and the more careful he was to obey his instructions in keeping the ground in order, the faster they grew. He was, however, careful to conceal the exploit from his father. Days and weeks had passed in this way.

The summer was now drawing toward a close, when one day, after a long absence in hunting, Wunzh invited his father to follow him to the quiet and lonesome spot of his former fast. The lodge had been removed, and the weeds kept from growing on the circle where it stood, but in its place stood a tall and graceful plant, with bright-colored silken hair, sur-

343

mounted with nodding plumes and stately leaves, and golden clusters on each side.

"It is my friend," shouted the lad; "it is the friend of all mankind. It is *Mon-daw-min*. We need no longer rely on hunting alone; for as long as this gift of corn is cherished and taken care of, the ground itself will give us a living." He then pulled an ear. "See, my father," said he, "this is what I fasted for. The Great Spirit has listened to my voice, and sent us something new, and henceforth our people will not alone depend upon the chase or upon the waters."

He then told his father the instructions given him by the stranger. He told him that the broad husks must be torn away, as he had pulled off the garments in his wrestling. And having done this, directed him how the ear must be held before the fire till the outer skin became brown, while all the milk was retained in the grain. The whole family then united in a feast on the newly grown ears, expressing gratitude to the Merciful Spirit who gave it. So corn came into the world.

THE HERMIT THRUSH

LONG AGO the birds had no songs. Only man could sing, and every morning man would greet the rising sun with a song. The birds, as they were flying by, would often stop and listen to the beautiful songs of man. In their hearts they wished that they too could sing. One day the Good Spirit visited the earth, inspecting the various things that he had created. As he walked through the forest, he noticed that there was a strange silence. Something seemed to be missing.

As the Good Spirit pondered, the sun sank behind the western hills. From the direction of the river, where was an Indian village, there sounded the deep, rich tones of an Indian drum followed by the sacred chanting of the sunset song. The Good Spirit listened. The song was pleasing to the ears of the Good Spirit. As he looked around, he noticed that the birds were also listening to the singing. "That is what is missing," said the Good Spirit. "Birds should also have songs."

The next day the Good Spirit called all the birds to a great council. From near and far they came. The sky was filled with flying birds. The trees and bushes bent to the earth under the weight of so many.

On the great Council Rock sat the Good Spirit. He waited until all of the birds had perched and had become quiet. The Good Spirit spoke. He asked the birds if they would like to have songs, songs such as the Indian people sang. With one accord the birds all chirped, "Yes, yes!"

"Very well," said the Good Spirit. "Tomorrow when the sun rises in the east, you are all to fly up in the sky. You are to fly as high as you can. When you can fly no higher you will find your song. That bird who flys the highest will have the most beautiful song of all of the birds." Saying these words the Good Spirit vanished.

Next morning, long before sunrise, the birds were ready. There were birds everywhere. The earth was covered with them. There was great excitement. However, one little bird was very unhappy. He was the little brown thrush. Perched beside him was the great eagle. As the little bird gazed at the eagle he thought, "What chance have I to compete with this great bird? I am so little and eagle is so large. I will never be able to fly as high as he."

As he was thus thinking, an idea entered his mind, "Eagle is so excited that he will not notice me." With this thought in mind, the little brown bird flew like a flash to the eagle's head and quickly hid under his feathers. The great eagle was so excited that he did not notice the little thrush. "With my great wings, I will surely win," thought he.

The sun finally looked over the eastern hill. With a great roar of wings the many birds took off. The air was so full of flying birds that for a time the sky was dark. Their bodies covered the face of the sun.

For a long time the birds flew upward. Finally the smaller, weaker, birds began to tire. The little hummingbird was the first to give up. His little wings beat the air so hard that to this day one can, if one listens, hear his humming wings. His little squeaking calls say, "Wait, wait for me," a very plain song.

The fat cowbird was the next to give up. As he floated down, he listened

345

and heard his song, a very common song. Other birds weakened and while flying earthward, listened and learned their songs.

At last the sun was at the end of the earth. The night sky began to darken the earth. By this time there were only a few birds left. They were the larger, strong-winged birds, the eagle, hawk, owl, buzzard, and loon. All night the birds flew up, ever up. When the sun rose next morning only the eagle, chief of all birds, was left. He was still going strong.

When the sun was halfway in the sky, he began to tire. Finally, with a look of triumph, for there were no other birds in sight, the tired eagle began to soar earthward. The little thrush, riding under the feathers of the great eagle, had been asleep all of this time. When the eagle started back to earth the little thrush awoke. He hopped off the eagle's head and began to fly upward. Eagle saw him go and glared with anger at him, but was powerless to stop him as he was completely exhausted.

The little thrush flew up and up. He soon came to a hole in the sky. He found himself in a beautiful country, the Happy Hunting Grounds. As he entered the Spirit World he heard a beautiful song. He stayed in heaven for a while learning this song. When he had learned it completely, he left the Land of Happy Spirits and flew back toward earth. He could hardly wait to reach the earth. He was anxious to show off his beautiful song.

As thrush neared the earth he glanced down at the Council Rock. There sat all of the birds, and on the Council Rock, glaring up at him was Akweks, the eagle. All the birds were very silent as they waited for thrush to light on the council ground. Suddenly the feeling of glory left the little thrush and he felt ashamed. He knew that he had cheated to get his beautiful song. He also feared Akweks, who might get even with him for stealing a free ride. He flew in silence to the deep woods, and in shame, with dragging heart, hid under the branches of the largest tree. He was so ashamed that he wanted no one to see him.

There you will find him today. Never does the hermit thrush come out into the open. He is still ashamed because he cheated. Sometimes, however, he cannot restrain himself, and he must sing his beautiful song. When he does this the other birds cease their singing. Well they know that the song of the hermit thrush, the song from heaven, will make their songs sound very weak.

That is why the hermit thrush is so shy. That is why his song is the most beautiful song of all of the birds. That is why this spirit song causes the sun to shine in the hearts of the Indian people who hear it as they go into the dark forest.

The old Six Nation People told this story to their children to teach them to be honest, that it does not pay to cheat.

THE ORIGIN OF STRAWBERRIES

WHEN the first man was created and a mate was given to him, they lived together very happily for a time, but then began to quarrel, until at last the woman left her husband and started off toward Nundagunyi, the Sun land, in the east. The man followed alone and grieving, but the woman kept on steadily ahead and never looked behind, until Unelanunhi, the great Apportioner, the Sun, took pity on him and asked him if he was still angry with his wife. He said he was not, and Unelanunhi then asked him if he would like to have her back again, to which he eagerly answered, "Yes."

So Unelanunhi caused a patch of the finest ripe huckleberries to spring up along the path in front of the woman, but she passed by without paying any attention to them. Farther on he put a clump of blackberries, but these also she refused to notice.

Other fruits, one, two, and three, and then some trees covered with beautiful red service berries, were placed beside the path to tempt her, but she still went on, until suddenly she saw in front a patch of large ripe strawberries, the first ever known.

She stooped to gather a few to eat, and as she picked them she chanced to turn her face to the west, and at once the memory of her husband came back to her, and she found herself unable to go on. She sat down, but the longer she waited, the stronger became her desire for her husband, and at last she gathered a bunch of the finest berries and started back along the path to give them to him. He met her kindly and they went home together.

347

OOT-KWA-TAH, THE PLEIADES

A LONG TIME AGO a party of Indians went through the woods toward a good hunting ground, which they had long known. They traveled several days through a very wild country, going on leisurely and camping by the way. At last they reached Kan-ya-ti-yo, "the beautiful lake," where the gray rocks were crowned with great forest trees. Fish swarmed in the waters, and at every jutting point the deer came down to bathe or drink of the lake. On the hills and in the valleys were huge beech and chestnut trees, where squirrels chattered, and bears came to take their morning and evening meals.

The chief of the band was Hah-yah-no, "Tracks in the water," and he halted his party on the lake shore that he might return thanks to Hawen-neyu, the Great Spirit, for their safe arrival at this good hunting ground. "Here will we build our lodges for the winter, and may the Great Spirit, who has prospered us on our way, send us plenty of game, and health and peace." The Indian is always thankful.

The pleasant autumn days passed on. The lodges had been built, and hunting had prospered, when the children took a fancy to dance for their own amusement. They were getting lonesome, having little to do while the others were busy, so they met daily in a quiet spot by the lake to have what they called their jolly dance, and very jolly they made it.

They had done this for some time, when one day a very old man came to them. They had seen no one like him before. He was dressed in white feathers, and his white hair shone like silver. If his appearance was strange, his words were unpleasant as well. He told them they must stop their dancing, or evil would come to them. Little did the children heed, and nothing did they say. They were intent on their sports. Again and again did the old man appear and repeat his warning. They danced on.

The mere dances did not afford all the enjoyment the children wished, and a little boy, who liked a good dinner, suggested a feast the next time they met. The food must come from their parents, of course, and they were asked for this food when the children returned home.

"You will waste and spoil good food," said one parent. "You can eat at home as you should," said another. "I have no time for such nonsense," said a third, and so they got nothing at all. Sorry as they were for this, they met and danced as before. A little to eat after each dance would have made them happy indeed. Empty stomachs bring no joy.

One day, as they danced, they found themselves rising little by little into the air, their heads being light through hunger. How this came about they did not know, but one said, "Do not look back, for something strange is taking place." A woman, too, saw them rise, and called them back, but with no effect. They still rose slowly from the earth. She ran to the camp, and all rushed out with food of every kind, calling piteously after them. The children would not and indeed could not return.

One did merely look back, and he became a falling star. The others reached the sky, and are now what we call the Pleiades, and the Onondagas, Oot-kwa-tah. Every falling or shooting star recalls the story to them, but the seven stars shine on continuously, a merry band of dancing children.

HOW TURQUOISES WERE OBTAINED

ONE DAY, long ago, the women and girls of Casa Grande were playing an ancient game called *toka*, formerly much in vogue at Casa Grande, but now no longer played by Pima. During the progress of the game, a blue-tailed lizard was noticed descending into the earth at a spot where the stones were green. The fact was so strange that it was reported to Morning Green, who immediately ordered excavation to be made.

Here they eventually discovered many turquoises, with which they made, among other things, a mosaic covering for a chair that used to stand in one of the rooms of Casa Grande. This chair was carried away many years ago and buried, no one knows where.

Morning Green also distributed so many turquoises among his people that the fame of these precious stones reached the ears of the Sun, in the east, who sent the bird with bright plumage to obtain them. When Parrot approached within a short distance of Casa Grande, he was met by one of the daughters of the chief, who returned to the town and announced to her father the arrival of a visitor from the Sun.

349

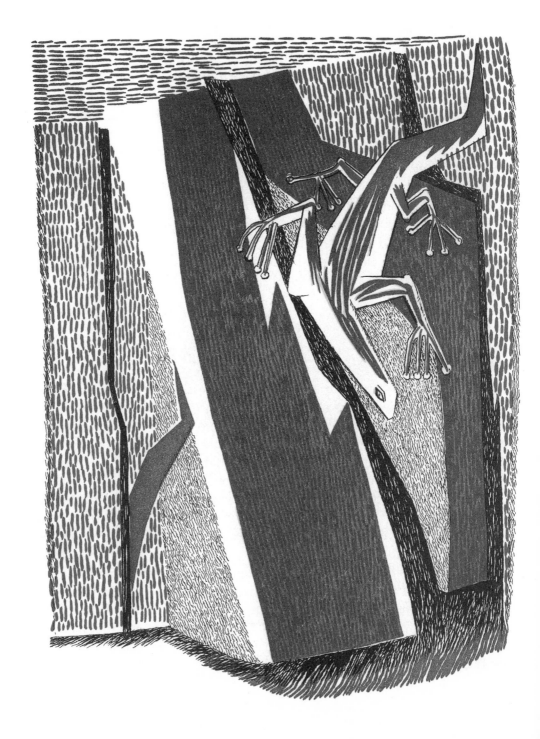

The father said, "Take this small stick, which is charmed, and when Parrot puts the stick into his mouth, you lead him to me." But Parrot was not charmed by the stick and refused to take it into his mouth, and the girl reported her failure.

The chief answered, "Perhaps the strange bird would eat pumpkin seeds," and told his daughter to offer these to him. She made the attempt without result and, returning, reported that the bird refused pumpkin seeds. The father then said, "Put the seed into a blanket and spread it before the bird; then perhaps you may capture him." Still Parrot would not eat, and the father thereupon suggested watermelon seeds. But Parrot was not tempted by these nor by seeds of cat's-claw, nor was he charmed by charcoal.

The chief of Casa Grande then told his daughter to tempt Parrot with corn, well cooked and soaked in water in a new food bowl. Parrot was obdurate and would not taste it, but noticing a turquoise bead of blue-green color, he swallowed it. When the two daughters of the chief saw this they brought him a number of blue stones, which the bird greedily devoured. Then the girls brought valuable turquoise beads, which Parrot ate; then he flew away. The girls tried to capture him, but without success. He made his way through the air to the home of the Sun in the east, where he drank an emetic and vomited the turquoises, which the Sun-god distributed among that people which reside near his house of rising, beyond the eastern mountains. This is the reason, it is said, why these people have many stone ornaments made of this material.

But when the chief of Casa Grande heard that Parrot had been sent to steal his turquoises, he was greatly vexed and caused a violent rain to fall that extinguished all fires in the east. His magic power over the Rain-god was so great that he was able even to extinguish the light of the Sun, making it very cold. Then the old priests gathered in council and debated what they should do. Man Fox was first sent by them into the east to get fire, but he failed to obtain it, and then Road Runner was commissioned to visit Thunder, the only one that possessed fire, and steal his lighted torch. But when Thunder saw him running off with the torch, he shot an arrow at the thief and sparks of fire were scattered around, setting afire every tree, bush, and other inflammable object, from which it happens that there is fire in everything.

THE ORIGIN OF THE BUFFALO AND OF CORN

WHEN the Cheyenne were still in the north, they camped in a large circle. At the entrance of the camp circle, there was a deep spring of water rapidly flowing from out the hillside. They camped near this spring so that they might get their water easily.

One bright day they were playing the game of ring and javelin in the center of the circle. The game consisted of a hoop painted red and black all over, and four throwing sticks which were to be thrown at the hoop when it was rolled. Two of the sticks were painted red, and two were painted black. The sticks were three or four feet long, and were tied together in pairs. The hoop was rolled along the ground, and as it rolled, the red or the black sticks were thrown at it, and the contestants won accordingly as the black or red portion of the ring fell upon the black or red sticks as it stopped. The owner of the stick which matched the color of that portion of the ring that fell on it won.

There was a large crowd of Cheyenne gathered in the middle of the camp, watching the game. As the players contested there came from the south side of the camp circle a certain young man to witness the game. He stood outside of the crowd to look on. He wore a buffalo robe with the hair side turned out, his body was painted yellow, and a yellow-painted eagle breath-feather stuck up on top of his head.

Soon there came from the north side of the camp circle another young man to see the game, and he was dressed exactly like the man who came from the south side. He also stood outside of the crowd, and opposite the first man, to view the game. When they saw each other they went inside the crowd and met face to face and asked each other questions. They were unacquainted with each other, and were surprised when they saw that they were dressed alike.

The crowd stopped playing the game, and stood around to hear what the two young men said. The man from the south said to the man from the north, "My friend, you are imitating my manner of dress. Why do you do it?" Then the man from the north said, "Why do you imitate my manner of dress?" At last each told the other the reason for his manner of dress on that day. Each claimed to have entered the spring that flowed out from the hillside at the entrance to the camp circle, where he had been instructed to dress after this fashion.

They then told the great crowd that they were going to enter the spring again, and that they would soon come out. The crowd watched them as they approached the spring. The man from the south side reached the spring, covered his head with his buffalo robe, and entered. The other young man did the same thing. They splashed the water as they went, and soon found themselves in a large cave.

Near the entrance sat an old woman cooking some buffalo meat and corn in two separate earthen pots. The woman welcomed them thus, "Grandchildren, you have come. I have been expecting you, and am cooking for you. Come and sit down beside me." They sat down, one on each side of her, and told her that their people were hungry, and that they had come to her for their relief. The woman gave them corn from one pot and meat from the other. They ate, and were filled, and when they were through the pots were as full as when they began.

Then the old woman told the young men to look toward the south. They looked, and they saw the land to the south covered with buffalo. She then told them to look to the west. They looked, and saw all manner of animals, large and small, and there were ponies; but they knew nothing of ponies in those days, for they never had seen any. She then told them to look to the north. They looked to the north, and saw everywhere growing corn.

Then said the old woman to them, "All this that you have seen shall in the future be yours for food. This night I cause the buffalo to be restored to you. When you leave this place, the buffalo shall follow you, and you and your people shall see them coming from this place before sunset. Take in your robes this uncooked corn. Every springtime plant it in low, moist ground, where it will grow. After it matures you will feed upon it. Take also this meat and corn which I have cooked, and when you have returned to your people, ask them all to sit down in the following order, to eat out of these two pots: first, all males, from the youngest to the oldest, with the exception of one orphan boy; second, all females, from the oldest to the youngest, with the exception of one orphan girl. When all are through eating, the contents of the pots are to be eaten by the orphan boy and the orphan girl."

The two young men went out and obeyed the old woman. When they passed out of the spring, they saw that their entire bodies were painted red, and the breath-feathers of their heads were painted red instead of yellow. They went to their people, and they ate as directed of the corn and the meat, and there was enough for all; and the contents of the pots was not diminished until it came time for the two orphan children, who ate all the food.

Toward sunset the people went to their lodges and began watching the spring closely, and in a short time they saw a buffalo jump from the spring. It jumped and played and rolled, and then returned to the spring. In a little while another buffalo jumped out, then another, and another, and finally they came out so fast that the Cheyenne were no longer able to count them. The buffalo continued to come out until dark, and all night and the following day the whole country out in the distance was covered with buffalo. The buffalo scented the great camp, for they left a long, narrow space where the wind went from the camp.

The next day the Cheyenne surrounded the buffalo. Though they were on foot they ran very fast. For a time they had an abundance of buffalo meat. In the springtime they moved their camp to low, swampy land, where they planted the corn they had received from the medicine spring. It grew rapidly, and every grain they planted brought forth strong stalks, and on each stalk grew from two to four ears of corn. The Cheyenne planted corn every year after this.

One spring, after the planting of their corn, the Cheyenne went on a buffalo hunt. When they had enough meat to dry to last them for a considerable time, they returned to their cornfields. To their surprise they found that their corn had been stolen by a neighboring tribe. Nothing but the stalks remained, not even a kernel for seed; so it was a long time before the Cheyenne planted any more corn. They trailed the footprints of the enemy for several days from their fields, though the thieves had visited them about one moon before. They fought with two or three tribes of Indians, but could not trace the thieves, nor could they learn anything regarding the stolen corn.

THE ORIGIN OF THE MEDICINE ARROWS

AFTER THE CHEYENNE had received their corn, and while they were still in the north, a young man and young woman of the tribe were married. The young woman became pregnant, and carried her child four years in her womb. The people observed the woman with great interest to see what would happen to her. During the fourth year she brought forth a beautiful boy. The child's father and mother died before he was able to take care of himself, and so his grandmother, who lived alone, took care of him. The Cheyenne regarded the birth of the child as extraordinary, and they looked upon him as supernatural.

Soon the boy walked and talked. As soon as the boy could walk, he was given a buffalo-calf robe to wear, and was shown how to wear it. He at once turned the hair side of the robe out. At that time the medicine men were the only ones who wore their robes in that way.

There were among the Cheyenne certain men of extraordinary intelligence and superhuman powers. At certain times these great medicine men would come together and put up a lodge, where they would sit in a large circle. They would chant and go through curious rituals. Each man would rise and by incantation perform before the crowd as no other man could perform.

When the boy was about ten years old he desired to go and take part in one of the magic dances given by the great medicine men. He insisted that his grandmother go to the chief of the medicine men and gain for him admission to the dance. His grandmother told one of the medicine men of the boy's desire, and so they let him enter the lodge. When the boy went into the lodge the chief said to him, "Where do you want to live?" (Where do you want to sit?) Without ceremony the boy took his seat beside the chief. He wore his robe, and had the man who brought him in paint his body red, with black rings around his face, and around each wrist and ankle. The performance began at one end of the circle.

When the boy's turn to perform came, he told the people what he was going to do. With sweet grass he burned incense. Through the incense he passed his buffalo-sinew bowstring east, south, west, and north. Then he asked two men to assist him while he performed. First he had them tie his bowstring around his neck, then cover his body with his robe, then pull at the ends of the string. They pulled with all their might, but they could not move him.

He told them to pull harder, and as they pulled at the string again, his head was cut off and rolled from under his robe, and his body was left under the robe. They took his head and placed it under the robe with his body. Next they removed the robe, and there sat a very old man in place of the boy. They covered the old man with the robe, and when they removed the robe again, there was a pile of human bones with a skull. They spread the robe over the bones, and when it was removed there was nothing there. Again they spread the robe, and when they removed it, there was the boy again.

After the magic dance, the Cheyenne moved their camp and hunted buffalo. The wonderful boy and a crowd of other boys went out by themselves to hunt buffalo calves that might be returning to the place where they last saw their mothers. They saw five or six calves, one of which was a two-year-old. The wonderful boy asked the other boys to surround the calves so that he might kill the two-year-old. They chased the calves and killed the two-year-old with their bows and arrows. The boys began to skin the buffalo calf with their bone knives. The wonderful boy told the other boys to skin it very carefully, for he wanted the skin for his robe. He told them to skin the whole head, and leave the hoofs on.

While they were skinning the calf, they saw a man coming toward them, driving a dog team. The man had come to the killing ground to gather what bones had been left. When the man saw the boys he went to them.

This man was Young Wolf, the head chief of the tribe. He said to the boys, "My children have favored me at last. I shall take charge of this whole buffalo. You boys can go off, for I have come. You cannot take this buffalo."

All the boys stopped skinning except the wonderful boy, who told the chief that he wanted only the hide for his robe, and that the boys were dressing it under his directions. The chief pushed the wonderful boy aside, but the boy returned and began skinning again. The chief jerked the boy away, and threw him down. The boy returned and began skinning again, and pretended that he was going to skin one of the hind legs, but he cut the leg off at the knee instead, and left the hoof on.

356

While the chief was skinning the calf, the boy struck him on the back of the head with the buffalo leg, and instantly killed him. The chief fell to the ground dead. The boys ran to their camp and told the people what the wonderful boy had done, and it caused great excitement. All the warriors assembled and resolved to kill the wonderful boy. They went out and found the body of their chief, but the wonderful boy had already returned to the camp with the other boys, and he was in his grandmother's lodge.

The old woman was cooking food for him in an earthen pot. Suddenly the old woman's tepee was raised completely by the warriors, who had returned from their hunt. The wonderful boy kicked over the cooking pot, and its contents went into the fire; and as the smoke rose, the boy, by mysterious means, went up with it, and the warriors saw the old woman sitting there alone. As they looked around, they saw the boy walking off toward the east at a distance of about a quarter of a mile from them. The warriors pursued him, but could not approach nearer to him, so they gave up the chase. Four times they chased him without avail.

Early one morning, while one of the young men was out hunting near their camp, he saw the wonderful boy down in a ravine, warming himself by a fire he had built. The young man returned to the camp at once, and notified the warriors, who immediately went out and surrounded the ravine. They saw the fire, but the boy had turned into a wolf, and jumped over a high bluff and ran away, howling at the crowd. They began to be afraid of him, for they could do nothing with him, but they still watched for him every day.

One day they saw him appear on the top of a near-by hill. Everyone's attention was attracted, and they went out to see him. He came to the top of the hill five times, and each time he was in a different dress. First he appeared in the Red Shield warrior's dress. He had a headdress made of buffalo skin; he had horns, a spear, a red shield, and two buffalo tails tied on each arm.

The second time he appeared in the Coyote warrior's dress. His body was painted black and yellow, with two eagle feathers sticking up on his head.

The third time he appeared in the dress of the Dog Men warriors. He had on a feathered headdress, an eagle-bone whistle, a rattle of buffalo hoof, and a bow and arrows.

The fourth time he appeared in the dress of the Hoof Rattle warriors. His body was painted, and he carried a rattle to sing by, also a spear about eight feet long, with a crook at one end, the end of the shaft being bent in semicircular form.

The fifth time he appeared with his body painted white, and on his forehead he wore a white-owl skin.

After his fifth appearance, the wonderful boy disappeared entirely. No one knew where he went, and he was soon forgotten, and people thought him dead. He was gone four years. He traveled alone into the highest peaks of the mountains. As he drew near to a certain peak, a door opened for him to enter. He passed through the door into the earth, and the opening closed after him. There he found men of all tribes, sitting around in a large circle.

Each man represented a tribe, and had a bundle. There was one bundle present that was unaccompanied, and as the Cheyenne boy entered, all welcomed him and pointed him to the unoccupied seat under the bundle that was wrapped in fox skin. Before taking this seat, the head man explained to him what he would expect of his people if he took the seat under the bundle, which was going to be his to take back to his people. The head man told him that he would have to stay here under the earth with them for four years, receiving instructions; that he was to become the prophet and counselor of the Cheyenne.

As the Cheyenne boy followed his instructions and accepted the bundle, all the men gave thanks to him. He sat down, and when his turn came to perform his bundle ceremony, they took down his bundle and went through the sacred ceremonies and sacred songs of his bundle, all in order. When they opened his bundle for him, there were four medicine arrows, each arrow representing something. They gave the young man instructions concerning the order of the bundle ceremony, and sacred songs in order, prophecies, magic, and material for warfare and hunting, to take back to his people at the end of his four years' stay.

After the Cheyenne had driven the wonderful boy from their camp, the whole country was visited by a four years' famine. The people became weak, and were threatened with starvation. All animals died of starvation. The people ate herbs. One day, as they were traveling in search of food, five children lingered behind in search of herbs and mushrooms. While they were eating them, there appeared the wonderful young man who had been driven from the camp.

The young man said, "My poor children, throw away those mushrooms. It is I who brought famine among you, for I was angry at your people, who drove me from their camp. I have returned to provide for you, so that you shall not hunger in the future. Go and gather me some dried buffalo bones and I will feed you." The boys ran and gathered buffalo bones and brought them to him. The wonderful boy made a few passes over them, and they were turned into fresh meat, and he fed the children with fat, marrow, liver, and other parts of the buffalo.

When they had eaten all they wanted, he gave them fat and meat and told them to take it to their people and tell them that he, Motzeyouf, had returned, and that they should no longer hunger. The boys all ran to the camp that their parents had made in the meantime. By magic, however, Motzeyouf reached the camp first. He entered the lodge of his uncle and lay down to rest, for he was tired. His uncle was sitting outside his lodge with his wife, and they did not see Motzeyouf enter.

When the Cheyenne heard from the boys what had happened, they became excited. All went to the lodge where Motzeyouf was. They came to Motzeyouf's uncle and began to question him, but his uncle knew nothing of what they said. His uncle's wife went into the lodge to get a pipe, and she saw Motzeyouf lying there, covered with a buffalo robe. She saw that his robe, shirt, leggings, and moccasins were painted red. She ran out of the lodge and told the men that someone was in there.

The men guessed that it was Motzeyouf, and they went inside. The uncle asked the strange man to sit up, and then all cried over him. The men observed that Motzeyouf had a bundle with him, and knowing that he had power, they asked him what they should do. He told them to camp in a circle, and have a large tepee put up in the center of the cirle. He called all the medicine men to bring their rattles and pipes to him. He went to the tepee and performed the ceremony and sang the sacred songs, as he had been instructed.

When he came to the part relating to the fourth arrow, and its song, it was night, and the buffalo had returned. The buffalo came like the roar of thunder, and it frightened the Cheyenne. They went to Motzeyouf and asked him what to do. He said, "Go and sleep, for the buffalo, your food, has returned to you." The buffalo continued to roar like thunder as long as Motzeyouf sang. The next morning the land was covered with buffalo, and the people went out and killed all they wanted. From that time forth the Cheyenne had plenty to eat and great power, owing to the power of the medicine arrows.

According to the account of Wolf Chief and his ancestors, the medicine arrows are from eighteen to twenty generations old. Motzeyouf brought them from the earth.

THE DISCOVERY OF FIRE

IN OLDEN TIMES when a Mohawk boy had reached the age of fourteen winters, it was customary for him to make a journey, accompanied by his father, to some sacred place up in the mountains. There, after receiving instructions from his father, the youth would remain alone for at least four days. During these four or more days, the Mohawk boy would perform a ceremony known as the Dream Fast. This Dream Fast was very important to the Indian boy of long ago. To be successful in the Dream Fast meant that the Indian was no longer a youth but a man. During the fast, the clan spirit of the young Mohawk would appear to him in a dream and reveal to him the bird, animal, or plant that was to be his guardian throughout his life. After the fast, he must secure something from the creature of his dream and must wear it in his medicine bag as a charm.

The Mohawk Iroquois had three clans which were, the Bear clan, Turtle clan, and Wolf clan. Should the dreamer belong to the Turtle clan, the spirit of the turtle would appear to him in a dream and show him his future guardian. If the clan spirit did not appear to him during the fast, his father who visited him daily would release him, and he departed home, a failure. He could not have two chances. The dreamer could leave his fasting place after sunset for brief periods. He could drink water to quench his thirst. He was not allowed to eat any food.

Otjiera belonged to the Bear clan and was the son of a famous leader. He had many honors to his credit. No youth of the Mohawks was fleeter on foot than he. He led in the games and was one of the best lacrosse players of his nation. He could shoot his arrow farther and straighter than any of his friends. He knew the forests and streams and would always return from the hunt loaded down with deer meat, which he always divided with the needy of his people. He could imitate the calls of the birds. They would come when he called and would sit on his shoulders. He was the pride of his people.

The time for the Dream Fast of Otjiera had come. It was in the Moon of Strawberries. Otjiera was eager to try the test of strength and endurance. High upon the mountain, on a huge ledge of rock, he built his lodge of young saplings. He covered it with the branches of the balsam to shelter it from the rains. He removed all of his clothing save his breechclout and moccasins. Appealing to his clan spirit, he entered the crude shelter.

Four suns had passed and yet the young warrior had not been visited by the clan spirit. The fifth sun had dawned when his father appeared. He shook the lodge poles and called for Otjiera to come forth. Otjiera in a low and weak voice begged his father to give him one more day. His father left, telling Otjiera that on the morrow he must return to his village.

That night Otjiera looked down from his lodge on the mountains. In the distance he heard low rumblings of thunder. As he listened, the thunder became louder and louder. Bright flashes of lightning lit up the heavens.

"Great Thunder Man, Ra-ti-we-ras," prayed the youth, "send my clan spirit to help me." He had no sooner spoken than a blinding flash of lightning lit the sky and a rumble of thunder shook the mountaintop. Otjiera looked and beheld his clan spirit. A huge bear stood beside him in his lodge. Suddenly the bear spoke, "This night, Otjiera, you shall have a magic that will not only aid you, but will also aid all of the Ongwe-Oweh, the Real People."

There was a blinding flash of lightning, and Otjiera awoke from his vision. He rubbed his eyes and looked for the clan spirit. The bear was gone. The youth wondered what his guardian helper would be. He looked out from his lodge. The storm had not yet left the mountain. Suddenly he heard a strange sound outside near the lodge. It was a dreadful screeching sound such as he had never heard before. He wondered what kind of animal or bird made such a dreadful noise. The sound had ceased. Then, almost over his head, he saw the cause of the sound. The wind was causing two balsam trees to rub their branches against each other. As the wood rubbed, the friction caused the strange, screeching sound. As Otjiera watched he saw a strange thing happen. The strong wind, rushing up the mountain, caused the trees to bend and sway more rapidly. Where the two trees rubbed against each other, a thin string of smoke appeared. As the boy watched, the wood burst into flame.

Otjiera was, at first, frightened. He started to run. None of his people had even seen fire so near, and it was feared. The boy remembered his clan spirit. "This must be what the great bear meant," thought the boy.

That day Otjiera took two pieces of dry balsam wood. He rubbed the wood together as he had seen the storm do the night before. He soon tired and was about to throw the wood away when he noticed a thin thread of smoke coming from the wood. He rubbed harder, and soon a tiny spark appeared. By using some dry cedar bark and grass he soon had a fire.

When his father and two chiefs came that noon, they found a happy Otjiera. He had a very powerful helper, a strong medicine which afterward was to help all of his people. That was how fire came to the Indian people of long ago.

THE ORIGIN OF WAMPUM

A MAN walking in a forest saw an unusually large bird covered with a heavily clustered coating of wampum, *oh-ko-ah*. He immediately informed his people and chiefs, whereupon the head chief offered as a prize his beautiful daughter to one who would capture the bird, dead or alive, which apparently had come from another world. Whereupon the warriors, with bows and arrows, went to the "tree of promise," and as each lucky one barely hit the bird it would throw off a large quantity of the coveted coating, which multiplied by being cropped.

At last, when the warriors were despairing of success, a little boy from a neighboring tribe came to satisfy his curiosity by seeing the wonderful bird of which he had heard. But as his people were at war with this tribe he was not permitted by the warriors to try his skill at archery, and was even threatened with death. But the head chief said, "He is a mere boy; let him shoot on equal terms with you who are brave and fearless warriors." His decision being final, the boy, with unequaled skill, brought the coveted bird to the ground.

Having received the daughter of the head chief in marriage, he divided the *oh-ko-ah* between his own tribe and that into which he had married, and peace was declared between them. Then the boy husband decreed that wampum should be the price of peace and blood, which was adopted by all nations. Hence arose the custom of giving belts of wampum to satisfy violated honor, hospitality, or national privilege.

THE FOUR WINDS

THE MIGHTY Master of the Winds of the Earth was sad. His sorrow was not because he was too weak. No. His sadness was caused because he was too strong. His giant strength made him a prisoner of his own power in the Western Sky, though he wished to roam in all directions. When he opened the doors of his Great Blue Wigwam, terrible winds shook the earth far below. He must divide his power, he decided, so that from each door of his great lodge in the sky would blow a separate wind.

He filled his mighty lungs with the loud, biting wind from the North and leaning far out of the North Door of his lodge, blew a bellowing breath to call the creatures of the earth to his aid. When he threw the North Door open, the fierce, whistling winter wind and driving snow which filled the somber sky was too strong and savage for most of the animals that heard the call. They could not fight their way through the storm. The Wind Master only saw some huge, battling shapes moving slowly in the direction of his wigwam. At last, with a great rumbling growl, a mighty, snow-covered bear, which had mastered the biting blast, stood at the door of the lodge.

"You are mighty, O Bear, and your powerful paws can hold my strongest winds in check. You will be the North Wind."

The head of the great beast swayed from side to side as the Master of the Winds took a collar of elk hide and fastened it securely around the animal's neck. With a strong leash he secured the Bear to the North Door of the Great Blue Wigwam.

Opening the massive door on the West side of his lodge, the Wind Master once again drew a deep breath and sent his summoning cry far out over the earth. As the door opened, dark, cold clouds filled the sky. Shrill shrieks and screams rent the air. Fierce fights raged around the lodge. Then, with a screeching snarl, a great green-eyed panther sprang into the doorway. Its eyes blazed like green fire. Its strong, lithe, tawny body quivered, and its long, heavy tail lashed from side to side.

"You are fierce, strong and fearless," praised the Master of the Winds. "You will be the West Wind." With a collar and leash of buffalo hide he bound the Panther to the West Door.

Striding to the eastern side of his lodge, the Master of the Winds flung the East Door wide and sent a piercing call echoing through the sky. At once, icy rain sleeted into the wigwam, and the world was shrouded in a gray mist. A crashing, trampling sound filled the air. The lodge shook. Suddenly a giant moose filled the doorway.

"Welcome, Moose of the misty breath, mighty antlers, and slashing hoofs which cut like a biting wind. You, too, can uproot trees like a storm. I choose you as the East Wind." So saying, the Wind Master took strong, green sinews and tied the Moose to the East Door of the wigwam.

One door still remained—the one on the southern side. The Master of the Winds opened it gently and called softly to the creatures. As the door opened, butterflies fluttered in amidst a shower of multicolored wild flowers. The lodge was filled with their perfume and the soft singing of balmy breezes. Light steps sounded outside and a little, graceful, spotted fawn stood trembling on slender legs at the entrance of the lodge.

"Enter, Little One," invited the Master of the Winds kindly. "You are all softness, beauty, and tenderness. Your step is light as the falling feather from a bird, and your breath sweet as the scent of flowers in the Moon of Roses. You shall be the South Wind." The Master stroked the silky head of the lovely little creature as he lightly wove a colorful collar of fragrant flowers around its slender neck. With a garland of varicolored vines he tenderly attached the dappled Fawn to the South Door of the Great Blue Wigwam, which is the sky.

From that time, when the wind from the North shook the elm-bark covering of their lodges, the Iroquois said, "Ho! The Bear growls."

When the wind whimpered from the West, the Iroquois mother told her children, "The Panther whines."

As the hunters on the trail of the deer felt the bite of the wind from the East, they observed, "The Moose breathes hard."

When the soft, serene breeze from the South sang in the pines, the children whispered, "Listen, the Fawn greets her mother."

THE GREAT GIFT

MANY YEARS AGO a band of Iroquois Indians were camped in a village on the Ohio River. At that early date the tobacco plant was unknown to the Ongwe-Oweh—the Indians.

One day, as the people of the Iroquois village were going about their regular work, a strange sound was heard coming from up the river. Immediately the people dropped their tasks and rushed to the riverbank to see where the strange sound was coming from. They stood looking at each other, listening to the weird sound which was sometimes like the howl of a strange animal and then again like the chant of singing people. As the people stood listening to the peculiar music, a loud voice was heard coming from up the river.

As they looked toward the sound of the voice, they saw, floating toward them, a large canoe filled with strange beings. These peculiar people were beating a big kettledrum that was in the center of the canoe and were singing a strange song. By their peculiar dress, the singers appeared to be medicine men. As the canoe floated toward the village, the loud voice was again heard coming from the canoe. It told the inhabitants of the village to go back to their homes and remain indoors. It said that, if they disobeyed, bad luck would come to them.

The people became very frightened, and most of them rushed for their houses. But there were some who refused to be frightened by these medicine people. They stood upon the bank of the river and watched the approaching canoe. As the canoe floated by them, these men who had remained on the bank fell dead upon the sandy beach. The canoe with the strange singing men continued floating on down the stream and disappeared around the bend of the river.

The next day one of the relatives of the dead men organized a war party. In their canoe they paddled down the river in search of the strange canoe. They were seeking revenge for the death of their friends. They followed the river for a long time. After days of travel they came upon the canoe floating in a sheltered bay. In each end of the canoe, fast asleep, was a strange being. As the warriors stood gazing at these sleeping beings, the voice was again heard coming from the canoe. The loud voice said that if these strange beings were destroyed, a great blessing would come to the Ongwe-Oweh.

After the strange voice had ceased speaking, the warriors hid in the forests bordering the stream. A single warrior approached the river. Taking a stone, he threw it at one of the beings who awoke with a shout. The single warrior stuck out his tongue at the strange creatures and pretended to run from them. Seeing this, the two beings beached their canoe and took after the fleeing Indian. The warrior led them to a near-by council house, and after he had decoyed them into it, he let out his war cry, and with his war club faced the two pursuers. At the sound of their comrade's war cry, the other warriors immediately came to the aid of their fellow warrior, and in a short time the two beings were killed.

Gathering a great pile of brush and placing the two dead creatures upon it, the warriors set fire to it, and soon the bodies were ashes. From the ashes of the dead bodies rose the tobacco plant. The voice was heard coming from the earth, instructing the Indian people how to use the tobacco.

THE ORIGIN OF TIDES

AGAIN RAVEN took his raven blanket and flew over the ocean with the firebrand in his hands. He arrived at the mainland and came to another house, which belonged to a very old woman, who held the tide line in her hand. At that time the tide was always high, and did not turn for several days, until the new moon came, and all the people were anxious for clams and other sea food.

Giant* entered and found the old woman holding the tide line in her hand. He sat down and said, "Oh, I have had enough, I have had all the clams I need!"

The old woman said at once, "How is that possible? How can that be? What are you talking about, Giant?"

"Yes, I have had clams enough."

The old woman said, "No, it is not true."

Therefore Giant pushed her, so that she fell back, and he threw dust into her eyes and her mouth. Then she let the tide line go, so that the tide ran out very low, and all the clams and shellfish were on the beach. So Giant carried up as much as he could. The tide was still low when he re-entered.

The old woman said, "Giant, come and heal my eyes. I am blind from the dust."

Giant said, "Will you promise to slacken the tide line twice a day?" She agreed, and Giant cured her eyes. He had eaten all the shellfish that he had carried up.

The old woman said, "How can you get water to drink, Giant?" He answered that it was under the roots of the little alder tree.

Soon Giant was thirsty, and he went to drink water, but he could not find any. Finally he went up Skeena River, and there he found water, because the old woman had dried up all the brooks and creeks. Therefore the tide turns twice every day, going up and down.

*See footnote on page 248.

XI

TALES INFLUENCED BY EUROPEAN FAIRY TALES AND FOLK TALES

THE MAGICAL FOOD, BELT, AND FLUTE

THERE WAS ONCE a king who owned a large farm in the neighborhood of the town where he resided; the farm was cultivated by a man who paid rent for it to the king. This man had but one child, a son, who was considered only about half-witted; he was very stupid, and was continually doing silly things.

After a while his father died; but as he had left a large store of money, the rent was easily met for a year or two. Finally a payday approached when there was no cash. The mother consulted with her son as to what was to be done. "The king will call in a day or two for his money, and we have none for him. What can we do?" He replies, "*Loooh*—I don't know." She concludes to select one of the finest cows, and send the boy off to market to sell it. He agrees to the proposal, and starts with the cow to market.

As he drives his animal along, he passes a house standing near the road; there is a man on the steps who has come out to hail him. He inquires, "Where are you going with that cow?" "I am driving her to market," Jack answers. "Come in and rest yourself," says the man, pleasantly. Jack accepts the invitation, goes in, and sits down.

"I want you to make me a present of that cow," says the man. "Can't do it," replies Jack; "but I will be glad to sell her to you, for we are in need of the money." The man replies that he will not buy the cow, but that he wants Jack to make him a present of her. This the boy refuses to do.

The man asks if he will have something to eat. He answers in the affirmative, and on a tiny dish is set before him a very small piece of food. The boy looks at the food, and ventures to taste it. He finds it very palatable, and eats away, but does not diminish the amount. After a while the distention of his stomach indicates that he has eaten sufficiently; but his appetite is as keen as ever, and the morsel that lies on the tiny plate is not in the least diminished.

He endeavors to stop eating, but finds that he cannot do so. He has to

371

keep on eating, whether he will or not. So he calls out to the man, "Take away your food." The man coolly answers, "Give me your cow, and I will." The boy answers indignantly, "I'll do no such thing; take your dish away." "Then eat on," quietly answers the man. And eat on he does, until he begins to think that his whole abdominal region will burst if he continues much longer.

He gives over the contest, cries for quarter, and yields up the cow. In return he receives the little dish with the food, undiminished in quantity or quality, remaining in it. He then returns home with the magical food in his pocket.

Arriving at his home, he is questioned as to the success of his mission. He relates his adventures and says, "I have been robbed of the cow." His mother calls him a thousand fools, upbraids him outrageously, and seizes the fire shovel in order to knock him down. He dodges her, however, and taking a particle of the magical food on the tip of his finger, adroitly touches her mouth with it as he jumps by her. She stops instantly, charmed with the exquisite taste, and inquires, "What is this that tastes so delicious?" Thereupon he hands the dish over to her; and she falls to eating greedily, while he quietly looks on.

But soon sensations and difficulties similar to those which he had himself experienced lead her to call out to him to remove the plate. "Will you beat me then?" he coolly asks. "I will," exclaims the mother, now more than ever enraged, finding herself thus caught in a trap. "Then you may eat away," says the boy. The indignant old lady eats on, until she can really stand the strain no longer, when she yields, and promises to lay aside the "rod of correction"; then he releases her by removing the tiny platter and its contents.

The next morning the old lady sends Jack off to market with another cow. Passing the same house, he is again accosted by the man, who is waiting on the doorstep to meet him. In the same manner as on the former occasion, the man makes the modest request that Jack give him the cow. Jack, however, has learned some wisdom by his late adventure, and has no idea of repeating the experiment. "*Jigulahse winsit*—Be off with you, you evil spirit," he exclaims. "You robbed me yesterday; you're not going to do it again today," and he hurries on.

The man takes off his belt, and throws it down in the middle of the road. Instantly the belt leaps up around both Jack and his cow, binds the animal's legs fast to her body, and lashes the boy to her side. There they lie, unable to stir. "*Apkwahle!*—Untie me!" shouts the struggling boy. "Give me your cow and I will," the man answers. "I won't do it," says Jack. "Then lie there!" is the answer. But the belt, like a huge boa constrictor, begins to contract, and to press upon Jack and his cow, so that they can scarcely draw their breath.

At length the poor fellow gives up the cow, is unfastened, receives the magic belt in return, and goes home. He informs his mother that the same man has again robbed him. The old woman is now more angry than ever. She calls him hard names, threatens to beat and even to kill him, and searches for a suitable weapon. Then Jack unclasps his belt, casts it upon the floor, and instantly the poor woman is bound hand and foot, and calls lustily to be released. Jack looks on and says, "*Mataedukstuh?*—Will you beat me, then?" "Yes, I will," she screams. "Untie me, you dog!" Jack pulls the magic cord a little tighter round her, and the violence of her wrath abates; she begins to gasp, and promises if he will let her go she will not beat him. Thereupon he unties her, and she keeps her word.

The difficulty still remains. The rent is not yet paid, and the mother determines to make one more attempt to sell a cow. Away goes the boy again toward the town, driving the third animal, when the same man again encounters him with the same proposal, "Give me your cow." "Give you my cow, indeed!" exclaims the boy in wrath. "I'll give a stone and hurl it at your head."

He is about to suit the action to the word, when the man pulls out a tiny flute and begins to play on it. Jack's muscles instantly contract in different directions. The stone drops from his hand, and literally charmed with the music, he begins to dance. The cow joins in the jig, and both dance away with all their might, unable to stop. "Hold! hold!" he exclaims at length; "stop your music! Let me get my breath!" "Give me your cow, and I will," answers the man. "I won't do it," Jack replies. "Then dance away!" is the answer; and the poor fellow dances until he nearly drops from weariness.

He then yields, gives up the cow, receives the magic flute, and returns to his mother to report his ill success for the third time. This time the old woman's rage knows no bounds. She will kill him outright. But while she is in the act of springing upon him with some deadly weapon, he commences operations on his magical flute. The old lady is enchanted with the music, drops her weapon, and begins to dance, but retains her wrath, and long persists in her determination to deal vengeance upon the boy.

Again and again she orders him to cease playing. But in answer to his question, "*Mataedukstuh?*—Will you beat me then?" she answers, "Indeed I will." Soon she becomes so weary that she can scarcely keep on her feet, but sways to and fro, almost sinking. Finally she falls and strikes her head with great force. She yields, and promises to let him alone, and he withdraws the enchantment of his music.

There was another effect produced by the magic flute when the man who met Jack commenced playing. No sooner had the boy and cow begun to dance than they were joined by a great swarm of hornets. These hornets hovered over them, and danced in concert in the air; they followed the flute; whenever it played they came, but they were invisible to all eyes except those of the musician, and his commands and wishes they implicitly obeyed.

The difficulty of paying the rent remains. The mother is still in trouble about it, but the boy quiets her fears, and undertakes to manage the affair. "Today," she says, "the king will be here. What can we do?" He says to her, "I'll pay him. Give yourself no uneasiness." He then takes a lot of earthen dishes and smashes them up fine, packs the pieces into a bag, and fills it so full that he can scarcely tie it up, then seals the strings with *upkoo-gum*.

Presently a carriage containing the king himself and two servants drives up to the door. They have come to collect the rent. They enter the house, and the terrified old woman runs and hides. The boy, however, meets them at the door, and politely conducts them to a seat. They sit down and wait, and he immediately fetches them what seems to be a well-filled money-bag, and sets it on the table, making it rattle and chink like a bag of money, as he sets it down.

He then produces his little magic platter and food, and gravely informs the king that his father, before he died, had given his instructions to set that before the king as a portion of exquisitely delicious food. The king takes the bait and falls into the trap; he first tastes a morsel, then falls to eating, and the two servants join him. Meanwhile the boy seems to be very busy getting ready to count out the cash, bustling round, going into another room where he remains a good while, then coming out and lifting up the bag, and as if having forgotten something, going back into some other apartment of the house.

Meanwhile the king and his servants become gorged with the food; but they can neither refrain from eating, nor push away from the enchanted platter. They call to the boy to come and remove his dish; but he is altogether too busy to hear or to notice them. Meanwhile their troubles increase. Their stomachs become distended beyond endurance, and they are glad to purchase a respite by giving up rent, house, stock, farm, and all. On these conditions, the dish and food are removed, and the king and his retinue return to the palace, leaving the good people in quiet possession of everything.

After they have retired, the old woman, who has been watching the maneuvers from her hiding place, comes out, and this time praises her boy for his adroitness. He makes over all the property to her, and starts off to seek his fortune and a wife, taking wth him the enchanted dish, belt, and flute.

So he travels on, and finally arrives at a town where a king resides who has one beautiful daughter. She has many suitors, for the king has promised her hand to the first one who will make her laugh three times in succession. Now, it happens that our hero is very ill-shaped, ugly-looking, and awkward, and can, by a little affectation, make himself appear much more so than he really is.

He strolls about the city, hears the current gossip, and learns about the domestic arrangements of the palace. So one day he strolls into the king's palace among the other suitors and visitors, and looks round at everything, and soon attracts the attention of the servants, who inquire what his business is there. At first he makes no reply. But he knows that, according to rule, unless he answers the third challenge, he will be summarily ejected. So he answers the second time, "Is it true, as I have heard, that the princess will marry the first man who can make her laugh three times in succession?" He is told that it is true, and he says he wishes to make the trial. So he is allowed to remain in the palace.

Being admitted into the apartment where the young lady is in waiting, surrounded by her suitors, who are to be umpires in the trial, he first brings out his magical dish with the enchanted food, and requests her to examine and taste it. She does this cautiously, following the bent of curiosity, and finds the taste so agreeable that she continues to eat, and offers it to the others, who also eat. To their astonishment the quantity of food does not diminish in the platter, nor does the taste become any less exquisite, although their distended stomachs protest against any further infliction.

Finally the protestations of the gastric regions overcome the clamors of the palate, and they attempt to stop eating and to push away the plate. But they can do neither the one nor the other, and so call upon the youth to take away his food. He will do so, but upon one condition: *The princess must laugh*. She hesitates; she had only thought of laughing from pleasure, not from pain. She refuses to comply, but he is inexorable; she may do what she pleases—laugh, or continue to eat. Finally she can hold out no longer, and she laughs, saying to herself, "He'll not make me laugh a second time."

As soon as he releases them from the enchantment of the food, they fly furiously at him to expel him from the palace. But they reckon without their host. Quick as lightning he unclasps the magic belt, tosses it on the floor, and instantly they are all bound together in a bundle, wound from head to foot, and lie in a helpless heap before him. "Untie us," shouts the tortured and terrified princess. "*Oosugawayan*—Laugh, then," he coolly answers.

But no, she will not laugh. However, he knows how to bring her to terms. He has but to will it, and the obedient belt will tighten its embrace.

When she and her guardians can endure the pressure no longer, she gives forth a forced and feeble laugh. Then they are all released. No sooner done, than the men draw their weapons and rush furiously at him. Before they reach the spot where he stands, however, he has the magic flute to his lips. Their steps are arrested, and princess, suitors, umpires, guards, and all are wheeling in the mazy dance. They are charmed, not figuratively but literally, with the music of the tiny magic flute.

At length they grow tired of the exercise, and vainly endeavor to stop, but they cannot do it. "Stop your playing!" they shout. "I will," he answers, when the princess laughs." She determines that she will not laugh this time, come what may. But the stakes are for a princess and a kingdom, and he will not yield. She dances till she can no longer stand. She falls upon the floor, striking it heavily with her head. She then yields to her fate, performs her part nobly, and gives forth *tokoo weskawake*—a hearty laugh. The music then ceases, the umpires are left to decide the case, and the young man walks away and leaves them.

The news of the affair reaches the ears of the king, and he commands that the young man shall be introduced into his presence. This is done; the king is disgusted with the looks and manners of the young man, and declares the contract null and void. But the matter must be hushed up, and not allowed to get abroad. The victor is to be privately despatched, and another more suitable match substituted in his place. By the king's direction, the stranger is seized, conveyed to the menagerie, and thrown in with the beasts. This is a large apartment surrounded by high walls. The ferocious animals rush upon him. But the magic belt is tossed down, and they are all tied up in a heap, their legs being bound fast to their bodies, while he sits quietly down awaiting the issue of events in one corner of the yard.

Meanwhile word is circulated that one of the suitors at the royal palace has won the princess's hand, and the wedding is to be celebrated that very evening. "All goes merrily as a marriage bell," until the hour arrives for the bridegroom to be introduced into the bridal chamber. There the whole affair is quashed. Hosts of invisible foes are there who have entered at the keyhole, and are waiting to vindicate the innocent, defend his rights, and punish the intruder. The victorious Jack has taken his flute and called the troops of hornets to his aid. He bids them enter the keyhole and wait until his rival has unrobed, and then ply him with their tiny weapons about his lower extremities. This they do; and the poor fellow, unable to see the hornets, but fully able to feel their stinging, begins to jump and scream like a madman.

The terrified princess rushes out of the room, and screams for help. The domestics run to her assistance, and she declares that the bridegroom is a maniac. They, hearing his screams and witnessing his contortions of countenance, and unable to learn the cause, come to the same conclusion, and hurry him away from the palace. Another bridegroom is substituted, who shares the same fate.

The king at length concludes that he is outgeneraled; that the young man who has won the hand of his daughter still lives; that he must be a remarkable personage, possessed of miraculous powers. He sends to the menagerie for him. The animals are all tied up; but a thick mist fills the place, and they cannot see the young man. They attempt to release the beasts, but find this impossible. They bring the report to the king.

"Ay," said he, "it is just as I said; he is a necromancer, a remarkable man. Go again, seek him carefully, and if you can find him bring him in."

This time they find him. They recognize him; but he is now transformed into a most lovely person. All admire his portly bearing and his polished manners. The wedding is consummated with great pomp. He builds a splendid palace, and, when the old king dies, is crowned in his place.

OOCHIGEOPCH, THE TRANSFORMED BRIDEGROOM

Two old Indians lived far away in the forest. They had no daughters, and only one son. When the boy was grown up, his mother advised him to begin housekeeping on his own. He made inquiries respecting the matter, and his mother gave him all due directions. She prepared his clothes for the occasion, and told him which way to go. He must follow the river, and go upstream. In due time he would come to a small Indian village; he would not find the wished-for girl there, but he would obtain directions. He must enter one of the humblest lodges, and make known his errand.

This all came out as foretold. He entered the lodge; and there was an old mother, who received him kindly, and a small boy, who took great pleasure in waiting upon him. The old lady had already divined his errand; and when he stated to her the particulars, she volunteered to assist him. She went over to a neighboring lodge, where two young men resided, and told them that a stranger had arrived—*wajoolkw*—and that a fine young man was on a marriage expedition and needed a guide. Would one of them accompany him? One consented, and his services as guide were accepted. The next day the two went on; they came to a second village, but their directions were to go on to a third. In due time this was reached; it turned out to be a very large one.

Here the young man entered one of the poorest and meanest-looking lodges, where an old grandmother and her little grandson, Marten, welcomed them. Before entering, the young candidate for matrimonial honors put off his fine, manly appearance, his ornaments, and his beauty, and assumed a mean garb and a rough, scabby face. Awkwardly entering the lodge, he managed to hit his face with the boughs that were woven by the side of the doorway to keep out the cold, and to set his face to bleeding. In this wretched plight he entered, and took his seat. The old lady knew well that all this was assumed for the purpose of seeing who would marry him notwithstanding his looks, intending that his bride should enjoy a pleasing surprise when she found out how handsome he really was.

His comrade informed the grandmother who her guests were, and what the object of their expedition was. She then went out to negotiate. There was a chief there who had a number of daughters, and to him the old woman made application. The old chief had a streak of magic in him; and despite the young stranger's appearance, he knew that there was something in him. "Let him come," said the chief, "and take his choice of my daughters."

The girls, all in a high state of expectation, were called in and seated round the lodge. At the word given, in blundered the would-be bridegroom. His face was covered with ugly sores, and he managed to stumble against the brush of the wigwam, so as to set them bleeding. In this condition he gazed around on the young women, in order to select the most beautiful and lovely one. They were horror-stricken, and screaming rushed out of the wigwam and hid their faces; but the youngest, who was the prettiest and best, kept her seat.

He went up and sat down by her side. This settled the matter. The parties were married, but the poor thing could not restrain her tears; these fell thick and fast. But her father told her to stop crying, "He is all right; you will soon find out that you have no reason to be sorrowful."

Meanwhile the other sisters could not restrain their taunts. But she waited patiently for some change. In the morning, when she awoke, what was her astonishment in beholding the transformation that had taken place! She could not believe this was the husband to whom she had been assigned; but her mother assured her that he was the very same one. Oh, how delighted she was! He had applied a little water and washing to his face, and removed all imperfections and impurities; his cheeks were red, his robes were splendid, and he had all the dignity and manly bearing of a chief. Upon this, the other sisters changed their tune, and were enraged at the good fortune of their sister.

A festival was planned, and they had eating, drinking, and games; and in due time the young couple arrived at their home. The friend of the bridegroom accompanied them as far as his own village, where he left the young married couple to go on. They arrived at their destination, and were welcomed by the bridegroom's mother.

THE POOR TURKEY GIRL

LONG, LONG AGO, our ancients had neither sheep nor horses nor cattle; yet they had domestic animals of various kinds, among them turkeys.

In Matsaki, the Salt City, there dwelt at this time many very wealthy families, who possessed large flocks of these birds, which it was their custom to have their slaves or the poor people of the town herd in the plains round about Thunder Mountain, below which their town stood, and on the mesas beyond.

Now in Matsaki at this time there stood, away out near the border of the town, a little tumble-down, single-room house, wherein there lived alone a very poor girl, so poor that her clothes were patched and tattered and dirty, and her person, on account of long neglect and ill fare, shameful to look upon, though she herself was not ugly, but had a winning face and bright eyes; that is, if the face had been more oval and the eyes less oppressed with care. So poor was she that she herded turkeys for a living; and little was given to her except the food she subsisted on from day to day, and perhaps now and then a piece of old, worn-out clothing.

Like the extremely poor everywhere and at all times, she was humble, and by her longing for kindness, which she never received, she was made kind even to the creatures that depended upon her, and lavished this kindness upon the turkeys she drove to and from the plains every day. Thus, the turkeys, appreciating this, were very obedient. They loved their mistress so much that at her call they would unhesitatingly come, or at her behest go whithersoever and whensoever she wished.

One day, this poor girl, driving her turkeys down into the plains, passed near Old Zuñi—the Middle Ant Hill of the World, as our ancients have taught us to call our home—and as she went along, she heard the herald priest proclaiming from the housetop that the Dance of the Sacred Bird (which is a very blessed and welcome festival to our people, especially to the youths and maidens who are permitted to join in the dance) would take place in four days.

Now, this poor girl had never been permitted to join in or even to watch the great festivities of our people or the people in the neighboring towns, and naturally she longed very much to see this dance. But she put aside her longing, because she reflected, "It is impossible that I should watch, much less join in the Dance of the Sacred Bird, ugly and ill-clad as I am." And thus musing to herself, and talking to her turkeys, as was her custom, she drove them on, and at night returned them to their cages round the edges and in the plazas of the town.

Every day after that, until the day named for the dance, this poor girl, as she drove her turkeys out in the morning, saw the people busy in cleaning and preparing their garments, cooking delicacies, and otherwise making ready for the festival to which they had been duly invited by the other villagers, and heard them talking and laughing merrily at the prospect of the coming holiday. So, as she went about with her turkeys through the day, she would talk to them, though she never dreamed that they understood a word of what she was saying.

It seems that they did understand even more than she said to them, for on the fourth day, after the people of Matsaki had all departed toward Zuñi and the girl was wandering around the plains alone with her turkeys, one of the big gobblers strutted up to her, and making a fan of his tail, and skirts, as it were, of his wings, blushed with pride and puffed with importance, stretched out his neck and said, "Maiden mother, we know what your thoughts are, and truly we pity you, and wish that, like the other people of Matsaki, you might enjoy this holiday in the town below. We have said to ourselves at night, after you have placed us safely and comfortably in our cages, 'Truly our maiden mother is as worthy to enjoy these things as any one in Matsaki, or even Zuñi'. Now, listen well, for I speak the speech of all the elders of my people. If you will drive us in early this afternoon, when the dance is most gay and the people are most happy, we will help you to make yourself so handsome and so prettily dressed that never a man, woman, or child among all those who are assembled at the dance will know you, but rather, especially the young men, will wonder whence you came, and long to lay hold of your hand in the circle that forms round the altar to dance. Maiden mother, would you like to go to see this dance, and even to join in it, and be merry with the best of your people?"

The poor girl was at first surprised. Then it seemed all so natural that the turkeys should talk to her, as she did to them, that she sat down on a little mound, and leaning over, looked at them and said, "My beloved Turkeys, how glad I am that we may speak together! But why should you tell me of things that you full well know I so long to, but cannot by any possible means, do?"

"Trust in us," said the old Gobbler, "for I speak the speech of my people, and when we begin to call and call and gobble and gobble, and turn toward our home in Matsaki, do you follow us, and we will show you what we can do for you. Only let me tell you one thing. No one knows how much happiness and good fortune may come to you if you but enjoy temperately the pleasures we enable you to participate in. But if, in the excess of your enjoyment, you should forget us, who are your friends, yet so much depend upon you, then we will think, 'Behold, this our maiden mother, though so humble and poor, deserves, forsooth, her hard life, because, were she more prosperous, she would be unto others as others now are unto her'."

"Never fear, O my Turkeys," cried the maiden, only half trusting that they could do so much for her, yet longing to try, "never fear. In everything you direct me to do I will be obedient as you always have been to me."

The sun had scarce begun to decline, when the turkeys of their own accord turned homeward, and the maiden followed them, light of heart. They knew their places well, and immediately ran to them. When all had entered, even their bare-legged children, the old Gobbler called to the maiden, saying, "Enter our house." She therefore went in. "Now, maiden, sit down," said he, "and give to me and my companions, one by one, your articles of clothing. We will see if we cannot renew them."

The maiden obediently drew off the ragged old mantle that covered her shoulders and cast it on the ground before the speaker. He seized it in his beak, and spread it out, and picked and picked at it. Then he trod upon it, and lowering his wings, began to strut back and forth over it. Then taking it up in his beak, and continuing to strut, he puffed and puffed, and laid it down at the feet of the maiden, a beautiful white embroidered cotton mantle. Then another gobbler came forth, and she gave him another article of dress, and then another and another, until each garment the maiden had worn was new and as beautiful as any possessed by her mistresses in Matsaki.

Before the maiden donned all these garments, the turkeys circled about her, singing and singing, and clucking and clucking, and brushing her with their wings, until her person was as clean and her skin as smooth and bright as that of the fairest maiden of the wealthiest home in Matsaki. Her hair was soft and wavy, instead of being an ugly, sunburned shock. Her cheeks were full and dimpled, and her eyes dancing with smiles, for she now saw how true had been the words of the turkeys.

Finally, one old turkey came forward and said, "Only the rich ornaments worn by those who have many possessions are lacking to thee, O maiden mother. Wait a moment. We have keen eyes, and have gathered many valuable things; as such things, being small, though precious, are apt to be lost from time to time by men and maidens."

Spreading his wings, he trod round and round upon the ground, throwing his head back, and laying his wattled beard on his neck; and presently beginning to cough, he produced in his beak a beautiful necklace. Another turkey brought forth earrings, and so on, until all the proper ornaments appeared, befitting a well-clad maiden of the olden days, and were laid at the feet of the poor turkey girl.

With these beautiful things she decorated herself, and thanking the turkeys over and over, she started to go. They called out, "O maiden mother, leave open the wicket, for who knows whether you will remember your turkeys or not when your fortunes are changed, and if you will not grow ashamed that you have been the maiden mother of turkeys? But we love you, and would bring you to good fortune. Therefore, remember our words of advice, and do not tarry too long."

"I will surely remember, O my Turkeys!" answered the maiden.

Hastily she sped away down the river path toward Zuñi. When she arrived there, she went in at the western side of the town and through one of the long covered ways that lead into the dance court. When she came just inside of the court, behold, everyone began to look at her, and many murmurs ran through the crowd—murmurs of astonishment at her beauty and the richness of her dress—and the people were all asking one another, "Whence comes this beautiful maiden?"

Not long did she stand there neglected. The chiefs of the dance, all gorgeous in their holiday attire, hastily came to her, and with apologies for the incompleteness of their arrangements—though these arrangements were as complete as they possibly could be—invited her to join the youths and maidens dancing round the musicians and the altar in the center of the plaza.

With a blush and a smile and a toss of her hair over her eyes, the maiden stepped into the circle, and the finest youths among the dancers vied with one another for her hand. Her heart became light and her feet merry, and the music sped her breath to rapid coming and going, and the warmth swept over her face, and she danced and danced until the sun sank low in the west.

But alas! in the excess of her enjoyment, she thought not of her turkeys, or if she thought of them, she said to herself, "How is this, that I should go away from the most precious consideration to my flock of gobbling turkeys? I will stay awhile longer, and just before the sun sets I will run back to them, that these people may not see who I am, and that I may have the joy of hearing them talk day after day and wonder who the girl was who joined in their dance."

So the time sped on, and another dance was called, and another, and never a moment did the people let her rest; but they would have her in every dance as they moved around the musicians and the altar in the center of the plaza.

At last the sun set, and the dance was well-nigh over, when suddenly breaking away, the girl ran out, and, being swift of foot—more so than most of the people of her village—she sped up the river path before anyone could follow the course she had taken.

Meantime, as it grew late, the turkeys began to wonder and wonder that their maiden mother did not return to them. At last a gray old gobbler mournfully exclaimed, "It is as we might have expected. She has forgotten us; therefore is she not worthy of better things than those she has been accustomed to. Let us go forth to the mountains and endure no more of this irksome captivity, inasmuch as we may no longer think our maiden mother as good and true as once we thought her."

So, calling and calling to one another in loud voices, they trooped out of their cage and ran up toward the Canyon of the Cottonwoods, and then round behind Thunder Mountain, through the Gateway of Zuñi, and so on up the valley.

All breathless, the maiden arrived at the open wicket and looked in. Behold! not a turkey was there! Trailing them, she ran and ran up the valley to overtake them; but they were far ahead, and it was only after a long time that she came within the sound of their voices, and then, redoubling her speed, well-nigh overtook them, when she heard them singing this song:

Kyaanaa, to! to!
Kyaanaa, to! to!
   Ye ye!
Kyaanaa, to! to!
Kyaanaa, to! to!
   Yee huli huli!

Hon awen Tsita
Itiwanakwin
   Otakyaan aaa kyaa;
Lesna Akyaaa

Shoya-koskwi
Teyathltokwin
  Hon aawani!

Ye yee huli huli,
Tot-tot, tot-tot, tot-tot,
  Huli huli!

Up the river, *to! to!*
Up the river, *to! to!*
  Sing *ye ye!*
Up the river, *to! to!*
Up the river, *to! to!*
  Sing *yee huli huli!*

Oh, our maiden mother
To the middle place
  To dance went away;
Therefore as she lingers,
To the Canyon Mesa
And the plains above it
  We all run away!

Sing *ye yee huli huli,*
Tot-tot, tot-tot, tot-tot,
  Huli huli!
Tot-tot, tot-tot, tot-tot,
  Huli huli!

Hearing this, the maiden called to her turkeys, called and called in vain. They only quickened their steps, spreading their wings to help them along, singing the song over and over until, indeed, they came to the base of the Canyon Mesa—Shoya-koskwi—at the borders of the Zuñi Mountains. Then singing once more their song in full chorus, they spread wide their wings, and *thlakwa-a-a, thlakwa-a-a,* they fluttered away over the plains above.

The poor turkey girl threw her hands up and looked down at her dress.

With dust and sweat, behold! it was changed to what it had been, and she was the same poor turkey girl that she was before. Weary, grieving, and despairing, she returned to Matsaki.

Thus it was in the days of the ancients. Therefore, where you see the rocks leading up to the top of Canyon Mesa, there are the tracks of turkeys and other figures to be seen. The latter are the song that the turkeys sang, graven in the rocks. And all over the plains along the borders of Zuñi Mountains since that day turkeys have been more abundant than in any other place.

After all, the gods dispose of men according as men are fitted; and if the poor be poor in heart and spirit as well as in appearance, how will they be aught but poor to the end of their days?

Thus shortens my story.

THE WIVES OF THE STORM-GOD

ONCE UPON A TIME a chief of Acoma had a lovely daughter. One day a handsome stranger stole her and took her away to his home, which was in the heart of the Snow Mountain—Mount San Mateo. He was none other than Mast-Truan, one of the Storm-Gods. Bringing his captive home, the powerful stranger gave her the finest clothing and treated her very nicely. But most of the time he had to be away from home, attending to the storms, and she became very lonesome, for there was no one to keep her company but Mast-Truan's wrinkled old mother.

One day when she could stand the loneliness no longer, she decided to take a walk through the enormous house and look at the rooms which she had not seen. Opening a door she came into a very large room toward the east; and there were a lot of women crying and shivering with cold, for they had nothing to wear. Going through this room she came to another, which was full of gaunt, starving women, and here and there one lay dead upon the floor. And in the next room were scores of bleached and ghastly skeletons. And this was what Mast-Truan did to his wives when he was tired of them. The girl saw her fate, and returning to her room, sat down and wept; but there was no escape, for Mast-Truan's old hag of a mother forever guarded the outer door.

When Mast-Truan came home again, his wife said, "It is now long that I have not seen my father. Let me go home for a little while."

"Well," said he, "here is some corn which must be shelled. When you have shelled it and ground it, I will let you out"; and he showed her four great rooms piled from floor to ceiling with ears of corn. It was more than one could shell in a year; and when her husband went out, she sat down again to cry and bemoan her fate.

Just then a queer little old woman appeared before her, with a kindly smile. It was a *cumush-quio*, fairy woman.

"What is the matter, my daughter?" asked the old fairy, gently, "and why do you weep?"

The captive told her all, and the fairy said, "Do not fear, daughter, for I will help you, and we will have all the corn shelled and ground in four days."

So they fell to work. For two days the girl kept shelling; and though she could not see the old fairy at all, she could always hear at her side the click of the ears together. Then for two days she kept grinding on her *metate*, apparently alone, but hearing the constant grind of another *metate* close beside her. At the end of the fourth day, the last kernel had been scrubbed into blue meal, and she was very happy.

Then the old fairy woman appeared again, bringing a large basket and a rope. She opened the doors to all the rooms where the poor women were prisoners, and bade them all get into the basket one by one. Mast-Truan had taken away the ladder from the house when he left, that no one might be able to get out. But with her basket and rope, the good old fairy woman let them all down to the ground, and told them to hurry home—which they did as fast as ever their poor, starved legs could carry them. Then the fairy woman and the girl escaped, and made their way to Acoma.

THE PRINCE AND THE PEASANT GIRL

THERE was once a king who had two sons and one daughter. He lived in a large town, and had many fine horses, many servants, and seven donkeys. He was in the habit of driving out in his carriage, and taking his queen and three children with him; but when he did so, he took, instead of horses, the seven donkeys to draw the carriage.

After the eldest son was grown up, he became dissatisfied with this arrangement, and questioned his mother about it; he got but little satisfaction, though he obtained permission to drive a pair of fine horses.

One day he drove out with his brother and sister and a couple of servants; he went beyond the limits of the town, and passing around the outskirts, came upon a very small, humble-looking house, where an old woman and a young girl—her granddaughter, whose parents were dead—resided. They were out of doors at their work in the garden. The prince halted at this house, and told the company that he would go in and ask for a drink of water. The servant remonstrated, and begged to be allowed to go for the drink; but the prince chose to go himself.

As soon as this splendid coach drove up to the door, the old woman and the girl fled into the house. The old woman, whose clothes were ragged, concealed herself; but the girl, on seeing that the coach halted, and that one of the young gentlemen was coming in, hastily tied on a clean apron, and adjusted her attire as well as the emergency would admit. As soon as she heard the rap at the door, she opened it cautiously a little way and looked out.

The young gentleman asked for a drink of water. She immediately took a pitcher, and obtained a fresh supply of the pure, cooling beverage; taking a tumbler in one hand, in which a clean towel was placed, and the pitcher in the other, she put both into the hands of the visitor. The prince walked back to the carriage, gave all a drink of water, and then returned the pitcher and tumbler to the girl, slipping two or three pieces of gold into the pitcher before he did so. She received them from his hand, and the royal party went on their way.

When the girl had set down the pitcher, she noticed the shining pieces lying at the bottom of the water, and not knowing what they were, she asked in surprise, "*Noogumee, cogoowa weget?*—Grandmother, what are these?" The old lady tells her it is *soolleawa*, money, and that they can now buy food and other things sufficient to make them comfortable for some time.

But the prince was wonderfully pleased with the beauty, modesty, neatness, and general appearance of the girl. He determined to make her another visit, and in case he could gain her consent, to make her his wife.

So a few days after, he arranged his plans to make another visit to the humble cottage. He told his mother that he would not be back to dinner, but would take some food and dishes with him; that he was going some distance into the country, and that he would call at some convenient place where he could have his dinner prepared for him.

When the coach arrived this time, the girl was absent, having gone out to obtain some seeds and other supplies for her garden, and no one was at home but the grandmother. The prince called again with the ever-ready excuse, the want of a drink of water. This the old lady gave him, but she did not know that it was the same young gentleman who had called on the previous occasion. When he had taken his drink, he proceeded to ask some questions of the old lady, in order to discover where the lovely object of his search was.

"Do you live here alone?" says he. "No," she answers, "I have a grandchild living with me." "Is your grandchild a boy or a girl?" he asks. "A girl," she answers. "How old is she?" says the prince. "Nineteen years old," she answers. "Where is she?" he inquires. "Gone to hunt up some seeds for our little garden," she answers. "Will she be back soon?" he asks. "She will," is the answer.

He then tells her that he is taking a drive out into the country, and that as he expects to be back a little before noon, he would like to come there and take lunch if she will allow him; he tells her at the same time that they have their provisions with them. The good woman modestly suggests that her accommodations are none of the best, and that she has no suitable cooking apparatus to answer his purpose. But he removes all her objections: her nice little room will just suit him; and as for cooking utensils, he has a supply of them with him. This arrangement being concluded, the coach moves off.

Soon after, the girl comes in from her begging expedition, and the old lady tells her what has occurred. She immediately goes to work and tidies up the room, and gets herself in as good trim as her limited circumstances will allow; and at the appointed time the coach arrives. The baskets and jars of provisions are brought in, and then the servant is sent away to some other place to attend to the horses and to get his own dinner; the old lady and her granddaughter assist in preparing for their guest.

When all is ready, he invites them to eat with him. But they hesitate; they are too bashful; they feel themselves unfit to eat with a gentleman. It requires some perseverance to overcome the bashfulness and hesitation of the girl; but she yields at last, and they eat and drink and enjoy themselves at their ease. After dinner he makes them a present of what is left—dishes, kettles, and all; for he had laid in his stores with an unstinted hand.

He then remains awhile longer, asks a great many questions respecting circumstances—*kakeiyesemilemaje*; and among other things, he learns how poor they are, and that they are sometimes pinched for seed. (Indians are always pinched for seed in the spring.) He inquires why they do not go and lay their troubles before the king. They tell him that they are too poor for this. But they are told that anyone can have access to the king who has any business of importance to transact with him.

Finally, the young prince, in a very businesslike way, asks her if she would be willing to be his wife. The poor girl looks upon the proposal as a joke, and refuses; when, however, he persists in his suit, and convinces her that he is in earnest, she argues very sensibly that she is too poor and incompetent to be the wife of a gentleman. But the old grandmother decides the question more promptly. She whispers to the girl. "*Tulim aa*—Tell him yes." Finally, she decides to think it over, and give him an answer by and by.

It is now time for the arrival of the servant, who has been told at what hour to come for his young master, and who has been enjoined to strict secrecy under a threat of being hanged if he should reveal aught. At the appointed hour he drives up with the coach, and the prince, who has not yet let slip a word about his rank, takes his leave, promising to return after seven days.

The coach then drives home, and the mother of the prince questions him as to where he has been. He tells her he has been over into another town in a neighboring kingdom, and the queen's curiosity is satisfied; she asks no more questions, and he tells her no more lies.

After a day or two, the prince intimates to his father that a widow and an orphan living in the outskirts of the town require a little looking after, and he requests him to call and see them. So one day he and his queen drive out that way; the king goes in, and being informed of their poverty, and of the difficulty of obtaining seed for their little patch of ground, inquires of the grandmother why she does not apply to the king for assistance. She says that she does not know the king, and doubts whether he would allow her to approach him, even if she did know him. But he tells her she is mistaken, that the king would assist her, did he know her case; and he encourages her to find him and try.

True to his promise, the young prince makes them another visit in seven days. They are expecting him, and are all ready to receive him. The pieces of gold left in the pitcher of water at his first visit have been well spent, and the inmates of this humble dwelling are arrayed in more comely suits of apparel; the house is made to look as tidy as possible. This time the prince is attended by two servants instead of one; but neither of them has been there before, and secrecy is enjoined upon them as upon the other, and under the same penalty of being hanged if they tell. He now inquires of the girl if there is any place where the horses can be fed. She says they can be accommodated in the small stable where they keep their cow, but there is no place for the coach. They manage, however, to hide the coach behind the stable.

This time all go in, get their dinner, and eat together. He now proposes to marry the girl; she finally agrees to think the matter over. He promises that she will hear from him in three days, and that he will come again, but he does not say when.

Three days after this he sends her a well-filled trunk, and when she opens it, she and her grandmother are astonished and delighted beyond measure at the contents. It is packed with clothes, jewels, and gold sufficient to make the possessor a princess. She arrays herself in her new robes, and tells her aged friend that she will marry the young man.

In due time he comes for her. He has told his father he is going for a wife, and in answer to the inquiries as to who and where she is, he tells him she lives in the next town, and is the daughter of the king of that place. So everything is prepared for the wedding; the oxen and the fatlings are killed, and he goes away in his coach to bring home the girl. In due time he arrives, and she is so beautiful and so splendidly arrayed that all hearts are captivated; the wedding festival is celebrated with great pomp, and no one ever mistrusts the ruse.

THE MAGICAL DANCING DOLL

THERE WAS ONCE LIVING in the forest an Indian couple who had seven sons, the oldest of whom was very unkind to the youngest. He used to impose hard tasks upon him, deprive him of his just allowance of food, and beat him. Finally, the lad determined to endure it no longer, and resolved to run away. His name, from his occupation, was Noojekesigunodasit, since his particular work was to take the rags from the moccasins, when pulled off, wring them and dry them.

So he requests his mother to make him a small bow and arrow, and thirty pairs of moccasins. She complies with his request, and when all are finished he takes the moccasins and his bow, and starts. He shoots the arrow ahead, and runs after it. In a short time he is able to outrun the arrow, and reach the spot where it is to fall before it strikes the ground. He then takes it up and shoots again, and flies on swifter than the arrow. Thus he travels straight ahead, and by night he has gone a long distance from home.

In the meantime his six brothers with their father have all been out hunting. When they return at evening, he is not there, and the older brother finding him absent is greatly enraged; he wants him to wring out and dry the wrappers of his feet. He inquires what has become of him. Being told that he has gone away, he resolves to pursue him and bring him back. So the next morning off he goes in pursuit, carefully following in his brother's tracks. For one hundred days in succession he follows on, halting every night and resting till morning. But during all this time he has only reached the spot where his brother passed his first night. He sees no sign before this of his having kindled a fire or erected a shelter; so he becomes discouraged, gives up the pursuit, and returns home.

The little boy in the meantime has been pursuing his way; he has met a very old man and had an interview with him. *"Tame aleen ak tame wejeen?*—Whither away, and where are you from?" the old man asks. "I have come a long distance," says the boy; "and you, where are you from?" "You say, my child, you have come a long distance," the old man replies; "but I can assure you the distance you have come is nothing in comparison with what I have traveled over; for I was a small boy when I started, and since that day I have never halted, and you see that now I am very old."

The boy answers, "I will try to go to the place from whence you came." "You can never reach it," the other answers. "But I will try," replies the boy. Seeing that the old man's moccasins are worn-out, the boy offers him a new pair; he accepts them gratefully and says, "I, in return, will do you a great favor. Here, take this box; you will find it of essential service to you in your travels." He then gives him a small box with a cover properly secured, which he puts in his pouch, and each goes his way.

After a while the boy begins to wonder what the box contains. He takes it out and opens it. As soon as he has removed the cover, he starts with an exclamation of surprise; for he sees a small image in the form of a man dancing away with all his might, and reeking with perspiration from the long-continued exertion.

As soon as the light is let in upon him, he stops dancing, looks suddenly up, and exclaims, "Well! what is it? What is wanted?" The truth now flashes over the boy. This is a supernatural agent, a Manito, a god from the spirit world, which can do anything that he is requested to do. "I wish," says the boy, "to be transported to the place from whence the old man came."

He then closes the box; suddenly his head swims, the darkness comes over him, and he faints. On coming to himself again, he finds himself near a large Indian village, and knows that this is the place from whence the old man had strayed. He walks into the first wigwam he comes to (a point of etiquette usually observed by the Indians on visiting a village), and is kindly received and invited up toward the back part of the wigwam, the place of honor.

There is but one person in the wigwam, and that is an old woman, who begins to weep bitterly as soon as the young man is seated. He asks the cause of her grief, and is told that it is on his account. She takes it for granted that he has come in quest of a wife, and that such hard conditions will be enjoined as the price of dower that he will be slain. This she proceeds to tell him, and to relate how many, who were much more brave and mighty than he appears to be, have fallen under the crafty dealings of their old chief, who imposes the conditions and works the death of those who come as suitors for his daughters. "Never mind," says our hero, "he'll not be able to kill me. I am prepared for any conditions he may be disposed to enjoin."

Meanwhile it is soon noised abroad through the village that a strange youth has arrived, to solicit in marriage one of the old chief's daughters. The chief sends him a somewhat haughty message to come and present himself before him. He answers the summons on a tone still more haughty. "Tell him I won't go," is the answer returned. The chief thereupon relaxes somewhat in his sternness, and sends a very modest request, intimating that he shall have one of his daughters in marriage, provided he will remove a troublesome object, a small nuisance, that hinders him from seeing the sun from his village until it is high up in the morning. This is a high granite mountain; he will please remove that out of the way. "All right," is the quiet response; and the young man sits down in great composure.

So, when the shades of evening have gathered over the village, he quietly takes out his little box and opens it. There, still dancing lustily, is his little comrade—*weedapcheejul*. He stops suddenly, looks up, and exclaims, "Well, what is it? What do you want of me?" "I want you to level down that granite mountain, and I want it done before morning." "*Ah*," is the answer, "*kesetulahdegedes*—I will have it done by morning." So he shuts up his little box, lies down, and goes to sleep. But all night long he hears the sound of laborers at their work. There is pounding, trampling, shouting, shoveling; and when he awakes, lo! the whole mountain has been removed.

When the chief awakes he hardly knows where he is; he is astonished out of measure. "He shall be my son-in-law," he exclaims; "go, call him, and tell him to come hither." The young man now obeys his summons. But the chief requires something further before he will give him the hand of his daughter. He happens to be at war with a powerful neighboring tribe, and he indulges the hope that, by engaging the young man in the war, he can cause him to fall by the hands of his enemies. He informs him that he wishes to surprise and destroy a village belonging to the enemy. "I will join you," says the young man. "Muster your warriors, and we will start tomorrow upon the expedition."

Arrangements are accordingly made, and everything is got ready for an early start. But our hero departs that very evening, and comes in sight of the village. There he uncovers his box and explains his wishes to the dancing doll. He then lies down and sleeps. All night long he hears the noise of war, the shouts of men, the clash of arms, the shrieks of women and children, and the groans of the wounded and dying. The noise and commotion grow fainter and fainter, and at length cease altogether. Morning dawns; he proceeds to view the village. All is silent and still; every soul is cut off —men, women, and children are all dead. He now returns, and on his way meets the chief and warriors moving on toward the enemy's village. He reports that he has destroyed the whole place as requested. They send, and find that it is even so.

The chief now inquires his name. He says, "Noojekesigunodasit." The chief is surprised, but fulfills his promise and gives him one of his daughters for a wife. He builds a large and commodious lodge, and takes up his residence there with his wife, and has a servant to wait upon him. He himself joins the hunters in their expeditions in the forest for game, and all goes on smoothly for a time. But alas for human happiness! There is always something to mar our repose. This servant manages to steal the dancing doll, and to run away with it—wife, wigwam, and all.

He accomplishes the feat thus. One day the master of the house went out a-hunting, and carelessly left his coat behind with the dancing doll stowed away in his pouch. Now it so happened that his servant had often been led to inquire in his own mind what could be the secret of his master's wonderful prowess. Seeing the coat on this occasion, he takes it up and slips it on. "Halloo! what is all this?" he exclaims, as he feels the box. He takes it out and opens it. "*Hie!* what are you?" he shouts, as his eyes rest on the dancing image. The little fellow stops his dancing suddenly, looks up, and exclaims, "Well, what is it? What do you want of me?"

The truth is now out. It flashes over the fellow. This is a Manito, and he it is that works all the wonders. The opportunity is not to be lost. "I want," says he, "this wigwam with all its contents removed to some spot where it cannot be discovered." The Manito replies, "I'll do it for you." Then the man grows dizzy, faints, and soon finds himself, wigwam, mistress, and all, far away in the depths of the forest, and surrounded on all sides by water. Of course he takes quiet possession, is lord of the place, the palace, and all.

But his triumph is brief. The original owner comes home, and finds himself minus wife, wigwam, magical box, and all. But he still has his magical bow and arrow; and shooting his arrow and giving chase, he is soon at the secluded wigwam, and has discovered his stolen home and wife.

No small management is required to regain the wonder-working box. He waits till nightfall; he looks in and sees the perfidious servant asleep with the coat under his head. He steals softly in, and directs the woman to withdraw it carefully from under him. He then slips it on, opens the box, and wishes himself back, wigwam, wife, servant and all, to their original home. No sooner said than done; and back the faithless servant is in his hands. Summary punishment is inflicted; he is killed, flayed, and a door blanket is made of his skin.

One more adventure and the story ends. The old chief himself is a great *boooin*, medicine man, or wizard, whose tutelar deity is a *chepechcalm*— a huge horned serpent or dragon, fabulous of course, but about the existence of which few doubts are entertained by the Indians. He is chagrined to find himself outdone by his son-in-law. So he makes one more effort to rid himself of him. He says quietly to him one day, "I want you to bring me the head of a *chepechcalm* for my dinner." "I will do so," he replies.

The dancing doll is commanded to bring one of these frightful monsters to the village. He does so. The inhabitants see the danger, and they scream and fly in every direction. Our hero walks out boldly to meet him, and gives battle. The fight is long and fearful, but finally victory declares for the man, and he severs the dragon's head from his trunk. He takes this head in his hand, and walks over to the chief's lodge and tosses it in. He finds the chief alone, weak and exhausted, and sitting bent nearly double. He walks up to him and pounds him on the head with the dragon's head. The old necromancer's magic is gone; his *teomul*, his medicine, his tutelary deity, is destroyed, and he falls and dies.

THE OLD MAN'S LESSONS TO HIS NEPHEW

A MAN and his nephew lived together in a solitary place. The old man one day said to his nephew, "You are now a young man. You should be hunting larger game—a bear or a deer—for our support." And he replied, "I will go."

Then the old man gave him the best bow and arrows, and in the morning he departed. When he returned home he brought that which he had killed—a deer—and thought himself lucky for a first attempt.

"I should like," he said to his uncle, "to go every day." Then the old man said, "Now and again you may see a bear go up a tree; if you see a hole in the tree and the marks of the bear's claws, you can be sure of the bear."

So one day as the young man was out he saw a hole in a tree, and he saw the claw marks of the bear, showing that he had gone up, so he returned and told his uncle, and in the morning they started together. The old man said, "I believe there is a bear inside now. Our plan is to knock around the outside of the tree and make the bear uneasy; presently he will come out." So they knocked, and the first thing they knew the bear was sticking his head out of the hole.

"Now," said the uncle, "I will tell you when to shoot. If you shoot just where there is no hair, you will surely kill him." The young man saw that the paws were without hair, and he hit the bear on the forepaw. "Shoot again," said the uncle. So he shot the other paw.

Then the old man pointed and said, "Shoot here." And the nephew aimed and shot the point of his uncle's finger. Then the old man's hand hurt him, so to direct his nephew he pursed out his lips and pointed with them, and the young man shot him through his lips.

Then the bear came down and made his way off, while the uncle was explaining that his meaning had been to shoot under the forelegs. The young man asked, "Why did you not say so?"

Then they started home for that day without game. "Tomorrow morning," said the uncle, "watch, for if you will look between the roots of the large trees, you may find a bear in that way."

Accordingly, the next day the young man found a hole near the root of the tree and saw a large bear inside. So he went home and asked his uncle for instructions how to get at the bear. The old man began to explain, but unfortunately in a way that his nephew could not understand.

He went into the cornfield, gathered the cornstalks and stuck them around the entrance to the hole, so that he surrounded the place where the bear must come out. Then he knocked on the other side of the tree, and the bear came out, as, of course, there was no reason why he should not, for the stalks fell before him. The young man took his arms and went home. Then the uncle asked him what he had done, and he told.

"You did not understand," said the old man. "You should have shot him as he left the den; first on one side then on the other."

"After this," argued the young man, "make your explanations clearer, and do not give so many illustrations. Had you told me this at first all would have been all right."

One day the old man said, "I'm going to make a feast. You can invite the guests. I cut sticks to represent so many friends. You invite them. Go to the highest tree you can find and leave this stick there. Then go along till you find a place all swamp—bad place—and leave one stick there." So the nephew went around and used up the sticks and returned.

"Have you done as I said?" asked the old man. "Yes," said he. Yet when the day came and the feast was ready, nobody came. "Why," asked the uncle, "has nobody come?" "How," inquired the young man, "could the tall tree and the swamp come here?"

So they ate together, and then the young fellow went off in the world to learn his lessons by experience, for he had become tired of his uncle's parables.

THE STORY OF JACK AND HIS BROTHER

JACK AND HIS ELDER BROTHER lived with their parents, who had a cook. They were enormous eaters; and when food was put on the table, they rapidly ate it all up, so that their parents had not enough. As they grew, they ate more; and at mealtime, even when the table was loaded with food, their parents had eaten only a few mouthfuls before all the food was finished.

Their parents made up their minds to get rid of them. They told the cook to provide them with a large lunch each, take them to a rough part of the mountains, and leave them. Jack read his parents' minds, and told his elder brother what was proposed. That day he went to a wise and friendly old woman who lived near by, and asked her for advice. She gave him a large reel of thread and told him what to do.

Next morning the cook provided them with packs of food, and told them he would take them to hunt grouse. They followed him; and as they went, Jack unrolled the thread unobserved by the cook. When the thread was almost all unrolled, the cook halted in a wild spot, saying, "We will camp here for tonight. I am going over yonder to shoot some grouse, and will be back before dusk." As soon as he was out of sight, the lads followed the thread back to their home, and arrived there shortly after the cook, and just as their parents were going to eat. Having left their lunch in the mountains, they were very hungry, and ate up the supper almost before their parents had commenced.

Their parents told the cook to take them farther away next time. Jack knew what they had arranged, and went to see the old woman again. She gave him a sack full of fine powder, which shone both by day and by night, but was brightest at night, and she told him what to do.

On the following morning the cook said he would take them hunting. As they followed the cook, Jack sprinkled the phosphorescent dust along the way. When the sack was about empty, the cook said, "We will camp here. I will go to yonder brush and shoot rabbits. Stay here until I return." As soon as he was out of sight, the boys ran back along the sprinkled trail. When they were about halfway back in a rough piece of country, they ran into a very large flock of small birds, and chased them hither and thither, trying to catch them.

In this way they lost their trail. They searched for a long time, but could not find it. They wandered on, not knowing where they were going. They descended from the mountains, and came to a plain where they saw a butte with a very tall pine tree growing on top. They went there. The elder brother tried to climb the tree, but he became dizzy and descended again. Then Jack went up, reached the top, and looked around. Far away he saw a column of smoke, and called to his brother to turn his face the way he pointed. Jack descended, and they traveled the way his brother was facing. At night they camped, and sat facing the same way, so that they might not go astray.

The next day they reached a large underground lodge. They were almost famished. Their shoes and clothes were in tatters. They found an old woman within, who fed them and then hid them in the cellar within the house. She told them that her husband was a cannibal. The cannibal and his wife had two children of the same size as Jack and his brother. Being young cannibals, they sniffed around Jack and his brother, and when they were in the cellar, continued to sniff about, so that their mother had to drive them away. Toward evening the cannibal approached the house, saying, "Nom, nom, nom, where can I get some meat?" On entering, he told his wife that he smelled game within the house; and she, on being threatened with a thrashing disclosed the fact that the boys were hidden in the cellar. Jack told his brother that he would influence the cannibal's mind, so that they might be spared.

The cannibal pulled them out of the cellar, and was about to eat them. Then he hesitated, and began to look them over. He said, "They are too thin." He put them back into the cellar, and told his wife to feed them well and give them a good place to sleep, that they might get fat and tender quickly. The next day the woman made a bed for them. After they had been in the house for some time, the cannibal told his wife the boys were now fit to eat, and he would kill them in the morning.

Jack knew his intention. He made the cannibal and his family sleep very soundly that night. The lads arose, and placed the cannibal's children in the bed in which they themselves had been, and put logs of rotten wood in the bed of the cannibal's children. They took the cannibal's magic staff of gold, four stones which, as learned afterward, were gold nuggets, and the key of his door. When anyone attempted to open the house door except with the proper key, a bell would ring.

In the morning, when the cannibal awoke, he immediately went to the bed in which the boys used to sleep, and killed his own children, whom he mistook for the captive boys. When about to eat them, he noticed their fingers, and thus realized that he had killed his own children. He uncovered what seemed to be children in the other bed, and found the logs of rotten wood.

The cannibal gave chase to Jack and his brother, who by this time were far away. When the lads saw that they would be overtaken, they hid themselves in the roots of a patch of tall grass. The cannibal, who had lost track of the boys, returned in another direction. As soon as he was out of sight, the lads ran on. Then the cannibal found their tracks again. The boys had just reached a broad lake, when he hove in sight. Jack threw his staff down on the water, and they crossed it as on a bridge. When they reached the opposite shore, he lifted it up, and the cannibal could not cross. He shouted, "I will forgive you, I will not harm you, if you will only give me back my staff!" But Jack stuck the staff in the ground at the edge of the lake, and left the cannibal crying.

Not far from here they came to a large town of white people, where there was a chief and many soldiers, also many houses, stores, and farms. The cannibal used to prey on these people, who were much afraid of him. Here Jack and his brother separated, each getting work on a different farm.

Jack's brother became jealous of him, and sought to accomplish his death by putting him in danger. He told his master that Jack intended to steal the large bell belonging to the cannibal. Jack's master heard of this, and asked him if it were true, adding that his elder brother had said so. Jack said, "Very well. I will go and get the bell. You will all see it."

The cannibal kept the bell on a wheeled vehicle alongside his house. It was very large. Jack went at night, and crossing the lake by means of the staff, he soon reached the cannibal's house. He caused a deep sleep to fall on the cannibal, his wife, and the bell. This bell could hear a long way off, and warned the cannibal of danger by ringing. Jack ran off with the bell, hauling it in a wagon. Just as he had reached the opposite side of the lake, the cannibal arrived at the shore. Jack drew in the staff, and stuck it in the ground. The cannibal begged for the staff, saying, "You may keep the bell, but give me back my staff, with which I cross water." Jack left him crying, and proceeded to town, where he displayed the bell to all the people.

After this, Jack's brother circulated the story that Jack intended to steal the cannibal's light. His master asked him about it, and he said he would do it. He took with him three small sacks of salt. When he came to the cannibal's house, he looked down the smoke hole. He saw the cannibal busy boiling a large kettle full of human flesh, which was now almost ready to be eaten. Jack emptied one sack full of salt into the kettle. The cannibal had a large spoon with which he was tasting the broth. When he took the next spoonful, he found the taste so agreeable that he forgot to eat any of the meat, and drank only of the soup. He said, "This must be delicious game I am boiling, to make the broth so nice."

Jack wanted to make him go to drink, so that he could steal the light. He threw in the other sack of salt. The cannibal went to the creek to drink, but instead of leaving the light, took it with him attached to his forehead. Jack ran down the trail and hid. When the cannibal was returning, he suddenly jumped up, and threw the salt in the cannibal's face and on the light, so that neither of them could see. The cannibal was so much startled that he ran away, and in his hurry and blindness struck his toe on a tuft of grass and fell down heavily. The light rolled off his head. Jack seized it and ran off.

This light could see a long way off, and told the cannibal what it saw. It saw farthest at night. The cannibal could not follow Jack, because it was very dark and he had no proper light. Jack carried the light to town, and displayed it to the people.

Next Jack's brother told that Jack was going to bring in the cannibal himself. His master asked him regarding it, and he said he would do it. He went to the blacksmith and had a large trunk made of iron, with a lid which shut with a spring. When it was finished, Jack went into it and tried it with all his strength. He found the box was too weak. Therefore he ordered the blacksmith to re-enforce it with heavy iron bands. He placed the trunk on a wagon, to which he harnessed a fine team, and drove to the cannibal's house, crossing the lake on the magic staff.

The cannibal came out and admired the team, wagon, and trunk. He did not recognize Jack, and thought he would kill the visitor and take his wagon, trunk, and team. The cannibal admired the trunk, which was polished and looked like steel. Jack opened the lid to show him the inside, which was decorated with carvings, pictures in colors, and looking glasses. Jack proposed to sell the trunk to the cannibal, and asked him to go in and try it. The cannibal told Jack to go in first. Jack went in, lay down at full length, and claimed that it was very comfortable. The cannibal then went in, and Jack shut the lid on him. The cannibal struggled to free himself, and at times nearly capsized the trunk; but Jack drove him into town, where he stopped in the square.

The chief and soldiers and all the people flocked to see the cannibal who had been killing them. They lifted him off the wagon, and asked Jack to liberate him. Jack said if he liberated him, he would kill all the people, and proposed to them to light a fire, and to roast him to death in the trunk. Jack's brother asked him to open the trunk, but he would not consent. Jack's brother said, "There is no danger. See these hundreds of armed soldiers." Jack said, "It matters not, for neither arrows, nor bullets, nor knives, can penetrate him. He will kill everybody." His brother laughed.

Jack said, "I will give you the key of the trunk, and you may open it in four hours from now." The white people wanted to have some fun with their enemy. When Jack had been gone four hours, and while he was sitting on the top of a distant hill overlooking the town, his brother opened the trunk. The cannibal, who was in a violent rage, killed every one of the people, including Jack's brother. There were none left. After this Jack traveled. Some say he turned foolish, and became Jack the Trickster.